Footprint Handbook
Borneo
SARAWAK • BRUNEI • SABAH
PAUL DIXON

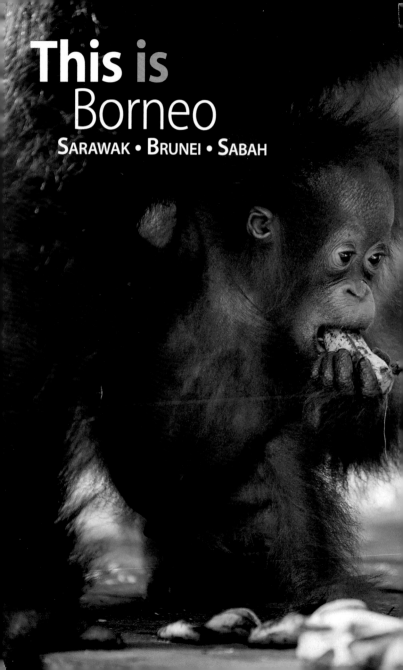

This is
Borneo
SARAWAK • BRUNEI • SABAH

The Malaysian states of Sabah, Sarawak and the tiny oil-rich sultanate of Brunei offer travellers genuine possibilities for untamed adventure. Lying along the northern coast of Borneo, the world's third largest island, bordered by the Celebes, Sulu and South China seas and blanketed in dense tropical forest, this great natural greenhouse has been attracting vistors for centuries. The first foreign settlers to the island battled murderous waves of cholera, typhoid and malaria alongside bloody warfare with local tribes to get their foot in the northern door of Borneo's resource-rich natural treasure house.

Sarawak, dominated by the crocodile-infested Rejang River, is renowned for its Headhunter's Trail and Iban, Melanau and Kenyah longhouses. Neighbouring Brunei glimmers with golden-roofed mosques whose calls to prayer ring out over the country's dense and pristine rainforest, filled with proboscis monkeys and lazy pythons, while offshore, flares from oil rigs light up the clouds in the tropical night.

The moody peak of Gunung Kinabalu, Borneo's highest mountain, has views down through the swirling clouds to Sabah's islands including Pulau Gaya, Layang Layang and Sipadan, which offer unparalleled underwater adventures. Sabah's jungle, though fast making way for endless plantations, still provides stunning jaunts for the hardy in the Maliau Basin, home to pygmy elephants, orang-utans and sun bears.

There are still ample opportunities to engage in Lost World fantasies here with stunning dive sites and hiking trails. These natural distractions, alongside diverse cultures, beguiling cities and some of the world's best food, make a trip to northern Borneo one of Southeast Asia's most sought-after experiences.

Paul

Best of
Borneo

top things to do and see in Sarawak, Brunei and Sabah

❶ Kuching

Kuching is Borneo's most charming city and an ideal introduction to the island with its cosmopolitan population, cat statues, abundance of Chinese shophouses and rakish colonial history. Check out the city's numerous cafés and bars to ease you out of your jetlag and into Borneo life. Take a sampan across the river to the Malay kampong or visit the nearby Sarawak Cultural Village to learn more about the region's ethnic groups. Page 36.

❷ Bako National Park

This is the oldest national park in Sarawak and makes a great side trip from Kuching. The park is home to groups of long-nosed proboscis monkeys, flying lizards and roaming gangs of cheeky macaques. There are well-marked hiking trails through thick dipterocarp forest dotted with small coves and beaches perfect for a quiet dip. Page 65.

❸ Gunung Mulu National Park

Make your way overland to this park and take your pick from a number of fantastic natural offerings: explore huge riverine cave systems, take night walks through the jungle, trek through the shard-like Pinnacles or test yourself on the four-day summit hike. This is also the starting point for the fabled Headhunter's Trail. Page 112.

③

❹ Bario trekking

Sit back and enjoy the prop flight into the interior as you make your way to Bario. In the tranquil Kelabit Highlands, Bario is the starting point for adventurous treks ideal for those seeking an escape from modern life. Check out ancient monoliths on a day trek, or treat yourself to the three-day walk to Bakalalan, a stunning hike that crosses into the Indonesian state of Kalimantan, staying in remote local villages. Page 121.

❺ Kampong Ayer

Bandar Seri Begawan is surely one of the world's most verdant capitals, surrounded by dense jungle and bisected by a meandering brown river. Though it may be a wealthy place, you never feel too far from the city's true origins, and this is never more evident than when exploring the city's Kampong Ayer (water village) where houses, hospitals, schools and fire stations sit precariously above the river in stilted structures. Page 147.

④

⑤

❻ Gunung Kinabalu

Dominating the skyline of northern Sabah, mighty Gunung Kinabalu is the tallest mountain in Borneo and a challenge for all who attempt its summit. Once you get there you'll be rewarded with staggering views over the island and the world's highest *via ferrata*. If the climb doesn't appeal, take a walk in the park around the base of the mountain to see amazing flora and fauna or have a soak in the Poring Hot Springs. Page 241.

❼ Sepilok Orang-Utan Rehabilitation Centre

This is the most famous place in the world to get a glimpse of the orang-utan. You'll need to battle your way through the crowds at feeding times, so don't expect great intimacy and jungle authenticity, but it's all fairly sensitively managed and offers an amazing close-up opportunity if you are pressed for time. There's also the Sun Bear Conservation Centre next door and a few decent cafés and restaurants nearby where you can laze away an afternoon. Page 266.

❽ Sungai Kinabatangan

The Kinabatangan is Malaysia's second longest river and is renowned for supporting some of Borneo's most diverse fauna. Stay in a riverside lodge on the wetlands and take boat trips to spot hornbills, pygmy elephants, orang-utans and proboscis monkeys alongside saltwater crocodiles, or visit one of the local minority communities for a spot of cultural exchange and a homestay experience. Page 270.

❾ Danum Valley Conservation Area

Jungle fans will relish the opportunity to trek in the Danum Valley Conservation Area, possibly Borneo's finest nature experience. Covering around 450 sq km in central Sabah, the area remains undisturbed by the horrors of logging and is packed full of amazing wildlife from vipers and cobras to gibbons, elephants, tarsiers, leopard cats and orang-utans. Entrance to the valley is strictly controlled so if you book well in advance, you can be assured of minimal human presence. Pages 276.

⑩ Pulau Sipadan

Sipadan is one of the world's most celebrated diving sites. Accommodation on the island has closed and slowly the island is returning to its pristine state while the waters around it remain a crystal-clear haven for marine life. Glide along coral walls with green turtles and manta rays, or drift with vast clouds of jackfish or barracuda, or perhaps the elusive hammerhead shark. If you are a diver, a visit to Sipadan is a must, but be sure to book early. Page 282.

KUALA
LUMPUR□
SINGAPORE□

South China Sea

Niah
National
Park ♦

Bintulu

MALAYSIA

Belaga

SARAWAK

Rejang

Sibu

Kapit

2 *Bako
National
Park* ♦

N

1 Kuching

Bandar
Sri Aman

80 km

*Gunung
Penrissen* ▲

80 miles

Kuching 1

Bako National Park 2

Gunung Mulu National Park 3

Bario trekking 4

Kampong Ayer 5

Kudat

Sulu Sea

Kota Belud
Gunung Kinabalu
(4095m) ▲ **6**
Kota Kinabalu

Sepilok
Orang-Utan
Rehabilitation ♦ **7**
Centre Sandakan

SABAH

Beaufort

Kinabatangan

Keningau

Danum Valley
Conservation ♦ **8** Lahad
Area Datu

5 BANDAR SERI
BEGAWAN

9

Magdalena ▲
(1347m) Semporna

BRUNEI

Ulu Temburong
National Park ▲

Tawau *Pulau Sipadan*

Gunung Mulu ♦
National Park **3**

10

Murudi ▲
(2423m)

Celebes Sea

4 Bario

INDONESIA
KALIMANTAN

6 Gunung Kinabalu

7 Sepilok Orang-Utan Rehabilitation Centre

8 Sungai Kinabatangan

9 Danum Valley Conservation Area

10 Pulau Sipadan

Route
planner

The Malaysian states of Sarawak and Sabah are by far the most visited regions of Borneo and – along with Brunei – they are the island's most accessible entry points. Rivers, rather than roads, have traditionally been the main arteries for travel though there are now excellent paved roads between the major coastal towns and cities. Northern Borneo can accommodate trips of anything from a couple of days to several weeks. If you intend to head upriver independently and stay in longhouses, the more time you have the better.

Crossing international borders between Sarawak, Brunei and Sabah is a fairly straightforward process. You should, however, allow time within your itinerary for immigration and custom formalities. Carefully planning a trip through Borneo is crucial, especially for those with restricted time. Certain places enforce strict visitor quotas: for example, dives on Sipadan and permits for Kinabalu. Slots for visiting the Turtle Islands are often booked up weeks in advance. It is important to think ahead about which sights and activities you most want to see and do and organize them before arrival. This does take some of the spontaneity out of travel, but saves the disappointment of being turned away.

Stopover

visit Brunei's stilt village and walk in the rainforest canopy

If you are just passing through, the tiny sultanate of Brunei makes a good stopover. Allow a day for the sights around the capital, **Bandar Seri Begawan**, including a tour of Kampung Ayer (water village) and a proboscis monkey river safari. Those with a few days to play with can head for the **Ulu Temburong National Park**, with its excellent canopy walkway. Longer stays in Brunei could take in **Tasek Merimbun**, Brunei's largest lake, or longboat journeys upriver to Iban longhouses.

Right: *tamu*, Kota Kinabalu
Opposite page: *sampan*, Kuching

Two weeks

a flying visit of the jungle, rivers, islands and beaches

Two weeks will fly by in Borneo. It's possible to take internal flights and speed about Sarawak and Sabah visiting the major highlights: **Kuching**, **Bako National Park**, the **Rejang River** and **Gunung Mulu National Park** in Sarawak; followed by **Mount Kinabalu**, **Sepilok Orang-Utan Rehabilitation Centre**, the **Turtle Islands** and the **Kinabatangan Wetlands** in Sabah. Alternatively, stick to one state and explore it in more depth. In Sarawak, a week could be spent in the tranquil **Kelabit Highlands** and another in the Kuching area; or climb Mount Kinabalu then spend a few days relaxing at a beach resort in Sabah. A few days in **Brunei** could also be incorporated, especially if this is your point of entry into Borneo. This kind of two-week itinerary allows very little time to solidify travel arrangements so ensure you make all your bookings in advance if there are specific activities you wish to do.

Four to eight weeks

trek to remote villages, head upriver to an Iban longhouse, climb Kinabalu and dive Sipadan's clear waters

With plenty of time on your hands, you could take in all the major sites of Sarawak, Brunei and Sabah. In six weeks, you'll be able to cover most of the suggestions detailed below, though, to avoid burnout, it's best to pick and choose between the national parks. Also, bear in mind that journeys deep into the jungle or upriver can be very expensive.

Above: Niah Caves
Opposite page top: Turtle Island
Opposite page middle: Danum Valley Conservation Area
Opposite page bottom: Sultan Omar Ali Saifuddien Mosque

You might begin in **Kuching**, the administrative capital of Sarawak, using this attractive riverside city as a base for forays deeper into the state. Destinations not to be missed in the region include **Bako National Park**, on the tip of the Santubong Peninsula; the **Sarawak Cultural Village**; and **Gunung Gading**, where giant rafflesia flowers bloom. Also head up the **Batang Ai River** to stay at an Iban longhouse. The mighty **Batang Rejang River** runs through the heart of Sarawak and a journey upriver is a great way to get a feel for the state, passing Iban, Kenyah and Kayan longhouses along the way. You might make a brief visit to the Melanau heartland, before heading along the coast to the magnificent **Niah Caves**. Inland from here is the **Gunung Mulu National Park**, one of Sarawak's highlights and home to the one of the world's largest caves, Deer Cave. The **Kelabit Highlands** offer a laid-back retreat high in the jungled mountains of Sarawak and have fantastic opportunities for hiking in a remote area.

From here, move on to Sabah via Brunei, stopping for a few days in the Brunei capital, **Bandar Seri Begawan**. Take a river trip in search of proboscis monkeys and enjoy tasty local fare at the night market, before exploring the incredible jungle at **Ulu Temburong**.

Next, press on to **Kota Kinabalu**, capital of Sabah, and prepare for the ascent of **Mount Kinabalu**. Afterwards, rest your limbs at the **Poring Hot Springs**, or jump on a launch to the islands of the **Tunku Abdul Rahman National Park**. Then, cross the state to **Sandakan**, your base for a trip to the idyllic **Turtle Islands National Park** and to the **Sepilok Orang-Utan Rehabilitation Centre**. Visiting the **Kinabatangan Wetlands** is your best chance of spotting wild elephants, orang-utans and proboscis monkeys. If you've got the time and money, spend a few days in the remarkable **Danum Valley Conservation Area**, which is rich in wildlife. Divers will want to head straight for Semporna for diving trips out to **Pulau Sipadan**, reckoned by some to be the best dive site in the world.

Best
dive sites

Sipadan Island Marine Reserve

The most famous of Borneo's dive destinations, Sipadan is a tiny spit of land off eastern Borneo with walls of coral dropping to well over 600 m creating a spectacular marine environment. If you're looking for big stuff, this is the place. Turtles are everywhere, hammerhead sharks are frequently sighted and huge schools of barracuda group to form a perfect spiral. Sipadan's nearest neighbour, Mabul, is known as a special place for spotting small creatures such as seahorses, frogfish and ghost pipefish. The offshore oil rig may be ugly but beneath it is one of the best muck dives in the region. The low-lying corals of Kapalai are a short motor from Sipadan. Above the sandbar is a water village

perched on stilts and the dive from the jetty is superb with blue-ringed octopus, batfish and even baby nurse sharks all within a couple of fin strokes. Page 282.

Lankayan

An hour by boat from Sandakan, idyllic Lankayan is ringed by an iridescent white beach and covered in a labyrinth of unruly jungle. The reefs surrounding the island are gently shelving, flat plateaux. A high concentration of plankton attracts animals that thrive in nutrient-rich conditions, including rare rhinopias and occasional whalesharks. Several

Left: pink soft coral
Above: emperor angel fish

Opposite page
Top: red lion fish
Bottom left: clownfish
Bottom right: barracuda

shipwrecks ensure good variety, including one straight off the jetty. Page 258.

Layang Layang

Some 300 km northwest of Kota Kinabalu, Layang Layang is a tiny, man-made island sitting on a stunning lagoon. Around the edge of the lagoon is a large atoll whose steep-sided walls drop off to unimaginable depths. Strong currents drag nutrients across the reefs which ensures prolific hard coral growth and creates a haven for masses of pelagic life. However, most people come for the curious hammerhead phenomena every Easter, when large schools swarm around the island for a few weeks. Page 211.

Pulau Labuan

A few kilometers off the west coast of Sabah, a short hop from Brunei, the marine park off Labuan's south coast consists of three small islands with pretty beaches, ringed by some shallow reefs that are suitable for snorkelling. However, the real draw is the cluster of accessible wrecks, a couple of which date from the Second World War. Page 218.

Miri

Miri sits on the mouth of a river that extends seawards as a flat plateau, never dropping far beyond 15 m. The area can be awash with sediment, caused by both man-made and natural erosion. But arrive on a clear day, when there has been little rain, and the diving can be excellent. Further offshore are some dive sites that reach 30 m and several oil rigs that make great artificial reefs, attracting pelagics like barracuda and turtles. Page 100.

Maigi Island, Semporna, Sabah

When to go

... and when not to

Climate

When planning a trip to Sarawak, Brunei and Sabah, you'll need to take the rainy season into account. The worst rains are usually from November to February and while main highways remain open, some roads are impassable in these months. Boat links to offshore islands and water visibility for diving can also be affected. However, travelling during the wet season can have its advantages: hotel prices can be negotiable and resorts that may be excessively crowded at peak times of year can be wonderfully quiet. Those grey days with stiff breezes also make travelling in the tropics quite bearable and locals actually look forward to the rainy season each year because of the coolness. Conversely in the dry season (July to September), some rivers become unnavigable due to low water levels, and accommodation and transport will need to be booked in advance.

In recent years, the onset of the wet and dry seasons in Borneo has become less predictable; environmentalists attribute this to deforestation and/or global warming. It can rain at any time of year, even in the dry season. It's also worth noting that the sky is often overcast rather than blue. However, even if it's overcast, always remember to slap on high factor sunscreen; the UV gets through the clouds and is much higher than in a European summer. It's also worth following the locals' lead and carrying an umbrella to protect you from

Weather Kuching

January	February	March	April	May	June
30°C	30°C	31°C	32°C	33°C	32°C
23°C	23°C	23°C	23°C	24°C	23°C
690mm	429mm	339mm	288mm	268mm	250mm

July	August	September	October	November	December
32°C	33°C	32°C	32°C	31°C	31°C
23°C	23°C	23°C	23°C	23°C	23°C
195mm	260mm	260mm	324mm	331mm	499mm

the sun; they offer better protection than a hat and are useful for keeping cool on roasting hot days in the city.

Festivals

Note that in Sabah and Sarawak, school holidays run from mid- to late February, mid-May to early June, mid- to late August and late November to early January. During these holiday periods room rates increase significantly and it is advisable to book hotels in advance. During Ramadan travel can be more difficult and many restaurants close during daylight hours. After dusk many Muslims break their fast at stalls, which do a roaring trade, although generally Ramadan is not a period when Muslims eat out, but instead dine at home.

Chinese New Year (usually late January or early February) is becoming an increasingly challenging time to travel in Sabah and Sarawak (though less so in Brunei). The increasing affluence of citizens of China means they often spend their Chinese New Year somewhere warmer than their own country and Borneo is a popular choice. Hotels are often fully booked during this time and plane ticket prices shoot up.

A great time to visit Brunei is the week of the sultan's birthday celebrations in mid-July. The event is celebrated with parties and fireworks and this is the only time when the palace grounds are open to the public. See also Practicalities, page 315, and Festival listings in the relevant town.

What to do

Birdwatching

Borneo is home to hundreds of birds, including many migratory species, and there are great facilities for birdwatchers. Some of the best spots are: **Bako National Park** (page 65) and **Gunung Mulu National Park** (page 112) in Sarawak; **Gunung Kinabalu Park** (page 241) and **Tempasuk River** (page 236) in Sabah; and **Ulu Temburong National Park** (page 166) in Brunei. For organized birdwatching holidays, check out highly experienced operator **Borneo Birding**, www.borneobirding.com, which offers tours across Sabah including the Danum Valley, Kinabatangan River and Kinabalu National Park.

Caving

Caving fanatics should head for the vast underground system beneath the **Gunung Mulu National Park** (page 112) in Sarawak, where guided expeditions explore some of the most spectacular and largest caves on the planet. Four of the caves here are open to the public, though adventure caving, including an overnight at the Sarawak Chamber, is available for intermediate and advanced cavers. Caves accesible for more general visits are the archeologically significant **Painted Cave** at Niah (page 97) in Sarawak and the **Gomantong Caves** (page 269) in Sabah; the huge limestone caverns here are famed for their swiftlet nests.

Climbing

The best-known climbing area in Sarawak is the **Fairy Cave** (page 58) just outside Bau, a short drive from Kuching. The area has around 80 climbs on its eight separate walls. The climbs here are suitable in any weather as the rock formations keep the rain off the wall. Contact **Outdoor Treks and Adventures**, www.bikcloud.com/rockropes.htm.

An up-and-coming area in Sarawak is **Bantang** near Serian, which has eight bolted climbs. In Sabah, **Berhala Island** (page 258) off Sandakan is generating a huge interest in the rock-climbing scene with its huge cliffs and crags jutting out of the sea.

Indoor climbers are catered for in Kota Kinabalu at the **Sabah Indoor Climbing Centre**, www.sicc.com.my/sabah_indoor_climbing_centre home_page.html, and in Kuching try **Climb Ascend**, www.climb asend.com, both of which are good places to meet like-minded people to team up with and organize climbing trips. See www.climb.my for more information on climbing in Malaysia.

Cookery courses

For those wishing to learn more about Malaysian cuisine, several state tourist boards offer short courses; enquire at **Tourism Malaysia** information centres. There are also a number of cookery courses offered privately in Sabah and Sarawak. In Kuching try **Bumbu Cooking Class**, Jln Carpenter, www.bumbucooking class.weebly.com. In Sabah, for a unique cooking experience, try the course offered at the **Upside Down House**, www.upside downhouse.com.my, in Tamparuli, a short drive from Kota Kinabalu.

Diving *For details of Borneo's most popular dive sites, see the colour section, pages 14-15.*

Washed by the South China, Sulu and Celebes seas, Borneo is one of the world's top diving destinations. Being surrounded by open currents makes for an incredibly diverse set of marine environments. The state of Sabah is *the* destination for those who come to Borneo for no other reason than to submerge. Ringed by a mass of idyllic islands and marine reserves, the diving here is superlative and the only problem is choosing where to go. Globally renowned **Pulau Sipadan** (page 283) is the stunning underwater jewel of Sabah, though other spectacular diving destinations include **Kapalai** (page 284) and **Lankayan** (page 258). A good website is www.scuba-junkie.com, with descriptions and maps detailing Sipadan and Mabul dives.

By contrast, the water around Sarawak tends to be shallow and somewhat murky,

attracting less marine life. However, the coastal region off **Miri** (page 100), in northern Sarawak, has a growing dive reputation. Miri sits on the mouth of a river that extends seawards as a flat plateau, never dropping far beyond 15 m. The area can be awash with sediment – caused by both man-made and natural erosion – but arrive on a clear day, when there has been little rain, and the diving can be excellent. Further offshore are some dive sites that reach 30 m and several oil rigs that make great artificial reefs, attracting pelagics like barracuda and turtles. The reefs here are 'undiscovered' but whether you enjoy the diving will depend much on the visibility. Contact **CoCo**, www.divemiri.com, for details on dive trips and packages.

The island of **Labuan** (page 218), which sits between the two states, has also gained a moderate dive reputation due to four well-known wrecks. Sea and wind conditions vary, so diving can be challenging but there are many places that are suitable for novices. **Tourism Malaysia**, www.tourism.gov.my, has plenty of diving information on its website.

Brunei offers much the same as Labuan and Miri: its murky waters are peppered with wrecks and reefs created by abandoned oil rigs. The leading operator in Brunei is PADI-affiliated **PONI Divers**, www.ponidivers.com.

Longhouses and homestays

Staying in a longhouse is a great way to experience the region's cultural diversity. These communal dwellings are the traditional houses for many of the communities in the region and can be

Diving practicalities

It is hard to be general about diving seasons across Borneo. Although it is hot and humid all year, each state is governed by different wind patterns and currents. No matter what time of year you visit, or what area, the water is invariably warm.

In terms of equipment, a 3 mm wetsuit is as much as you're likely to need, unless you plan to do more than three dives a day. Almost every dive centre will rent good-quality equipment but bringing your own will considerably reduce costs. Prior to departure, check the baggage allowance with your airline and see if you can come to some arrangement for the extra weight.

While there are highly professional dive operations in Sabah, the unpredictable nature of the diving in Brunei, Labuan and Sarawak means that the industry and its dive facilities are less developed. It's always worth asking around to find out what's on offer. See also Dive safety, page 319.

visited on a day trip or overnight visit, though it is crucial to have an invitation before showing up (usually arranged via a guide or tourist agency). Many of the longhouses visited by tourists are located around the **Skrang River** (page 70) area in Sarawak, though there are some excellent opportunities for authentic longhouse visits around **Kapit** (page 80), **Belaga** (page 85) and **Batang Ai** (page 70). Typically, you'll be welcomed with a meal, and a bit of a song and dance, and you'll be expected to contribute to the fun with a rendition of your favourite number suitably fortified with a few glasses of *tuak* (rice wine). If you don't have time to make it upriver, you can get an idea of what a longhouse is like at the **Sarawak Cultural Village** (see page 61) near Kuching.

Another excellent way to get in touch with local communities is a homestay, where you can join in with daily activities and get an insight into village life. The Malaysian government runs an excellent

homestay programme. In Sarawak check www.right.sarawak.gov.my/homestay and for Sabah visit www.sabahhomestay.my to find out more. There are a few homestays in Brunei, notably around the **Kampong Ayer** (page 147) in Bandar Seri Begawan, which make a nice contrast to the business hotels that litter the city.

Mountain biking

Sabah has diverse opportunities for mountain biking, including day trips around villages in **Tuaran** (page 210) and three-day trips around the foothills of **Gunung Kinabalu** (page 246) to explore the countryside and communities, or to beaches around **Lahad Datu** (page 273). See www.bikeborneo.com or www.bikeandtours.com.

Mountain biking is less well established for tourists in Sarawak though numerous companies offer trips, such as **Borneo Adventure**, www.borneoadventure.com. Serious mountain bikers will want to head to the **Sikoh Trail** or the **Kampong Opar**

Trail near Kuching. For true enthusiasts the longhouses and villages around the **Penrissen Highlands** (page 56) along the Indonesian border or the **Kelabit Highlands** (page 121) near Bario are all connected with trails that are ideally suited to serious mountain bikers.

Trekking

Sabah, Sarawak and Brunei all offer bountiful trekking opportunities, and most of the national parks have well-marked hiking trails and opportunities for camping. One of the most popular hikes is the ascent of **Gunung Kinabalu** (page 246) in Sabah. Since the 2015 earthquake, the number of people allowed to climb the summit has been restricted, making the climb much quieter and more pleasant. Aim to get to the summit by sunrise for spectacular views over Sabah and its coastline. The Via Ferrata here is an interesting option on Gunung Kinabalu for those who wish to spend a bit of time clambering over the face of the mountain. Sabah has plenty of other trekking options from the glorious heights of the **Crocker Range** (page 228) to the dense and wildlife-rich jungles in the **Danum Valley** (page 276) and **Maliau Basin** (page 290).

Notable hiking options in Sarawak include fantastic multi-day off-the-beaten-path trekking around **Bario** and the **Kelabit Highlands** (page 121) and trekking in the **Gunung Mulu National Park** (page 112) with options to ascend the tough **Pinnacles** or the **Peak**. Also in Sarawak is the **Headhunter's Trail**, named after Kayan war parties who followed the route on their raids, and is a great alternative to flying into Mulu.

In Brunei, **Ulu Temburong National Park** (page 166) offers trekking in pristine rainforest with kayaking and tubing extensions.

Whitewater rafting

Wild or whitewater rafting is becoming an established activity in Sabah, and there are some good spots to take to the rapids. Tour operators such as **Riverbug**, www.riverbug.asia, can organize rafting. Some of the best rivers are **Kiulu** (Grade II) and **Liwagu** (Grade I) and a 9-km trip down the muddy **Padas River** (Grade III); see page 205.

The scene is less established in Sarawak, though there is an annual **River Safari** in Padawan which involves teams racing on bamboo rafts or Kayaks.

Where to stay

from five-star luxury to longhouses and jungle camps

Sarawak and Sabah

Superb guesthouses and boutique hostels are well established in major towns such as Kuching and Kota Kinabalu, and stiff competition often means excellent value for money. Many of the major international chains have hotels on Borneo, including **Hilton**, **Holiday Inn** and **Hyatt**. Rates have been fairly stable for the last few years and the generally depressed economy has kept prices relatively low.

It is often possible to stay with families in Malay kampongs (villages) as part of the so-called homestay programme or in longhouses, where rates are at the discretion of the visitor (see page 72). For accommodation in national parks it is necessary to book in advance through the National Parks Booking Office for Sarawak (see page 47), Brunei (see page 154) and Sabah (see page 189). It's also possible to camp and many of the national parks have campsites with facilities and often have equipment to hire.

Room rates are subject to 10% tax and 6% goods and services tax. It is also worth noting that in tourist resorts, many hotels have different room tariffs: one for weekdays, one for weekends and, sometimes, a third for holiday periods. Room rates can vary substantially between these periods.

Tip...
For homestays in Sarawak, contact the government homestay programme, www.right.sarawak.gov.my/homestay. For Sabah contact www.sabahhomestay.my or ask a local tourist office or travel agent for information.

Price codes

Where to stay	Restaurants
$$$$ over US$150	$$$ over US$12
$$$ US$66-150	$$ US$7-12
$$ US$30-65	$ under US$7
$ under US$30	

Price of a double room in high season, including taxes.

Price for a two-course meal for one person, excluding drinks or service charge.

Brunei has a real dearth of good value and engaging places to stay and accommodation is significantly more expensive than in neighbouring Sarawak and Sabah. Most of the hotels are functional business-oriented places and there are virtually no budget options, apart from the excellent and extraordinarily quiet youth hostel (**Pusat Belia**, see page 155) in Bandar Seri Begawan and the indigenous longhouses, some of which offer homestay programmes. At the top end, Brunei boasts the outrageously decadent six-star **Empire Hotel and Country Club** (see page 164), one of the world's flashiest hotels.

With relatively small visitor numbers, there shouldn't be a problem finding a room, whatever your budget. What's more, the top-end hotels frequently offer promotions. Book online as early as possible to get the best discounts.

Shopping tips

Except in the larger fixed-price stores, bargaining (with good humour) is expected; start at 50-60% lower than the asking price. Do not expect to achieve instant results; if you walk away from the shop, you will almost certainly be followed with a lower offer. If the salesperson agrees to your price, you should feel obliged to purchase; it is considered very ill-mannered to agree on a price and then not buy the article.

Sarawak and Sabah

The traditional handicraft industry is flourishing in Sarawak (see page 53). **Kuching**, the state capital, is full of handicraft and antique shops selling tribal pieces collected from upriver; those going upriver themselves can often find items being sold in towns and even longhouses en route. Typical handicrafts include woodcarvings, *pua kumbu* (rust-coloured tie-dye blankets), beadwork and basketry (see page 139).

Larger urban areas may have a Chinatown (with a few curio shops and a *pasar malam*, or night market) and an Indian quarter; these are the best places to buy sarongs, *longis*, *dotis* and saris (mostly imported from India) as well as other textiles. Malay handicrafts are usually only found in markets or government craft centres. The island of **Labuan** has duty-free shopping, and is a good place to pick up cheap textiles from India and Indonesia as well as cheap whisky and rum for those lonely tropical nights in Brunei.

Brunei

Compared to Malaysia, Brunei is not up to much when it comes to shopping; the range of goods on offer is limited and the prices much higher. That said, you'll have no trouble finding international branded and luxury items.

Food
& drink

from Malay *nasi lemak* to Chinese *dim sum*

Sarawak and Sabah

Malaysians love their food and the dishes of the three main communities, Malay, Chinese and Indian, comprise a hugely varied national menu. Even within each ethnic cuisine, there is a vast choice; for example, there are North Indian, South Indian and Indian Muslim dishes. Malaysia also has great seafood, which the Chinese do best. The various tribal specialities offered in Sabah and Sarawak further add to this ethnic culinary smorgasbord. For non-meat eaters, there are numerous Chinese and Malay vegetarian dishes, although it is not unusual to find slivers of meat even when a vegetable dish is specifically requested. Most major towns have an Indian district where vegetarians will be able to sit down and enjoy a pure veg (vegetarian) feast.

Food

The best **Malay** food is usually found at stalls in hawker centres. The staple diet is rice and curry, which is rich and creamy due to the use of coconut milk. Herbs and spices include chilli, ginger, turmeric, coriander, lemongrass, anise, cloves, cumin, caraway and cinnamon.

Cantonese and **Hainanese** cooking are the most prevalent Chinese cuisines. Some of the more common dishes are Hainanese chicken rice (rice cooked in chicken stock and served with steamed or roast chicken), *char kway teow* (Teochew-style fried noodles, with eggs, cockles and chilli paste), *luak* (Hokkien oyster omelette), *dim sum* (steamed dumplings and patties), *bak kut teh* (Hokkien herbal pork stock soup with pork ribs) and *yong tow foo* (beancurd and vegetables stuffed with fish). Good Chinese food is available in restaurants, coffee shops and from hawker stalls.

Indian cooking can be divided into three schools: northern and southern (no beef) and Muslim (no pork). Northern dishes tend to be more subtly spiced, use more meat and are served with breads. Southern dishes use fiery spices, emphasize vegetables and are served with rice. The best known North Indian food is tandoori, which is served with delicious fresh naan breads, baked in ovens. Other pancakes include roti, *thosai* and chapati. Malaysia's famous *mamak* men are Indian Muslims who are highly skilled at making everything from *teh tarik* (see below) to rotis.

The Kadazan form the largest ethnic group in Sabah and their **Sabahan** food tends to use mango and can be on the sour side. Check out their *sambal tuhau*, a condiment heavy on ginger and chili, lime and prawn paste for a really mind-blowing accompaniment.

The Bajau sea nomads are well known for their *siput kima*, a raw snail dish prepared with lime and lashings of local black pepper.

The Murut do great things with wild boar and river fish and when in Sarawak, it is imperative to try the Melanau dish, *umai*, a sprightly salad of raw fish, limes, onion, chilli and salt.

The cheapest places to eat are in hawker centres and roadside stalls (often concentrated in or close to night markets) where it is possible to eat well for less than RM5. Stalls may serve Malay, Indian or Chinese dishes and even pseudo-Western (think deep-fried chicken chop, chips and cold baked beans). Next in the sequence of sophistication and price come the ubiquitous *kedai kopi* (coffee shops), where a meal will cost upwards of RM5. Usually run by Chinese or Indian families, rather than Malay, they open at around 0900 and close in the early evening. Some open at dawn to serve dim sum to people on their way to work and they are also the only coffee shops where it is possible to track down a cold beer. Malay-run *kedai kopi* are good for lunch with their *nasi campur* (buffet) spreads. Hotel restaurants regularly lay on buffet spreads, which are fair value at around RM40-50, often much cheaper than the price of a room would suggest; these are also usually open to non-residents.

Drink

Soft drinks, mineral water and freshly squeezed fruit drinks are available. Anchor and Tiger beer are widely sold and are cheapest at the hawker stalls (RM6-8 per bottle). A beer will cost RM8-15 per bottle in coffee shops. The potent Malaysian brewed Guinness Foreign Extra is popular, mainly because the Chinese believe it has medicinal qualities. Local Chinese men often go all out on the Guinness and mix it 50-50 with lager for a potent syrupy cocktail. Malaysians like strong coffee and unless you specify *kurang manis* (less sugar), *tak mahu manis* (no sugar) or *kopi kosong* (black, no sugar), it will come with lashings of condensed milk. Those who want their drinks without milk and sugar should ask for *teh/kopi o kosong*.

One of the most interesting cultural refinements of the Indian Muslim community is the *mamak* man, who is famed for *the tarik* (pulled tea), which is thrown across a distance of about a metre, from one cup to another, with no spillages. The idea is to cool it for customers but it's become an art form; *mamak* men cultivate a nonchalant look when pouring. Malaysian satirist Kit Lee says a tea stall *mamak* "could 'pull' tea in free fall without spilling a drop, while balancing a *beedi* on his lower lip and making a statement on Economic Determinism".

Brunei

Food

The variety and quality of food in Brunei is good, with a medley of restaurants, market stalls and food courts offering a wide range of cuisines from Malay, Chinese and Indian, to Indonesian, Thai and Japanese. Because of Brunei's relative wealth, there isn't the same density of street food as elsewhere in Borneo. Nevertheless, the informal local restaurants and food courts are still the best places to sample good local cuisine – and at great prices.

Drink

Brunei is a 'dry' country: sale of alcohol is banned, while consumption is prohibited for Muslims. Certain restaurants will allow non-Muslims to bring their own alcohol to drink with the meal, but always check in advance. Life without booze is quite manageable in Brunei as they have an excellent selection of amazing tropical fruits to whizz up and coffee shops and cafés can be found all over the country. Like Malaysians, the people of Brunei like their drinks sweet so specify if you want no sugar.

Menu reader

assam sour; tamarind
ayam chicken
babek duck
babi pork
belacan hot fermented prawn paste
buah fruit
daging meat
es krim ice cream
garam salt
gula sugar
ikan fish
kacang tanah peanut
kambing mutton
ketupat cold, compressed rice
kopi coffee
lombok chilli
manis sweet
mee noodles
minum drink
nasi rice
roti bread, pancake
sambal spicy relish side dish
sayur vegetables
sejuk crab
susu milk
tahu beancurd
telur egg
udang prawn

Rice dishes
nasi biryani saffron rice flavoured with spices and garnished with cashew nuts, almonds and raisins (Sarawak).

nasi campur Malay curry buffet of rice served with meat, fish, vegetables and fruit.
nasi dagang glutinous rice cooked in coconut milk and served with fish curry, cucumber pickle and *sambal*.
nasi goreng rice, meat and vegetables fried with garlic, onions and *sambal*.
nasi lemak a breakfast dish of rice cooked in coconut milk and served with prawn sambal, *ikan bilis*, hard-boiled egg, peanuts and cucumber.
nasi puteh plain boiled rice.
nontong rice cakes in a spicy coconut milk topped with grated coconut and sometimes bean curd and egg (Sarawak).

Soup
lontong cubed, compressed rice served with mixed vegetables in coconut milk. Sambal is the accompaniment. Popular for breakfast.
soto ayam a spicy chicken soup served with rice cubes, chicken and vegetables, popular for breakfast in Sarawak.
sup manuk on hiing chicken soup with rice wine (Sabah).
sup terjun jumping soup – salted fish, mango and ginger (Sabah).

Meat, fish and seafood
hinava marinated raw fish (Sabah).
pan suh manok chicken cooked in bamboo cup, served with *bario* (Kelabit mountain rice) (Sarawak).

satay chicken, beef or mutton marinated and skewered on a bamboo, barbecued over a brazier. Usually served with *ketupat*.
Sayur masak lemak deep-fried marinated prawns (Sarawak).
tapai chicken cooked in rice wine (Sabah).
ternbok fish, which has been either grilled or steamed (Sarawak).

Noodles
kway teow flat noodles fried with seafood, egg, soy sauce, beansprouts and chives.
laksa johor noodles in fish curry sauce and raw vegetables.
mee goreng fried noodles.
mee jawa noodles in gravy, served with prawn fritters, potatoes, tofu and beancurd.
mee rebus noodles with beef, chicken or prawn with soybean in spicy sauce. In Sarawak, it's yellow noodles served in a thick sweet sauce made from sweet potatoes and garnished with sliced hard-boiled eggs and green chillies.
mee siam white thin noodles in a sweet and sour gravy made with tamarind (Sarawak).

Salad
gado-gado cold dish of bean sprouts, potatoes, long beans, tempeh, bean curd, rice cakes and prawn crackers, topped with a spicy peanut sauce.

rojak Malaysia's answer to Indonesia's *gado gado* –mixed vegetable salad served in peanut sauce with *ketupat*. Indian rojak is a different beast entirely of a selection of deep fried fritters served with a sweet spicy sauce.

Vegetables
kang-kong belacan water spinach fried in chilli-shrimp paste.
pakis ferns, which are fried with *belacan* and mushrooms. Sometimes ferns are eaten raw, with a squeeze of lime (*sayur pakis limau*) (Sabah).
sayur manis sweet vegetables; vegetables fried with chilli, *belacan* and mushrooms.

Sweets (kueh)
apam Indian steamed rice cakes.
es delima a dessert of water chestnut in sago and coconut milk.
hinompula a dessert made from tapioca, sugar, coconut and the juice from screwpine leaves (Sabah).
ice kachang similar to Chinese *chendol*, a cone of ice shavings topped by syrup and other ingredients, but with evaporated milk instead of coconut milk.
nyonya kueh Chinese *kueh*, among the most popular is *yow cha koei* – deep-fried kneaded flour.
pulut inti glutinous rice served with sweetened grated coconut.

Improve your travel photography

Taking pictures is a highlight for many travellers, yet too often the results turn out to be disappointing. Steve Davey, author of Footprint's *Travel Photography*, sets out his top rules for coming home with pictures you can be proud of.

Before you go

Don't waste precious travelling time and do your research before you leave. Find out what festivals or events might be happening or which day the weekly market takes place, and search online image sites such as Flickr to see whether places are best shot at the beginning or end of the day, and what vantage points you should consider.

Get up early

The quality of the light will be better in the few hours after sunrise and again before sunset – especially in the tropics when the sun will be harsh and unforgiving in the middle of the day. Sometimes seeing the sunrise is a part of the whole travel experience: sleep in and you will miss more than just photographs.

Stop and think

Don't just click away without any thought. Pause for a few seconds before raising the camera and ask yourself what you are trying to show with your photograph. Think about what things you need to include in the frame to convey this meaning. Be prepared to move around your subject to get the best angle. Knowing the point of your picture is the first step to making sure that the person looking at the picture will know it too.

Compose your picture

Avoid simply dumping your subject in the centre of the frame every time you take a picture. If you compose with it to one side, then your picture can look more balanced. This will also allow you to show a significant background and make the picture more meaningful. A good rule of thumb is to place your subject or any significant detail a third of the way into the frame; facing into the frame not out of it.

This rule also works for landscapes. Compose with the horizon two-thirds of the way up the frame if the foreground is the most interesting part of the picture; one-third of the way up if the sky is more striking.

Don't get hung up with this so-called Rule of Thirds, though. Exaggerate it by pushing your subject out to the edge of the frame if it makes a more interesting picture; or if the sky is dull in a landscape, try cropping with the horizon near the very top of the frame.

Fill the frame

If you are going to focus on a detail or even a person's face in a close-up portrait, then be bold and make sure that you fill the frame. This is often a case of physically getting in close. You can use a telephoto setting on a zoom lens but this can lead to pictures looking quite flat; moving in close is a lot more fun!

Interact with people

If you want to shoot evocative portraits then it is vital to approach people and seek permission in some way, even if it is just by smiling at someone. Spend a little time with them and they are likely to relax and look less stiff and formal. Action portraits where people are doing something, or environmental portraits, where they are set against a significant background, are a good way to achieve relaxed portraits. Interacting is a good way to find out more about people and their lives, creating memories as well as photographs.

Focus carefully

Your camera can focus quicker than you, but it doesn't know which part of the picture you want to be in focus. If your camera is using the centre focus sensor then move the camera so it is over the subject and half press the button, then, holding it down, recompose the picture. This will lock the focus. Take the now correctly focused picture when you are ready.

Another technique for accurate focusing is to move the active sensor over your subject. Some cameras with touch-sensitive screens allow you to do this by simply clicking on the subject.

Leave light in the sky

Most good night photography is actually taken at dusk when there is some light and colour left in the sky; any lit portions of the picture will balance with the sky and any ambient lighting. There is only a very small window when this will happen, so get into position early, be prepared and keep shooting and reviewing the results. You can take pictures after this time, but avoid shots of tall towers in an inky black sky; crop in close on lit areas to fill the frame.

Bring it home safely

Digital images are inherently ephemeral: they can be deleted or corrupted in a heartbeat. The good news though is they can be copied just as easily. Wherever you travel, you should have a backup strategy. Cloud backups are popular, but make sure that you will have access to fast enough Wi-Fi. If you use RAW format, then you will need some sort of physical back-up. If you don't travel with a laptop or tablet, then you can buy a backup drive that will copy directly from memory cards.

Recently updated and available in both digital and print formats, Footprint's Travel Photography by Steve Davey covers everything you need to know about travelling with a camera, including simple post-processing. More information is available at www.footprinttravelguides.com

Sarawak

Sarawak, the 'land of the hornbill', is the largest state in Malaysia, covering an area of nearly 125,000 sq km in northwest Borneo with a diverse population of 2.5 million.

Sarawak has a swampy coastal plain, a hinterland of undulating foothills and an interior of steep-sided, jungle-covered mountains. The lowlands and plains are dissected by a network of broad rivers which are the main arteries of communication and where the majority of the population is settled. In the mid-19th century, Charles Darwin described Sarawak as "one great wild, untidy, luxuriant hothouse, made by nature for herself".

Sarawak is Malaysia's great natural storehouse, where little more than half a century ago great swathes of forest were largely unexplored and where tribal groups, collectively known as the Dayaks, would venture downriver from the heartlands of the state to exchange forest products of hornbill ivory and precious woods. Today these ethnic groups have largely been integrated into mainstream Malaysian society and the market economy has infiltrated the lives of the great majority of the population. But much remains unchanged. The forests, although much reduced by a rapacious logging industry, are still some of the most species-rich on the globe; the government claims more than 70% of the land is forested and has pledged to keep a minimum of 60% covered though these numbers are contested by environmentalists.

Best for
Indigenous culture ▪ Longhouses ▪ River trips ▪ Trekking

Kuching

Kuching & around 36
Bandar Sri Aman & around 69
Sibu, Kapit & Belaga. 74
North coast 90
Northern Sarawak 112
Background 126

Footprint
picks

★ **Kuching**, page 36

Visit Sarawak's best museum and stroll along the waterfront.

★ **Bako National Park**, page 65

Get nose to nose with the proboscis monkey; it's one of the best places in Sarawak for seeing them.

★ **Longhouse stay**, page 72

Secure an overnight invitation to an Iban, Badayuh or Orang Ulu village.

★ **Sungai Rejang**, page 83

Ride the rapids or head upriver from Kapit or Belaga to visit remote longhouses.

★ **Niah National Park caves**, page 96

Admire prehistoric cave art and see huge clouds of bats and swiftlets at sunset.

★ **Gunung Mulu National Park**, page 112

Trek through the Melinau Gorge to the spectacular Pinnacles.

★ **Kelabit Highlands**, page 121

Hike from village to village and enjoy unspoiled rural Borneo.

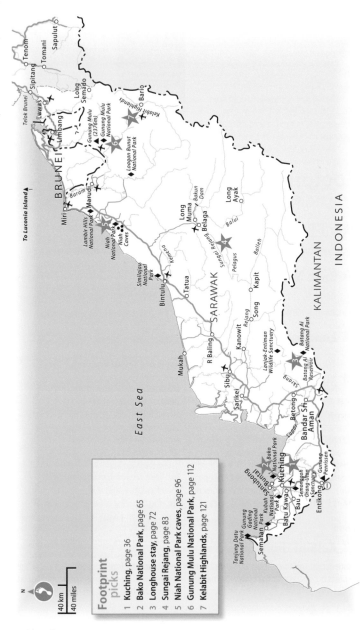

N

40 km
40 miles

To Luconia Island ▲

East Sea

BRUNEI

SARAWAK

KALIMANTAN

INDONESIA

Tenom
Tomani
Sapulut
Sipitang
Long Semado
Bario
Kelabit Highlands
Gunung Mulu (2376m)
Gunung Mulu National Park
Tawau
Telok Brunei
Limbang
Lawas
Marudu
Miri
Baram
Loagan Bunut National Park
Lambir Hills National Park
Niah National Park
Niah Caves
Long Muma
Belaga
Bakun Dam
Balui
Long Ayak
Similajau National Park
Bintulu
Tatua
Kemena
Sungai Rejang
Pelagus
Balleh
Kapit
Mukah
R Baling
Kanowit
Rejang
Song
Batang Ai National Park
Batang Ai Reservoir
Lanjak-Entiman Wildlife Sanctuary
Sibu
Sarikei
Betong
Skrang
Bandar Sri Aman
Tuang
Entikong
Gunung Penrissen
Semenggoh Orang-Utan Sanctuary
Bako National Park
Kuching
Santubong
Sematan
Tanjung Datu National Park
Semantan Park
Kubah National Park
Gunung Gading National Park
Bau
Batu Kawa

Footprint picks

1 Kuching, page 36
2 Bako National Park, page 65
3 Longhouse stay, page 72
4 Sungai Rejang, page 83
5 Niah National Park caves, page 96
6 Gunung Mulu National Park, page 112
7 Kelabit Highlands, page 121

Getting around

Air

Sarawak has a good internal flight network, as well as regular connections with Brunei and Sabah. Kuching is the main international gateway. **MASwings** flies regularly to Kuching, Kota Kinabalu, Miri and Sibu, as well as more remote locations such as Limbang, Lawas and Gunung Mulu National Park. **Air Asia** operates between Kuching, Kota Kinabalu, Miri, Bintulu and Sibu. Bario, in the remote Kelabit Highlands, can be reached by plane from Miri, Lawas and Marudi. **Royal Brunei Airlines** flies from Kuching to Bandar Seri Begawan. For airport information, see www.malaysiaairports.com.my.

River

River travel is used for exploring the interior of Sarawak, though road travel has dramatically improved in recent years. An express boat runs daily between Kuching and Sibu (five hours); a beautiful journey via Sarakei. From Sibu there are regular express boats along the Batang Rejang to Kapit (two to three hours); and, in the wet season when the river is high enough, they continue to Belaga (five to six hours; permits required), from where it's possible to arrange longhouse visits.

Ferries also run internationally, between Lawas, Limbang and Brunei. If there is no scheduled boat, it is often possible to charter one though this can be expensive. For up-to-date river information, contact the **Sarawak Rivers Board**, www.srb.sarawak.gov.my.

Road

The Trans-Borneo Highway runs almost the entire length of Sarawak from Kuching to the Brunei border at Kuala Belait. Long-distance express buses connect Kuching with major towns including Sibu (seven hours), Bintulu (11 hours) and Miri (15 hours). There are several car hire firms in Kuching.

When to go

The main tourist season is July to September, when flights and treks need to booked well in advance. While heavy showers can happen at any time of year, they are more likely during the rainy season (November to February), which could make trekking and coastal travel difficult. River travel may not always be possible in the dry season due to low water levels.

Time required

A two-week visit, using internal flights to cover long distances, would allow time to spend a few days in Kuching, with side trips to the Damai Peninsula and Bako National Park, a river trip up the Rejang for a longhouse stay, and trekking in Gunung Mulu National Park. Allow a couple of extra days to explore the tranquil Kelabit Highlands.

Useful websites

www.mot.sarawak.gov.my
Ministry of Tourism
www.museum.sarawak.gov.my
Sarawak Museums Department
www.right.sarawak.gov.my
Sarawak Homestay Association
www.sarawaktourism.com
Sarawak Tourism Board

National parks information

For information and accommodation booking for many of Sarawak's national parks, including Bako, Gunung Gading and Kubah and Matang Wildlife Centre, contact the **National Parks and Wildlife Booking Office** in Kuching (see page 47). Also see **www.sarawakforestry.com** (click on online services, and then booking of national park) and **www.ebooking.com.my**.

Kuching
& around

Due to Kuching's relative isolation (population 325,000) and the fact that it was not bombed during the Second World War, Sarawak's state capital has retained much of its 19th-century dignity and charm, despite the increasing number of modern high-rise buildings. Colourful Chinese shophouses still line many of the narrow streets. Kuching is a great introduction to the state and there are many sights within its compact centre, including the renowned Sarawak Museum and the Petra Jaya State Mosque.

Within easy reach is the Semenggoh Wildlife Centre and the national parks of Gunung Gading, Kubah and Tanjung Datu. North of Kuching is the Damai Peninsula, featuring the worthwhile Sarawak Cultural Village and Bako National Park on the Muara Tebas Peninsula.

Essential Kuching

Finding your feet

Kuching Airport is 10 km south of Kuching. At the time of research, the public bus service to and from the airport had been suspended due to lack of custom. However, those watching their pennies can still a bargain bus into town by making the 1-km walk to the Kuching Sentral Bus Station and taking a city-bound bus (3A, 6, 8 or 9). The bus terminal is west of the airport, so turn left as you exit Arrivals, and then turn left again at the first major junction. To take a taxi into town, buy a fixed-price coupon (RM30) from the counter in Arrivals. Or catch the **Tune Hotel** shuttle bus which departs every hour 0800-2000 (RM10). This service drops passengers off at the **Tune Hotel** on Jalan Borneo.

Best experiences

Explore the Sarawak Museum and wince at the display of *palang*, pages 39 and 138
Walk along Kuching's bustling waterfront promenade, snacking on *ais cream goring* (fried ice cream), page 41
Climb to the top of the Kuching Civic Center for panoramic views over the city, page 44
Visit Malaysia's first planetarium, page 44
Take a sampan across the river to visit the Astana, Fort Margherita and the Malay kampongs, pages 44, 45 and 46
Wander around Kuching's massive Sunday market, page 53
Take a day trip to the Sarawak Cultural Village, the state's 'living museum', page 61

Getting around

The central part of the city, which is the most interesting, can be negotiated on foot. Sampans (flat-bottomed Chinese wooden boats, also known as *perahu tambang*) operate as river taxis and are a bargain at 50 sens per trip. There are three city bus companies that provide a cheap and fairly efficient service. It's possible to hire bicycles from some of the guesthouses in town, notably on Jalan Carpenter. Taxis are found outside many of the larger hotels and at designated taxi stands. There are several international as well as local self-drive car hire firms in Kuching. See Transport, page 55.

When to go

The **Kuching Marathon**, www.marathon kuching.com, is held annually in August. There's also the popular **Rainforest Music Festival** (see page 64), held every August at the Sarawak Cultural Village. May and June are the months for **Gawai Padi** (see page 60), a kind of harvest festival and a time for feasting and partying.

Weather Kuching

January 30°C 23°C 690mm	**February** 30°C 23°C 429mm	**March** 31°C 23°C 339mm
April 32°C 23°C 288mm	**May** 33°C 24°C 268mm	**June** 32°C 23°C 250mm
July 32°C 23°C 195mm	**August** 33°C 23°C 260mm	**September** 32°C 23°C 260mm
October 32°C 23°C 324mm	**November** 31°C 23°C 331mm	**December** 31°C 23°C 499mm

BACKGROUND

Kuching

Shortly after dawn on 15 August 1839, the British explorer James Brooke sailed around a bend in the Sarawak River and, from the deck of his schooner, *The Royalist*, had his first view of Kuching. According to the historian Robert Payne, he saw "…a very small town of brown huts and longhouses made of wood or the hard stems of the nipah palm, sitting in brown squalor on the edge of mudflats." The settlement, 32 km upriver from the sea, had been established less than a decade earlier by Brunei chiefs who had come to oversee the mining of antimony in the Sarawak River valley. The antimony – used as an alloy to harden other metals, particularly pewter – was exported to Singapore where the tin plate industry was developing.

By the time James Brooke had become rajah in 1841, the town had a population of local Malays, Dayaks and Cantonese, Hokkien and Teochew traders. Chinatown dominated the south side of the river while the Malay kampongs were strung out along the riverbanks to the west. A few Indian traders also set up in the bazaar among the Chinese shophouses. Under Charles Brooke, the second of the White Rajahs (see page 294), Kuching began to flourish; he commissioned most of the town's main public buildings. Brooke's wife, Ranee Margaret, wrote:

"I wish I could give a description of our home in Kuching as it appeared to me then and as I think of it now. How I delighted in those many hours spent on the broad verandah of our house, watching the life going on in the little town the other side of the river. I think I have said before that at high tide the breadth of the river where it runs under the banks of our garden is as broad as the Thames at Westminster Bridge. The little town looked so neat and fresh and prosperous under the careful jurisdiction of the Rajah and his officers, that it reminded me of a box of painted toys kept scrupulously clean by a child. The Bazaar runs for some distance along the banks of the river, and this quarter of the town is inhabited almost entirely by Chinese traders, with the exception of one or two Hindoo shops. The Chinese shops look very much like those in small towns on the Italian Lakes. Groceries of exotic kinds are laid out on tables near the pavement, from which purchasers make their choice. At the Hindoo shops you can buy silks from India, sarongs from Java, tea from China, and tiles and porcelain from all parts of the world, laid out in picturesque confusion, and overflowing into the street. Awnings from the shops and brick archways protect purchasers from the sun, whilst across the road all kinds of boats are anchored, bringing produce from the interior of Sarawak, from the Dutch Settlement, from Singapore, and from adjacent islands". (Brooke, Margaret, *My Life in Sarawak*, pages 62-63. London Forgotten Books [London, 2013]. Original work published 1913.)

ON THE ROAD

Hazy days in Kuching

Of all the cities in Malaysia, Kuching has been the worst affected by the smog – euphemistically known as 'the haze' – that periodically engulfs large areas of Borneo and the Indonesian island of Sumatra, and affects Singapore, Peninsular Malaysia, Thailand and, in 2015, was causing problems in Vietnam, Cambodia and the southern Philippines. This haze is largely blamed on slash-and-burn deforestation in Kalimantan and Sumatra. This was most severe in mid-1997, but occurs to some extent every year. At the peak of the 'emergency' – for that is what it became – in late September 1997, Kuching came to a standstill. It was too dangerous to drive and, seemingly, too dangerous to breathe. People were urged to remain indoors. Schools, government offices and factories closed. The port and airport were also closed. Tourism traffic dropped to virtually zero and for 10 days the city stopped. At one point there was even discussion of evacuating the entire population of Sarawak. People began to panic buy and the prices of some commodities rose 500%. The haze in 2015 was somewhat different in nature. It was prolonged over several months and though the intensity of it on a daily basis did not reach the levels of 1997, the consistency of it caused a greater amount of damage to economies throughout the region. Sarawak was one of the worst affected regions, with schools being closed for several days as the air quality was declared hazardous. Visitors should note the haze season, which usually starts around June, and plan accordingly. Travelling, or even being outside when it is hazy, is unpleasant and unhealthy.

Sights

the charming state capital, with heritage architecture and a long riverfront esplanade

Sarawak's capital is divided by the Sarawak River; the south is a commercial and residential area, dominated by Chinese, while the north shore is predominantly Malay in character with the old kampong houses lining the river. The Astana, Fort Margherita and the Petra Jaya area, with its modern government offices, are also on the north side of the river. The two parts of the city are very different in character and even have separate mayors. Kuching's cosmopolitan make-up is immediately evident from its religious architecture: Chinese and Hindu temples, the imposing state mosque and Protestant and Roman Catholic churches.

★ Sarawak Museum

Jln Tun Haji Openg, T082-244232, www.museum.sarawak.gov.my, Mon-Fri 0900-1645, Sat, Sun and public holidays 1000-1600 (closed on 1st day of longer public holidays), free. There is a library and a bookshop attached to the museum as well as a gift shop, the Museum Shoppe, all proceeds of which go to charity. Permits to visit Niah's Painted Cave can be obtained, free of charge, from the curator's office.

Kuching's biggest attraction is this internationally renowned museum, housed in two sections on either side of Jalan Tun Haji Openg. The old building to the east of the main road is a copy of a Normandy town hall, designed by Charles Brooke's French valet. The rajah was encouraged to build the museum by the naturalist Alfred Russel Wallace, who spent over two years in Sarawak, where he wrote his first paper on natural selection. The museum was opened in 1891, extended in 1911, and the 'new' wing built in 1983. Its best-known curators have been naturalist Eric Mjoberg, who made the first ascent of Sarawak's highest peak – Gunung Murudi (see page 121) – in 1922, and ethnologist and explorer Tom Harrisson, whose archaeological work at Niah made world headlines in 1957. The museum overlooks pleasant botanical gardens and the **Heroes Memorial**, built to commemorate those that died in the Second World War, the Communist insurgency and the confrontation with Indonesia. Across the road, and linked by a footbridge, is the Dewan Tun Abdul Razak building, the newer extension of the museum.

The museum has a strong ethnographic section, although some of its displays have been superseded by the Sarawak Cultural Village (see page 61). The old museum's

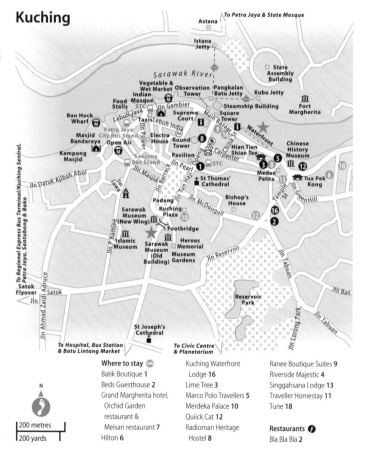

Kuching

Where to stay 🛏
Batik Boutique **1**
Beds Guesthouse **2**
Grand Margherita hotel,
    Orchid Garden
    restaurant &
    Meisan restaurant **7**
Hilton **6**

Kuching Waterfront
    Lodge **16**
Lime Tree **3**
Marco Polo Travellers **5**
Merdeka Palace **10**
Quiick Cat **12**
Radioman Heritage
    Hostel **8**

Ranee Boutique Suites **9**
Riverside Majestic **4**
Singgahsana Lodge **13**
Traveller Homestay **11**
Tune **18**

Restaurants 🍴
Bla Bla Bla **2**

ethnographic section includes a full-scale model of an Iban longhouse, a reproduction of a Penan hut and a selection of Kayan and Kenyah woodcarvings. There is also an impressive collection of Iban war totems (*kenyalang*) and carved Melanau sickness images (*blum*) used in healing ceremonies. The museum's assortment of traditional daggers (*kris*) is the best in Malaysia. The Chinese and Islamic ceramics include 17th- to 20th-century Chinese jars, which are treasured heirlooms in Sarawak (see box, page 45). Temporary exhibitions are held, often sponsored by major corporations, with a small entry fee (RM5).

The natural history collection, covering Sarawak's flora and fauna, is also noteworthy. The Tun Abdul Razak ethnological and historical collection includes prehistoric artefacts from the Niah Caves, Asia's most important archaeological site (see page 96). There is even a replica of Niah's Painted Cave – without the smell of guano.

To Cultural Village & Resort Hotels

Jln Tunku Abdul Rahman

Riverside Shopping Complex

Petanak

Jln Petanak

Jln Abell

Jln Padungan

UTC Sarawak

MAS

Jln Bukit Mata Kuching

Jln Song Thian Cheok

Great Cat of Kuching Statue

To Sin Kheng Hong Wharf (Boats to Sibu)

Royal Brunei Airlines

Hock

Jln Central Timur

To **11**, Turf Club, Regional Express Bus Terminal, Airport & Immigration Office

Black Bean Café **3**
James Brooke Bistro & Café **12**
The Junk **16**
Lepau **4**
Life Café **5**
Little Lebanon **8**
The Living Room **1**

Lok Thian **13**
Lyn's Thandoori Kitchen **7**
My Little Kitchen **11**
See Good **6**
Tom's **10**
Top Spot Food Court **9**
Zhun San Yen **14**

Sarawak Islamic Museum

Jln P Ramlee, T082-244232, Mon-Fri 0900-1645, Sat, Sun and public holidays 1000-1600 (closed on 1st day of longer public holidays), free.

Just south of the Sarawak Museum, this collection is housed in the restored Maderasah Melayu Building, an elegant, single-storey colonial edifice. As its name suggests, the museum is devoted to Islamic artefacts from all the ASEAN countries, with the collection of manuscripts, costumes, jewellery, weaponry, furniture, coinage, textiles and ceramics spread over seven galleries, each with a different theme, and set around a central courtyard.

★ Waterfront

Around Main Bazaar are some other important buildings dating from the Brooke era; most of them are closed to the public. The **Supreme Court** on Main Bazaar was built in 1874 as an administrative centre. State council meetings were held here from the 1870s until 1973, when it was converted to law courts. In front of the grand entrance is a memorial to Rajah Charles Brooke (1924) and on each corner there is a bronze relief representing the four main ethnic groups in Sarawak – Iban, Orang Ulu, Malay and Chinese. The clocktower was built in 1883. The **Square Tower**, also on Main Bazaar, was built as an annexe to Fort Margherita in 1879 and was used as a prison. Later in the Brooke era it was used as a ballroom. The

ON THE ROAD

A town called Cat

There are a few explanations as to how Sarawak's capital acquired the name 'Cat'. (*Kuching* means 'cat' in Malay, although today it is more commonly spelt *kucing* as in modern Bahasa 'c' is pronounced 'ch'.)

Local legend has it that James Brooke, pointing towards the settlement across the river, enquired what it was called. Whoever he asked mistakenly thought he was pointing at a passing cat. If that seems a little far-fetched, the Sarawak Museum offers a few more plausible alternatives. Kuching may have been named after the wild cats (*kucing hutan*) which, in the 19th century, were commonly seen along jungled banks of the Sarawak River. Another theory is that it was named after the fruit *buah mata kucing* ('cat's eyes'), which grows locally. Yet another theory speculates that Kuching comes from Chinese ku meaning old and ching meaning 'water well' and is related to a well in Chinatown that was the only source of crucial clean water during the 1888 cholera epidemic. Most likely, however, is the theory that the town may originally have been known as *Cochin* (port), a word commonly used across India and Indochina.

square tower marks one end of Kuching's waterfront esplanade which runs alongside the river for almost 900 m to the **Hilton**.

The waterfront has been transformed into a landscaped esplanade through restoration and a land-reclamation project. It has become a popular meeting place, with foodstalls, restaurants and entertainment facilities including an open-air theatre used for cultural performances. There is a restored Chinese pavilion, an observation tower, a tea terrace and musical fountains, as well as a number of modern sculptures. During the day, the waterfront offers excellent views of the Astana (palace), Fort Margherita and the Malay kampongs that line the north bank of the river. At night, the area comes alive as younger members of Kuching's growing middle class make their way here to relax.

A good way to see the Sarawak River is to take a 90-minute **cruise** ⓘ *tickets from Layar Warisan, 98 Main Bazaar, Lebuh Temple, T082-240366, or from tourist agencies, hotels or at the waterfront booths halfway along the esplanade, RM60, children RM30, with a minimum of 2 passengers, 3 departures daily at 0900, 1200 and 1500, or in the early evening at 1730.* Some cruises include folk dancers and a buffet meal or snacks and soft drinks.

The **General Post Office**, with its majestic Corinthian columns, stands in the centre of town, on Jalan Tun Haji Openg. Dating back to 1931, it was one of the few edifices built by Vyner Brooke, the last rajah. It has been renovated and is now the home of the **Sarawak Art Museum** ⓘ *T082-244232, for information see www.museum.sarawak.gov.my, Mon-Fri 0900-1645, Sat, Sun and public holidays 1000-1600 (closed on 1st day of longer public holidays), free.* This museum is home to ethnic art and crafts, as well as contemporary sculptures and modern styles. Attention is focused on local Malay artists.

The **Courthouse complex**, was built in 1871 as the seat of Sarawak's government and was used as such until 1973. It remains one of Kuching's grandest structures. The buildings have *belian* (ironwood) roofs and beautiful detailing inside and out, reflecting local art forms. It also continues to house the state's high court and magistrates' court as well as several other local government departments. The colonial-baroque **clocktower** was added in 1883 and the **Charles Brooke Memorial** in 1924. The complex also includes the

Pavilion Building which was built in 1907 as a hospital. During the Japanese occupation it was used as an information and propaganda centre and it is now undergoing renovation with a view to making it the home of a new textile museum. Opposite the Courthouse is the **Indian Mosque (Mesjid India)** on Lebuh India. It was originally built with an *atap* roof and *kajang* (thatch) walls; in 1876 *belian* (ironwood) walls were erected. The mosque was built by South Indians and is in the middle of an Indian quarter where spices are sold along the Main Bazaar. When the mosque was first built only Muslims from South India were permitted to worship here; even Indian Muslims from other areas of the subcontinent were excluded. In time, as Kuching's Muslim population expanded and grew more diversified, this rigid system was relaxed. It is hard to get to the mosque as it is surrounded by buildings. However, a narrow passage leads from Lebuh India between shop Nos 37 and 39.

The **Round Tower** on Jalan Tun Abang Haji Openg (formerly Rock Road) was originally planned as a fort in 1886, but was never completed. The whole area is undergoing restoration for future art galleries and cultural exhibits. The **Steamship Building** ⓘ *52 Main Bazaar*, was built in 1930 and was previously the offices and warehouse of the Sarawak Steamship Company. It has been extensively restored and now houses a restaurant, souvenir stalls, a handicrafts gallery and an exhibition area.

The **Bishop's House** ⓘ *off Jln McDougall, near the Anglican Cathedral of St Thomas*, is the oldest surviving residence in Sarawak. It was built in 1849, entirely of wood, for the first Anglican Bishop of Borneo, Dr McDougall. The first mission school was started in the attic and developed into St Thomas's and St Mary's School, which is now across the road on Jalan McDougall.

Chinatown

Kuching's Chinese population, part of the town's community since its foundation, live in the shophouses lining the narrow streets around **Main Bazaar**. This street opposite the waterfront is the oldest in the city, dating from 1864. The Chinese families who live here still pursue traditional occupations such as tinsmithing and woodworking. Kuching's highest concentration of antique and handicraft shops is to be found here. **Jalan Carpenter**, parallel to Main Bazaar, has a similar selection of small traders and coffee shops, as well as foodstalls and two small Chinese temples. Off **Lebuh China** (Upper China Street), there is a row of perfectly preserved 19th-century Chinese houses. The oldest Chinese temple in Kuching, **Tua Pek Kong** (also known as Siew San Teng), in the shadow of the **Hilton** on Jalan Tunku Abdul Rahman, was built in 1876, although it is now much modernized. There is evidence that the site has been in use since 1740 and a Chinese temple was certainly here as early as 1770. The first structure was erected by a group of Chinese immigrants thankful for their safe journey across the hazardous South China Sea. New immigrants still come here to give thanks for their safe arrival. The **Wang Kang Festival** to commemorate the dead is also held here. Just to the east of here, **Jalan Padungan** has some of Kuching's finest Chinese shophouses. Most were built during the rubber boom of the 1920s and have been restored. There are also some great coffee shops in this quarter of town. Further east still, the kitsch statue of the **Great Cat of Kuching** – the sort of thing to induce nightmares in the aesthetically inclined – mews at the junction of Jalan Padungan and Jalan Central.

The **Chinese History Museum** ⓘ *on the waterfront opposite Tua Pek Kong temple, T082-231520, Mon-Fri 0900-1645, Sat, Sun and public holidays 1000-1600 (closed on 1st day of longer public holidays), free*, documents the history of the Chinese in Sarawak, from the early traders of the 10th century to the waves of Chinese immigrants in the 19th century. This museum is small and easily managed in an hour and provides an excellent insight into the city's Chinese communities. The building itself is simple, with a flat roof, and shows English colonial influences. It was completed in 1912 and became the court for the Chinese population of Kuching. The Third Rajah was keen that the Chinese, like other ethnic groups, should settle disputes within their community in their own way and he encouraged its establishment. From 1912 until 1921, when the Chinese court was dissolved, all cases pertaining to the Chinese were heard here in front of six judges elected from the local Chinese population. In 1993 it was handed over to the Sarawak Museum and was turned into a museum.

Also of interest in Chinatown is the **Hian Tien Shian Tee** (Hong San) temple, at the junction of Jalan Carpenter and Jalan Wayang, which was built in 1897. The Moorish, gilt-domed **Masjid Bandaraya** (Old State Mosque), near the market on the west side of town, was built in 1968 on the site of an old wooden mosque dating from 1852.

Civic Centre and Planetarium

Jln Taman Budaya, T082-415806, www.planetarium-sarawak.org. Mon-Thu 0915-1730, Sat 0915-1800, viewing platform 0900-1700. Planetarium shows, RM2 (6 shows daily). Take STC bus K10 from the Saujana Bus Terminal on Jln Masjid and Jln P Ramlee.

On the south side of the river, the extraordinary-looking Civic Centre is Kuching's stab at the avant garde. As well as the viewing platform for panoramas of Kuching and the surrounding countryside including the mountains of Kalimantan on a clear day, the Civic Centre complex houses an art gallery with temporary exhibits (mainly of Sarawakian art), a restaurant and a pub-cum-karaoke bar one floor down, together with a public library. Malaysia's first planetarium is also within the complex: **Sultan Iskandar Planetarium** has a 15-m dome and a 170-seat auditorium.

Astana

Take a tambang across the river from the Pangkalan Batu jetty next to Square Tower on the waterfront to the Astana and fort, around RM0.50 with other passengers one way. The boats can also be hired privately for around RM30 per hr.

Apart from the Sarawak Museum, the White Rajahs bequeathed several other architectural monuments to Kuching. The Astana, a variant of the usual spelling *istana* (palace), was built in 1870, two years after Charles Brooke took over from his uncle. It stands on the north bank of the river almost opposite the market on Jalan Gambier. The Astana was hurriedly completed for the arrival of Charles' new bride (and cousin), Margaret. It was originally three colonial-style bungalows, with wooden shingle roofs, the largest being the central bungalow with the reception room, dining and drawing rooms. The crenellated tower on the east end was added in the 1880s at her request. Charles Brooke is said to have cultivated betel nut in a small plantation behind the Astana, so that he could offer fresh betel nut to visiting Dayak chiefs. Today, it's the official residence of the Governor of Sarawak and is only open to the public on **Hari Raya Puasa**, a day of prayer and celebration to mark the end of Ramadan. To the west of the Astana, in the traditionally Malay area, are many old wooden kampong houses.

A ceramic inheritance

Family wealth and status in Sarawak was traditionally measured in ceramics. In the tribal longhouses upriver, treasured heirlooms include ancient glass beads, brass gongs and cannons and Chinese ceramic pots and beads (such as those displayed in the Sarawak Museum). They were often used as currency and dowries. Spencer St John, the British consul in Brunei, mentions using beads as currency on his 1858 expedition to Gunung Mulu. Jars (*pesaka*) had more practical applications; they were (and still are) used for storing rice, brewing *tuak* (rice wine) or for keeping medicines.

Their value was dependent on their rarity: brown jars, emblazoned with dragon motifs, are more recent and quite common while olive-glazed dusun jars, dating from the 15th-17th centuries, are rare. The Kelabit people, who live in the highlands around Bario, in particular treasure the dragon jars. Although some of the more valuable antique jars have found their way to the Sarawak Museum, many magnificent jars remain in the Ian and other tribal longhouses along the Skrang, Rejang and Baram rivers. Many are covered with decoratively carved wooden lids.

Chinese contact and trade with the north coast of Borneo has gone on for at least a millennium, possibly two. Chinese Han pottery fragments and coins have been discovered near the estuary of the Sarawak River and, from the seventh century, China is known to have been importing birds' nests and jungle produce from Brunei (which then encompassed all of north Borneo), in exchange for ceramic wares. Chinese traders arrived in the Nanyang (South Seas) in force from the 11th century, particularly during the Sung and Yuan dynasties. Some Chinese pottery and porcelain even bore Arabic and Koranic inscriptions – the earliest such dish is thought to have been produced in the mid-14th century. In the 1500s, as China's trade with the Middle East grew, many such Islamic wares were traded and the Chinese emperors presented them as gifts to seal friendships with the Muslim world, including Malay and Indonesian kingdoms.

Fort Margherita
Jln Sapi, T082-231520, Mon-Fri 0900-1645, Sat, Sun and public holidays 1000-1600 (closed on 1st day of longer public holidays), free. To get to the fort, see Astana, above.

Not far away from the Astana, past the Kubu jetty, is this fort. It was also built by Rajah Charles Brooke in 1879 and named after Ranee Margaret, although there was a fort on the site from 1841 when James Brooke became Rajah. It commanded the river approach to Kuching, but was never used defensively, although its construction was prompted by a near-disastrous river-borne attack on Kuching by the Ibans of the Rejang in 1878. Even so, until the Second World War a sentry was always stationed on the lookout post on top of the fort; his job was to pace up and down all night and shout 'All's well' on the hour every hour until 0800. The news that nothing was awry was heard at the Astana and the government offices.

After 1946, Fort Margherita was first occupied by the Sarawak Rangers and was converted into a police museum in 1971. However, in 2008 this museum was closed and the exhibits moved back into police custody. The fort is now open to visitors once more with simple exhibits about the building. There is a cemetery dedicated to those who fought in the Second World War, which has good views of the city.

Towering above Fort Margherita is Sarawak's **State Assembly building** (Dewan Undangan Negeri). In a break from the norm, this huge structure resembles a cross between Brunei's Bolkiah Mosque and an Apollo moon lander. It's a fitting tribute to the rapid modernization of East Malaysia.

The **Malay kampongs** along the riverside next to Fort Margherita are seldom visited by tourists, despite their beautiful examples of traditional and modern Malay architecture.

Petra Jaya

The new **State Mosque** is situated north of the river at Petra Jaya and was completed in 1968. It stands on the site of an older mosque dating from the mid-19th century and boasts an interior of Italian marble.

Kuching's architectural heritage did not end with the White Rajahs; the town's modern buildings are often based on local styles. The new administration centre is in Petra Jaya: the **Bapak** (father) **Malaysia** building is named after the first prime minister of Malaysia and houses government offices; the **Dewan Undangan Negeri** (State Legislative Assembly of Sarawak) next door, is based on the Minangkabau style. Kuching's latest building is the ostentatious **Masjid Jamek**.

Also in Petra Jaya, like a space launch overlooking the road to Damai Peninsula, is the **Cat Museum** ⓘ *T082-446608, daily 0900-1700 (closed public holidays), free, camera RM3, take Petra Jaya bus K15 from Saujana Bus Stand*, which houses everything you ever wanted to know about cats with four extensive galleries displaying more than 4000 artefacts.

Nearby, the **Timber Museum** ⓘ *Wisma Sumber Alam (next to the stadium), T082-473000, www.sarawaktimber.org.my, Mon-Thu 0800-1630, Fri 0830-1130 and 1430-1630, closed weekends and public holidays, take a taxi, RM15 as there is no bus*, is meant to look like a log. It was built in the mid-1980s to engender a better understanding of Sarawak's timber industry. The museum, which has many excellent exhibits and displays, toes the official line about forest management and presents facts and figures on the timber trade, along with a detailed history of its development in Sarawak. The exhibition provides an insight into all the different forest types. It has information on and examples of important commercial tree species, jungle produce and many traditional wooden implements. The final touch is an air-conditioned forest and wildlife diorama, complete with leaf litter; all the trees come from the Rejang River area. A research library is attached to the museum. While it sidesteps the more delicate moral issues involved in the modern logging business, its detractors might do worse than to brush up on some of the less emotive aspects of Sarawak's most important industry.

Tourist information

Kuching Visitor Information Centre
UTC Sarawak, Jln Padungan, T082-410994.
Daily 0800-2100 (closed public holidays).
Staff are very knowledgeable and friendly and it's well stocked with maps and pamphlets. The desk at the airport has information on bus routes, approved travel agents and itineraries.

National Parks and Wildlife Booking Office
At the time of writing in 2016 the booking office was being relocated to new offices at UTC Sarawak, Jln Padungan, T082-248088. Mon-Fri 0800-1700. Check http://sarawak tourism.com/temporary-relocation-of-national-park-booking-office-kuching for the latest information.
For information and accommodation booking for the national parks of Bako, Gunung Gading and Kubah and Matang Wildlife Centre. Bookings can also be made online through the Sarawak Forestry Department (see below) or http://ebooking.sarawak.gov.my.

Sarawak Forestry Department
Wisma Sumba Alam, Jln Stadium, Petra Jaya, T082-442180, www.sarawakforestry.com.
Click on online services, and then booking of national park.

Sarawak Tourism Board
5th-7th floor, Bangunan Yayasan Sarawak, Jln Masjid, T082-423600, www.sarawak. tourism.com. Also at Kuching International Airport, T082-450944.

Tourism Malaysia
Parcel 297-2-1, Level 2, Riverbank Suites, Jln Tunku Abdul Rahman T082-246575, www. malaysia.travel. Also at Kuching International Airport, Lot L1A, Level 1, T082-627741.
Has information on Sarawak and Sabah and a good stock of brochures.

Tourist Police
Kuching Waterfront, T082-250522.

Where to stay

It is possible to negotiate over room rates and many of the hotels offer special deals. There is a good choice of international-standard hotels in Kuching. The Sarawak Tourism Board website (see above) has additional listings of hotels and resorts.

Recent years have seen unprecedented growth in mid- to budget-priced accommodation and Kuching has an excellent selection of guesthouses. With so many options to choose from, finding a bed is rarely a problem. However, guesthouses are booked solid for the annual Rainforest Music Festival and finding somewhere to sleep during this time could be problematic.
 Alternatively, you could try the **Homestay Programme**, www.right. sarawak.gov.my/homestay.

$$$$ Hilton
Jln Tunku Abdul Rahman, T082-248200, www.hilton.com.
Minimalistic but very stylish accommodation and the best hotel facilities in town, with several restaurants, gym, tennis courts and pool. Often has major discounts, making it great value. Good for a treat after a tough jungle trek.

$$$ Grand Margherita
Jln Tunku Abdul Rahman, T082-423111, www.grandmargherita.com.
Recently renovated, this towering edifice with 288 rooms is popular with weekday business folks and tour groups. Good weekend discounts available. The more expensive rooms have river views. Rooms are comfortable, with a faux bamboo theme, and have bathrooms with bathtubs, cable TV, safety box and fridge. There is a pool at the back of the hotel and a bar with live music, popular with expats at the weekend.

$$$ Merdeka Palace
Jln Tun Haji Openg, T082-258000,
www.merdekapalace.com.
Central location overlooking a playing field.
Pool, health club and business facilities, with
6 bars and restaurants on site. The 214 rooms
have minibar and satellite TV. Great value.

$$$ Ranee Boutique Suites
7 Main Bazaar, T082-258833,
www.theranee.com.
For those after something a little distinctive
and sophisticated in town, this is surely the
best offering. Decorated with antiques and
beautifully crafted furniture, this hotel is
perfect for a bit of Borneo romance. Rooms
are spacious and elegant. The suites are
particularly opulent, each with a unique
design, wide windows and a veranda
overlooking the river.

$$$ Riverside Majestic
Jln Tunku Abdul Rahman, T082-247777,
www.riversidemajestic.com.
Located in a shopping centre with a cinema,
this business hotel has a slightly dated feel but
rooms and suites are spacious. On the lower
floors, views are blocked by luxury suites.

$$ Batik Boutique Hotel
38 Jln Padungan, T082-422845,
www.batikboutiqehotel.com.
You won't miss the swirly whirly frontage
on this sophisticated offering which has
understated batik accents throughout.
Rooms are surprisingly generous and include
rain showers, iPod docks and large TVs.
There's a comfortable social area downstairs
with a dining area that serves up up a fair
approximation of a fried breakfast complete
with tasty wholegrain bread.

$$ Kuching Waterfront Lodge
Main Bazaar, T082-231111, www.
kuchingwaterfrontlodge.com.
Located along the bustling Main Bazaar, this
hotel is filled with artefacts from around the
region with beautifully carved tables and
tribal door frames; a stay here will not be

short on atmosphere. The dorms are a little
dark, as are some of the double rooms on the
top floor. Slightly overpriced but excellent
location in the heart of town.

$$ Lime Tree Hotel
Lot 317, Jln Abell, T082-414600,
www.limetreehotel.com.my.
Well-run mid-range option a short walk from
the town centre. The hotel has hints of lime
in every corner so those with a citrus aversion
would do well to avoid, but for everyone
else, this place represents good value with
spacious, spotless rooms, excellent daily
breakfast, fast Wi-Fi and a rooftop terrace
with good views over the town.

$$ Tune Hotel
Jln Borneo, T082-238221,
www.tunehotels.com.
Chain hotel based on the budget airline
model: the earlier you book, the cheaper the
room. Rooms are spotless, a little sterile, but
comfortable. A/c, towels and Wi-Fi are all
chargeable add-ons. Not the most exciting
place to stay but offers all the mod cons at
a fair price.

$ Beds Guesthouse
Lot 91, Section 50, Jln Padungan, T082-
424229, www.bedsguesthouse.com.
This small and friendly place has a stylish
and comfortable social area, a dining room
at the back which is a popular spot for a
glass of longhouse *tuak* in the evenings
and a light bit of guitar interaction, and
Wi-Fi access throughout. Rooms are
comfortable and stylish and kept spotlessly
clean. Staff are friendly and knowledgeable.
Decent breakfast.

$ Marco Polo Travellers
236 Jln Padungan, T082-332061.
This place gets plus points for its quiet and
verdant outdoor veranda and super-friendly
staff. Many of the rooms are windowless
though are comfortable and spotlessly clean.
General old school backpacker charm with
spotless shared bathrooms.

$ Quiik Cat
12B Jln Wayang, T013-8310020,
www.quiikcat.com.
Owner Akiew is very friendly and a superb
source of local knowledge and can point out
all the best dining hot spots in Kuching. His
hostel is a simple cat-themed place with fan
and a/c rooms, Wi-Fi throughout and bargain
RM20 beds in mixed dorms. Bathrooms are
shared and kept clean.

$ The Radioman Heritage Hostel
1 Jln Wayang, T082-248816.
Located a 1-min stroll from the waterfront
and just around the corner from the gourmet
delights on Jln Carpenter, this hostel is
brimming with character and off-beat artistic
flourishes. Simple rooms and cheap dorms
with free Wi-Fi throughout.

$ Singgahsana Lodge
1 Lebuh Temple, T082-429277,
www.singgahsana.com.
Well-established guesthouse owned by
Donald and Marina Tan whose travel photos
from around the world adorn the corridors.
Staff here are efficient and the hotel is a
well-run and cheerful place with funky decor,
a rooftop bar open until the wee hours
and free internet and Wi-Fi access. There is
a selection of rooms, from large dorms to
the stylish and sensual honeymoon suites
with attached bathroom. The double rooms
on the ground floor have an interesting
mezzanine level, although suffer from a lack
of natural light. This is probably the most
popular budget haunt in town and is a good
option for sociable types.

$ Traveller Homestay
240 Jln Padungan, T082-414093.
Located at the far flung reaches of town,
this small operation only has 5 rooms so is
perfect for those looking for a bit of peace
and quiet. The owner, Moi, is a goldmine of
local knowledge and can help organize a
variety of local tours. Well decorated with
interesting art prints leading down a steep
flight of stairs to a café which serves up

decent fare and plays a blinding selection of
80s and 90s tunes.

Restaurants

Kuching, with all its old buildings and
godowns along the river, seems made for
open-air restaurants and cafés but good
ones are notably absent and there seems
to be quite a high turnover. However,
the town is not short of hawker centres.
Local dishes worth looking out for include
umai (a spicy salad of raw marinated fish
with limes and shallots) and *laksa* (spicy
noodles – a Malaysia-wide dish, but
especially good here). Other distinctive
Sarawakian ingredients are *midin* and *paku*
(jungle fern shoots).

All the major hotels have Chinese restaurants;
most open for lunch and dinner, closing in
between. There are several cheap Indian
Muslim restaurants along Lebuh India.
Seafood is also excellent.
   In Kampong Buntal, 25 km north
of Kuching, there are several seafood
restaurants on stilts over the sea. It's popular
with Kuchingites.

$$$ Meisan
Grand Margherita Hotel (see Where to stay),
Jln Tunku Abdul Rahman.
Head here on Sun for a massive dim sum
blowout and join local Chinese families on
their Sun lunch treat.

$$$ Tom's
82 Jln Padungan, T082-247672.
Tue-Sun 1130-2300.
Excellent Western dishes including steaks
and salads in a slick modern setting. There's
a good beer garden out the back, ideal for
a pre-dinner tipple. The dessert selection
is very good and many locals consider it a
must-visit for guests in town.

$$ Bla Bla Bla
27 Jln Tabuan, T082-233944.
Tasty pan-Asian fare with plenty of seafood
options with dominant Thai and Indonesian

flavours. Beautiful interior with lots of calming foliage and serene Buddha statues.

$$ James Brooke Bistro and Café
Facing the river near the Chinese museum, Main Bazaar, T082-412120.
Open-air restaurant in fine Casablanca style, especially the mirrored bar. Fairly expensive but fine food from Malaysian curries to colonial favourites.

$$ The Junk
80 Jln Wayang, T082-259450. Closed Tue.
Beautifully atmospheric restaurant filled with antiques like old cash registers and lit by lanterns. Serves good but not fantastic pasta, steaks and other Western and Asian dishes.

$$ Lepau Restaurant
395 Jln Ban Hock, T019-880 5383.
Ever wondered what Sarawakian food tasted like? Well here is your chance to get familiar with indigenous dishes and a few Malaysian standards served in a tranquil setting with local music and friendly staff. On the menu look for *umai* (a delicious Sarawakian salad), tapioca prawns and *ayam kachangma* (a delicious local chicken dish).

$$ Life Café
108 Jln Ewe Hai, T082-425707.
Open 1000-2330.
Taiwanese noodle joint in a beautifully decorated restaurant with bamboo, Chinese art and an antique or 2. The food is consistently high quality with diners able to select the spiciness of their noodles, chomp into the signature pork leg or try local steamed vegetables. The ice-cold papaya juice goes down a dream after a morning of sightseeing.

$$ Little Lebanon
The Old Courthouse, Jln Barrack, T082-233523.
A small place with outdoor seating, *sheesha* pipes with a range of flavoured tobacco, and a long menu of Lebanese favourites including kebabs, tabbouleh and hummus. Those in the know swear by the felafels.

$$ The Living Room
23 Jln Tabuan, T082-426608.
Stylish and sophisticated restaurant with magnificent lighting and divided into several distinct sections, one of which is a tranquil Japanese garden and a lovely spot to unwind in. Come here for the pizzas, salads and a glass of wine after the sun has gone down.

$$ Lok Thian
1st floor, Bangunan Beesan, Jln Padungan, T082-331310.
This restaurant is very highly regarded by locals for the way it has gradually improved standards over time. The food is very good with lots of sticky and sweet Shanghainese dishes. Gets busy at weekends and would suit groups rather than individual diners. Booking advisable.

$$ Lyn's Thandoori Kitchen
No 7, Lot 267, Jalan Song Thian Cheok.
Probably the best bet in town for a decent tandoori chicken meal with good paneer dishes, pakora, dahls and freshly cooked naan. This should sort out any Indian food cravings and marks a pleasant departure from the stodgy biryanis that dominate Malaysian Indian food. Be prepared for a bit of a wait in the evenings.

$$ My Little Kitchen
56 Upper China St, T016-858 6669.
Scandinavian bistro serving up big portions of meatballs, mashed potatoes and coleslaw in an unpretentious, friendly environment.

$$ Orchid Garden
Grand Margherita Hotel (see Where to stay), Jln Tunku Abdul Rahman.
Good breakfast and evening buffets, international and local cuisine.

$$ See Good
Lot 228-229, No 53, Jalan Ban Hock.
Closed 4th and 18th of every month.
Extensive range of seafood at superb prices and a surprisingly good wine list. Good robust and spicy sauces, lots of herbs, extensive and exotic menu with a few nods

to indigenous fare, unlimited free bananas. Recommended by locals.

$ Zhun San Yen Vegetarian
Jln Chan Chin Ann, T082-230068.
This place is a vegetarian's dream with huge plates of Chinese vegetarian options and a daily buffet from 1200-1400. There is more than enough variety to keep you coming back for days. The fruit juices are great too.

Coffee shops
There are several Malay/Indian coffee shops on Lebuh India including **Madinah Café**, **Jubilee** and **Malaysia Restaurant**. Many Chinese coffee shops serve excellent *laksa* (breakfast) of curried coconut milk with a side plate of *sambal belacan* (chillied prawn paste).

Black Bean Café
87 Jln Ewe Hai, T082-420290.
Serves fantastic Malaysian coffee in a smart little café setting in the heart of town. Pop in here for a the refreshing a/c and enjoy your Borneo coffee with a chocolate walnut cookie or 2. Good place to pick up edible Borneo snacks and souvenirs if you are on your way back home.

Foodstalls and food centres
There are great open-air informal places along the waterfront selling everything from kebabs to *ais cream goreng* (fried ice cream) that start opening towards the evening. It makes a great place for an evening meal. Most of the foodstalls are clustered around the **Hilton** end of the promenade selling Malay dishes and fruit juices (no alcohol). There are beautiful views of the river, accompanied by popular Malay love songs.
Some of the best food centres are located in the suburbs; a taxi is essential.

Batu Lintang open-air market
Jln Rock (to the south of town, past the hospital).

Chinese Food Centre
Jln Carpenter (opposite temple).
Chinese foodstalls offering hot and sour soups, fish balls and more.

Hock Hong Garden
Jln Ban Hock, opposite Grand Continental.
Finest hawker stall food in Kuching, little English spoken but definitely worth trying to be understood.

King's Centre
Jln Simpang Tiga (bus No 11 to get there).
Large range of foodstalls, busy and not many tourists.

Kubah Ria Hawker stalls
Jln Tunku Abdul Rahman (on the road out of town towards Damai Beach, next to Satok Suspension Bridge).
Specialities include *sop kambing* (mutton soup).

Petanak Central Market
Jln Petanak, above Kuching's early morning wet market.
Light snacks, full seafood selection, good atmosphere, especially early in the morning.

The Spring Food Bazaar
Spring Mall, Jln Simpang Tiga.
A clean and comfortable setting to eat with a selection of Asian favourites, from Japanese teppanyaki to Sarawak *laksa*.

Top Spot Food Court
Jln Bukit Mata Kuching, top floor of a car park.
Range of stalls, deservedly popular and well worth a visit.

Bars and clubs

There are enough clubs, pubs and bars to keep most people reasonably happy. Clubs and discos usually have a cover charge, although there is often a drink or 2 thrown in with the price. Expect to pay around RM15 for a beer and RM25 for spirits.

Most places have happy hours and 2-for-1 offers. Bars tend to close around 0100-0200, a little later in hotels. Most bars are along Bukit Mata off Jln Pandungan and along Jln Borneo next to the Hilton.
The main centres of evening entertainment are along Jln Tunku Abdul Rahman, Jln Mendu,

Jln Padungan and Jln Petanakin, an area known locally as Travillion.

99
Jln Green Hill.
Quiet during the weeks but livens up at weekends and is a good spot to watch the football.

Fire
Jln Petanak.
New and friendly spot with a long happy hour and a crowd that grooves to Chinese dance music.

Grappa
58 Jln Padungan.
Stylish place popular with the young crowd. Music is famously loud and the beer some of the cheapest in town.

Kilkenny's
66 Jln Padungan.
Kilkennys on tap, tapas on the menu and good happy hour deals.

Mojo@Denise
On the junction of Jln Padungan and Jln Abell.
Wine and cocktail bar with themed evenings including poetry nights and live music.

Monsoon
Riverside Complex, Jln Tunku Abdul Rahman.
Balcony jutting out over the river. Good mix of locals and tourists.

Music Café
100 Jln Petanak, 1800-0200.
Good spot to meet locals with live music, DJs and big jugs of beer.

Rajang Lobby Lounge
Grand Margherita Hotel (see Where to stay).
Small but popular and with plenty of good drinks promotions.

Soho
64 Jln Padungan.
One of the most happening spots in town with Latin dance nights, club nights and lethal cocktails. Good for a spot of weekend clubbing oblivion.

Tribes
Downstairs at Grand Margherita Hotel (see Where to stay). Open 1600-0100.
Ethnic food, tribal decor and a variety of live music.

Entertainment

Also see the Sarawak Cultural Village (page 61), which puts on displays of tribal dance routes and cultural shows.

Cinemas
GSC City One Megamall, *3rd Floor, Jln Song.*
MBO Cinemas, *Lot 214, 2nd Floor, Spring Shopping Mall (see below).*
Star Cineplex, *Level 9, Medan Pelita, top floor of car park on Temple St.*

Festivals

See also the **Rainforest Music Festival**, page 64, and **Gawai Padi**, page 60.
Aug   Kuching Marathon, www.marathonkuching.com.

Shopping

When it comes to choice, Kuching is the best place in Malaysia to buy tribal handicrafts, textiles and other artefacts, but they are not cheap. In some of Sarawak's smaller coastal and upriver towns, you are more likely to find a better bargain and more authentic items, although the selection is not as good. If buying several items, it's a good idea to find a shop that sells the lot, as good discounts can be negotiated. It is essential to shop around: the best-stocked handicraft and antique shops in and near the big hotels are usually the most expensive. It is possible to bargain everywhere. Many shops are closed on Sun.

It is illegal to export any antiquity without a licence from the curator of the Sarawak Museum. An antiquity is defined as any object made before 1850. Most things sold as antiquities are not; some very convincing weathering and ageing processes are used.

Antiques, art and handicrafts

Most handicraft and antique shops are along **Main Bazaar**, **Lebuh Temple** and **Lebuh Wayang**, with a few in the Padungan area.

The **Sun market** on Jln Satok (see Markets, below) has a few handicraft stalls.

There are rows of pottery stalls along **Jln Penrissen**, out of town, take an STC bus (No 3, 3A, 6 or 2) or taxi to Ng Hua Seng Pottery bus stop. Antique shops sell this pottery too.

Artrageously Ramsay Ong, *94 Main Bazaar, T082-424346, www.artrageouslyasia.com.* Art gallery of Sarawak artiste extraordinaire Ramsay Ong who made fame with his tree bark works. Exhibits an eclectic collection of contemporary Malaysian art including some beautiful pieces by celebrated Bidayuh artist Narong Daun.

Fabriko, *56 Main Bazaar, www.fabriko.com.my.* Set in a beautifully restored Chinese shop-house, interesting souvenirs and gallery.

Galleri M, *lobby of Hilton hotel (see Where to stay).* Exclusive jewellery, bead necklaces and antiques, best available Iban hornbill carvings. Also paintings from Sarawakian artists.

Karyaneka (handicrafts) Centre, *Cawangan Kuching, Lot 324 Bangunan Bina, Jln Satok.*

Lov Gallery, *38 Jln Padungan, www.lov gallery.weebly.com.* Contemporary art by local artists. Well worth a look if you are in that part of town.

Sarakraf Pavilion, *78 Jln Tabuan, www. sarakraf.com.my.* Wide range of souvenirs and handicrafts and live demonstrations in a Chinese mansion. Craft courses are offered here. Outlets in major hotels in Kuching, Damai, Sarawak Cultural Village and Miri airport (chain set up by the Sarawak Economic Development Corporation).

Sarawak Batik Art Shop, *1 Lebuh Temple.* Excellent selection of local textiles including Iban *pua kumbu* (traditional patterned cloth).

Sarawak House, *67 Main Bazaar.* More expensive but better quality crafts, carvings, fabrics and pots.

Unika Borneo Arts and Crafts, *5 Jln Wayang.* Good selection of products from the interior.

Books and maps

Berita Book Centre, *Jln Haji Taha.* Good selection of English language books.

HN Mohd Yahia & Sons, **Holiday Inn**, *Jln Tunku Abdul Rahman, and in the basement of the Sarawak Shopping Plaza.* Sells a 1:500,000 map of Sarawak.

Popular Bookstore, *Boulevard Shopping Mall.* Fair selection of English language bestsellers.

Markets

Vegetable and wet markets are on the riverside on Jln Gambier; further up is the **Ban Hock Wharf market**, now full of cheap imported clothes. The **Sunday Market** on Jln Satok sells jungle produce, fruit and vegetables (there are a few handicraft stalls) and all sorts of intriguing merchandise; it starts on Sat night and runs through to Sun morning and is well worth visiting. There is a jungle produce market, **Pasar Tani**, on Fri and Sat at Kampong Pinang Jawa in Petra Jaya.

Shopping malls

Boulevard Mall, *Mile 4 Kuching–Serian Rd.* Books, sushi and fast food in a clean mall environment.

Riverside Shopping Complex, *next to Riverside Majestic.* Has **Parkson Department Store** and good supermarket in basement.

Sarawak Plaza, *next to the Holiday Inn, Jln Tunku Abdul Rahman.* Recently renovated and looking all the better for it.

The Spring, *Jln Simpang Tiga, on the way to the airport.* Standard shopping mall with a range of high street shops and a good food court.

What to do

Climbing

Outdoor Treks and Adventures, *www. bikcloud.com/rockropes.htm.* Organized rock-climbing trips to the Batman Wall at the Fairy Caves outside Bau (see page 58). There are 20 routes of up to 40 m.

Diving

Southern Sarawak has yet to open up as a popular diving centre. Visibility is generally poor most of the year, perhaps due in part to the vast amounts of silt being carried down the major rivers. But the marine life (if you can see it) is rich and relatively undisturbed, so there's a lot of potential for exploration. Apr-Sep are considered the best diving months. Also see **Aquabase** at the Damai Puri Resort & Spa (page 63).

Kuching Scuba Centre, *159 Jln Chan Chin Ann, T082-428842, www.kuchingscuba.com*.

Fishing

Seaworld NMS, *www.seaworldfishing. blogspot.sg*. Offshore fishing from Santubong or deep-sea game fishing at Tanjung Datu (near the Indonesian border).

Golf

Damai Golf & Country Club, *www.damaigolf.com*. See page 64.

Hornbill Golf & Jungle Club, Borneo Highlands Resort, *Padawan, T082-790800, www.borneohighlands.com.my*. 18-hole golf course at 1000 m.

Kelab Golf Course, *Petra Jaya, T082-440966, www.kgswak.com*. An 18-hole course.

Mountain biking

There are good trails at **Kamppung Singgai**, about 30 mins from Kuching (across the Batu Kawa bridge). There's a beginner to intermediate trail near **Kampong Apar** and an advanced trail at **Batang Ai**. Alternatively, hire a bike from Kuching (Singgahsana Lodge) and tour the Malay villages adjacent to the Astana and Fort Margherita. Cross the Sarawak River by sampan (around RM2 for you and your bike) and then follow the small road that runs parallel to the river.

Borneo Adventure, *see Tour operators, below*. Rents mountain bikes and can arrange specialized tours.

Spectator sports

Football See Malaysia Cup football matches in the **Stadium Negeri Sarawak**, Petra Jaya.

Horse racing The **Kuching Turf Club** (Serian Rd), is the biggest in Borneo (see newspapers for details of meetings).

Swimming

Kuching Municipal Pool, *next to Kuching Turf Club, Serian Rd. Mornings only*.

Water sports

Permai Rainforest Resort, *see page 64*. Aimed at families, with many activities on offer, including kayaking, windsurfing, sailing and rafting. Also offers trekking.

Tour operators

Most tour companies offer city tours as well as trips around Sarawak to **Semenggoh**, **Bako**, **Niah**, **Lambir Hills**, **Miri**, **Mulu** and **Bario**. There are also competitively priced packages to longhouses (mostly up the Skrang River, see page 70). It is cheaper and easier to take organized tours to Mulu, but arrange these in Miri (see page 100) as they are much more expensive if arranged from Kuching. Other areas are easy to get to independently.

Borneo Adventure, *No 55 Main Bazaar, T082-245175, www.borneoadventure.com*. Known for its environmentally friendly approach to tourism. Offers tours all over Sarawak as well as Brunei and Sabah. Recommended.

Borneo Exploration, *76 Jln Wayang, T082-252137, www.borneoexplorer.com.my*. Organizes a variety of longhouse tours, a city tour and trips to the national parks.

Borneo Touch Eco Tour, *www.borneo ecotours.com*. Award-winning agency with 37 years of experience and based in Sabah but offering very good Sarawak Tours at good prices. There's no office in Kuching but consultations are available on Skype.

Borneo Trek and Kayak Adventure, *T082-240571, www.rainforestkayaking.com*. Highly regarded outfit that offers kayaking trips combined with other cultural activities.

Rainforest kayak trips from RM188 per person. Specializes in jungle experiences for children. Recommended.

CPH Travel Agency, *70 Jln Padungan, T082-243708, www.cphtravel.com.my*. Longhouse trips, national park tours, day trips to the Kuching wetlands. Recommended.

Ibanika Tours and Travel, *ground floor, Lot 10528, Blok 16, KCLD, Jln Tun Jugah, T082-571133, ibanika@ace.cdc.abu.com*. Long-established company offering longhouse and more general tours.

Interworld, *1st floor, 161/162 Jln Temple, T082-252344/424515*. Can arrange packages to the Rainforest Music Festival (see page 64).

Transport

Air

Kuching Airport, T082-457373, is 10 km south of Kuching. For details of transport from the airport to Kuching centre, see Essential box, page 37.

Regular connections with **KL** (8-10 flights daily), **Kota Kinabalu** (**KK**) and **Brunei**. AirAsia (Wisma Ho Ho Lim, ground floor, 291 Jln Abell, T082-283222) flies to **KL**, **KK**, **JB**, **Miri**, **Bintulu** and **Singapore**; book online for the best rates. **Silk Air** also connects **Singapore** with Kuching. **Xpress Air** (www.xpressair.co.id) flies to **Pontianak** in West Kalimantan then on to **Bandung** in West Java.

Malaysian Airlines subsidiary **MASwings** (Level 3 Departures, Kuching Airport, T082-220 618) has a fleet of Twin Otters, Fokker F50s and ATR 72-500s which fly to smaller destinations in Sabah and Sarawak. Tickets can be purchased online. Destinations include **Bintulu**, **Mukah**, **Tanjung Manis**, **Gunung Mulu National Park** via **Miri** and **Sibu** and **Pontianak** in Indonesia. There are also connections to **KK**.

Boat

Sampans cross the Sarawak River from next to the Square Tower on Main Bazaar to **Fort Margherita** and the **Astana** on the north bank for around RM0.50. Small boats and some express boats connect with outlying kampongs on the river. Sampans can also be hired by the hour (RM40) for a tour up and down the river.

Express boats leave from the Sin Kheng Hong Wharf, 6 km out of town (take a taxi from Kuching, RM20), T082-410076. Turn up at the ferry 30 mins before departure to get a ticket. There is 1 daily departure for **Sibu** via Sarakei at 0830 (5 hrs, RM55).

Bus

Local 3 bus companies operate in Kuching. Yellow and white **Petra Jaya City Buses** serve Bako, Buntal and Kota Samarahan and the Damai Peninsula; buses depart from the open-air market near Electra House. The green and yellow **Sarawak Transport Company** (**STC**) buses serve the Kuching city area and southwestern Sarawak and leave from the post office and Jln Masjid. **Bau Transport Company** buses depart from Saujana Bus Stand and head for Bau Town.

Long distance Buses depart from the **Regional Express Bus Terminal** also known as **Kuching Sentral**, a short walk from the airport on the edge of town, about a 20-min drive from the city centre on Jln Penrissen (a taxi ride costs around RM20). You either have to buy tickets at the bus station itself or buy online in advance with a small booking fee with **Easy Book** (http://www.easybook.com). Buses to **Sibu** (0730-2200, RM50, 7 hrs), **Bintulu** (RM70) and **Miri** (0630-2200, RM80, 15 hrs). There are several morning daily departures to **Pontianak** in Kalimantan, from 0700, RM60.

International The Indonesian border crossing at Entikong has VOA (Visa On Arrival) status, meaning tourists can get a 30-day visa (US$35) on arrival. However, the visa situation in Indonesia is extremely volatile and it is imperative that travellers contact the consulate in Kuching for the latest updates (see page 322). Buses leave from Kuching Sentral. Interior towns are sometimes difficult to access by road.

Car

It is possible to enter Sarawak from Kalimantan driving a private vehicle (including rental vehicles) as long as it has international insurance cover.

Car hire **Flexi Car Rental**, Lot 7050, 2nd floor, Jln Sekama, T082-335282, www.flexicarrental.com. Also at the airport. **Golden System Car Rental & Tours**, 58-1B, 1st floor, Block G, Pearl Commercial Centre, Jln Tun Razak, T082-333609. **Pronto**

Car Rental, 1st floor, 98 Jln Padungan, T082-236889. **Wah Tung Travel Service**, 7 Jln Ban Hock, T082-248888, www.wahtunggroup.com.my.

Taxi

Local taxis congregate at the taxi stand on Jln Market, or outside the big hotels; they don't use meters, so agree a price before setting off. 24-hr radio taxi service, T082-341 818 or T082-242821. Short distances around town should cost RM10-15.

Around Kuching

giant rafflesias at Gunung Gading and gawai celebrations with the Bidyayuh in Bau

There is a wealth of places a short drive from Kuching that can be visited on a day trip or short overnight trip. Public transport is generally readily available as are good value taxis and minibuses. For more out of the way places, check with a local tour operator.

Semenggoh Nature Reserve and Wildlife Centre

30 km south of Kuching. Daily 0800-1700, RM3. For information contact Sarawak Forestry, www.sarawakforestry.com, T082-248088. Take STC bus No 6 (RM4) to the main gate and be prepared for a 20-min walk into the reserve. The last bus back to Kuching departs at 1700. A taxi to the reserve costs around RM55 one way plus RM15 per hr of waiting time. Feeding times 0900-1000 and 1500-1530.

Semenggoh, on the road to Serian, became the first forest reserve in Sarawak when the 800 ha of jungle were set aside by Rajah Vyner Brooke in 1920. They were turned into a wildlife rehabilitation centre for monkeys, orang-utans, honey bears and hornbills in 1975. All were either orphaned as a result of logging or were confiscated, having been kept illegally as pets. The aim has been to reintroduce as many of the animals as possible to their natural habitat. In late 1998 many of the functions that previously attracted visitors to Semenggoh were transferred to the Matang Wildlife Centre (see page 58). However, there are a few trails around the park including a plankwalk and a botanical research centre dedicated to jungle plants with medicinal applications. Semi-wild orang-utans still visit the centre for food handouts and can be seen at feeding times. Even when Semenggoh was operating as an orang-utan rehabilitation centre, it did not compare with Sepilok (see page 266) in Sabah, which is an altogether more sophisticated affair.

Gunung Penrissen

100 km south of Kuching. There are no buses so visitors will need to charter a taxi from Kuching to get there (RM350 per day).

This is the highest peak in the mountain range south of Kuching running along the Kalimantan border (altitude 1329 m). The mountain was visited by naturalist Alfred Wallace in 1855. Just over 100 years later the mountain assumed a strategic role in Malaysia's *Konfrontasi* with Indonesia (see page 130) – there is a Malaysian military post on the summit. Gunung Penrissen is accessible from Kampong Padawan; it lies a few kilometres south of Anna Rais, right on the border. It is a difficult mountain to climb requiring two long days, but affords views over Kalimantan to the south and Kuching and the South China Sea to the north. Prospective climbers are advised to see the detailed trail guide in John Briggs' *Mountains of Malaysia*, usually available in the Sarawak Museum bookshop.

Gunung Gading National Park

65 km northwest of Kuching, T082-735144, RM20. The park is 5 mins' drive from Lundu; taxis charge around RM15. From Kuching take STC bus No EP7 (RM12) to Lundu from Kuching Sentral (near the airport).

This park was constituted in 1983 and covers 4104 ha either side of the River Lundu. There are some marked trails, the shortest of which takes about two hours and leads to a series of waterfalls on the river. Gunung Gading and Gunung Perigi summit treks take seven to eight hours; it is possible to camp at the summit. Bring enough food and water. The park is made up of a complex of mountains with several dominant peaks including Gunung Gading (906 m). The rafflesia, the world's largest flower (see box, page 227), is found here but if you're keen to see one in bloom, phone the Park HQ first, since it has a very short flowering period. Basic chalet accommodation can be booked through the **National Parks and Wildlife Booking Office** (see page 47).

Around Kuching

Where to stay
Damai Puri Resort **2**
Permai Rainforest Resort **1**

Santubong Kuching Resort **3**

Lundu and Sematan

Bau Transport Company bus 2, or STC bus No 2, run from Jln Masjid to Bau (I hr), from where there are buses on to Lundu (2½ hrs). STC bus No EP07 goes directly to Lundu from Kuching Sentral (near the airport).

These villages have beautiful, lonely beaches and there is a collection of deserted islands off Sematan. One of the islands, **Talang Talang**, is a turtle sanctuary and permission to visit it must be obtained from the **Sarawak Forestry Department** in Kuching (see page 47).

Bau

60 km southwest of Kuching. Take STC bus No 2 from Jln Masjid; the journey takes 1 hr. Tour companies also organize trips.

Bau, which had its five minutes of fame during the 19th century as a small mining town, is today a market town and administrative centre. There are several caves close by; the **Wind Cave** is a popular picnic spot. The **Fairy Cave**, about 10 km from Bau, is larger and more impressive, with a small Chinese shrine in the main chamber and varied vegetation at the entrance. A torch is essential. Another reason to go to Bau is to see the Bidayuh celebrating their **Gawai Padi**, a festival with animistic roots which gives thanks to the gods for an abundant rice harvest. Singing, dancing, massive consumption of *tuak* (rice wine) and colourful shamans make this a highlight. It's held at the end of May and beginning of June. Ask at the tourist office in Kuching for details.

Kubah National Park

20 km west of Kuching, T082-845033, but the National Parks and Wildlife Booking Office in Kuching, see page 47, is likely to be more helpful; RM20. The park is easy to visit as a day trip, but there is no scheduled bus service. Matang Transport Company bus No 21 runs to Kubah Park HQ from the bus station near Saujana Bus Stand in Kuching but the service is very irregular (RM3.50, 40 mins). A minibus also departs when full. Far easier is to charter a taxi (one-way RM60) from Kuching. Travel agents also arrange tours.

This is a mainly sandstone, siltstone and shale area covering some 2230 ha, with three mountains: **Gunung Serapi**, **Gunung Selang** and **Gunung Sendok**. There are at least seven waterfalls and bathing pools. Vegetation includes mixed dipterocarp and *kerangas* (heath) forest, wild orchids and palms (of which there are 93 species). Wildlife includes bearded pigs, mouse deer, hornbills and numerous species of amphibians and reptiles. Unfortunately for visitors here, Kubah's wildlife tends to stay hidden; it's not really a park for 'wildlife encounters'.

There are four marked trails, ranging from 30 minutes to three hours. The **Rayu Trail** passes through rainforest containing a number of bintangor trees (believed to contain two chemicals that have showed some evidence of being effective against HIV). Visitors may be able to see trees that have been tapped for this potential rainforest remedy. There is a variety of accommodation available for those wishing to stay longer, from a cheap hostel (RM15 a bed) to air-conditioned chalets.

The **Matang Wildlife Centre** ⓘ *T082-225012, animal feeding times vary (orang-utans, sambar deer and crocodiles),* is part of the Kubah National Park. It houses endangered wildlife in spacious enclosures which are purposefully placed in the rainforest. The key attraction are the orang-utans, which are rehabilitated here for release back into the wild. Other animals include sambar deer, sun bears, civets and bear cats. There is accommodation, an information centre and education programmes to enable visitors to learn more about the conservation of Sarawak's wildlife. The centre has also established a series of trails.

Pulau Satang Besar
Boats leave from either Kampong Telaga Air or Santubong and take 35 mins. Buses run to Kampong Telaga Air from Kuching Sentral (45 mins). Petra Jaya bus K15 runs to Santubong (every 40 mins, RM8, 45 mins), or take a shuttle bus from Singgahsana Hostel or Hotel Margherita (see page 61). Ask at the Visitor Information Centre overlooking the Padang in Kuching, T082-410942, for boat departure times, or enquire at travel agencies in town.

North of the fishing village of Kampong Telaga Air, Pulau Satang Besar has been designated a **Turtle Sanctuary** to protect the green turtles that come ashore here to lay their eggs. It's an excellent spot for snorkelling and relaxing on the beach.

Tanjung Datu National Park
100 km from Kuching, at the westernmost tip of Sarawak. Take STC bus No EP7 (RM12) to Lundu Kuching Sentral (near the airport), and on to Sematan. At the jetty in Sematan, hire a boat (40 mins, RM120 to hire the whole boat; there is no scheduled service). The seas are too rough for the journey Oct-Feb. The boat will drop you off at the Park HQ's jetty. Alternatively, from Sematan you can jump in a boat to Teluk Melano (more regular, takes about 40 mins), and then hire a 10-min boat trip to the park.

This is the newest and smallest park in Sarawak, first gazetted in 1994. It is covered with mixed dipterocarp forest, rich in flora and fauna, and beautiful beaches with crystal-clear water and coral reefs offshore. Keep an eye out for venomous sea snakes here. There is some rudimentary accommodation available within the park, but an altogether more interesting option would be the Telok Melano homestay, which offers all-inclusive packages for groups of up to five visitors. Contact **PNK Sematan** ⓘ *T082-711101*, for information.

Listings Around Kuching *map page 57.*

Where to stay

Gunung Penrissen

$$$ Hornbill Golf & Jungle Club
Borneo Highlands Resort, Jln Borneo Heights, Padawan, T082-578980, www.borneohighlands.com.my.
As its name suggests, this is a mountain hideaway for golf fanatics. There are luxurious chalets and suites beautifully furnished with golfing touches like paintings of greens. The resort lies at 1000 m and so the weather is cooler and more spring-like. The resort offers golf, jungle treks and longhouse tours, a rabbit farm, spas and flower gardens.

Gunung Gading National Park

$$-$- National park accommodation
Bookings taken through the National Parks and Wildlife Parks Booking Office in Kuching (see page 47), T082-248088, www.sarawakforestry.com.
Chalets with 2-3 bedrooms (RM140 per chalet) and a hostel (RM15 per person in a 6-bed dorm or RM40 for the entire room). Camping for RM5 per head, although visitors need to bring their own equipment.

Lundu and Sematan

$$$ Sematan Palm Beach Resort
Lot 295, Kpg Sungai Kilong, Jln Seacom, Sematan, T082-712388, www.spbresort.com.

Family-friendly place with brightly coloured A-frame chalets and bungalows on a long stretch of beach. Rooms are well furnished and newly painted and all have a/c and TV. There is access to a pool and that inviting beach is just a short leap away. Bikes can be hired to explore the surrounding countryside.

$ Sematan Hotel
162 Sematan Bazaar, Sematan.
Functional place with green walls and old rooms with a/c. Whilst this place is in need of a bit of a loving touch up, it is a passable place to crash out for the night.

Kubah National Park

$$$-$ National park accommodation
Bookable through the National Parks and Wildlife Booking Office in Kuching (see page 47), T082-248088 or www.sarawak forestry.com.
There are fan chalets (RM150), an 8-room hostel (RM15.75) and 5 huge bungalows at the Park HQ with full kitchen facilities,

4 beds (2 rooms), a/c, hot water, TV and veranda (RM225 for the whole chalet). Bring your own food.

Festivals

Bau
May-Jun Gawai Padi is celebrated by the indigenous Bidayuh with singing, dancing, drums and plenty of rice wine. The festival has animistic roots and shamanistic rituals give thanks to the gods for an abundant rice harvest. Ask at the tourist office in Kuching for details.

What to do

Climbing
Outdoor Treks and Adventures, *www. bikcloud.com/rockropes.htm*. Based in Kuching, this company offers organized rock-climbing trips to the Batman Wall at the Fairy Caves outside Bau (see page 58). There are 20 bolted routes of up to 40 m.

Damai Peninsula
Sarawak's 'living museum' and river cruises to spot crocodiles and dolphins

The Damai Peninsula, 35 km north of Kuching, is located at the west mouth of the Santubong River and extends northwards as far as Mount Santubong, a majestic peak of 810 m. Its attractions include the Sarawak Cultural Village, trekking up Mount Santubong, fantastic sunset river cruises, sandy beaches, a golf course, adventure camp and a number of decent places to stay.

Santubong and Buntal
Petra Jaya bus K15 to Damai goes to Buntal and Santubong.

The village of **Santubong** itself, located at the mouth of the Santubong River, is small and quiet. Formerly a fishing village, most of the villagers now work in one of the nearby resorts. However, some fishing still goes on and the daily catch is still sold every morning at the quayside. Nearby are two or three Chinese-run grocery stores and a coffee shop. The rest of the village is made up of small houses strung out along the road, built in the Malay tradition on stilts – many are wooden and painted in bright colours. Another village here is **Buntal**, which is just off the Kuching–Santubong road and is popular with local Kuchingites, who visit at the weekends for the seafood restaurants.

Sarawak Cultural Village

35 km north of Kuching, T082-846108, www.scv.com.my. Daily 0900-1700, cultural shows at 1130 and 1600 (45 mins). RM60, children (6-12 years) RM30, prices include cultural show. A regular shuttle bus service operates from the Grand Margherita hotel in Kuching. Sometimes it's cheaper to buy both the entrance ticket and bus tickets from tour agencies or the Grand Margherita where they often have special offers.

The Sarawak Cultural Village (Kampong Budaya Sarawak) was the brainchild of the **Sarawak Development Corporation** which built Sarawak's 'living museum' at a cost of RM9.5 million to promote and preserve Sarawak's cultural heritage, opening it in 1990. With increasing numbers of young tribal people being tempted from their longhouses into the modern sectors of the economy, many of Sarawak's traditional crafts have begun to die out. The Cultural Village set out to teach traditional arts and crafts to new generations. For the State Development Corporation, the concept had the added appeal of creating a money-spinning 'Instant Sarawak' for the benefit of tourists lacking the time or inclination to head into the jungle. While it is rather contrived, the Cultural Village has been a great success and contains some superb examples of traditional architecture. It should be on the sightseeing agenda of every visitor to Kuching, if only to provide an introduction to the cultural traditions of all the main ethnic groups in Sarawak.

Each tribal group is represented by craftsmen and women who produce handicrafts and practise traditional skills within houses built to carefully researched design specifications. Many authentic everyday articles have been collected from longhouses all over Sarawak. In one case the village has preserved a culture that is already effectively dead: today the Melanau people all live in Malay-style kampongs, but a magnificent traditional wooden Melanau house has been built at the Cultural Village and is now the only such building in Sarawak. Alongside it there is a demonstration of traditional sago processing. A resident Melanau craftsman makes sickness images (*blum*), each representing the spirit of an illness, which were floated downriver in tiny boats as part of the healing ritual.

There are also Bidayuh, Iban and Orang Ulu longhouses, depicting the lifestyles of each group. In each there are textile or basket weavers, woodcarvers or swordmakers. There are exhibits of beadwork, bark clothing, and *tuak* (rice wine) brewing. At the Penan hut there is a demonstration of blowpipe making and

Essential Damai Peninsula

Finding your feet

Petra Jaya bus K15 runs regularly to the Damai Peninsula from the open-air market near Electra House (RM8).

There is a more comfortable shuttle bus service offered by **Aquabase**, www.aquabase-kuching.com/shuttle_time_schedule.html, which starts at **Singgahsana Lodge** and picks up at hotels in town and runs to the resorts in Damai (eight daily, 0715-2200, RM10, 45 minutes).

Another shuttle bus leaves from the **Grand Margherita Hotel**, https://www.grandmargherita.com/facility.php, and runs to Damai resort hotels and the Sarawak Cultural Village (leaves Kuching at 1015, 1415 and 1815, returns from Damai Beach Resort at 0919 and 1315, RM12 single/RM20 return, 40 minutes).

A taxi from Kuching should cost RM50-60 one way, depending on your bargaining skills. Tour companies offer packages for various prices including transport, entry to the Sarawak Cultural Village and lunch.

ON THE ROAD

The Penan: museum pieces for the 21st century?

Economic progress has altered many Sarawakians' lifestyles in recent decades; the oil and natural gas sector offers many employment prospects and upriver tribespeople have been drawn into the logging industry. But it is logging that has directly threatened the 16,000-strong Penan tribe's traditional way of life.

Sarawak's nomadic hunter-gatherers emerged as 'the noble savages' of the late 20th century, as their blockades of logging roads drew world attention to their plight. In 1990, Prince Charles's remarks about Malaysia's "collective genocide" against the Penan prompted an angry letter of protest from former Prime Minister Dr Mahathir Mohamad. He is particularly irked by western environmentalists – especially Bruno Manser, who lived with the Penan in the late 1980s. "We don't need any more Europeans who think they have a white man's burden to shoulder", Dr Mahathir said.

Malaysia wants to integrate the Penan into mainstream society, on the grounds that it is morally wrong to condemn them to a life expectancy of 40 years, when the average Malaysian lives to almost 80. "There is nothing romantic about these helpless, half-starved, disease-ridden people", Dr Mahathir said. The government has launched resettlement programmes to transform the Penan from hunters into fishermen and farmers. One of these longhouses can be visited in Mulu (see page 112). It has failed to engender much enthusiasm from the Penan, although the majority have now been resettled. Environmentalists countered that the Penan should be given the choice, but, the government asks, what choice do they have if they have only lived in the jungle?

The Sarawak Cultural Village, opened by Dr Mahathir, offered a compromise of sorts – but the Penan had the last laugh. One tribal elder, Apau Madang, and his grandson were paid to parade in loincloths and make blowpipes at the Penan hut while tourists took their snapshots. The arrangement did not last long as they did not like posing as artefacts in Sarawak's 'living museum'. They soon complained of boredom and within months had wandered back to the jungle where they could at least wear jeans and T-shirts. Today, the Penan hut is staffed by other Orang Ulu. There are thought to be only 200 Penan still following their traditional nomadic way of life.

visitors are invited to test their hunting skills. There is a Malay house and even a Chinese farmhouse with a pepper garden alongside. The tour of the houses, seven in all (you can collect a stamp from each one for your passport) is capped by an Andrew Lloyd Webber-style cultural show which is expertly choreographed, if rather ersatz. It is held in the air-conditioned onsite theatre.

Special application must be made to attend heritage centre workshops where courses can be requested in various crafts such as woodcarving, mat weaving or batik painting; they also run intensive one-day and three- to four-day courses. There is a restaurant and craft shop, **Sarakraf**, at the village.

> **Tip...**
> The Cultural Village is also the venue for the fabulous annual **Rainforest Music Festival** (see page 64).

Gunung Santubong

Take the bus to Damai Beach from Kuching or a minivan from the open-air market on Jln Masjid.

Situated on the Santubong Peninsula, Gunung Santubong's precipitous southwestern slopes provide a moody backdrop to Damai Beach. The conical peak – from which there are spectacular views – is most accessible from the eastern side, where there is a clear trail (taking seven to nine hours; the last stretch is a tough scramble) to the top. The trail starts at **Santubong Mountain Trek Canteen** ① *opposite the Palm Beach Seafood Restaurant and Resort, about 2.5 km before the Holiday Inn Damai Beach, T082-846153.* Follow the numbered trees (there are 250 in all). After 30 minutes of walking you'll reach a junction and see trails marked red or blue. To get to the summit follow the red trail. The blue trail leads to a waterfall and then heads back down to the main road. Take your own food and water supplies. Guides are not necessary (but can be provided); check with hotel recreation counters or at the Santubong Mountain Trek Canteen. The official *Damai Guide* provides a more detailed description of the trek.

Kuching Wetlands National Park

Most tours depart from Santubong Boat Club or Damai Beach; from here it's only a 20- to 30-min boat ride to the park. Reliable agencies include Aquabase Kuching (see page 61), www.aquabase-kuching.com, and CPH Travel Agency, 70 Jln Padungan, Kuching, T082-243708, www.cphtravel.com.my.

Designated in 2002 this relatively small national park encompasses 6610 ha of dense mangrove and heath forest where the Sibu and Salak rivers meet the South China Sea. The area is rich in wildlife and an important site for a range of water birds, crocodiles and primates, including the proboscis monkey. One of park's truly distinctive inhabitants is the Irrawaddy dolphin, a small slow swimming mammal that lives in shallow seas – and often far up major rivers into freshwater areas – throughout Southeast Asia. The dolphin is rare almost everywhere, but the Kuching wetlands is one of the best places to see them in Malaysia.

Several Kuching tour agencies offer dolphin and wildlife spotting boat tours of the park's waterways. A number of agencies around town also run cruises (three hours, RM220 including snacks and drinks on the boat). It is recommended to start this trip around 1600 to maximize the variety of wildlife seen from the cruise and to have a chance to experience the glorious Sarawak sunset from the river. The boats glide quietly pass riverbanks with proboscis monkeys, through waters filled with saltwater crocodiles and Irrawaddy dolphins and the cruise finishes with a performance from fireflies on the river banks after the sun has gone down. It's an excellent introduction to the diversity of wildlife of Sarawak and thoroughly recommended.

Listings Damai Peninsula

Where to stay

$$$ Damai Puri Resort
Damai Beach, T082-846900,
www.damaipuriresort.com.
Just below a mansion belonging to the Sultan of Brunei, this upmarket hotel has 207 elegant rooms offering stunning views either of the rainforest and Gunung Santubong on one side or the sea on the other. Facilities include a pool, tennis courts and full spa centre. Discounts available.

$$$ One Hotel Santubong Kuching Resort
Jln Pantai Damai, Santubong, PO Box 2364, T082-846888, www.sarawak-hotels.com/one-hotel-santubong.

Surrounded by the Damai golf course, and with more than 300 a/c rooms in 5 towers, this sprawling hotel is looking a tad rough round the edge nowadays. It has a restaurant, large pool surrounded by greenery, chalets with jacuzzis, and offers tennis, basketball, volleyball, gym and mountain biking. Nestling beneath Mt Santubong, this low-rise resort is particularly popular with golfers who come to hit a few rounds on the Arnold Palmer-designed golf course. Keep your expectations in check and you'll have a fair stay.

$$$ Permai Rainforest Resort
Pantai Damai Santubong, PO Box B91, Satok Post Office, T082-846487, www.permairainforest.com.

At the foot of Mt Santubong, this resort markets itself as a low impact eco-resort and offers lots of green and healthy activities from jungle trekking and night mangrove cruises to sea kayaking. There are comfy a/c treehouses, built on stilts 6 m above ground and with attached hot water bathroom, or for those with less cash to splash, there are 23 comfortable a/c cabins a little closer to the earth. Camping is also available at RM10 per person. Cafeteria and tents and camping equipment for hire.

$$$ The Village House
Santubong Village, T082-846166, www.villagehouse.com.my/villagehouse.

Gorgeous little place with smallish rooms with ethnic motifs, spacious social area with pool, restaurant and abundant Sarawakian tribal art in the heart of Santubong Village. It might not be the most convenient place to stay but more than makes up for it in relaxed atmosphere.

$ BB Bunkers
Unit C1, Damai Central, Pantai Damai Santubong, T082-846835, www.bbbunkers.com.

Brand new place in the heart of the Damai Peninsula principally catering to budget travellers. It's an unusual concept and designed like a warehouse with beds divided by grills and curtains rather than by walls. Nevertheless, it's great value, friendly, has very clean bathrooms and plenty of space for socializing, making this the best budget option in Damai.

Bars and clubs

Gecko
Damai Puri Inn, Damai Beach.

Lovely tropical-style bar with plenty of comfy seats and a good selection of drinks. Simple Asian and Western snacks served.

Entertainment

Cultural shows
Sarawak Cultural Village, *see page 61.* Shows daily at 1130 and 1600. Cultural shows, with stylized and expertly choreographed tribal dance routines.

Festivals

Jun/Jul/Aug **Rainforest World Music Festival**, www.rwmf.net. Held at the Sarawak Cultural Village (see page 61), this festival attracts musicians from around the world. There are stages set up with live music offerings from groups around the world, foodstalls and jamming sessions are held in the different sections, culminating in a great evening show.

What to do

Golf
Damai Golf & Country Club, *Jln Santubong, PO Box 400, T082-846088, www.damaigolf.com.* International-standard, 18-hole golf course designed by Arnold Palmer, laid out over approximately 6.5 km, 10-bay driving range right on the sea. A very long 18 holes, with electric buggies to stop you expiring through perspiring. Caddies, clubs and shoes

for hire, spacious clubhouse, restaurant, bar, pro shop, tennis, squash and pool are also available. Really busy at weekends and worth booking in advance.

Mountain biking
Damai Cross-Country Track, *close to Permai Rainforest Resort*. This is a purpose-built track where visitors can get very hot, sweaty and dirty as they career around the 3.5-km track; bikes can be hired from hotels.

Water sports
Damai Puri Resort, *see page 63*. A range of water sports from jet skiing to sailing. Snorkelling trips also arranged.
Permai Rainforest Resort, *see page 64*. A slightly more limited range of water sports in natural surroundings.

★ Bako National Park

walking trails, empty beaches and diverse flora and fauna

Bako is situated on the beautiful Muara Tebas Peninsula, a former river delta which has been thrust above sea level. Its sandstone cliffs, which are patterned and streaked with iron deposits, have been eroded to produce a dramatic coastline with secluded coves and beaches and rocky headlands. Millions of years of erosion by the sea has resulted in the formation of wave-cut platforms, honeycomb weathering, solution pans, arches and sea stacks. Bako's most distinctive feature is the westernmost headland – Tanjung Sapi – a 100-m-high sandstone plateau, which is unique in Borneo. Established in 1957, Bako was Sarawak's first national park. It is very small (2742 ha) but it has an exceptional variety of flora and guaranteed wildlife spotting. Its beaches and accessible trails make it a wonderful place to relax for a few days.

Flora and fauna
There are seven separate types of vegetation in Bako. These include mangroves (*bakau* is the most common stilt-rooted mangrove species), swamp forest and heath forest, known as *kerangas*, an Iban word meaning 'land on which rice cannot grow'. Pitcher plants (*Nepenthes ampullaria*) do however grow in profusion on the sandy soil. There is also mixed dipterocarp rainforest (the most widespread forest type in Sarawak, characterized by its 30- to 40-m-high canopy), beach forest, and *padang* vegetation, comprising scrub and bare rock from which there are magnificent views of the coast. The rare *daun payang* (umbrella palm) is also found in Bako; it is a litter-trapping plant as its large fronds catch falling leaves from the trees above and funnel them downwards where they eventually form a thick organic mulch enabling the plant to survive on otherwise infertile soil. There are also wild durian trees in the forest, which can take up to 60 years to bear fruit.

Bako is one of the few areas in Sarawak inhabited by the rare proboscis monkey (*Nasalis larvatus*), known by Malays as Orang Belanda (Dutchmen) or even Pinocchio of the Jungle, because of their long noses (see box, page 163). Bako is home to approximately 275 proboscis monkeys. They are most often seen in the early morning or at dusk in the Teluk Assam and Teluk Delima areas (at the far west side of the park, closest to the headquarters) or around Teluk Paku (a 45-minute walk from the Park HQ). Another good place to spot them is on the beach when the tide is out and they come down, so you can see them up close.

The park also has resident populations of squirrels, mouse deer, sambar deer, wild pigs, long-tailed macaques, flying lemur, silver leaf monkeys and palm civet cats. Teluk Assam, in the area around the Park HQ, is one of the best places for birdwatching: over 150 species

Essential Bako National Park

Finding your feet

Bako lies 37 km north of Kuching, an hour's bus journey (RM3.50) or a 40-minute drive. Take Rapid Kuching bus No 1 (every 30 minutes 0700-1800, RM3.5) from just below Electra House on Lebuh Market to Kampong Bako (Bako Village). The bus continues just beyond the village to the Bako National Park boat jetty. There are also minibuses (no fixed schedule) from Lebuh Market (RM4) or you can charter a minibus or a taxi for RM60. The last buses returning to Kuching depart around 1730 – ask the driver on your way to Bako to confirm the day's last bus. From Kampong Bako, head to the office of **Koperasi Warisan Pelancongan Bako** at the boat jetty (T011-2513 2711 mob) to buy tickets for the 30-minute boat trip to Sungai Asssam near the Park HQ (departs hourly, RM20 per person). Parking is safe at Kampong Bako and the park offices.

Getting around

It also is possible to hire boats around the park: speed boats (for up to six) charge a negotiable rate, usually around RM400 per day, good for exploring the park's beaches and the island of Pulau Lakei.

Park information

On arrival visitors are required to register at the Park HQ, a short walk from where the boat lands, and pay the entrance fee (RM20, children RM7). The information centre next door has a small exhibition on geology and flora and fauna within the park. Visitors can ask to see a 40-minute introductory video to the park. The Park HQ has a simple canteen.

To arrange accommodation in the park and any necessary permits, contact the the **National Parks and Wildlife Booking Office** in Kuching, T082-248088 (see page 47). Professional photography and filming permits cost RM300.

have been recorded in the park, including pied and black hornbills. Large numbers of migratory birds come to Bako between September and November. Other inhabitants of the park are the blue fiddler crab, which has one big claw and is forever challenging others to a fight, and mudskippers, evolutionary throwbacks (resembling half-fish, half-frog), which are common in mangrove areas.

Also in the park there are two species of otter: the oriental small clawed otter and the hairy nosed otter (the best area to see them is at Teluk Assam). The Bornean bearded pig is the largest mammal found in Bako and can often be seen snuffling around the Park HQ. There are many lizards too, the largest being the water monitor which is often found near the accommodation. Snakes include the gorgeous but venomous bright green Wagler's pit viper and sometimes pythons and tree snakes can be seen on night walks. Nocturnal animals include flying lemur, pangolin, mouse deer, bats, tarsier, slow loris and palm civet; the beach by the Park HQ is a great place for a night-time stroll.

Treks

There are several well-marked trails throughout the park – more than 30 km in total. All paths are colour coded, corresponding to the map available from Park HQ. The shortest trek is the steep climb to the top of **Tanjung Sapi**, overlooking Telok Assam, with good views of Gunung Santubong, on the opposite peninsula, to the west. The 3.5-km trek to **Tajor Waterfall** is among the most popular, with varied terrain (including some steep climbs), spectacular views and a chance of a refreshing swim at the waterfall. A few meters further on you reach a secluded beach.

The longest trek is to **Telok Limau**; a five- to seven-hour walk. You can arrange with Park HQ for a boat to bring you back (RM200-250 depending on your negotiating skills). Some trails are temporarily closed for maintenance – always check with Park HQ. Full-day treks and overnight camping expeditions can be arranged. There are plank walkways with shelters at intervals to provide quiet watching spots, particularly required for viewing the proboscis monkey in the early morning.

Beaches

There are seven beaches around the park, but some are rather inaccessible, with steep paths down to the cliffs. The best swimming beach is at **Telok Pandan Kecil**, about 1½ hours' walk, northeast from the Park HQ. It is also possible to swim at **Telok Assam** and **Telok Paku**. Enquire about jellyfish at the Park HQ before swimming in the sea; it is advisable not to swim in March and April. In the monsoon season, between November and February, the sea can be rough.

Listings Bako National Park *map below.*

Where to stay

All bookings to be made at the **National Parks and Wildlife Booking Office**, Kuching, T082-248088 (see page 47). Hostels (RM42.40 per room/RM15.90 per person) have mattresses, kerosene stoves and cutlery. Chalets (RM159 per house/RM106 per room) offer electricity and fridges. Both have fans. Checkout time is 1200. Accommodation is always booked up, so you should reserve as early as possible before you want to go. Bako can be visited on a day trip, although this gives almost no opportunity to explore the parks trails – an overnight or 2-night/3-day trip would be preferable.

Bako National Park trails

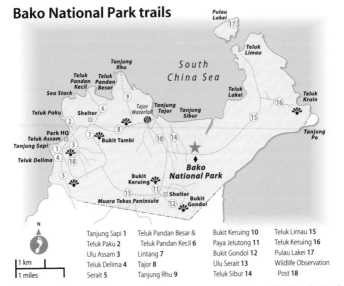

Tanjung Sapi **1**	Teluk Pandan Besar &	Bukit Keruing **10**	Teluk Limau **15**
Teluk Paku **2**	Teluk Pandan Kecil **6**	Paya Jelutong **11**	Teluk Keruing **16**
Ulu Assam **3**	Lintang **7**	Bukit Gondol **12**	Pulau Lakei **17**
Teluk Delima **4**	Tajor **8**	Ulu Serait **13**	Wildlife Observation
Serait **5**	Tanjung Rhu **9**	Teluk Sibur **14**	Post **18**

1 km
1 miles

Camping

Unless you are intending to trek to the other side of the park, it is not worth camping as monkeys steal anything left lying around and macaques can be aggressive. In addition, the smallest amount of rain turns the campsite into a swimming pool. It is, however, necessary to camp if you go to the beaches on the northeast peninsula. Tents can be hired for RM8 (sleeps 4); campsite RM5.

Homestays

It's worth checking with the **Sarawak Tourist Board**, www.sarawaktourism.com, for their latest recommendations and advice on homestay programmes. You can research and make bookings at the official **Sarawak Homestay Association** website: www.right. sarawak.gov.my/homestay/prices are usually all-inclusive and these homestays are a great way to get a feel for local life.

Restaurants

The canteen is open 0700-2100. It serves local food at reasonable prices and sells tinned foods and drinks. No need to take food, there is a good seafood restaurant near the jetty.

Bandar Sri Aman
& around

Previously called Simmanggang, Bandar Sri Aman lies on the Batang Lupar, a three- to four-hour journey southeast from Kuching, and is the administrative capital of the Second Division. The river is famous for its tidal bore. Several times a year a wall of water rushes upstream wreaking havoc with boats and divides into several tributaries; the Skrang River is one of these. It is possible to spend the night in longhouse homestays on the river. The Batang Ai National Park is home to hornbills, orang-utans and gibbons.

Sights

Most tourists do not stop in the town but pass through on day trips from Kuching to visit traditional Iban longhouses sited along the Skrang River. The route to Bandar Sri Aman goes through pepper plantations and many 'new' villages. During Communist guerrilla activity in the 1960s (see page 130), whole settlements were uprooted in this area and placed in guarded camps.

There is, however, one major sight: the defensive and recently restored **Fort Alice**. Constructed in 1864, it has small turrets, a central courtyard, a medieval-looking drawbridge and is surrounded by a fence of iron spikes. Rajah Charles Brooke lived in the Batang Lupar district for about 10 years, using this fort – and another downriver at Lingga – as bases for his punitive expeditions against pirates and Ibans in the interior. The fort is the only one of its type in Sarawak and was built commanding this stretch of the Batang Lupar River as protection against Iban raids. The original fort here was built in 1849 and named Fort James; the current fort was constructed using much of the original material. It was renamed Alice in honour of Ranee Margaret

Essential Bandar Sri Aman and around

Finding your feet

Bandar Sri Aman is accessible from Kuching and Sibu by bus. To reach Skrang longhouses, buses and then chartered boats must be arranged. There is one hotel in Batang Ai National Park, which arranges transport for its guests. Trips to longhouses and the national park can be organized through **Borneo Adventure Travel Company**, www.borneoadventure.com (see page 73).

Brooke (it was her second name). It is said that every evening, until the practice was ended in 1964, a policeman would call from the fort (in Iban): "Oh ha! Oh ha! The time is now eight o'clock. The steps have been drawn up. The door is closed. People from upriver, people from downriver, are not allowed to come to the fort anymore." (It probably sounded better in Iban.)

Skrang longhouses

traditional Iban longhouses and jungle treks

The Skrang River was one of the first areas settled by Iban immigrants in the 16th to 18th centuries. The slash-and-burn agriculturalists originally came from the Kapual River basin in Kalimantan. They later joined forces with Malay chiefs in the coastal areas and terrorized the Borneo coasts; the first Europeans to encounter these pirates called them Sea Dayaks (see box, page 134). The Ibans took many heads. Blackened skulls – which local headmen say date back to those days – hang in some of the Skrang longhouses. In 1849 more than 800 Iban pirates from the Batang Lupar and Skrang River were massacred by Rajah James Brooke's forces in the notorious Battle of Beting Marau. Four years later the Sultan of Brunei agreed to cede these troublesome districts to Brooke; they became the Second Division of Sarawak.

There are many traditional Iban longhouses along the Skrang River, although those closer to **Pias** and **Lamanak** (the embarkation points on the Skrang) tend to be very touristy – they are visited by tour groups almost every day. **Long Mujang**, the first Iban longhouse, is an hour upriver. Pias and Lamanak are within five hours' drive of Kuching. Jungle trekking is also available (approximately two hours); the guide provides an educational tour of the flora and fauna.

Batang Ai River and Batang Ai National Park

The Batang Ai River, a tributary of the Batang Lupar, has been dammed to form Sarawak's first hydroelectric plant, which came into service in 1985; it provides 60% of Sarawak's electricity supply, transmitting as far as Limbang. The area was slowly flooded over a period of six months to give animals and wildlife a chance to escape, but it has affected no fewer than 29 longhouses, 10 of which are now completely submerged causing the necessary resettlement of 3000 longhouse dwellers. The rehousing of the longhouse community has been the topic of fierce controversial debate. The communities were moved into modern longhouses and given work opportunities in local palmeries. However, it now seems that the housing loans that were initially given were not commensurate with local wages and have been very difficult for the longhouse communities to pay off. In addition, modern longhouses were not provided with farmland, so many local people have returned to settle on the banks of the reservoir. Near the dam there is a freshwater fish nursery. These fish are exported to South Korea, Japan and Europe. Those families displaced by the flooding of the dam largely work here and many of the longhouses surrounding the dam depend upon this fishery for their own fish supply.

The Batang Ai dam has created a vast and picturesque man-made lake covering some 90 sq km, stretching up the Engkari and Ai rivers. Beyond the lake, more than an hour's boat ride upriver from the dam, it is possible to see beautiful lowland mixed dipterocarp forest.

The longhouse: prime location apartments

Most longhouses are built on stilts, high on the riverbank, on prime real estate. They are 'prestigious properties' with 'lots of character', and with 'commanding views of the river', they are the condominiums of the jungle. They are long-rise rather than high-rise, however, and the average longhouse has 20-25 'doors' (although there can be as many as 60). Each represents one family. The word 'long' in a settlement's name – as in Long Liput or Long Terawan – means 'confluence' (the equivalent of *kuala* in Malay), and does not refer to the length of the longhouse.

Behind each of the doors – which even today, are rarely locked – is a *bilik* (apartment), which includes the family living room and a loft, where paddy and tools are stored. In Kenyah and Kayan longhouses, paddy (which can be stored for years until it is milled) is kept in elaborate barns, built on stilts away from the longhouse, in case of fire. In traditional longhouses, the living rooms are simple with *atap*-roofs and bamboo floors; in modern longhouses, designed on the same principles, living rooms have sofas, lino floors, TV and en suite bathroom.

At the front of the *bilik* is the *dapur*, where the cooking takes place. All *biliks* face out onto the *ruai* (gallery), which is the focus of communal life and is where visitors are usually entertained. The width of the wall which faces onto the *ruai* indicates the status of that family. Attached to the *ruai* there is usually a *tanju* (open veranda) running the full length of the house – where rice and other agricultural products are dried. Long ladders – notched hardwood trunks – lead up to the *tanju*; they can get very slippery and do not always come with handrails.

The **Batang Ai National Park**, 250 km from Kuching and two hours from the jetty by boat, covers an area of over 24,040 ha and was inaugurated in 1991. It protects the much-endangered orang-utan and is home to a wide variety of other wildlife, including hornbills and gibbons. As yet there are no visitor facilities, but five walking trails have been created, one of which takes in an ancient burial ground. Trips to one of the 29 longhouses surrounding the dam and to Batang Ai National Park are organized by the **Borneo Adventure Travel Company** (see What to do, page 73).

Listings Bandar Sri Aman and around

Where to stay

Bandar Sri Aman

$$-$ Seri Simanggang Hotel
*Lot 1518, Block 2, Plot 49, Simanggang Town District, T6083-322699, www.
serisimangganghotel.com.*
Easily the best bet in town with clean rooms and standard mid-range facilities though in need of a sprucing up. It's the tallest building in town with 150 rooms, pool and restaurants.

Skrang longhouses
All longhouses along the Skrang River are controlled by the Ministry of Tourism so rates are the same. Resthouses at most of the longhouses can accommodate 20-40 people; mattresses and mosquito nets are provided in a communal sleeping area with

★ Visiting longhouses: house rules

There are more than 1500 longhouses in Sarawak. They are usually located along the big rivers and their tributaries, notably the Skrang (see page 70), the Rejang (see page 83) and the Baram (see page 103). The Iban, who are characteristically extrovert and hospitable to visitors, live on the lower reaches of the rivers. The Orang Ulu tribes – mainly Kayan and Kenyah – live further upriver and are generally less outgoing than the Iban. The Bidayuh live mainly around Bau and Serian, near Kuching. Their longhouses are usually more modern than those of the Iban and Orang Ulu, and are visited less often for that reason. The Kelabit people live on the remote plateau country near the Kalimantan border around Bario (see page 121).

The most important ground rule is not to visit a longhouse without an invitation. People who arrive unannounced may get an embarrassingly frosty reception. Tour companies offer the only exception to this rule, as most have tribal connections. Upriver, particularly at Kapit, on the Rejang (see page 80), such 'invitations' are not hard to come by; it is good to ensure your host actually comes from the longhouse you are being invited to. The best time to visit Iban longhouses is during the *gawai* harvest festival at the beginning of June, when communities throw an open house and everyone is invited to join the festivities.

On arrival, visitors should pay an immediate courtesy call on the headman (the *tuai rumah* in Iban longhouses). It is normal to bring him gifts; those staying overnight should offer the headman around RM20 per person. The money is kept in a central fund and saved for use by the whole community during festivals. Small gifts such as beer, coffee, biscuits, whisky, batik and food (especially rice or chicken) go down well. It is best to arrive at a longhouse during late afternoon after people have returned from the fields. Visitors who have time to stay the night generally have a much more enjoyable experience than those who pay fleeting visits. They can share the evening meal and have time to talk and drink.

If you go beyond the limits of the express boats, it is necessary to charter a longboat. Petrol costs RM2.50-4 a litre, depending on how far upriver you are. Guides charge approximately RM80-100 a day and sometimes it is necessary to hire a boatman or frontman as well. Prices increase in the dry season when boats have to be lifted over shallow rapids. Permits are required for most upriver areas; these can be obtained at the residents' or district office in the nearest town.

few partitions. Facilities are basic but include flush toilet and shower. Local food, phone and a clinic are available nearby. If the stay is for 2 nights, on the 2nd night it's possible to camp in the jungle and then get a return boat ride to the longhouse. Most visitors arrange package trips with tour operators in Kuching with 3-day/2-night packages costing around RM1400.

Batang Ai and Batang Ai National Park
Tour companies provide accommodation in longhouses here, in a much more central location within the park than the **Hilton**.

$$$ Hilton International Batang Ai Longhouse Resort
On the eastern shore of the lake, T083-584388, www.hilton.com.

Opened in 1995, the resort is made up of 11 longhouses, built of the local *belian* (ironwood) to traditional designs. Despite its lakeside location there are no views, except from the walkways, as longhouses are built, for purposes of defence, to face landwards – in this case, over the buggy track. However, there are compromises to modern comforts: all 100 rooms have a/c, fan, TV, shower room, minibar. Other facilities include an outdoors pool paddling pool, excellent restaurant, 18-km jogging track, and shuttle bus from **Kuching Hilton International** tour desk. The hotel arranges transport.

$ Kooperasi Serbaguna Ulu Batang Ai
The Iban have formed this cooperative to provide longhouse homestay accommodation. Contact **Sarawak Tourism** in Kuching to put you in touch with the group.

Restaurants

Bandar Sri Aman

$ After Six Café
No 9, Jln Pasir Panas.
Western fare. Lots of fried food, coleslaw and baked beans.

$ Benak Sensation
Lot 869, Block 2, Jln Club, Simanggang Town District.
Serves Japanese-style omelettes with ketchup designs and pseudo-Western dishes such as cheesy chicken chops. Some reasonable Asian fare including *lok lok* (satay sticks cooked in a sauce on the table).

$ Tandang Sri Aman
2 GF, Jln Club, Bangunan Yayasan Sarawak.
Muslim Indian and Malay dishes to fill up on. The roti canai makes for a solid late evening snack.

What to do

Bandar Sri Aman
Many of the restaurants in the resort are staffed by locals and discreet enquiries may get you an invitation to a longhouse and/or Batang Ai National Park for considerably less than the **Borneo Adventure Travel Company** charge.
Borneo Adventure Travel Company, *55 Main Bazaar, Kuching, T082-410569, www.borneoadventure.com, and at the Hilton Batang Ai Longhouse Resort.* Reliable operator offering a selection of tour packages in Sarawak, Sabah and Brunei. Good selection of longhouse and culture-based activies and a number of worthwhile wildlife tours. Not cheap but worth the money.

Transport

Bandar Sri Aman
Bus
Regular connections with **Kuching**, RM25 (135 km) and **Sibu** (via Sarikei).

Skrang longhouses
Bus
From Bandar Sri Aman, take bus Nos 14 and 19 to **Pias** and bus No 9 to **Lemanak**. Self-drive car rental (return) or minibus (8-10 people, return) from **Kuching** to **Entaban**. From these points it is necessary to charter a boat to reach the nearest longhouses. Many of the Kuching-based tour agencies offer cut-price deals for 1- to 2-day excursions to Skrang and Lemanak river longhouses (see box, opposite). Unless you are already part of a small group, these tours work out cheaper because of the boat costs.

Sibu, Kapit
& Belaga

The third largest town in Sarawak, Sibu is sited at the confluence of the Rejang and the Igan rivers, 60 km upstream from the sea. It is the starting point for trips up the Rejang to the Kapit and Belaga. The Rejang is an important thoroughfare and Malaysia's longest river at 563 km. Tours to upriver longhouses can be organized from Sibu or more cheaply from Kapit and Belaga.

Sibu

waterfront town with a Chinese influence; a jumping-off point for journeys into the interior

Sibu is a busy Chinese trading town – the majority of the population came originally from China's Fujian Province – and is the main port on the Rejang (also spelt Rajang). In 1899, Rajah Charles Brooke agreed with Wong Nai Siong, a Chinese scholar from Fujian, to allow settlers to Sibu. Brooke had reportedly been impressed with the industriousness of the Chinese: he saw the women toiling in the paddy fields from dawn to dusk and commented: "If the women work like that, what on earth must the men be like?"

The Kuching administration provided these early agricultural pioneers with temporary housing on arrival, a steamer between Sibu and Kuching, rice rations for the first year and tuition in Malay and Iban. The town grew rapidly (its expansion is documented in a photographic exhibition in the Civic Centre) but was razed to the ground in the great fire of 1828. The first shophouses to be constructed after the fire are the three-storey ones still standing on Jalan Channel. At the beginning of the 20th century, Sibu became the springboard for Foochow migration to the rest of Sarawak. Thanks to the discovery of the Kuala Paloh Channel in 1961, Sibu is accessible to boats with a sizeable draft. Today it is an industrial and trading centre for timber, pepper and rubber, and home to some of Sarawak's wealthiest families, mostly timber *towkays* (merchants).

Sights
The old trading port has now been graced with a pagoda, a couple of big hotels and a smart esplanade. The 1929 **shophouses** along the river are virtually all that remains of the old town. The seven-storey **pagoda**, adjacent to **Tua Pek Kong Temple**, cost RM1.5 million to build; there are good views over the town from the top, especially at sunset though you'll need to ask for the key. In the **Sibu Civic Centre** ① *2.5 km out of town on Jln Tun*

Abang Haji Openg, Tue-Sun 0800-1700; take Sungei Merah bus No 1A or 4 from the bus terminal and ask for the Civic Centre (90 sen), there is an exhibition of old photographs of Sibu and a mediocre tribal display. This serves as Sibu's municipal museum. Five aerial photographs of the town, taken since 1947, chart the town's explosive growth.

Those with an interest in medicine will enjoy popping into the **Lau King Howe Hospital Museum** ⓘ *Jln Pulau, www. lkhhmm.org, Tue-Sun 0900-1700, free*, which offers a fascinating glimpse into the history of medical care in Sarawak. The museum has lots of old medical machines, nurses uniforms and photos to browse.

There are a couple of interesting Chinese temples out of town. The **Taoist Tiger Temple** ⓘ *take a taxi to Jln Trusan, off Jln Teku (RM15)*, is unique in that it is the only temple in Malaysia dedicated to the seven tiger deities. The temple has the tigers in various fierce poses dressed in human clothes. The myth goes back to the mountains of rural China, where after years of being attacked and killed by the local human population, seven tiger brothers took their revenge and went on a violent killing spree until they were caught and imprisoned by Kuan Keng, a Chinese general from the Three Kingdoms period.

Essential Sibu

Finding your feet

The airport is 23 km southeast of Sibu and has connections with Kuala Lumpur, Johor Bahru, Kuching and Kota Kinabalu. To get from the airport by taxi you need to buy a taxi coupon (RM35). For those on a budget, walk 400 m from the airport to the bus stand and hop on a bus to Sibu Jaya (RM2). Buses pass the airport from 0600 to 1815.

The long-distance bus station is about 3 km out of town on Jalan Pahlawan. Take a taxi, RM20, or a Lorong Road bus (no number) or Sungei Merah bus No 12 or 17 to the local bus station near the ferry terminal. There are daily connections with Bintulu and Miri, and Kuching via Sarikei.

Boats from Kuching and Sarikei dock at two wharves close to the town centre.

Getting around

Although this is Sarawak's third largest town, it's still possible to see most of Sibu's sights on foot. The local bus station is on Jalan Khoo Peng Loong.

The tigers were released after 400 years of captivity, by which time they had become half human and had vowed to become strict vegetarians. Each of the statues in the temple represents the qualities of a different deity; the tiger nearest the entrance is in charge of the environment, and next to him is Tsai Shen, the fifth tiger deity and God of Wealth. The tigers receive vegetarian offerings from the local Chinese population.

Recently completed, the **Yu Lung San Tian Ensi (Jade Dargon Temple)** ⓘ *T019-892 8128, take Lanang bus No 2 (hourly from 0515, RM4) from Jln Maju, a taxi costs around RM35*, is the largest Chinese temple in Southeast Asia. It's the temple that turns heads on the road from Bintulu with its enormous size, sweeping gables and multi-coloured buildings.

Tourist information

Residents Office
T084-321963.

Sibu Visitor Information Centre
*Sublot 3a & 3b, Sibu Heritage Centre,
Jln Central, T084-340980, www.sarawak
tourism.com. Mon-Fri 0800-1700 (closed
on public holidays).*
Very friendly and helpful. As well as
information on Sibu they can advise for trips

onwards to Kapit and Belaga. A visit here is
highly recommended.

Where to stay

Cheaper hotels tend to be around the night
market in Chinatown, but there's also a
selection within walking distance of the jetty.

$$$ Kingwood
*12 Lorong Lanang 4, T084-335888,
kingwood.sibu@yahoo.com.my.*

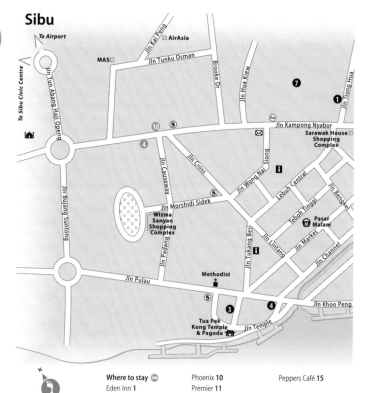

Sibu

Where to stay 🛏
Eden Inn **1**
Garden **5**
Kingwood **6**
Li Hua **7**

Phoenix **10**
Premier **11**
RH **4**
Tanahmas, Loong Jin
   restaurant &

Peppers Café **15**

Restaurants 🍴
Café Café **3**
Jack Pork **4**

This business hotel might not be the most exciting option, and some rooms have a noticeably smoky air, but it's comfortable and has cable TV and Wi-Fi (weak connection). Some rooms have town views and the more expensive ones have fantastic views over the river. There is a top Chinese restaurant, **Mingziang**, pool and fitness centre.

$$$ RH Hotel
Jln Kampong Nyabor, T084-365888, www.rhhotels.com.my.
A huge hotel overlooking the **Wisma Sanyan** shopping complex and Sibu's spacious town square. It's a fairly bog standard business hotel which, despite being fairly new, is starting to fade fairly quickly. The rooms are spacious and well decorated. It has a pool and steam bath, and rooms have Wi-Fi (slow), cable TV and safety deposit boxes. The **Oriental Bistro** serves good coffee and international dishes. Huge discounts often available. Good.

$$$ Tanahmas
Jln Kampong Nyabor, T084-333188, www.tanahmas.com.my.
One of the better options in town with central location. Rooms are well furnished and have Wi-Fi; those on higher floors command good views over the city centre. There's a pool, karaoke lounge and good restaurant. Possibly the best option in this price range.

$$ Premier
Jln Kampong Nyabor, T084-323222, www.premierh.com.my.
This place offers very reasonable value with large, clean rooms with Wi-Fi, bath, and for the lucky ones, a river view. The hotel is located in the centre of town next to **Sarawak House Shopping Centre and Cinema**, discounts often available.

$$-$ Garden
1 Jln Huo Ping, T084-317888, gardenhotel_sbw@yahoo.com.
The entrance of this hotel is a bit clubby with mirrors all over the place. Rooms are comfortable, but furnishings are a little scuffed. Renovations are on the cards. Staff are friendly and there is Wi-Fi access throughout. Generic buffet breakfast included in the price.

$ Eden Inn
1 Jln Lanang, T084-337277.
Next to the 1960s-style Sacred Heart Church, this well-run place is owned by a local Catholic association and has a selection of large, spotless a/c rooms with TV and attached bathroom. Excellent value and full of positive retro vibes.

Mr & Mrs Yeo's Stall **1**
Noodle House **7**
Payung Café **9**
Sri Meranti **2**
Sri Meranti
Chicken Rice **8**

$ Li Hua
18 Lorong 2, Jln Lanang, T084-324000,
Run by one of the local Chinese associations, and often packed with visiting ethnic Chinese, this friendly place has simple, large rooms with TV and attached bathroom. Many rooms offer sweeping views over the Rejang and the dense forest beyond. Don't expect glam and glitz, but do expect excellent value.

$ Phoenix
1 & 3 Jln Kai Peng (off Jln Kampong Nyabor), T084-313877.
Spotless, slightly old hotel with a selection of clean a/c rooms with attached bathroom and TV. Good value.

Restaurants

With such a large Chinese population, it's no surprise that the many coffee shops and hawker centres are packed with Chinese eateries. One Sibu speciality is *kampua mee*, a fatty dish of noodles and pork lard served with roasted pork or pork balls with soup.

$$ Café Café
10 Jln Chew Geok Lin, T084-328101.
Open 1200-1600 and 1800-2300.
Cosy place, popular with families and couples out for a spot of romancing over plates of Asian and Western dishes including macaroni cheese and delicious *nasi lemak*.

$$ Loong Jin
Tanahmas Hotel (see Where to stay), Jln Kampong Nyabor.
Halal Cantonese and Sichuan with promotion deals at weekends.

$$ Peppers Café
Tanahmas hotel (see Where to stay), Jln Kampong Nyabor.
A favourite with visitors, this hotel eatery has a good selection of Western and local food. Popular and open until 0200.

$ Jack Pork
8 Jln Chew Geok Lin.
Fantastic lunch promos and a menu encompassing all things porky including belly pork, pulled pork sandwiches and burgers and some excellent local dishes including Sarawak laksa with pork balls and, for a bit of relief from pork, chicken *mee sua*.

$ Kasturi
18 Jln Tunku Osman.
One of the town's most celebrated Malay places with great curries and seafood. Also a selection of Melanau dishes and including *tebaloi* and *umai* (raw fish salad). Delicious.

$ Mr and Mrs Yeo's Stall
Lorong Tiong Hua. Mornings only.
This friendly local spot dishes up a local speciality, *konpia*, a fresh bread roll served with pork broth and slices of pork. This is a must-visit to get in touch with local flavours.

$ Noodle House
2B Lorong Laichee, T084-338480.
It is not all noodles here and the locals pour in to chomp down the chocolate lava cake and desserts. However, look for minced pork porridge, pork ribs and braised Sarawak noodles with chicken for satisfying savouries.

$ Payung Café
20F Jln Lanang, T016-890 6061.
Daily for lunch and dinner.
Payung is a fantastic place to eat with its menu of local favourites, cooked healthily and with fresh local ingredients. The place is beautifully decorated with artwork and coloured parasols. Great dishes to try include the *otak otak*, salads, soups and curries.

$ Sri Meranti
1A Jln Hardin.
Friendly staff, good seafood, nice sitting-out area with cold beer and tablecloths.

$ Sri Meranti Chicken Rice
26 Jln Mission, T084-316 904. Open 0830-2100.
Functional a/c restaurant offering chicken rice in every conceivable form with good Chinese vegetable dishes in sauces including *sambal belacan*.

Foodstalls

Jln Market Food Court
Jln Market, near Premier Hotel.
Good selection of Chinese and Malay stalls.

Sibu Central Market
1st floor.
Over 30 stalls serving mainly Chinese dishes, but with a few interesting local offerings.

Taman Muhibah Food Court
Jln Pedade.
Cendol (a refreshing shaved ice concoction), spicy *sotong* and a whole host of bargain basement local favourites.

Shopping

Handicrafts
Stalls along express boat wharves at Jln Channel, mainly selling basketware.
Chop Kion Huat, *Jln Market.* Sarawak handicrafts including batik, basketware, T-shirts and carvings.
Sibu Heritage Handicrafts, *Sibu Heritage Centre, Jln Central.* Get digging in this fantastic little store which is packed full of Penan, Kayan and Melinau crafts along with other bits and bobs from the region.

Markets
Native market, *at the Sibu Central Market, Jln Channel.* This is Malaysia's largest indoors market and home to a fascinating array of local produce from jungle foodstuffs, and ethnic clothing made of coloured beads.
Pasar Malam (night market), *High St, Jln Market and Lembangan Lane, Chinatown.* This place is an unmissable destination for any visit to Sibu. Things start up in the late afternoon, so pack your camera for an evening of snapping, snacking and browsing of goods. It's vibrant and fun and a great way to try some local delicacies. Sago worms anyone?

Pottery
There are 2 potteries at Km 7 and 12 Ulu Oya Rd.

Shopping malls
Wisma Sanyan Shopping Centre, *1 Jln Sanyan.* Located in the tallest building in Sarawak, this place has all the standard mall offerings including several internet cafés and a big branch of **Giant Supermarket** which is good for stocking up on things before jungle trips. If you are here in Sep, look for the **Sibu BASE Jump** event, when people from around the world hurl themselves off the building and land at Sibu Town Square a few mins later, hopefully in one piece.

What to do

Golf
Sibu Golf Club, *Km 10, Ulu Oya Rd, www. kelabgolfsibu.com.* RM95/RM64 for a round on weekends/weekdays.

Tour operators
Most companies run city tours plus tours of longhouses, Mulu National Park and Niah Caves. It is cheaper to organize upriver trips from Kapit or Belaga than from Sibu.
Greatown Travel, *No 6, 1st floor, Lorong Chew Siik Hiong 1A, T084-211243, www. greatown.com.* Currently the leading operator offering longhouse tours and rainforest treks. Highly recommended.
Sazhong Trading & Travel, *4 Jln Central, T084-336017.* Can arrange budget stays for groups in an Iban longhouse or longhouses in Kapit and beyond.
Travel Consortium, *14 Jln Central, T084-334455.* Good for arranging air tickets.

Transport

Air
The airport is 23 km southeast of town, T084-307770/307755. **MASwings** (T084-326861) has regular connections with **Kuching**, **Bintulu**, **Miri** and **KK**. MAS and **Air Asia** fly to **Kuala Lumpur**. **Air Asia** also flies to **Johor Bahru**. Airlines offices are at the airport terminal building.

Boat

All boats leave from the wharf. The time of the next departure is shown by big clock faces on whiteboards; just buy the ticket at the jetty. **Ekspress Bahagia** (T084-319228) runs 1 express boat daily between Sibu and **Kuching** (economy class RM45/1st class RM50, 5 hrs), which leaves at 1130.

This boat stops off at **Sarekei** (RM10) and **Tanjung Manis** and is a beautiful journey. There are regular express boats to **Kapit** (every 30 mins 0535-1530, RM25 economy/RM30 2nd class/RM35 1st class, 2-3 hrs), and in the wet season, when the river is high enough, they continue to **Belaga** (5-6 hrs). It is not possible to travel up river to Belaga in a day, as you need a permit from the Resident's Office in Kapit. However, if the situation changes, there is a daily boat from Sibu to Belaga (RM50) at 0615 when the water is high enough. This service doesn't usually run in the dry season (Jul-Sep). Some Sibu–Kapit boats stop off at **Kanowit** and **Song** on their way upriver. For up-to-date river information, contact the **Sarawak Rivers Board**, T084-339936 (24 hrs).

Bus

Local Buses leave from the bus station on Jln Khoo Peng Loong.

Long distance Buses leave from the long-distance bus terminal at Jln Pahlawan. To get there take a taxi (a negotiable RM15), or bus No 12 or No 17 from the local bus station. There are 3 main long-distance bus companies: **Biaramas Express**, **Borneo Highway Express** and **Suria Express** which all have routes from Sibu to Bintulu, Miri and Kuching. Buses run more or less hourly 0700-0030 to **Bintulu** (RM28, 4 hrs) and **Miri** (RM40, 6-7 hrs). It's best to purchase tickets the day before departure – there are ticket offices for the different companies around the jetty or buy direct from the bus station. Early morning buses to Bintulu connect with the buses direct to **Batu Niah** (see page 96). There are also daily connections with **Kuching** (RM40, 8 hrs) via **Sarikei** (RM10, 2 hrs). There are around 10 daily departures 0700-2400.

International There are a number of departures to **Pontianak**, Kalimantan (earliest at 1000, RM95, 16 hrs).

Kapit

riverside settlement with a decrepit colonial fort and a base for longhouse expeditions

Kapit (population 100,000), which means 'twin' in local dialect, is the capital of Sarawak's Seventh Division, through which flows the Rejang River and its main tributaries, the Batang Baleh, Batang Katibas, Batang Balui and Sungai Belaga. In a treaty with the Sultan of Brunei, Rajah James Brooke acquired the Rejang Basin for Sarawak in 1853. Kapit is the last big town on the Rejang and styles itself as the gateway to 'the heart of Borneo', after Redmond O'Hanlon's *Into the Heart of Borneo*, which describes his adventure up the Batang Baleh in the 1980s. Kapit is full of people who claim to be characters in this book.

The main sights are Fort Sylvia and the Kapit Museum but, like O'Hanlon and his journalist companion James Fenton, most visitors simply use the town as a pit stop before continuing their adventures into the interior to explore the upper Rejang and its tributaries, where there are many Iban and Orang Ulu longhouses.

Sights

Fort Sylvia, near the wharves, was built of *belian* (Borneo ironwood) by Rajah Charles Brooke in 1880, and is now occupied by the Kapit Museum. It was originally called Kapit Fort but was renamed in 1925 after Rajah Vyner Brooke's wife. Most of the forts built during this time were designed to prevent the Orang Ulu going downriver; Fort Sylvia was built to stop the belligerent Iban headhunters from attacking Kenyah and Kayan settlements upstream.

Kapit Museum ⓘ *Fort Sylvia, Mon-Thu 0800-1230 and 1400-1700, Friday 0800-1145 and 1415-1700 (if closed at these times search for the curator to open it), free*, was enlarged in the 1990s and moved to Fort Sylvia. It has exhibits (all labelled in English) on Rejang tribes and the local economy. Set up by the Sarawak Museum in Kuching, it includes a section of an Iban longhouse and several Iban artefacts including a wooden hornbill. The Orang Ulu section has a reconstruction of a longhouse and a mural painted by local tribespeople. An Orang Ulu *salong* (burial hut), totem pole and other woodcarvings are also on display. The museum has representative exhibits from the small Malay community and the Chinese. Hokkien traders settled at Kapit and Belaga and traded salt, sugar and ceramics for

Essential Kapit

Visiting longhouses

Maps of the Kapit Division and other parts of Sarawak are available from the **Land Survey Department**, Jalan Beletik on Jalan Airport. Permits for upriver trips are available from the **Government Administration Centre**, Resident Office, Kapit Division, ninth floor, Kompleks Kerajaan, Negeri Bahagain Kapit, Jalan Bleteh, T084-796230,

http://www.sarawak.gov.my/web/home/list_agency/230/, Monday-Thursday 0800-1300 and 1400-1700, Friday 0800-1145 and 1415-1700, which is 2 km outside town. Take one of the local buses heading 'downstream' from Kapit town centre for around RM2. Tourists going up the Balleh River or Upper Rejang must sign a form saying they understand they are travelling at their own risk.

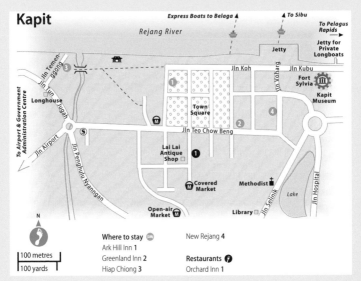

Kapit

Express Boats to Belaga ▲   ▲ To Sibu

Rejang River

To Pelagus Rapids ▶

Jetty for Private Longboats

Jetty

Jln Temenggong

Jln Koh

Jln Yohang

Jln Kubu

Fort Sylvia

Kapit Museum

Jln Jugah

Longhouse

Town Square

Jln Teo Chow Beng

To Airport & Government Administration Centre

Jln Airport

Jln Penghulu Nyangan

Lai Lai Antique Shop

Covered Market

Methodist ✝

Lake

Jln Selinik

Jln Hospital

Open-air Market

Library

N

100 metres
100 yards

Where to stay 🛏
Ark Hill Inn 1
Greenland Inn 2
Hiap Chiong 3

New Rejang 4

Restaurants 🍴
Orchard Inn 1

BACKGROUND

Kapit

There are only a few tens of kilometres of surfaced road in and around Kapit, but the small town has a disproportionate number of cars. It is a trading centre for the tribespeople upriver and has grown enormously in recent years with the expansion of the logging industry upstream. Logs come in two varieties: floaters and sinkers. Floaters are pulled downstream by tugs in huge chevron formations. Sinkers – like *belian* (ironwood) – are transported in the Chinese-owned dry bulk carriers that line up along the wharves at Kapit. When the river is high these timber ships are able to go upstream, past the Pelagus Rapids. The Rejang at Kapit is normally 500 m wide and, in the dry season, the riverbank slopes steeply down to the water. When it floods, however, the water level rises more than 10 m, as is testified by the high-water marks on Fort Sylvia.

pepper, rotan and rubber; they were followed by traders from Fujian. The Chinese exhibit is a shop. In addition, there are also displays on the natural history of the upper Rejang and modern industries such as mining, logging and tourism.

Kapit has a particularly colourful daily **market** in the centre of town. Tribeswomen bring in fruit, vegetables and animals to sell; it is quite normal to see everything from turtles, frogs, birds and catfish to monkeys, wild boar and even pangolin and pythons. **Note** If you do see animals such as monkeys, pangolins, wild cats or birds, please remember that most of them are protected species and in serious danger of extinction, due to the wildlife 'pet' trade and the rising demand for 'traditional' medicines like ground bone and body parts such as monkey gall bladders. Please do not buy them or in any way encourage this business.

★ Pelagus Rapids

Some 45 minutes upstream from Kapit on the Rejang River, this 2.5-km-long series of cataracts and whirlpools is the result of a sudden drop in the riverbed, caused by a geological fault line. Express boats can make it up the Pelagus to Belaga in the wet season (September-April) and at times of high water the rest of the year, but the rapids are still regarded with some trepidation by the pilots. When the water is low, they can only be negotiated by the smallest longboats. There are seven rapids in total, each with local names such as The Python, The Knife and one, more ominously, called The Grave. In 2013 the government invested over 9.8 million ringgit in blasting away at the rocks that had been causing many of the riverine issues along this stretch of water and though the river has been somewhat tamed, there are still some underwater rocks which pose a threat to boats. At the end of 2015 there were reports that no vessels had come to any harm along the Pelagus Rapids since the blasting process begun.

★ Longhouses

To go upriver beyond Kapit it is necessary to get a permit (no charge) from the offices in the State Government Complex (see page 81). The permit is valid for travel up the Rejang as far as Belaga and for an unspecified distance up the Baleh. For upriver trips beyond Belaga another permit must be obtained there; however, these trips tend to be expensive and dangerous.

Some longhouses are accessible by road and several others are within an hour's longboat ride from town. In Kapit you are likely to be invited to visit one of these. Visitors are strongly advised not to visit a longhouse without an invitation, ideally from someone who lives in it (see box, page 72). As a general rule, the further from town a longhouse is, the more likely it is to conform with the image of what a traditional longhouse should be like. That said, there are some beautiful traditional longhouses nearby, which are mainly Iban. One of the most accessible is **Rumah Seligi**, about 30 minutes' drive from Kapit. Cars or vans can be hired by the half day. Only a handful of longhouses are more than 500 m from the riverbanks of the Rejang and its tributaries. Most longhouses still practise shifting cultivation; rice is the main crop but under government aid programmes many are now growing cash crops such as cocoa. Longhouses are also referred to as *Uma (Sumah)* and the name of the headman, ie Long Segaham is known locally as *Uma Lasah* (Lasah being the chief).

Longhouses between Kapit and Belaga on the upper Rejang River are accessible by the normal passenger boats, but these express boats travel a limited distance on the Baleh River (2½ hours). To go further upriver it is necessary to take a tour or organize your own guides and boatmen. The sort of trip taken by Redmond O'Hanlon and James Fenton (as described in O'Hanlon's book, *Into the Heart of Borneo*) would cost more than RM2000 a head. Large-scale logging operations are currently underway on the Baleh River and although this may increase boat traffic and the opportunities to access this part of Sarawak, brace yourself for a very different experience from that described in O'Hanlon's book. See What to do, page 85.

The vast majority of the population, about 68%, in Sarawak's Seventh Division is Iban. They inhabit the Rejang up to and a little beyond Kapit, as well as the lower reaches of the Balleh and its tributaries. The Iban people are traditionally the most hospitable to visitors but, as a result, their longhouses are the most frequently visited by tourists. Malays and Chinese account for 3.4% and 7% of the population respectively. The Orang Ulu live further upriver; the main tribes are the Kayan and the Kenyah (12%) and a long list of sub-groups such as the Kejaman, Beketan, Sekapan, Lahanan, Seping and Tanjong. In addition there are the nomadic and semi-nomadic Penan, Punan and Ukit. Many tribal people are employed in the logging industry and, with their paid jobs, have brought the trappings of modernity to even the most remote longhouses. There are a number of longhouses that can be visited on outings from Kapit for a small charge of around RM25 per visitor a day or RM70 for an overnight stay. Longhouses that accept uninvited travellers from Kapit include: **Rumah Bundong**, an Iban longhouse around 12 km away; **Rumah Lulut Tisa**, which has a homestay and involves a bus to Rumah Masam and then a two-hour boat journey; and **Nanga Mujong** which is an Iban longhouse and accessible by bus and short river crossing. To get to these longhouses, sharpen up your bargaining skills and keep an eye on minivans departing from Pasar Teresang.

Listings Kapit *map page 81.*

Where to stay

The following places are within walking distance of the wharf.

$ Ark Hill Inn
Lot 451, Jln Penghulu Gerining (off the Town Square), T084-796168, arkhill@streamyx.com.
Fair value place with 20 a/c rooms with attached bath and TV. The single rooms here are small, but doubles offer greater value. Although clean, the walls could do with a lick of paint. Wi-Fi access available.

$ Greenland Inn
463 Jln Teo Chow Beng, T084-796388
This clean place offers 19 well-maintained spacious rooms with a/c, TV and attached bathroom and moody Wi-Fi. Often full at weekends. A little expensive given the competition in town.

$ Hiap Chiong
33 Jln Temenggong Jugah, T084-796314.
This place has a strangely institutional feel but has survived the test of time. Rooms, though old, are reasonable value with TV and attached bathroom. Room 307 is huge and offers the finest river views of any hotel in town.

$ New Rejang Inn
28 Jln Temenggong Jugah, T084-796600.
Friendly hotel with 4 flights of steep steps and spotless a/c rooms with TV and Wi-Fi. Room 410 has a good view of the Rejang working its murky magic. Powerful showers and liberally scattered bibles.

Restaurants

There is nothing very exciting about dining in Kapit. Most of the locals are content with eating and relaxing in the town's many coffee shops. Food to look out for includes fresh river fish (including the very expensive emparau, Borneo masheer), and Rejang prawns. You should also be able to find

local boar dishes (*babi hutan*) if you keep your eyes peeled.

$$ Madam Ma's
Hotel Meligai, 334 Jln Airport.
Come here for friendly service and a well-made selection of Malaysian classics.

$$ Orchard Inn Restaurant
Jln Teo Chow Beng, T084-796325.
A/c restaurant with a simple menu of Chinese seafood and meat dishes. Not a bad choice for a meal and beer. Popular with the local Chinese.

$ Ah Kau
Jln Berjaya.
Good spot for local seafood dishes.

$ Chun Cheng
Jln Pedral.
Held in high regard among the locals, this place offers mainly Chinese and some halal Malay dishes.

Bakeries and coffee shops

Chuong Hin
Opposite the Sibu wharf.
The best-stocked coffee shop in town.

Ung Tong Bakery
Opposite the market.
A very friendly family-run bakery offering sweet treats, simple breakfasts and Asian-style (soft and sweet) fresh bread. There's a large selection of rolls and good coffee and fresh bread is baked daily (1500). Recommended.

Foodstalls

Gelanggang Kenyalang
Opposite the Orchard Inn.
Look for the brightly painted exterior of this covered food court. It's usually the first place recommended by locals and has a range of Chinese and Malay stalls. Here you can find a Kapit speciality, the heart-stoppingly

unhealthy, but fiendishly tasty, deep-fried *roti canai*, found at the Malay stall on the 1st floor.

Taman Selera Empurau
Jln Kapit Bypass.
Lively with a great selection of Malay dishes and local favourites. It's a good place to linger over a cup of tea and a plate of satay.

Shopping

Handicrafts
Din Chu Café, *next to Methodist Guesthouse.*
Sells antiques and handicrafts.
Sula Perengka Kapit, *Shop 21, 2nd floor of the Gelanggang Kenyalang complex (see above).*
There's a small range of woven rugs/sarongs in this Iban-run shop. Prices are high but similar to the starting prices at longhouses.

Shopping centres
Riverside Shopping Mall. Department store, cinema, ATMs and supermarket.

What to do

Tour operators
There have been a number of complaints made by tourists who feel they have been overcharged for unsatisfactory tours.

Often the guides are young local men with a fair command of English but limited experience in guiding foreigners who are paying handsomely for the experience. The Sarawak Tourist Information Office in Sibu (see page 76) and the Kapit Resident's Office (see page 81) recommend using guides from **Alice Tours and Travel**, Lorong 6 Jln Airport (a good 25-min walk from town in a residential area past the overgrown airport), T019-859 3126, atta_kpt@yahoo.com. Day trips to visit the longhouse at Bundong start at RM250, and an overnight trip including a stay at the longhouse starts at RM325. Owner Alice Chua recommends booking tours at least a week in advance. Some hotels will help organize trips, or ask at the police station.

Transport

Boat
All 3 wharves are close together. There are regular boats to **Sibu** (0630-1500, RM25-35 depending on class, 2-3 hrs) from the **Kapit/ Sibu Express Boat Terminal** which opened in 2009. There is a daily express boat to **Belaga** (0900, RM55, 5 hrs) only in the wet season. Large express boats do not run in the dry season (Jul-Sep) but smaller speedboats sometimes go upriver (RM60-100 per person).

Belaga
scruffy but engaging upriver settlement; starting point for jungle treks and longhouse visits

This is the archetypal sleepy little town where most people while away the time in coffee shops. These are the best places to watch life go by and there are always interesting visitors in town, from itinerant wild honey collectors from Kalimantan to Orang Ulu who have brought their jungle produce downriver to the Belaga Bazaar or those who are heading to the metropolis of Kapit for medical treatment. At night, when the neon lights flicker on, coffee shops are invaded by thousands of cicadas, beetles and moths.

A few Chinese traders set up shop in Belaga in the early 1900s and traded with the tribespeople upriver, supplying essentials such as kerosene and cooking oil. The Orang Ulu brought their beadwork and mats as well as jungle produce such as beeswax, ebony, *gutta-percha* (rubbery tree gum) and, most prized of all, bezoar stones. These are gallstones found in certain monkeys (the wah-wahs, jelu-merahs and jelu-jankits) and porcupines. To the Chinese, they have much the same properties as rhinoceros horn

Essential Belaga

Finding your feet

There is a daily boat from Kapit in the wet season; the journey takes around five hours. In the dry season smaller speedboats still run (see Kapit transport, above) but when the river is very low the only option is to drive to Belaga from Bintulu.

and, even today, they are exported from Sarawak to Singapore, where they fetch S$300 per kilogram.

Belaga serves as a small government administration centre for the remoter parts of the Seventh Division as it is the last settlement of any size up the Rejang. It's also a major centre for the illegal logging business, with many locals having been paid off handsomely to say nothing negative regarding the huge-scale logging operations close to the Kalimantan border. For such a small village Belaga boasts a large number of expensive cars and 4WDs, and the money's not from ecotourism.

Belaga is also a good place to arrange visits to the Kayan and Kenyah longhouses on the Linnau River. There is a very pretty Malay kampong, **Kampong Bharu**, along the esplanade downriver from the Belaga Bazaar. The **Kejaman burial pole** on display outside the Sarawak Museum in Kuching was brought from the Belaga area in 1902.

Upriver from Belaga

To go upriver beyond Belaga it is technically necessary to obtain a permit from the Residents' Office, T084-321963 and permission from the police station. The situation 'on the ground' is usually a lot more relaxed, with local guides and boat owners able to travel with the minimum of paperwork; ask in Belaga hotels and coffee shops on arrival.

When the river is high, express boats go upstream as far as the vast **Bakun Dam** (see box, opposite). From the dam a paved road connects to Bintulu on the coast, around four hours away, providing the main artery of supply for the Bakun project. Several basic shops and even a couple of 'motels' have been set up in the area to provide for the needs of the workers employed here. Beyond the Bakun dam itself logging roads continue further into the interior and it's sometimes possible to hire a driver and 4WD to explore.

Many low-lying areas are to be flooded on completion of the dam and boat transport may again be more organized further upriver. Indigenous communities above the Bakun Dam have been resettled in the Sungai Asap area some 40 km away on the Bintulu road. It's possible to stop at Asap when heading back to Bintulu on the coast.

Although these communities have been given compensation, land and housing, it seems they had little choice once the dam scheme was finalized. No financial compensation or land was given to upriver longhouses beyond the direct area of flooding in the Bakun Basin – for example, the Kayan Longhouses of Long Benalui, Long Ayak and Uma Batu Kalo. These communities still reside in their original homes.

The biggest impact of this project seems to have been felt by the nomadic and semi-nomadic Penan people. Due to their non-agricultural way of life little or no land rights or compensation have been provided, despite having lived in the area for hundreds, perhaps thousands, of years. Logging – and its associated disturbance of the forest – means nomadic people are finding it increasingly difficult to find enough food and make a living in the Upper Rejang basin.

Many of the **longhouses** around Belaga are quite modern, although several of the Kenyah and Kayan settlements have beautifully carved wooden *salongs* (tombstones) nearby. All the longhouses beyond Belaga are Orang Ulu, upriver tribal groups. Even

ON THE ROAD

Build and be dammed: an ecological time bomb

The Bakun Dam Scheme, upriver from Belaga on the upper Rejang and 400 km east of Kuching, has had more twists and turns than the river on which it has been built.

The RM9.12 billion project to build Southeast Asia's largest dam was on and off the books countless times. In 1990 it was scrapped for environmental reasons, but was back on again in 1993. Again, in late 1997, in the midst of Malaysia's economic crisis, when money was scarce, it was shelved only to be restarted in 2001. In 2004, with the government struggling to find buyers for the dam's electricity, it was rumoured that the project would again be scrapped or postponed. Government figures were determined to see the project through, although its original completion date of 2003 was pushed back to late 2007 and then onto 2010. The project finally came to fruition in August 2011 – much to the disappointment of environmental groups and many of the indigenous communities in the surrounding region.

The dam itself flooded a 700-sq-km tract of virgin rainforest that supported at least 43 species of endangered mammals and birds and had some of the highest rate of species endemism on earth. As well as flooding, the construction of the dam required 230 sq km of virgin rainforest to be cut down for to make way for roads to bring building materials and engineering equipment to the remote site above the Bakun Rapids. Malaysian lobby groups, such as the Environmental Protection Society, predict the project will cause severe soil erosion in an area already suffering from the effects of logging. In the early 1990s the river water was clear and fish were abundant; now the river is a muddy brown and water levels fluctuate wildly.

In addition to the catastrophic damage to the rainforest, the local Kayan and Kenyah communities suffered, with over 9000 longhouse residents displaced from their ancestral homelands and moved to longhouse settlements in Sungai Asap. Activists claim that many tribespeople were promised jobs on the dam that never materialized. As money concerns have crept in, many of these once proud subsistence farmers have turned to the bottle for comfort.

The project is not even a long-term solution: even the government admits its productive life is likely to be in the region of 20 years before it silts up. In the meantime, Bakun is expected to generate 2400 MW of electricity. The power was initially proposed to be consumed within Sabah and Sarawak, and possibly Brunei and Kalimantan, and will involve the construction of 800 km of high-voltage power lines. However, it seems there is an increasing demand for energy in Peninsular Malaysia and plans for an undersea cable more than 600 km long have been revived.

Film maker Chou Z Lam made a five-part documentary series showing the effect of the dam on local communities, particularly focussing on the challenges these communities face when displaced in terms of farming, education and lack of medical and transport facilities. The series, Documentary Series on Bakun Dam' (in Malay but with English subtitles) was considered 'sensitive' and taken off air when shown on Malaysian TV, but can now be watched on YouTube.

longhouses which seem to be very remote (such as Long Busang) are now connected by logging roads from Kapit, only four hours' drive away. To get well off the beaten track, into Penan country, it is possible to organize treks from Belaga towards the Kalimantan border, staying in longhouses en route.

About 2 km up the Batang Belaga from Belaga are the **Pasang Rapids** (hire a boat from Belaga), the biggest in Sarawak. No one has deliberately tried to shoot them as they are too dangerous. Boats can get reasonably close, however, and in the dry season it is possible to climb up to a picnic area overlooking the white water.

Listings Belaga

Tourist information

District Office
On the far side of the basketball courts, T086-461326.
This is the place to organize upriver permits.

Residents' Office
T084-321963.

Where to stay

In keeping with Belaga's frontier ambience, don't expect much luxury in this town's hostelry.

$ Belaga B&B
4 Belaga Bazaar (upstairs from Worldwide Exploration Travel and Tour office), T086-461512.
This mellow place has a dorm and a double room with fan and a/c on offer. It's a good place to source local information and guides.

$ Belaga Hotel
14 Belaga Bazaar, T086-461244.
Basic rooms with a/c, restaurant and coffeeshop to drink away the hours. Friendly owner. Reasonable option.

$ Daniel Levoh's Guesthouse
Jln The Ah Kiong, T084-461997, daniellevoh@hotmail.com.
Small backpacker place run by one of Belaga's best-known guides. There are 4 simple rooms and a communal area to share upriver tales.

$ Sing Soon Huat
26-27 New Bazaar, T086-461413.
Simple friendly place with comfortable social area and basic rooms. Not a bad choice.

Restaurants

Several small, cheap coffee shops along Belaga Bazaar and Main Bazaar.

Shopping

Handicrafts
Chop Teck Hua, *Belaga Bazaar.* An intriguing selection of tribal jewellery, old coins, beads, feathers, woodcarvings, blowpipes, parangs, tattoo boards and other curios buried under cobwebs and gecko droppings at the back of the shop.

What to do

Tour operators
Pop into **Daniel's Corner** (Jln The Ah Kiong, T013-848 6351), for a chat with Daniel Levoh about his tour prices. He runs trips to Kayan-Kenyah longhouses as well as jungle treks and other jungle fun. A 2-night longhouse trip starts at around RM250. The **Belaga Hotel** will contact guides for upriver trips and the **District Office** (see above) can also recommend a handful of experienced guides. In this part of Sarawak, guides are particularly expensive – sometimes up to RM120 a day, mainly because there are not enough tourists to justify full-time work. It is necessary to hire experienced boatmen too, because of the numerous rapids. Contact

Sarawak Tourism (see page 47) for their list of recommended guides. Guides with decent reviews include **John Belakirk**, T086-461512, johneddie1@hotmail.com; **Hamdani Louis**, T086-461039, hamdani@hotmail.com; and **Andreas Bato**, T019-3722972, niestabato@yahoo.com, an Orang Ulu guide with perfect English. Prices for longhouse trips upriver vary according to distance and water level, but are similar to those in Kapit. English is not widely spoken upriver so basic Malay comes in handy.

Transport

Air

At the time of research the airport was looking distinctly overgrown and flights between Belaga and Bintulu had been suspended. Check www.maswings.com.my for updates.

Boat

There is a daily boat to **Kapit** leaving at 0730, RM55, only in the wet season; the journey takes around 5 hrs. In the dry season speedboats RUN TO Kapit, from around RM60-100 per person if the water is high enough.

To **Tubau** and on to **Bintulu**: it is possible to hire a boat from Belaga to Kestima Kem (logging camp) near Rumah Lahanan Laseh (RM70 per person in a group or RM300 for 2-3 people); from there logging trucks go to Tabau on the Kemena River. Logging trucks leave irregularly and you can get stuck in logging camps. It is a 3-hr drive to Tabau;

this trip is not possible in the wet season. There are regular express boats from Tabau to Bintulu (RM12). This is the fastest and cheapest route to Bintulu, but not the most reliable. It is necessary to obtain permission from the Residents' Office and the police station in Belaga to take this route (see Tourist information, above).

Car

At the moment Belaga is comparatively isolated and overland links are poor. During the dry season it is possible to travel by 4WD overland to **Bintulu** (see page 90). The Bakun to Bintulu road has been gradually upgraded and is now surfaced along almost its full length. To charter a 4WD for the whole journey to Bintulu costs RM400 for 5 people and the journey takes 5 hrs. Vehicles leave from outside **Belaga B&B** at around 0700 so be there earlier to grab a place. Try Daniel Levoh of **Daniel's Corner** or **Hasbee Enterprises** (4 Belaga Bazaar), for help arranging a 4WD or try **Hap Kiat Transport**, T013-807 5598. They have a Toyota Landcruisers leave Belaga daily at 0700 and return from Bintulu at 1400 (RM60-70). Those wishing to travel overland from Bintulu must report to the Bintulu Resident's Office and the Belaga Resident's Office. For more information phone the Kapit Resident's Office, T084-796445. Keep a close eye on people's driving abilities in this area – many drive while drunk and large logging trucks speeding round the sharp bends are a significant danger.

North
coast

The north coast of Sarawak is fairly remote, with Bintulu, Miri and Marudi being the only significant towns. Close to Bintulu is Similajau National Park where green turtles lay their eggs. Niah National Park boasts famous limestone caves and is home to jungle birds and primates. Miri is the launch pad for river trips into the interior and Marudi is an upriver trading post and the start of a cross-border trek. Bintulu is accessible by air, boat (from Tubau in the interior) and bus. Miri is accessible by air and bus, and Marudi by air and boat.

Bintulu

rapidly developing town with a seedy edge but good local Melanau food

On the Kemena River, Bintulu is in the heart of Melinau country and was a fishing and farming centre until the largest natural gas reserve in Malaysia was discovered offshore in the late 1970s, making Bintulu a boom town overnight. Shell, Petronas and Mitsubishi then moved into the town in force. Modern Bintulu has a frontier town atmosphere, with muddy 4WDs ploughing streets lined with an inordinate number of short-stay hotels and sleazy *dangdut* and karaoke lounges popular with stimulation-starved oil men on boozy weekend escapades.

Few tourists stay long in Bintulu, despite it being the jumping-off point for the Similajau National Park and the Niah Caves. The longhouses on the Kemena River are accessible, but tend not to be as interesting as those further up the Rejang and Baram rivers. The Penan and Kayan tribes are very hospitable and eager to show off their longhouses and traditions to tourists.

Sights

Bintulu has a modern Moorish-style mosque called the **Masjid Assyakirin**; visitors may be allowed in when it is not prayer time. There is a colourful, centrally located Chinese temple called **Tua Pek Kong**. The **Pasar Bintulu** is an impressive

Tip...
The word Bintulu is believed to be a corruption of Mentu Ulau, which translates as 'the place for gathering heads'.

Bintulu

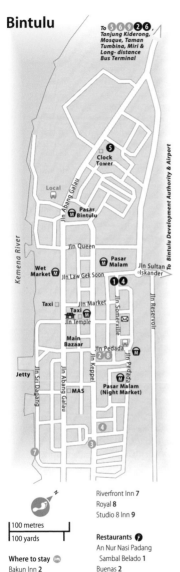

To ⑤⑥⑨❷❻,
Tanjung Kiderong,
Mosque, Taman
Tumbina, Miri &
Long- distance
Bus Terminal

Clock
Tower ⑤

Jln Abang Galau

Local

Pasar
Bintulu

Kemena River

Jln Queen

Pasar
Malam

Jln Sultan
Iskander

Wet
Market

Jln Law Gek Soon

To Bintulu Development Authority & Airport

Taxi

Jln Market

Taxi

Jln Somerville

Jln Temple

Jln Reservoir

Main
Bazaar

Jln Pedada

Jln Keppel

Jln Pedada

Jetty

Jln Sri Dagang

Jln Abang Galau

MAS

Pasar Malam
(Night Market)

④

③

⑦

100 metres
100 yards

Where to stay 🛏
Bakun Inn **2**
Kemena Plaza **3**
Kintown Inn **4**
My Inn **5**
New World Suites **6**
Riverfront Inn **7**
Royal **8**
Studio 8 Inn **9**

Restaurants 🍴
An Nur Nasi Padang
 Sambal Belado **1**
Buenas **2**
Nasi Ayam Singapore **4**
Popular Corner **5**
Sera Café **6**

building in the centre of town, built to house a local jungle produce market, foodstalls and some limited handicrafts stalls. The remnants of the old fishing village at Kampong Jepak are on the opposite bank of the Kemena River. During the Brooke era the town was a small administrative centre. The **clocktower** commemorates the meeting of five members of the Brooke government and 16 local chieftains, creating Council Negeri, the state legislative body.

A landscaped wildlife park, **Taman Tumbina** ⓘ *www.tumbina.com.my, daily 0800-1630, RM2*, has been developed on the outskirts of town, on the way to Tanjong Batu. It is a local recreational area and contains a small zoo, including a hornbill collection, a botanic garden (the only one in Sarawak) and the latest attraction, **Butterfly World**.

Some 20 km north of town is **Tanjong Kidurong**, Bintulu's main industrial area. The first project to break ground in Bintulu was the RM100-million crude oil terminal at Tanjong Kidurong from which 45,000 barrels of petroleum are exported daily. A deep-water port was built and the liquefied natural gas (LNG) plant started operating in 1982. The abundant supply of natural gas also created investment in related downstream projects. The **viewing tower** at Tanjong Kidurong gives a panoramic view of the new-look Bintulu and out to the timber ships on the horizon. They anchor 15 km offshore to avoid port duties and the timber is taken out on barges.

Longhouses

Trips to the longhouses on the Kemena River (which are rarely visited) can be organized from Bintulu. There are more than 20 longhouses, reached by road or river, within 30 minutes of the town. Iban longhouses are the closest; further upriver are the more traditional Kayan and Kenyah longhouses. Overpriced tours are organized by **Similajau Adventure Tours** (see page 93) or hire a boat from the wharf.

Tourist information

Bintulu Development Authority
Jln Tanjung Kidurong T086-332011,
www.bda.gov.my.
The best place for tourist information
in Bintulu.

Sarawak Forestry Department
www.sarawak.forestry.gov.my.
Provides information on the national parks
around Bintulu.

Where to stay

There aren't any places specifically geared
towards budget travellers here, and there
are plenty of seedy short-stay hotels that
are worth avoiding.

$$$ New World Suites
Park City Commerce Square, Lot 3971,
Jln Tun Ahmad Zaidi, T086-331122,
www.newworldsuites.net.
Comfortable and modern place a short
distance from the traditional heart of
town. Rooms, though very beige, are good
value. This hotel has excellent service and
significant discounts can be found online.

$$ Kemena Plaza
116 Taman Sri Dagang, Jln Abang Galau,
T086-335111, www.kemenahotelgroup.com/
kemena-plaza-hotel-home/.
Mid-range hotel with grandiose designs in
the heart of town. Rooftop pool with good
views over the town and standard mid-range
rooms with rooms with bath tubs. There is a
reasonable restaurant and a bar downstairs
and Wi-Fi throughout.

$$ Kintown Inn
93 Jln Keppel, T086-333666.
Large orange building offering a selection
of carpeted a/c rooms with TV and attached
bathroom with Wi-Fi. It's getting a bit rough
round the edges and showing its age.

$$ Riverfront Inn
256 Taman Sri Dagang, T086-339577.
One of the best options in town for those
on a mid-range budget, this place is popular
with foreign oil workers looking to relax at
the weekend. The rooms are comfortable,
modern and clean; those on the higher floors
at the front of the hotels have fantastic river
views. However, there is a lingering odour of
cigarette smoke throughout the hotel which
is off-putting. Wi-Fi available throughout.

$$ Royal
12 Jln Pedada, T086-315888.
Fair-value oldish mid-range hotel offering
carpeted a/c rooms with attached bathroom
and cable TV. Wi-Fi access throughout. There
are some decent eateries and shops around
the hotel making this a convenient spot.

$ Bakun Inn
7 Jln Pedada, T086-311111.
Fair budget digs in the heart of town.
Rooms are basic and clean and come
with cable TV and Wi-Fi. Very reasonable
value for a short stay.

$ My Inn
Sublot 197, Lot 960, Block 31, Kemena Land
District, Kemena Commercial Centre, Tanjung
Batu Rd, T086-318113.
Like many of the new budget business
hotels in Bintulu, this place is a bit of a
walk from town but has big TVs, Wi-Fi,
comfortable beds and excellent discounts
if booked online.

$ Studio 8 Inn
Sublot 4, Wisma PRC, Lot 472, Block 31,
T086-338838, www.studio8inn.com.
Located far from the old heart of town on the
way to Kidurong and slightly inconvenient
if you are a late eater, this hotel has 48 new
comfortable budget rooms with a lift to save
the legs. Fast Wi-Fi throughout. Good value.

Restaurants

A typical Melanau speciality is umai: raw fish pickled with lime or the fruit of *assam* (wild palms) and mixed with salted vegetables, onions and chillies. Bintulu is famed for its *belacan* (prawn paste). In the local dialect, prawns are called *urang*, not *udang* as elsewhere.

$ An Nur Nasi Padang Sambal Belado
39 Jln Somerville.
It's worth getting here early when there is still a good selection of tasty Indonesian-style curries and vegetable dishes.

$ Buenas
Opposite Parkcity Mall, Jln Tun Ahmad Zaidi.
Filipino place selling a variety of dishes including fried pork, crispy *prata* and ice *kachang*. However, if you make the effort to get here the one dish you must try is *umai*, Bintulu's celebrated raw fish speciality.

$ Nasi Ayam Singapore
Jln Somerville.
Large place offering up plates of steamed and roast Hainan chicken rice. Good spot for lunch.

$ Popular Corner
Opposite the hospital.
This place is definitely one of the better places to eat in Bintulu with a range of good fresh seafood dishes, dim sum at lunchtime and refreshing juices.

$ Sera Café
Lot 8138, Sibuyu, T019-438 4454.
Located a short drive from downtown Bintulu, this modest eatery serves up hearty plates of Iban specialities. Check out the various *pansuh* (cooked in bamboo) dishes, such as intestines with pineapple, and local vegetable dishes. This is a great opportunity for adventurous eaters to get a real taste of Borneo.

Markets

The Pasar Malam, off Jln Abang Galau, is a fun place to wonder and get stuck in to a selection of grilled seafood and meats.

Pasar Tamu and Pasar Utama are also fun places to browse local produce. The cone-shaped roofs are designed to look like Melanau headwear and the Pasar Utama has a foodcourt on the 2nd floor dishing up local favourites.

Shopping

Handicrafts
Dyang Enterprise, *Plaza Hotel, lobby floor, Jln Abang Galau.* Rather overpriced because of the hotel's more upmarket clientele.
Li Hua Plaza, *near the Plaza Hotel.* The best place for handicrafts.

What to do

Golf
Tanjong Kidurong, *north of town (regular buses), T08-651852.* A golf course by the sea, built by the Bintulu Development Authority. This is a 9-hole course with pleasant coastal breezes and sea views.

Sports complex
Bintulu Sports Complex, *1 km from town centre, fork right from the Miri road at the Chinese temple.* Swimming pool (RM2), tennis, football.

Tour operators
Deluxe Travel, *No 86, ground floor, Jln Abang Galau, Pusat Taman Medan Sepadu, T086-335313.*
Hunda Travel Services, *8 Jln Somerville, T086-331339.*
Similajau Adventure Tours, *105, 4359 Medan Jaya Commercial Centre, T086-331552.* Offers tours around the city, and to Niah caves, longhouses and Similajau National Park.

Transport

Air
Bintulu Airport is 5.5 km southwest of town. AirAsia and MAS (Jln Masjid, T086-331554) have regular connections with **Kuala Lumpur** and **Kuching**. MAS flies to **Miri**, **Sibu** and **Kota Kinabalu**.

Boat

Enquire at the wharf for times and prices. Regular connections with **Tubau**, last boat at 1400 (2½-3 hrs, RM22). There are connections with **Belaga**, via the logging road, see page 86; this route is popular with people in Belaga as it is much cheaper than going from Sibu. However, tourists need a permit to get to Belaga, and there is no accommodation in Tubau for those who get stuck. If you really want to do this, call Mr Hasbee in Belaga (T013-842 9767) or Daniel Levoh (T084 461 997, daniellevoh@hotmail.com) and see if any drivers are making the return trip to Belaga from Bintulu (RM60). If travelling overland from Bintulu, report to the Bintulu Resident's Office and the Belaga Resident's Office. For more information, call the Kapit Resident's Office, T084-796445.

Bus

There are 2 bus stations in town. The local bus terminal is in the centre. The long-distance Medan Jaya station is 10 mins by taxi from the centre, on the road towards Miri (RM15) or by bus 29 from the town centre. Regular connections with **Miri** (RM27), **Batu Niah** (RM20) and **Sibu** (RM20) and **Kuching** (RM70). There are at least 10 bus companies, and buses leave frequently all day. One of the more organized companies ploughing the bumpy roads is **Biaramas**, T086-314 999, www.busasia.net.

Taxi

For **Miri** and **Sibu**, taxis leave from Jln Masjid. Because of the regular bus services and the poor state of the roads, most taxis are for local use only and chartering them is pricey.

Similajau National Park

long, thin coastal park with sandy beaches and nesting green turtles

Lying 20 km northeast of Bintulu, Similajau is a coastal park with sandy beaches, broken by rocky headlands. It is Sarawak's most unusually shaped national park, being more than 32 km long and only 1.5 km wide. Similajau was demarcated in 1978, but has only been open to tourists since the construction of decent facilities in 1991.

Pasir Mas (Golden Sands) is a beautiful 3.5-km-long stretch of coarse beach, to the north of the Likau River, where green turtles come ashore to lay their eggs between July and September. A few kilometres from the Park HQ at **Kuala Likau** is a small coral reef, known as **Batu Mandi**. The area is renowned for birdwatching. Bintulu is not on the main tourist route and consequently the park is very quiet. Its seclusion makes it a perfect escape.

The beaches are backed by primary rainforest: peat swamp, *kerangas* (heath forest), mixed dipterocarp and mangrove (along Sungai Likau and Sungai Sebubong). There are small rapids on the Sebulong River. Sadly, the rivers, particularly the beautiful **Sungai Likau**, have been polluted by indiscriminate logging activities upstream.

Flora and fauna

On arrival at Kuala Likau there is a prominent sign advising against swimming in the river and to watch your feet around the Park HQ area; Similajau is well known for its saltwater crocodiles (*Crocodylus perosus*) though there have been no reported attacks on humans here. The best time to see the crocodiles is after dark and you can organize a boat tour at Park HQ and see their menacing eyes slipping in and out of the water reflected in the guide's torchlight. There are also false gharials, which resemble the crocs but have a diet of fish and are harmless to humans. The park is home to 24 resident species of mammal (including gibbons, Hose's langurs, banded langurs, long-tailed macaques, civets, wild boar, porcupines and squirrels) and 185 species of birds (including many migratory species). There are some good coral reefs to the north and marine life includes five different species of dolphins, porpoises and turtles. Pitcher plants grow in the *kerangas* forest and along the beach.

Treks
Several longish but not-too-difficult trails have been created from the Park HQ. One path follows undulating terrain, parallel to the coast. It is possible to cut to the left, through the jungle, to the coast, and walk back to Kuala Likau along the beach. The main trail to **Golden Beach** is a three- to four-hour walk crossing several streams and rivers where estuarine crocodiles are reputed to lurk. Most of these crossings are on 'bridges', which are usually just felled trees with no attempt made to assist walkers; a good sense of balance is required. Another enjoyable walk is the trail to **Selansur Rapids**, around 2½ hours in total. Follow the trail to Golden Beach; after about an hour a marked trail leads off into the forest. The walk ends at the rapids where it is possible to take a dip and cool off.

Essential Similajau National Park

Finding your feet

There is no regular bus service to the park. From Bintulu, a taxi (T086-332009) costs RM50 one-way/RM100 return and takes 30 minutes. Boats can be chartered from the wharf at Bintulu, costing from RM200.

Park information

Permits are available from the **Bintulu Development Authority** (see page 92). There's an information centre at Park HQ at the mouth of Sungai Likau, across the river from the park, T086-391284. A boat is needed to cross the 5 m of crocodile-infested river. Because the park facilities are outside the park boundaries, visitors do not need a permit to stay there. This has led to the 'park' becoming popular with Bintulites at the weekend.

Listings Similajau National Park

Where to stay

$ National park accommodation
Contact Similajau National Park HQ, T086-391284.
There are 2 chalets and 2 'forest' hostels a short walk from the beach with bargain-basement dorm beds and 24-hr electricity. The **hostels** have attractive polished hardwood decor. The more expensive accommodation is in the **chalets**, which have 8 beds to a room, sofas and a sea view. The canteen at Park HQ serves basic food and there are picnic shelters at Park HQ. You can camp for RM5 a night. This place can get very busy at weekends and can be block-booked, so arrange your stay well in advance.

★ Niah National Park

one of Borneo's prime archaeological sites, with huge caves and swiftlet collectors' precipitous ladders

Niah's famous caves, tucked into a limestone massif called Gunung Subis (394 m), made world headlines in 1958, when they were confirmed as the most important archaeological site in Asia. The park is one of the most popular tourist attractions in Sarawak and more than 15,000 visitors come here every year. The caves were declared a national historic monument in 1958, but it was not until 1974 that the 30 sq km of jungle surrounding the caves were turned into a national park to protect the area from logging.

Park Information Centre
Park HQ, Mon-Fri 0800-1230 and 1400-1615, Sat 0800-1245, Sun 0800-1200.

At the Park HQ is this centre, with displays on birds' nests and flora and fauna. The exhibition includes the 37,000-year-old human skull which drew world attention to Niah in 1958. Also on display are 35,000-year-old oyster shells and palaeolithic pig bones, monkey bones, turtle shells and crabs, found littering the cave floor. There are also burial vessels dating from 1600 BC and carved seashell jewellery from 400 BC.

Essential Niah National Park

Finding your feet

The nearest town to the park is Batu Niah. There are regular buses to Batu Niah from Miri (RM12, two hours), Bintulu (six buses daily, RM20, two hours) and Sibu. From Batu Niah it is around 3 km to the Park HQ; it's a 45-minute walk through the forest, or take a longboat from near the market in Batu Niah (RM 15 per person; or RM3 per person if more than five people). A taxi to Park HQ costs RM20 (25 minutes) from the bus station at Batu Niah but the riverboat is far more scenic.

Getting around

From Park HQ there are well-marked trails to the caves. Guides are not essential but they provide information and can relate legends about the paintings. Even with a guide, visitors cannot cross the barrier 3 m in front of the cave wall. Guides charge RM40 for groups of up to 20 and can be hired from the Park HQ. Longboats can be hired from Park HQ for upriver trips (maximum of eight people per boat). Bring a powerful torch for the caves. Walking boots are advisable during the wet season as the plankwalk can get very slippery.

Park information

Park HQ is at Pangkalan Lubang next to Sungai Niah. The park is open daily 0800-1700 and the caves can be visited daily 0800-1630. Entry costs RM20, children RM7 (camera RM5, video RM10, professional photography RM200). For more information on the park, contact the Deputy Park Warden, Niah National Park, PO Box 81, Miri Post Office, Batu Niah, T085-737454. A useful website is: http://www.sarawakforestry.com/htm/snp-np-niah.html.

ON THE ROAD

Niah's guano collectors: scraping the bottom

Eight bat species live in the Niah Caves. Some are quite common, such as the horseshoe bat and fruit bats, while other, more exotic, varieties include the bearded tomb bat, Cantor's roundleaf horseshoe bat and the lesser bent-winged bat.

The ammonia-stench of bat guano permeates the humid air. People began collecting guano in 1929 and it is used as a fertilizer and to prevent pepper vines from rotting. Guano collectors pay a licence fee for the privilege of sweeping up *tahi sapu* (fresh guano) and digging up *tahi timbang* (mature guano), which they sell to the Bat Guano Cooperative at the end of the plankwalk.

The caves

To reach the caves, take a longboat across the river from Park HQ at Pangkalan Lubang to the start of the 4-km belian (ironwood) plankwalk to the entrance of the **Great Cave**. Take the right fork 1 km from the entrance. The remains of a small kampong, formerly inhabited by birds' nest collectors (see below) and guano collectors, is just before the entrance, in the shelter of overhanging rocks. It is known as **Traders' Cave**. Beware of voracious insects; wear long trousers and plenty of repellent. There are no lights in the Great Cave, so torches are needed.

The **Painted Cave** is beyond the Great Cave. Prehistoric wall paintings – the only ones in Borneo – stretch for about 32 m along the cave wall. Most of the drawings are of dancing human figures and boats, thought to be associated with a death ritual. On the floor of the cave, several 'death-ships' were found with some Chinese stoneware, shell ornaments and ancient glass beads. These death-ships served as coffins and have been carbon-dated to between AD 1 and AD 780. By around AD 700 there is thought to have

Niah National Park

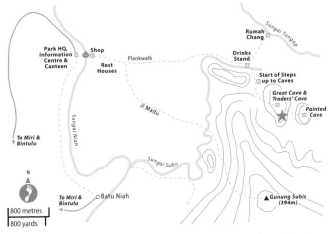

BACKGROUND

Niah National Park

About 40,000 years ago, when the Gulf of Thailand and the Sunda Shelf were still dry ground and a land bridge linked the Philippines and Borneo, Niah was home to *Homo sapiens*. It was the most exciting archaeological discovery since Java man (*Homo erectus*).

Scientist and explorer A Hart Everett led expeditions to Niah Caves in 1873 and 1879, after which he pronounced that they justified no further work. Some 79 years later, Tom Harrisson, ethnologist, explorer, conservationist and curator of the Sarawak Museum, confirmed the most important archaeological find at that time in Southeast Asia at Niah. He unearthed fragments of a 37,000-year-old human skull – the earliest evidence of *Homo sapiens* in the region – at the west mouth of the Niah Great Cave itself. The skull was buried under 2.4 m of guano. His find debunked and prompted a radical reappraisal of popular theories about where modern man's ancestors had sprung from. A wide range of palaeolithic and neolithic tools, pottery, ornaments and beads was also found at the site. Anthropologists believe Niah's caves may have been permanently inhabited until around AD 1400. Harrisson's excavation site, office and house have been left intact in the mouth of the Great Cave. A total of 166 burial sites have been excavated, 38 of which are Mesolithic (up to 20,000 years ago) and the remainder neolithic (4000 years ago). Some of the finds are now in the Sarawak Museum in Kuching.

been a flourishing community based in the caves, trading hornbill ivory and birds' nests with the Chinese in exchange for porcelain and beads. But then it seems the caves were suddenly deserted in about 1400. In Penan folklore there are references to 'the ancestors who lived in the big caves' and tribal elders are said to be able to recall funeral rites using death boats similar to those found at Niah.

Flora and fauna

The park primarily comprises alluvial or peat swamp and mixed dipterocarp forest. Long-tailed macaques, hornbills, squirrels, flying lizards and crocodiles have all been recorded here. There are also bat hawks, which provide an impressive spectacle when they home in on one of the millions of bats which pour out of the caves at dusk. The caves here are also renowned throughout Asia for their swiftlet activity and therefore for the bird's nest soup industry. Every inch of the cave roofs in which the birds nest is owned by private entities that have the sole right to collect the nests. These are collected by candlelight by using bamboo ladders that can reach up to 30 or more metres and the nests are harvested every six months and sent around Asia to be made into bird's nest soup.

Treks

A lowland trail called **Jalan Madu** (Honey Road), traverses the peat swamp forest and ascends Gunung Subis; it is not well marked. Return trips need a full day. The trail leads off the plankwalk to the right, about 1 km from Pangkalan Lubang (Park HQ). The left fork on the plankwalk, before the gate to the caves, goes to an Iban longhouse, **Rumah Chang** (40 minutes' walk), where cold drinks can be bought.

ON THE ROAD

How to make a swift buck

The Malay name for the Painted Cave is Kain Hitam (black cloth), because the profitable rights to the birds' nests were historically exchanged for bolts of black cloth.

The Chinese have had a taste for swiftlets' nests for well over 1000 years, and the business of collecting them from 60 m up in the cavernous chamber of the Great Cave is as lucrative – and as hazardous – a profession now as it was then. The nests are used to prepare bird's nest soup – blended with chicken stock and rock salt – which is a famous Chinese delicacy, prized as an aphrodisiac and for its supposed remedial properties for asthma and rheumatism.

Birds' nests are one of the most expensive foods in the world: they sell for up to US$2500 per kg in Hong Kong (a bowl of the soup costs US$30-50), where over 100 tonnes of them are consumed annually. The Chinese communities of North America import 30 tonnes of birds' nests a year. Locally, they fetch up to RM5000 per kg, depending on the grade.

Hundreds of thousands – possibly millions – of swiftlets (of the *Collocalia* swift family) live in the caves. Unlike other parts of Southeast Asia, where collectors use rotan ladders to reach the nests (see Gomantong Caves, Sabah, page 269), Niah's collectors scale *belian* (ironwood) poles to heights of more than 60 m. They use bamboo sticks with a scraper attached to one end (called *penyulok*) to pick the nests off the cave roof. The nests are harvested three times each season (the seasons run from August to December and January to March). On the first two occasions, the nests are removed before the eggs are laid and a third are left until the nestlings are fledged. Nest collectors are now all supposed to have licences but, in reality, no one does. Although the birds' nests are supposed to be protected by the national park in the off-season, wardens turn a blind eye to illegal harvesting; the collectors also know many secret entrances to the caves. Officially, people caught harvesting out of season can be fined RM2000 or sent to jail for a year, but no one's ever caught.

Despite being a dangerous operation (there are usually several fatal accidents at Niah each year), collecting has become so popular that harvesters have to reserve their spot with a lamp. Nest collecting is run on a first-come, first-served basis. Nests of the white-nest swiftlets and the black-nest swiftlets are collected – the nests of the mossy-nest and white-bellied swiftlets require too much effort to clean. The nests are built by the male swiftlets using a glutinous substance produced by the salivary glands under the tongue which is regurgitated in long threads; the saliva sets like cement producing a rounded cup which sticks to the cave wall. In the swifts' nest market, price is dictated by colour: the best are the white nests which are without any plant material or feathers. Most of the uncleaned nests are bought up by middle-men, agents of traders in Kuching, but locals at Batu Niah also do some of the cleaning. The nests are first soaked in water for about three hours and, when softened, feathers and dirt are laboriously removed with tweezers. The 'cakes' of nests are dried over-night: if left in the sun they turn yellow.

Listings Niah National Park *map page 97.*

Where to stay

$$-$ National park accommodation
It's advisable to book accommodation at least 2-3 days in advance, through Niah National Park (T085-737454 or T085-737450) or the National Parks Booking Office in Miri (see page 105) or Kuching (T082-248088). Bookings can also be made online at http://ebooking.sarawak.gov.my.
There's a **family chalet** (RM159 per room or RM239 per chalet), similar to a hostel but with cooker and a/c, 2 rooms with 4 beds in each. There is a slightly cheaper **chalet** (RM105 per room or RM159 per house) with fan. There are 5 **hostels** (RM42.50 for 1 room, 04 RM15.90 per bed), each with 4 rooms of 4 beds each; all rooms have private bathrooms, clean, and Western-style with shower, toilet, electric fans, fridges, large sitting area and kitchen. No cooking facilities, but kettle, crockery and cutlery provided on request. All accommodation has 24-hr electricity and treated water.

$ Camping
There is a campsite with space for 30, RM5 per night. Tents can be hired from Park HQ or from the site.

Batu Niah

$ Niah Caves Inn
621 Batu Niah Bazaar, T085-737333.
With a/c, TV, shower and spacious, fully carpeted rooms. Reasonable value.

Restaurants

The **Guano Collectors' Cooperative** shop at the beginning of the plankwalk sells basic food and cold drinks and camera film. There is another basic shop/restaurant just outside the park gates. There is a canteen at Park HQ (open 0700-2300 but timing is a little erratic), which serves good-value local food and full Western breakfast. A barbecue site is provided.

Miri and the Baram River

seafood nirvana and home to Sarawak's first oil well

Miri is the starting point for adventurous trips up the Baram River to Marudi, Bario and the Kelabit Highlands. Also accessible from Miri and Marudi is the incomparable Gunung Mulu National Park with the biggest limestone cave system in the world and one of the richest assemblages of plants and animals.

The capital of Sarawak's Fourth Division is a prosperous, predominantly Chinese town with one of Malaysia's best selections of restaurants and back streets filled with karaoke lounges and ladies of the night. While there isn't a great deal to do in the town itself, many visitors find Miri a good place to recuperate after the rigours of the road and often spend a couple of days enjoying the bustling streets and bountiful food on offer. The waterfront development on the north side of town has a marina; there is a pleasant walk on the peninsula here across the Miri River, and some good fishing.

Sights

Juxtaposed against Miri's modern boom-town image is **Tamu Muhibba** ⓘ *opposite the Park Hotel in a purpose-built concrete structure with pointed roofs on the roundabout connecting Jln Malay and Jln Padang, open 24 hrs*, the native jungle produce market. The Orang Ulu come downriver to sell their produce and a walk around the market provides an illuminating lesson in jungle nutrition. Colourful characters run impromptu stalls from rattan mats, selling yellow cucumbers that look like mangoes, mangoes that look like turnips, huge crimson durians, tiny loofah sponges, sackfuls of fragrant Bario rice (brown and white), every shape, size and hue of banana, *tuak* (rice wine) in old Heineken bottles and a menagerie of jungle fauna – including mouse deer, falcons, pangolins and the apparently delicious long-snouted *tupai* (jungle squirrel). There are handicrafts and a large selection of dried and fresh seafood: fish and *bubok* (tiny prawns) and big buckets boiling with catfish or stacked with turtles.

For more tropical market action, head to **Saberkas Weekend Market** ① *Jln Miri Pujut, 3 km from the centre of town, RM16 taxi ride, Sun 0800-1200*. This is a cheerful place packed full of Sarawak goodies and snacks and well worth a Sunday morning visit.

For great views of the city and an insight into the importance of oil in the development of the city make your way to the **Petroleum Museum** ① *Bukit Tenaga, Tue-Fri 0900-1645, Sat, Sun 1000-1600, free.* Here you can see the Grand Old Lady, the first oil pump erected in Miri and Shell Oil's first ever pump, a change that altered the fate of the city forever, and kept on bringing oil out of the ground from 1910 until 1972. It's worth coming up here for the breezes and the views alone, but the museum is an added bonus. To get here, walk from town or jump in a cab.

Essential Miri

Finding your feet

The airport is close to the centre of town. A taxi from the airport into town costs RM25. Buses from the airport run almost hourly 0720-1850 and drop passengers at the local bus terminal near the tourist information centre on Jalan Melayu. Miri is a hub for **MASwings** and has flights to many of the smaller towns in the interior (see Transport, page 111).

The long-distance bus terminal is at Pujuk Padang Kerbau, 4 km from the centre. A taxi costs RM20 into town, or bus No 33 runs to the tourist information centre.

Park information

National park accommodation can be booked at the visitor information centre in Miri (see page 105) or through the relevant national park offices: for **Gunung Mulu**, T085-792300; for the **Lambir Hills**, T085-471609; for **Loagan Bunut**, T019-861 0994; for **Niah**, T085-737454; and for **Similajau**, T085-391284.

For further information visitors can also contact the **National Parks and Wildlife Office**, Level 11, Wisma Pelita Tunku, Jln Puchong, T085-438455.

Head to **Miri City Fan** on Jalan Kipas to enjoy a relaxed park with plenty of seating areas, jogging track and a large swimming pool (RM1).

The coast around Miri

Hawaii Beach ① *15-min taxi ride from Miri (RM20) or take bus No 13 (RM2.60)*, is a pristine, palm-fringed beach, popular for picnics and barbecues. It's privately owned and visitors are asked to pay RM12 to enter. There are a couple of other beaches closer to Miri including **Luak Bay** and **Taman Selera**. Bus No 11 (RM1) runs to both these spots. Don't expect anything akin to Mauritius here; these places are mellow city escapes.

Although visibility might not be comparable to better known sites, such as Sipadan off the east coast of Sabah, the extensive **coastal reefs** of Miri are an area of rich marine life and unexploited hard and soft coral gardens. With patch reefs, steep drop-offs

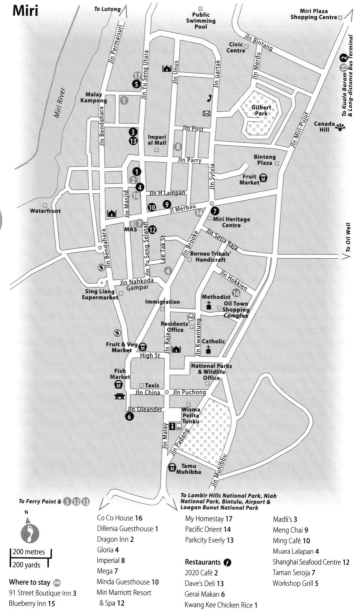

Miri

To Lutong
Public Swimming Pool
Miri Plaza Shopping Centre
Civic Centre
Jln Bintang
Jln Merdu
To Kuala Baram & Long-distance Bus Terminal
Jln Permaisuri
Jln Yu Seng Utara
Jln Unus
Jln Gartak
Gilbert Park
Canada Hill
Malay Kampong
Jln Bendahara
Jln Post
Jln Miri-Pujut
Imperial Mall
Jln Parry
Bintang Plaza
Jln Sylvia
Fruit Market
Jln Masjid
Jln H Lampan
Jl Merbau
Waterfront
Miri Heritage Centre
MAS
Jln Yu Seng Selatan
Lee Tak St
Jln Brooke
Jln Setia Raja
To Oil Well
Borneo Tribals' Handicraft
Jln Nahkoda Gampar
Jln Hokkien
Sing Liang Supermarket
Methodist
Oil Town Shopping Complex
Immigration
Residents' Office
Jln Raja
Jln Kwantung
Catholic
Fruit & Veg Market
High St
National Parks & Wildlife Office
Fish Market
Taxis
Jln China
Jln Puchong
Jln Oleander
Wisma Pelita Tunku
Jln Malay
Jln Padang
Tamu Muhibba
Jln Muhibbu
To Ferry Point & 3 12 13
To Lambir Hills National Park, Niah National Park, Bintulu, Airport & Loagan Bunut National Park

N

200 metres
200 yards

Where to stay
91 Street Boutique Inn **3**
Blueberry Inn **15**

Co Co House **16**
Dillenia Guesthouse **1**
Dragon Inn **2**
Gloria **4**
Imperial **8**
Mega **7**
Minda Guesthouse **10**
Miri Marriott Resort & Spa **12**

My Homestay **17**
Pacific Orient **14**
Parkcity Everly **13**

Restaurants
2020 Café **2**
Dave's Deli **13**
Gerai Makan **6**
Kwang Kee Chicken Rice **1**

Madli's **3**
Meng Chai **9**
Ming Café **10**
Muara Lalapan **4**
Shanghai Seafood Centre **12**
Taman Seroja **7**
Workshop Grill **5**

descending into the depths and diverse wreck sites, there's something to interest divers of any level of experience. Combine that with world-beating biodiversity and divers are in for a little known adventure. So, why isn't this one of the world's most popular diving areas? The answer is that visibility is often low, at many sites 10 m or less, with bad weather sometimes making diving impossible. Miri's sites are fairly easy to access and the Miri-Sibuti area has recently been declared a conservation zone. Some of the more distant regions offshore seem to have become more difficult to access.

Luconia Shoals, more than a day's sail from Miri, is a good example of this with few boats (liveaboards required) prepared to sail out to this area, charging prohibitive fees. A few years ago, some in the diving world claimed that Luconia was one of Malaysia's greatest diving sites, and while that may still be the case, several sources suggest that illegal dynamite fishing has inflicted a heavy price recently. For more detailed and up-to-the-minute information, contact Co Co Dive (www.divemiri.com), the best organized diving outfit in town. They also have a popular backpackers' lodge in town.

Lambir Hills National Park
19 km south of Miri, T085-471609, RM20, children RM7, photography RM5, video camera RM10, professional camera RM200; to get there, take Bekenuor Bakong bus from Park Hotel (RM5, 40 mins) and ask the driver to drop you off outside the Park HQ – the last bus goes back to Miri at around 1730, or go by taxi (RM70, 30 mins).

Lambir Hills, just visible from Miri, mainly consists of a chain of sandstone hills bounded by rugged cliffs. The main attractions are the many beautiful waterfalls. *Kerangas* (heath forest) covers the higher ridges and hills while the lowland areas are mixed dipterocarp forest. Bornean gibbons, bearded pigs, barking deer and over 230 species of bird have been recorded in the park. There is only one path, across a rickety suspension bridge, at present, but there are numerous waterfalls, tree towers for birdwatching, and several trails which lead to enticing pools for swimming. The park attracts hordes of day trippers from Miri at weekends. It's possible to stay overnight (see Where to stay, page 107). The Park HQ is close to the Miri–Niah road and contains an audiovisual room.

Marudi
Four major tribal groups – Iban, Kelabit, Kayan and Penan – come to Marudi to do business with Chinese, Indian and Malay merchants. Marudi is the furthest upriver trading post on the Baram and services all the longhouses in the Tutoh, Tinjar and Baram river basins. Most tourists only stop long enough in Marudi to down a cold drink before catching the next express boat upriver; as the trip to Mulu National Park can now be done in a day, not many have to spend the night here. Because it is a major trading post, however, there are a lot of hotels, and the standards are reasonably good.

Fort Hose was built in 1901, when Marudi was still called Claudetown, and has good views of the river. It is named after the last of the rajah's residents, the anthropologist, geographer and natural historian Dr Charles Hose. The fort is now a **museum** ⓘ *Tue-Sun 0900-1800, free*, with a selection of some of Hose's ethnographic collection as well as handicrafts produced by the region's diverse population. Also of note is the intricately carved **Thaw Peh Kong Chinese Temple** ⓘ *diagonally opposite the express boat jetty*, also known as Siew San Teen. The temple was shipped from China and erected in in the early 1900s, although it was probably already 100 years old by the time it began life in its new location.

If you are lucky, you might be able to catch the **Baram Regatta**, which takes place over three days in August, and features races between boat crews from different local

BACKGROUND

Miri

In the latter years of the 19th century, a small trading company set up in Sarawak to import kerosene and export polished shells and pepper. In 1910, when 'earth oil' was first struck near Miri, the small trading company took the plunge and diversified into the new commodity, creating Sarawak's first oil town in the process. The company's name was **Shell**. Together with the Malaysian national oil company, **Petronas**, Shell has been responsible for discovering, producing and refining Sarawak's offshore oil deposits. Oil is a key contributor to Malaysia's export earnings and Miri has been a beneficiary of the boom. There is a big refinery at Lutong to the north, which is connected by pipeline with Seria in Brunei. Lutong is the next town on the Miri River and the main headquarters for Shell.

The oil boom in this area began on Canada Hill, behind the town (incidentally, this limestone ridge provides excellent views). **Oil Well No 1** was built by Shell and was the first oil well in Malaysia, spudded on 10 August 1910. The well was still yielding oil 62 years later, but its productivity began to slump. It is estimated that a total of 600,000 barrels were extracted from Well No 1 during its operational life. It was shut off in 1972. There are now 624 oil wells in the Miri Field, producing 80 million barrels of oil a year.

communities. Apparently the Berawan crews from Mulu have the upper hand as they are able to practise every day after work. The **Sape Festival** is held at the same time as the regatta with people from many different ethnic groups coming together and mingling over food, traditional music and plenty of rice wine. The next regatta will be held in August 2017.

The **Marudi Kampong Teraja log walk** is normally done from the Brunei end, as the return trek – across the Sarawak/Brunei border – takes a full day, from dawn to dusk. It is, however, possible to reach an Iban longhouse inside Brunei without going the whole distance to Kampong Teraja. The longhouse is on the Sungai Ridan, about 2½ hours down the jungle trail. The trail starts 3 km from Marudi, on the airport road. There's no customs post on the border; the trail is not an official route into Brunei. Trekkers are advised to take their passports in the unlikely event of being stopped by police, who will probably turn a blind eye. Kampong Teraja in Brunei is the furthest accessible point that can be reached by road from Labi.

Three **longhouses** – Long Seleban, Long Moh and Leo Mato – are accessible by 4WD from Marudi.

Loagan Bunut National Park

120 km (3 hrs) by road southeast of Miri, T085-779410, take a local bus from Miri to Lapok Bridge and then hire a car/taxi for the remaining 10 km to the park. A number of travel agents in Miri offer tours.

Located in the upper reaches of the Sungai Bunut, the park contains Sarawak's largest natural lake covering approximately 650 ha. The water level in the lake is totally dependent on the water level of the rivers Bunut, Tinjar and Baram. The level is at its lowest in the months of February, May and June and sometimes, for a period of about two to three weeks, the lake becomes an expanse of dry, cracked mud. The lake's main cultural attraction is the traditional method of fishing (*selambau*), which has been retained by the Berawan fishermen. It is possible to charter a boat with one of the fisherman for an informative tour of the lake. The fishermen are highly knowledgeable about the ecosystem and often speak a fair level of English. Boats can be hired for RM60 per hour and for four people; additional passengers cost RM15 per hour. The surrounding area is covered with peat swamp forest. Common larger birds found here are darters, egrets, herons, bittern, hornbill and kites. Gibbons are also common.

Listings Miri and the Baram River *map page 102.*

Tourist information

Miri Visitor Information Centre
Lot 452 Jln Melayu (next to the local bus station and just across from the Park Hotel), T085-434181, www.sarawaktourism.com. Mon-Fri 0800-1700 and Sat, Sun and public holidays 0900-1500.
Maps and tourist information. Bookings for accommodation at Mulu, Lambir Hills, Loagan Bunut, Niah and Similajau can be made here.

National Parks and Wildlife Office
Level 11, Wisma Pelita Tunku, Jln Puchong, T085-438455.

Police station
Jln Kingsway, T085-433730.

Residents' Office
Jln Kingsway, T085-427254.

Where to stay

Miri
Most people going to Mulu will have to spend at least a night in Miri. The town has a fair selection of dreary mid-range accommodation and a couple of excellent new budget options. Many mid-range hotels are around Jln Yu Seng Selatan. Being an oil town, and close to Brunei, Miri has a booming prostitution industry and the warblings from the karaoke bars go on late into the night.

$$$ Imperial
Part of the Imperial Shopping Mall, Jln Post, T085-431133, www.imperial.com.my.

Set in a towering block to the east of the town centre, this hotel offers comfortable rooms or apartments with cable TV and internet access. The suites here are massive and come with large sofas. There's a lovely poolside area with café, offering excellent views over the city, particularly at sunset. Apartments feature a fully equipped kitchen, and, in some cases, a washing machine. Rooms in the newer wing are the best bet and have been recently renovated.

$$$ Miri Marriott Resort & Spa
Jln Temenggong Datuk Oyong Lawai, a short taxi ride from Miri, T085-421121, www.marriotthotels.com.
This best in town, this luxurious resort-style hotel overlooks the sea and has 220 a/c rooms, all with minibar, TV and Wi-Fi. 5-star comforts include Balinese-style spa and massage parlour, the largest swimming pool in the Miri area, with a good shallow pool for kids, tennis, a 24-hr gym and a health centre. **Wildlife Expeditions** arrange tours from their office in the lobby.

$$$ Parkcity Everly
Jln Temenggong Datuk Oyong Lawai, 2 km from town centre, T085-440288, www.vhhotels.com.
At the mouth of the Miri River, this hotel curves around the South China Sea and offers 168 a/c rooms with cable TV, bathroom, minibar and balcony. The colourful but noisy river traffic is an entertaining diversion. The beach is too near town to be clean and the sea is not safe for swimming but is good for sunset strolls.

There's a palm-lined free-form pool with swim-up bar and a jacuzzi. Facilities include a coffee house, Chinese restaurant, bar, bakery/deli, fitness centre and sauna. The hotel is looking a bit ragged and needs a bit of investment to renovate and bring it back to its former glory.

$$ Blueberry Inn
Lot 8007-8008, 1st and 2nd floor, Bandar Baru Permyjaya, T085-421175.
Far from the centre of town but offering a quiet respite from the city centre, this friendly motel-style place has comfortable doubles with old-school wallpaper. There's a social area just over the road from Permy Mall.

$$ Dragon Inn
Lot 355, Jln Masjid, T085-422266.
The clashing psychedelic carpet and flowery wallpaper in the corridors and can be a little disturbing after a few hours in the sun, but thankfully, decor in the rooms is toned down. Rooms have comfy beds, flatscreen TV, kettle, fridge and free Wi-Fi access. It's in a good location in the heart of the city with plenty of eating options nearby.

$$ Gloria
27 Jln Brooke, T085-416699.
A selection of bright carpeted a/c rooms with cable TV and attached bathroom with bathtub. There's free Wi-Fi in the lobby and a good Chinese restaurant downstairs. Rooms here are fair value, but nothing special. Some of the cheaper rooms are windowless so ask to see a selection.

$$ Grand Palace
2 km Jln Miri-Pujut, Pelita Commercial Centre, T085-428888, www.grandpalace hotel.com.my.
Like many of the hotels in the mid- to upper-range price brackets in Miri, time has stood still here. Rooms are clean and spacious but haven't been upgraded for some time. The 125 comfortable rooms have dreary carpets and intense burgundy curtains, cable TV, a/c

and a smart attached bathroom. There's a pool and a couple of good restaurants with occasional themed buffets.

$$ Mega
Jln Merbau, T085-432432, www.megahotel.com.my.
Another beast of a building, with its 293 rooms towering over the town. Rooms are comfortable and functional though not particularly inspiring and could do with a bit of a sprucing up. There is an oddly shaped pool with a jacuzzi and lounge chairs, bar and karaoke lounge and good Chinese restaurant. Free Wi-Fi throughout. There is a shopping mall below the hotel. Good discounts for online bookings.

$$ Pacific Orient
49 Jln Brooke, T085-413333, pohotel@streamyx.com.
Dated mid-range business hotel that is somewhat lacking in character. Aiming for domestic business travellers, rooms are comfortable, plain and have a/c, TV and attached bathroom. There's free Wi-Fi in the lobby and a cheap food court on the ground floor offering local delights.

$ 91 Street Boutique Inn
Lot 2016-2018, Jln MS 1/1, Marina Square 1, Marina Park City, T085-321591, www.91boutiqueinn.com.
This place is a bit of a trek from the commercial heart of Miri but has spotless rooms, powerful a/c and is surrounded by decent places to eat. Staff are friendly and the Wi-Fi is fast.

$ Coco House
Lot 2117, Block 9, Miri-Pujut Rd, Miri Concession Land District (MCLD), T085-417051, www.cocohouse.com.my.
This is a good spot for divers as it's located above the best dive shop in town and is a source for excellent aquatic information. There's a selection of dorm rooms and doubles with good breakfast included and cheap beer for evening socializing.

$ Dillenia Guesthouse
Lot 846, 1st floor, Jln Sida, T085-434204, dillenia.guesthouse@gmail.com.
This excellent guesthouse has been offering superb-value backpacker accommodation for almost 10 years and still continues to pull in the crowds with its simple, clean rooms, Wi-Fi and fantastic breakfast buffet with tropical fruits. Shared bathroom facilities are well equipped and the lounge area is a good place to exchange travel tips with fellow guests

$ Minda Guesthouse
Lot 607, 1st floor, Jln Yu Seng Utara, T085-411422, www.mindaguesthouse.com.
A backpacker haunt with social area, clean dorms and Wi-Fi access, breakfast and a good travellers' noticeboard. The roof terrace has a few loungers and nice views over the rooftops; it's a good spot for a sunset beer.

$ My Homestay
Lot 1091, Jln Merpati, T085-429091, www.staymyhomestay.blogspot.sg.
A good backpacker option not far from the action with a selection of neat dorms and comfortable, simple double rooms and spotless shared bathrooms.

Lambir Hills National Park

$$$-$$ Borneo Rainforest Resort
38 KM Miri–Bintulu Rd, Lot 15, Block 2, Sibuti Land District, T019-885 2193, www.borneorainforestresort.com.
A lovely little resort, 5 mins from Lambir Hills, with eco ideals and handily located for exploring the nearby national parks, this resort has a variety of full board packages and accommodation in wooden chalets and longhouse rooms and free access to a water park and swimming pool making this an ideal spot for families visiting the area. The staff can organize a variety of adventures including outward bound and wildlife spotting boat trips.

$ National park accommodation
Book accommodation through the National Parks Booking Office in Kuching (T082-248088) or phone the Park HQ directly T085-471609.
There's plenty of choice here, from 2-room a/c chalets (RM150 per chalet or RM100 per room) and fan chalets (RM75 per chalet or RM50 per room; 2 beds in a room). There is no dorm accommodation available here. Camping costs RM5 per person.

Marudi

$ Grand
Lot 350 Backlane, T085-755711.
A large hotel close to the jetty with restaurant, 30 clean rooms with cable TV and some a/c. Has information on upriver trips and Wi-Fi.

$ Marudi Hotel
3 Queen Square, T085-755911.
Central and close to the river, this place has moderately clean double rooms with attached bathrooms. Some rooms are windowless so make sure you ask to see a selection. Wi-Fi available throughout.

$ Mount Mulu Hotel
Lot 80 & Lot 90, Marudi Town District, T085-756671.
A/c and internet access. Discounts are often available, making this place excellent value.

Loagan Bunut National Park

$ National park accommodation
To book call the national park direct, T019-861 0994, or contact the National Parks Booking Office in Kuching (T082-248088). Bookings can also be made online at http:// ebooking.sarawak.gov.my.
There is 1 forest hostel with 4 rooms, each with 7 double bunk beds with fan and own toilet. The park has a canteen. Electricity is available 0600-0200. There is also a hostel, the **Mutiara Hostel**, run by a local Berawan family with 9 twin rooms and a 15-bed dorm. Grocery items are available from the floating

grocery store and meals can be arranged in advance through Mr Meran Sulang T011-292164. Bookings for the hostel can be made through the booking office in Miri.

Restaurants

Miri

Locals take their food pretty seriously in Miri and there are more than enough good places to choose from. A walk after dark along Jln Yu Seng will reveal an array of eateries, from simple Malay stalls to top-notch seafood joints. Below is a selection of the better ones.

$$ Dave's Deli
Jln Yu Seng Utara. Open 0900-2300.
The Peninsula has **Kenny Rogers** and Miri has **Dave's** to satisfy the local craving for roast chicken and mash. An interesting menu of American-themed Western food including the mighty 1-ft-long sausage. Ice cream, creamy soups and plenty of cholesterol.

$$ Meng Chai
Jln Merbau. Open from 1700.
Members of the local Chinese community rave about this place, with a variety of types of fish and shellfish cooked myriad ways. The grilled fish here is an excellent choice.

$$ Shanghai Seafood Centre
Jln Yu Seng Selatan. Lunch and dinner.
Another popular seafood place where customers happily get stuck into treats such as prawns cooked in Chinese wine and steamed seafish alongside deer and honey-glazed bbq pork ribs. Come with an appetite and preferably in a group to maximize the experience.

$$ The Workshop Grill
Lot 865, ground floor, Block 9, Jln Merpati.
If you have been missing out on pork on your travels then look no further than this place with its famed pork burgers. There is also a local Sarawak dish or 2 lurking on the menu including pork and catfish *pansuh*, where the fish is cooked inside bamboo.

$ 2020 Café
Jln Pelita 2. Daily 0500-1200.
Sprint here for your dim sum fix as this is one of the best places in town to spend a morning chowing down these delightful little treats from dumplings to yam cakes, it's all delicious. There is also an excellent range of local noodle dishes, including Sarawak *laksa*.

$ Kwang Kee Chicken Rice
Jln Yu Seng Utara.
Plates of delicious fresh chicken rice. Busy at lunchtimes.

$ Madli's
Jln Merpati.
A top joint for Malay staples with lots of noodle dishes such as *laksa* and *mee kolok*. Come here for a gut stuffing breakfast of *roti canai* and sweet *teh tarik* to keep up your calorie quota.

$ Ming Café
On the corner of Jln Merbau and Jln Yu Seng Utara. Open 0800-2400.
A collection of different hawker stalls offering some good Indian fare, Chinese beef noodles and pseudo-pizza. This place is popular with tourists and locals and gets a bit boozy in the evenings with its numerous drinks promotions including imported ciders and lagers and loud, but inoffensive, music.

$ Muara Lalapan
Jln Yu Seng Utara.
If you are a sambal lover this is the place to come. Lalapan is a plate of veggies, tempe and fried chicken served with a generous dollop of intensely spicy *sambal belacan*. If that's too hot to handle, give the *nasi lemak* a try. The restaurant isn't the most stunning of eateries in appearance, but all eyes should be on the food here.

Foodstalls

Gerai Makan
Near the Chinese temple at the end of Jln Oleander.
Malay food.

Taman Seroja
Jln Brooke.
Malay food, best in the evenings.

Tamu Muhibba (Native Market)
Opposite Park Hotel on roundabout connecting Jln Malay and Jln Padang.
Best during the day.

Tanjong seafood stalls
Tanjung Lobung (south of Miri).
Best in the evenings.

Marudi
There are several coffee shops in town.

Rose Garden
Opposite Alisan Hotel.
A/c coffee shop serving mainly Chinese dishes.

Festivals

Miri
May **Borneo Jazz Festival**, www. jazz borneo.com. Held annually at the Parkcity Everly Hotel with bands from around the world playing their own brands of jazz. Tickets cost around RM80 for a day, though can be 25% cheaper if booked in advance.
Aug **Baram Regatta**. 3-day festival featuring boat races between different local communities. Next in Aug 2017. The **Sape Festival**, held at the same time as the regatta, sees people from many different ethnic groups coming together and mingling over food, traditional music and plenty of rice wine.

Shopping

Miri
Books
Parksons Department Store, *Bintang Plaza.*
Pelita Book Centre, *1st floor, Wisma Pelita Tunku department store.*

Handicrafts
Borneo Arts, *Lot 548, Jln Yu Seng Selatan. Daily 0900-2100.* T-shirts, pottery, handicrafts, wood carvings, batik, Iban textiles, Chinese porcelain, kris daggers, Dayak warrior swords and shields.
Miri Heritage Centre, *Jln Brooke (about 15 mins' walk from the local bus station).* Stalls with local artists' batik, beads, basketry, musical instruments and some tourist tack, café. Worth checking out.
Tiang Heng and Sons, *51 Jln Bendahera.* Good selection of handicrafts, curios and a few antiques alongside lots of fishing gear.

Markets
Miri has a number of interesting markets selling local products.
Fish Market, *Jln Bendahera.* This is a good place to go for a bit of early morning tourism and to see the catch of the day being unloaded and snapped up. The marketers here are well known for their fish displays, which are minor works of art.
Saberkas Weekend Market, *at the Saberkas Commercial Centre on the Pujut –Lutong Rd.* Rammed at weekends with people hunting down jungle produce, Miri snacks and plastic bits and bobs from China. Bring your camera.
Tamu Muhibbah, *opposite the central bus station.* The place to check out a selection of jungle products and to pick up a bag of Bario rice.

Shopping complexes
Bintang Megamall, *off Jln Merbau.* Shops, supermarket, cinema and a bowling alley. Perfect for a spot of a/c consumerism.
Boulevard (BSC), *Jln Pujut Lutong.* One of Miri's bigger shopping complexes with a food court, supermarket, department store and boutiques.
Imperial Mall, *part of the Imperial hotel complex.* Money-changers, a department store and supermarket in the basement.

What to do

Miri
Diving
Co Co Dive, *Lot 2117, Block 9, Jln Miri–Pujut, T085-417053, www.divemiri.com.* A well-

organized outfit offering a variety of PADI dive courses and trips off the coast of Miri to spots such as Atago Maru, a Second World War Japanese wreck that is home to trevally, jack and barracudas, and to the Sea Fan Garden with its gorgeous gorgonian sea fans. **Red Monkey Divers**, *Unit 1, Kelab Gymkhana Miri, Jln Dato Abang Indeh, T014-699 8296, www.redmonkeydivers.com*. PADI courses and exciting offshore dives.

Golf

Eastwood Valley Golf and Country Club, *Lot 1379, Block 17, Jln Miri-bypass, T085-421010, www.eastwoodvalley.com*. Located out near the Miri bypass, this lovely new place has good facilities. A round of 18 holes starts at RM232, or you can hit a few balls up the driving range at RM12 for 100 balls.

Mountain biking

Miri Mountain Bike Club, *T085-423589*. Contact the bike club for details on joining a bike ride on many of the challenging trails around the city.

Running

Join the **Hash House Harriers** (T019-855 8582) for a bit of a run and then a boozy evening out in town.

Swimming

There's a swimming pool at the Miri City Fan area around Jln Merpati and Jln Kipas, RM1.

Tour operators

Although most tour companies specialize in trips up the Baram River to Mulu National Park, some are much better than others in terms of facilities and services offered. Every agency in Miri has a Mulu National Park itinerary covering the caves, pinnacles and summits. It is also possible to trek to Bario and Mount Murud as well as to Limbang from Mulu. Most agencies employ

experienced guides who will be able to advise on longer, more ambitious treks. The Mulu National Park is one destination where it is usually cheaper to go through a tour company than to try to do it independently. Costs vary considerably according to the number of people in a group. For a 3-day **Mulu** trip, a single tourist can expect to pay at least RM480 with all accommodation, food, travel and guide costs included. A 5-day **Headhunter's Trail** trek costs around RM1800. An 8-day tour of **Ulu Baram longhouses** would cost RM2200 for 1 person and RM1500 per person in a group of 10. A 20-day trek will cost 2 people (minimum number) around RM2500 each, and a group of 6-10, RM1700 a head. For remote longhouses, tour companies present by far the best option. Tour fees cover 'gifts' and all payments to longhouse headmen for food, accommodation and entertainment. Recommended companies include:
Borneo Mainland, *Lot 1081, Jln Merpati, T085-433511, www.borneomainland.com*. For longhouse tours and longer jungle treks.
JJ Tour Travel, *Lot 231, Jln Maju Taman, Jade Centre, T085-418690, www.jjtourservice.com*. Local tours and ticketing agents.
KKM Travel & Tours, *236 Jln Maju, T085-417899, www.kkmtravelntours.com*.
Limbang Travel Service, *1G Park Arcade (near Park Hotel), T085-413228*. Efficient ticket service;
Borneo Jungle Safari, *Lot 1396, 1st floor, Centre Point Commercial Centre II, Jln Kubu, T085-422595*.
Tropical Adventure Tours and Travel, *Lot 906, No 12, ground floor, Soon Hup Tower Shopping Complex, Jln Merbau, T085-419337, www.borneotropical adventure.com*. A professional outfit with lots of experience. Offers tailor-made trips throughout Malaysia and Indonesia. There are some excellent offers for those with residence permits in Singapore, Malaysia or Brunei.

Miri

Air

Miri Airport, *T085-615433,* is a few km south of town. To get there, take bus No 28 (hourly 0700-1800, RM2.60) from the tourist information centre but ask the driver to drop you off outside the terminal, otherwise you will be dropped off on the highway, a 10-min trek. Or take a taxi for RM22.

AirAsia (main terminal building, T03-7651 2222) and **MAS** fly to **Kuching**, **Kota Kinabalu** and **Kuala Lumpur**. AirAsia also flies to **Johor Bahru**, **Penang** and **Singapore**. Miri is a hub for **MASwings** with flights to **Ba'kelalan**, **Bario**, **Bintulu**, **Lawas**, **Limbang**, **Long Akah**, **Long Banga**, **Long Lellang**, **Long Seridan**, **Marudi**, **Mukah**, **Mulu**, **Sibu** and **Labuan**.

Note that it is crucial to book the excellent-value flights to Bario and Mulu in advance. Travellers hoping to show up and get on a flight will probably be disappointed. There are no flights between Miri and **Brunei**.

Boat

From Miri, take a bus or shared taxi (RM50) to **Kuala Baram** from where there are express boats upriver to **Marudi** (roughly 1 boat every 2 hrs from 0800, last boat 1500; RM25; 3 hrs), providing there are enough passengers. This is the 1st leg of the journey to Mulu and the interior.

Bus

The long-distance bus terminal is at Pujuk Padang Kerbau, Jln Padang, around 4 km from the town centre. A taxi to the terminal costs around RM20. Or take bus No 33 from outside the tourist centre. There are regular connections from early morning to mid-afternoon with **Batu Niah** (2 hrs, RM12-15),

Bintulu (4 hrs, RM27), **Sibu** (7 hrs, RM50), **Kuching** (13 hrs, RM90), and **KK** (8 hrs, RM90). Buses connect with **Kuala Baram** (1st bus 0530), and the express boat upriver to **Marudi** (see above). There is a daily bus service to **Kota Kinabalu** leaving at 0830 (RM93). This travels via **Limbang** and **Lawas** and takes 9-10 hrs. There are also 4 daily buses to **Pontianak** departing daily (RM96) which travel via **Kuching**.

There are 2 departures a day to **Bandar Seri Begawan** in Brunei. Buses leave from Miri's central bus station, by the tourist information centre on Jln Melayu (RM40, 2-3 hrs) and travel via the Sungai Tujuh checkpoint. These buses are run by **Borneo Express** and PHLS.

Car

Car hire Avis, Lot 616, Permaisuri Rd, T085-430222; and **Greenax**, Lot 8503, Jln Dato Permaisuri, RPR Permai Jaya, Bandar Baru Permy Jaya, T013-813 1003, www.grenaxmiri.com, have a decent range of cars starting at RM160 a day. They also offer driver services for trips to longhouses and the interior.

Marudi

Air

The airport is 5 km from town and has connections with **Miri**, **Bario**, **Long Akah** and **Long Lellang** with MASwings.

Boat

These leave opposite the Chinese temple. There are connections with **Kuala Baram** (4 boats daily 0700-1500, RM25); **Tutoh**, for longboats to **Long Terawan** (1 boat daily at 1200, RM25); and **Long Lama**, for longboats to **Bario** (1 boat every hour 0730-1400). From **Long Terawan** the longboat journey to Mulu Park, via the Sungai Tutoh, takes up to 2 hrs (RM60 each for group of 5 or more).

Northern
Sarawak

The impressive peak of Gunung Mulu is the centrepiece of the eponymous national park. The luscious jungle, home to orchids and hornbills, also boasts the largest limestone cave system on the planet. The cooler climes of the Kelabit Highlands provide good walking opportunities around Bario. Limbang is frontier country and the start of a cross-border trek.

★ Gunung Mulu National Park

an extraordinary cave system and challenging treks, including The Pinnacles and Gunung Mulu

Tucked in behind Brunei, this 529-sq-km park lays claim to Gunung Mulu, which at 2376 m is the second highest mountain in Sarawak, and has the biggest limestone cave system in the world. Mulu is basically a huge hollow mountain range, covered in 180-million-year-old rainforest. Its primary jungle contains an astonishing biological diversity and was awarded UNESCO World Heritage status in 2000. Just outside the national park boundary on the Tutoh River there are rapids which it is possible to shoot; this can be arranged through tour agencies.

Flora and fauna

In the 1960s and 1970s, botanical expeditions were beginning to shed more light on the Mulu area's flora and fauna: 100 new plant species were discovered between 1960 and 1973 alone. Mulu Park encompasses an area of diverse altitudes and soil types – it includes all the forest types found in Borneo except mangrove. About 20,000 animal species have been recorded in Mulu Park, as well as 3500 plant species and 8000 varieties of fungi (more than 100 of these are endemic to the Mulu area). Mulu's ecological statistics are astounding: it is home to 1500 species of flowering plant, 170 species of orchid and 109 varieties of palm. More than 280 butterfly species have been recorded. Within the park boundaries, 262 species of bird (including all eight varieties of hornbill), 67 mammalian species, 50 species of reptile and 75 amphibian species have been recorded.

Mulu's caves contain an unusual array of flora and fauna too. There are three species of swiftlet, 12 species of bat and nine species of fish, including the cave flying fish (*Nemaaramis everetti*) and blind catfish (*Silurus furnessi*). Cave scorpions (*Chaerilus chapmani*) – which are poisonous but not deadly – are not uncommon. Other subterranean species include albino crabs, huntsman spiders, cave crickets, centipedes and snakes (which dine on

Essential Gunung Mulu

Finding your feet

There is an airstrip just downriver from Park HQ which receives flights from Miri, Kota Kinabalu and Kuching; book well in advance. The price of a flight is only marginally more expensive than taking the bus and boat from Miri (see page 111) and is significantly quicker.

Park information

Entry permits are valid for five days (RM30, children RM10) and can be bought at Park HQ, T085-792300. Up-to-date information is available from can be found on www.mulupark.com, which has a detailed description of the treks and tours offered at the park. You can also book guided treks through the website. There is accommodation and a café at Park HQ (see page 120), and a simple hostel at Camp 5.

Guides

Some treks around the park that can be done without a guide. However, most of the Mulu Park guides are very well informed about flora and fauna, geology and tribal customs. Mulu Park and various Miri-based tour agents (see page 110) organize treks and include guides as part of their fee. Popular treks include the **Mulu summit trips** (RM504 per person, minimum three people; four days, three nights), and **Melinau Gorge and Pinnacles** (RM406 per person, minimum three people; three days, two nights). If you book online and are a solo traveller, organizers will try to put you into a group of three to save costs. If you want to go alone, expect costs to rise significantly. For example a solo traveller doing the Pinnacles Trek will be charged RM1000 plus porterage fees. Ornithological guides may be available from the Park HQ though expect to pay a little extra for their services. It is usual to tip guides and porters.

Porters

For longer treks, guide fees are included in the cost but porterage isn't. Porters will carry a load of 10 kg for RM30 per day, RM1 for each extra kilo. Mulu summit: minimum RM100 plus 15 for park admission and RM10 per night accommodation fee. Melinau Gorge (Camp 5): minimum RM100.

Caving

Visitors are not permitted to enter the caves without an authorized guide; guides can be arranged from Park HQ or booked in advance from the national parks office in Miri, see page 105. For cavers wishing to explore caves not open to the public (those open to visitors are known as 'show' caves), there are designated 'adventure caves' within an hour of Park HQ. Experienced cave guides can be organized from Park HQ. The most accessible adventure cave is the one-hour trek following the river course through **Clearwater Cave**. Cavers should bring their own equipment. Tougher caves such as the Sarawak Chamber can only be visited by advanced cavers who have some experience.

Equipment

A small store at the Park HQ sells basic necessities; there is also a small shop just outside the park boundary, at Long Pala. A sleeping bag is essential for Gunung Mulu trips; other useful items include a good insect repellent, water bottle, wet weather gear and a powerful torch.

When to go

It is best to avoid visiting the park during school and public holidays. June, July, August and September are the peak months to visit Mulu and booking tours and treks in advance is essential.

Gunung Mulu National Park

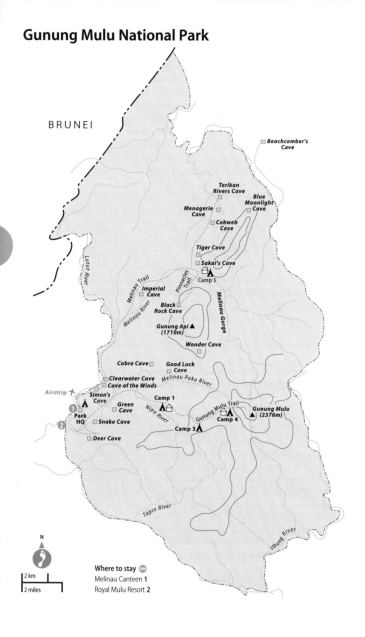

BRUNEI

Beachcomber's Cave

Terikan Rivers Cave

Blue Moonlight Cave

Menagerie Cave

Cobweb Cave

Tiger Cave

Sakai's Cave

Camp 5

Melinau Trail

Imperial Cave

Pinnacles Trail

Black Rock Cave

Melinau River

Melinau Gorge

Gunung Api (1710m)

Wonder Cave

Cobra Cave

Good Luck Cave

Melinau Paku River

Clearwater Cave

Cave of the Winds

Airstrip

Simon's Cave

Green Cave

Camp 1

Nipa River

Gunung Mulu Trail

Gunung Mulu (2376m)

Camp 4

Park HQ

Snake Cave

Camp 3

Deer Cave

Lutut River

Tapin River

Ubung River

N

2 km

2 miles

Where to stay
Melinau Canteen **1**
Royal Mulu Resort **2**

An alternative way of entering or leaving Mulu Park is via the Headhunter's Trail from Limbang. The walk takes around two days and is most commonly arranged through a tour agency with a guide. This trek includes river travel on longboats, treks through undisturbed jungle and a night at a longhouse following the route used by Kayan raiding parties who paddled upstream to the Melinau Gorge before pulling their war canoes through the rainforest for 3 km until reaching the Sungai Terikan. And that was only where the fun began. From here they would launch raids against the indigenous communities around Limbang and get as many heads as possible to take back home with them.

You'll need to charter a boat from Park HQ to Kuala Berar and walk for at least three hours until you get to Camp 5. From here there is a 12-km trail to Kuala Terikan which takes between five and six hours before getting back in a longboat and for four hours until you reach the longhouse at Rumah Bala Lesong, where you will spend the night. The next morning you can hop back in the boat down to Naga Medamit where you can use the road to get to Limbang. The trek can be done in reverse starting in Limbang and makes a refreshing change from flying into Mulu. It all sounds quite challenging but there is actually a lot of time spent admiring the scenery from a longboat.

Rates for an all-inclusive hike along the Headhunter's Trail from Mulu National Park to Limbang or vice-versa start at around RM1600 per person. Book through agencies in Miri or via www.mulunationalpark.com.

swiftlets and bats). These creatures have been described as "living fossils... [which are] isolated survivors of ancient groups long since disappeared from Southeast Asia."

Gunung Mulu

The minimum time to allow for the climb is four days, three nights. The main summit route starts from the plankwalk at Park HQ heading towards Deer Cave. The Mulu walkway forks left after about 1 km. From the headquarters it is a tough six- to eight-hour trek to Camp 3. The second day is an easier four-hour trek up to Camp 4 (1800 m), where there is also a shelter. From Camp 3, the trail climbs steeply up Bukit Tumau, which affords good views over the park, and above which the last wild rhinoceros in Sarawak was shot in the mid-1940s. There are many pitcher plants (*Nepenthes lowii*) along this stretch of trail. From Camp 4, known as 'The Summit Camp', the path passes the helicopter pad, from where there are magnificent views of Gunung Benarat, the Melinau Gorge and Gunung Api. The final haul to the summit is steep; there are fixed ropes. Around the summit area, the *Nepenthes muluensis* pitcher plant is common – it is endemic to Mulu. From Camp 4 it takes 1½ hours to reach the summit, and a further eight to ten hours back down the mountain to Camp 3.

Tents are not required if you stay at Camp 1. Camps 3 and 4 have water (providing the tank has been filled by rain water). Water should be boiled before drinking. It is necessary to bring your own food; in the rainy season it is wise to bring a gas cooking stove. A sleeping bag and waterproofs are also necessary and spare clothes, wrapped in a plastic bag, are a good idea.

BACKGROUND

Gunung Mulu

In Robin Hanbury-Tenison's book *The Rain Forest*, he says of Mulu: "All sense of time and direction is lost." Every scientific expedition that has visited Mulu's forests has encountered plant and animal species unknown to science. In 1990, five years after it was officially opened to the public, the park was handling an average of 400 visitors a month. Numbers have increased markedly since then – the area is now attracting more than 15,000 tourists a year – and as the eco-tourism industry has extended its foothold, local tribespeople have been drawn into confrontation with the authorities. In the early 1990s, a series of sabotage incidents was blamed on the Berawan tribe, who claim the caves and the surrounding jungle are a sacred site.

In 1974, three years after Mulu was gazetted as a national park, the first of a succession of joint expeditions led by the British Royal Geographical Society (RGS) and the Sarawak government began to make the discoveries that put Mulu on the map. In 1980 a cave passage over 50 km long was surveyed for the first time. Since then, a further 137 km of passages have been discovered. Altogether 27 major caves have now been found speleologists believe they may represent a tiny fraction of what is actually there. The world's biggest cave, the **Sarawak Chamber**, was not discovered until 1984.

The first attempt on Gunung Mulu was made by Spencer St John, the British consul in Brunei, in 1856 (see also his attempts on Gunung Kinabalu, page 244). His efforts were thwarted by "limestone cliffs, dense jungle and sharp pinnacles of rock". Dr Charles Hose, Resident of Marudi, led a 25-day expedition to Gunung Mulu in 1893, but also found his path blocked by 600-m-high cliffs. Nearly 50 years later, in 1932,

Treks from Camp 5

For a three-day trip, a longboat will cost about RM450. It takes two to three hours, depending on the river level, from Park HQ to Kuala Berar; it is then a two- to three-hour trek (8 km) to Camp 5. Visitors to the Camp 5 area are also advised to plan their itinerary carefully as it is necessary to calculate how much food will be required and to carry it up there. There is a fairly well-equipped shelter with kitchen, bathrooms with shower and communal sleeping space which can house a maximum of 50 people. The camp is next to the Melinau River; river water should be boiled before drinking. There is a solar power generator to power radios, pump river water and for low lighting after dark.

Camp 5 is about four to six hours upstream from the Park HQ, at the base of the Melinau Gorge. From the camp it is possible to trek up the gorge as well as to the Pinnacles on Gunung Api. It is advisable to hire a longboat for the duration of your time at and around Camp 5. The boat has to be abandoned at Kuala Berar, at the confluence of the Melinau and Berar rivers. It is only used for the first and last hours of the trip but necessary in case of emergency, as there are no trails leading back to the Park HQ.

Melinau Gorge

Camp 5 nestles at the end of the gorge, across a fast-flowing section of the Melinau River and opposite the unclimbed 1580-m Gunung Benarat's sheer limestone cliffs. The steep limestone ridges, which lead eventually to Gunung Api, comprise the east wall of the gorge. Heading out from Camp 5, the trail fizzles out after a few minutes. It

a Berawan rhinoceros hunter called Tama Nilong guided Edward Shackleton's Oxford University expedition to the summit. One of the young Oxford undergraduates on that expedition was Tom Harrisson, who later made the Niah archaeological discoveries, see page 129. Tama Nilong, the hunter from Long Terawan, had previously reached the main southwest ridge of Mulu while tracking a rhinoceros.

The cliffs of the Melinau Gorge rise a sheer 600 m, and are the highest limestone rock faces between north Thailand and Papua New Guinea. The limestone massifs of Gunung Api and Gunung Benarat were originally at the same elevation as Gunung Mulu, but their limestone outcrops were more prone to erosion than the Mulu's sandstone. Northwest of the gorge lies a large, undisturbed alluvial plain which is rich in flora and fauna. Penan tribespeople (see page 136) are permitted to maintain their lifestyle of fishing, hunting and gathering in the park. At no small expense, the Malaysian government has encouraged them to settle at a purpose-built longhouse at **Batu Bungan**, just a few minutes upriver from the Park HQ, but its efforts have met with limited success because of the desire of many Penan to maintain their travelling lifestyle. Penan shelters can often be found by riverbanks.

Reeling from international criticism, the Sarawak state government set aside 66,000 ha of rainforest as what it called 'biosphere', a reserve where indigenous people could practise their traditional lifestyle. Part of the reserve lies within the park. In Baram and Limbang districts, the remaining 300 Penan will have a reserve in which they can continue their nomadic way of life. A further 23,000 ha has reportedly been set aside for 'semi-nomadic' Penan.

In 1961 geologist Dr G Wilford first surveyed Deer Cave and parts of the Cave of the Winds. But Mulu's biggest subterranean secrets were not revealed until the 1980s.

takes an arduous two to three hours of endless river crossings and scrambles to reach a narrow chute of whitewater, under which is a large, deep and clear jungle pool with a convenient sandbank and plenty of large boulders to perch on. Alfred Russel Wallace's *Troides brookiana* – the majestic Rajah Brooke's birdwing – is particularly common at this little oasis, deep in undisturbed jungle. The walk involves criss-crossing through waist-deep, fast-flowing water and over stones that have been smoothed to a high polish over centuries: strong shoes are recommended as is a walking stick. Only occasionally in the walk upstream is it possible to glimpse the towering 600 m cliffs. Mulu can also be climbed from the south ridge of Melinau Gorge; it is three hours to Camp 1, five hours to Camp 3, a steep four- to five-hour climb to Camp 4, and finally two hours to the top.

The Pinnacles

The Pinnacles are a forest of sharp limestone needles three-quarters of the way up Gunung Api. Some of the pinnacles rise above treetops to heights of 45 m. The trail leaves from Camp 5 and climbs steeply all the way. A maximum time of three to four hours is allowed to reach the pinnacles (1200 m); otherwise you must return. There is no water source en route. It is not possible to reach Gunung Api from the Pinnacles. It is strongly recommended that climbers wear gloves as well as long-sleeved shirts, trousers and strong boots to protect themselves against cuts from the razor-sharp rocks. Explorers on Spenser St John's expedition to Mulu in 1856 were cut to shreds on the Pinnacles: "three of our men had already been sent back with severe wounds, whilst several of those left were much injured," he wrote, concluding that it was "the world's most nightmarish surface to travel over".

Gunung Api (Fire Mountain)

The vegetation is so dry at the summit of Gunung Api that it is often set ablaze by lightning in the dry season. The story goes that the fires were once so big that locals thought the mountains were volcanoes. Some of the fires could be seen as far away as the Brunei coast. The summit trek takes a minimum of three days. At 1710 m, it is the tallest limestone outcrop in Borneo and, other than Gunung Benarat (on the other side of the gorge), it is probably the most difficult mountain to climb in Borneo. Many attempts to climb it ended in failure; two Berawans from Long Terawan finally made it to the top in 1978, one of them the grandson of Tama Nilong, the rhinoceros-hunter who had climbed Gunung Mulu in 1932. It is impossible to proceed upwards beyond the Pinnacles.

Limbang Trail

Camp 5, cross the Melinau River and head down the **Limbang Trail** towards Lubang Cina. Less than 30 minutes down the trail, fork left along a new trail which leads along a ridge to the south of Gunung Benarat. Climbing higher, after about 40 minutes, the trail passes into an area of leached sandy soils called *kerangas* (heath) forest. This little patch of thinner jungle is a tangle of many varieties of pitcher plants. It is possible to continue to Limbang from here, although it is easier to do it the other way (see page 123).

Clearwater Cave

This part of the Clearwater System, on a small tributary of the Melinau River, is 107 km long, 75 km of which have been explored. The cave passage links Clearwater Cave (Gua Ayer Jernih) with the **Cave of the Winds** (Lubang Angin), to the south. It was discovered in 1988. Clearwater is named after the jungle pool at the foot of the steps leading up to the cave mouth, where the longboats moor. Two species of monophytes – single-leafed plants – grow in the sunlight at the mouth of the cave. They only grow on limestone. A lighting system has been installed down the path to **Young Lady's Cave**, which ends in a 60-m-deep pothole.

On the cave walls are some helictites – coral-like lateral formations – and, even more dramatic, are the photokarsts, tiny needles of rock, all pointing towards the light. These are formed in much the same way as their monstrous cousins, the Pinnacles, by vegetation (in this case algae), eating into and eroding the softer rock, leaving sharp points of harder rock which 'grow' at about 0.5 mm a year. Clearwater can be reached by a boat tour up the Melinau River organized by the park which includes a visit of a Penan market and the Cave of the Winds. Once at the cave your guide will lead you to a gorgeous pool at the entrance to the cave where you can take a refreshing dip. There are daily scheduled guided tours of the cave at 0845 and 0915 (RM65 per person; four hours).

Deer Cave and Lang's Cave

This is another of Mulu's record breakers: it has the world's biggest cave mouth and the biggest cave passage, which is 2.2 km long and 220 m high at its highest point. Before its inclusion in the park, the **Deer Cave** had been a well-known hunting ground for deer attracted to the pools of salty water running off the guano. The silhouettes of some of the cave's limestone formations have been creatively interpreted; notably the profile of Abraham Lincoln. Adam's and Eve's Showers, at the east end of the cave, are hollow stalactites. This darker section at the east end of Deer Cave is the preferred habitat of the naked bat. Albino earwigs live on the bats' oily skin and regularly drop off. The cave's east entrance opens onto 'The Garden of Eden', a luxuriant patch of jungle, which was once part of the cave system until the roof collapsed. This separated Deer Cave and **Green Cave**, which lies adjacent to the east mouth; the latter is open only to caving expeditions. The west end of the cave is home to several million wrinkle-lipped and horseshoe bats. Hundreds of thousands of these bats pour out of the cave at dusk. Bat hawks can often be seen swooping in for spectacular kills. The helipad, about 500 m south of the cave mouth, provides excellent vantage points. VIPs' helicopters, arriving for the show, are said to have disturbed the bats in recent years. From the analysis of the tonnes of saline bat guano, scientists conclude that they make an 80-km dash to the coast for meals of insects washed down with seawater. Cave cockroaches eat the guano, ensuring that the cavern does not become choked with what locals call 'black snow'.

Part of the same hollow mountain as Deer Cave, **Lang's Cave** is less well known but its formations are more beautiful and it contains impressive curtain stalactites and intricate coral-like helictites. The cave is well lit and protected by bus-stop-style plastic tunnels.

There are guided tours to Deer Cave and Lang's Cave departing from the office at 1400 and 1430 (RM30). Tours last around three hours and coincide with the great bat exodus at sunset. The trek to the cave is along a plankwalk and takes about an hour.

Sarawak Chamber

Discovered in 1984, this chamber is 600 m long, 450 m wide and 100 m high – big enough, it is said, to accommodate 40 jumbo jets wing-tip to wing-tip and eight nose-to-tail. It is the largest natural chamber in the world. It is now possible for cavers with some experience to visit the cave, with the approval of the park manager. It is a three-hour trek to the cave following the summit trail. Access to the cave is through Gua Nasib Bagus, following a river trail bordered by 50-m-high sheer rock faces on both sides for 800 m. After a further scramble, cavers reach the dark mouth of the chamber. It is not permitted to enter any further as it is considered too dangerous. Guided trips to the Sarawak Chamber are offered starting at 0630 (RM280 per person) from the Park HQ office.

Listings Gunung Mulu National Park map page 114.

Where to stay

$$$ Mulu Marriot Resort and Spa
Sungai Melinau, Muku, Miri, a 20-min boat ride downstream from Park HQ, T085-792338, www.marriott.com.
This resort has 101 longhouse-inspired rooms and suites with cable TV, a/c. There is also a pool, a gym, a spa and restaurants. Travellers who are desperate to visit the park in peak summer months and find that all the other accommodation is booked can usually find a bed here. It has sparked much resentment among local tribespeople. The Berawan claim the resort's land as theirs by customary right.

$$-$ National park accommodation
The park offers its own good quality and fair value accommodation. Bookings can be made through www.mulupark.com or contact **Borsarmulu Park Management** in Miri (T085-792300). Top of the range are the **deluxe garden houses** ($$) which have a double bed and a single bed, attached bathroom and a/c. For 3 people sharing, it works out at RM86 each and breakfast is included. The standard **longhouse rooms** ($$) are spacious with attached bathrooms and can sleep up to 4. Sharing here works at just over RM53 per person. There is also a **hostel** ($) with 20 dorm beds, fan and shared bathrooms for RM53 per person. There are also simple wooden shelters on the summit

trail and a simple hostel at Camp 5; bring your sleeping bag.

$$ Benarat Lodge
Just outside the park and located across the river from the Marriot, T012-8703541.
One of several hostels a short walk downstream from the Park HQ, this family-oriented place has fan and a/c rooms. The price includes 2-way airport transfers.

Restaurants

There are stoves and cooking utensils available and the small store at Park HQ also sells basic supplies. There is a small shop with basic supplies at Long Pala. As an alternative to the café at Park HQ, cross the suspension bridge and walk alongside the road to the guesthouses lining the river.

Café Mulu
Park HQ. Daily 0730-2030.
The café has a range of simple Asian and Western dishes, alongside some local vegetable dishes including Paku fern. Alcohol is available and guests are able to enjoy a glass or 2 on the patio, but don't expect a particularly wide selection or a boozy party.

What to do

Visitors are recommended to go book through **Mulu Park** (www.mulupark.com), or through one of the Miri-based travel agents (see page 110). The average cost of a Mulu package (per person) is RM1200 (4 days/3 nights) or RM2188 (5 days/4 nights). These prices don't include transport to and from Mulu. Independent travellers will find it cheaper to arrange accommodation, flights, permits and guided treks than using an agency.

Transport

Air
MASwings currently runs 2 daily flights between Mulu and **Miri** (28 mins); book well in advance. The airline operates flights to **Kuching** and daily flights to **Kota Kinabalu**.

Boat hire
Longboats can be chartered privately from Park HQ to travel back to Long Terawan or to Kuala Berar to begin the Headhunter's Trail (maximum 10 people per boat). The cost is calculated on a rather complicated system which includes a rate for the boat, a charge for the engine based on its horsepower, a separate payment for the driver and frontman, and then fuel. Total costs can be over RM150. How far these boats can get upriver depends on the season. They often have to be hauled over rapids whatever the time of year.

Bus/boat/taxi
Take a bus or taxi from **Miri** to **Marudi**, where express boats leave from the jetty near **Kuala Baram** at mouth of the Baram River (see page 111). Express boats from Kuala Baram to **Marudi** (RM25, 3 hrs) run from 0720 until about 1500, depending on demand; there might be up to 4 departures a day. From Marudi, one express boat per day runs to **Long Terawan** (leaves at 1200, RM25) on the Tutoh River, via **Long Apoh**. During the dry season express boats cannot reach Long Terawan and terminate at Long Panai on the Tutoh River, where longboats continue to Long Terawan (RM25). Longboats leave Long Terawan for **Mulu Park HQ**: this used to be regular and relatively cheap; now that most people travel to Mulu by air, longboats need to be privately chartered – an expensive business at RM450 a pop. Mulu Park HQ is 1½ hrs up the Melinau River, a tributary of the Tutoh. As you approach the park from Long Terawan the Tutoh River narrows and becomes shallower; there are 14 rapids before the Melinau River, which forms the park boundary. When the water is low, the trip can be very slow and involve pulling the boat over the shallows; this accounts for high charter rates. The first jetty on the Melinau River is **Long Pala** accommodation and from there the Park HQ is another 15 mins upriver. Longboats returning to Long Terawan leave Park HQ at dawn each day, calling at the various jetties en route.

superlative walking opportunities in unspoilt rural setting

Bario (Bareo) lies in the Kelabit Highlands, a plateau 1000 m above sea level close to the Kalimantan border in Indonesia. The undulating Bario Valley is surrounded by mountains and fed by countless small streams that in turn feed into a maze of irrigation canals.

Treks around Bario

Because of the rugged terrain surrounding the plateau, the area mainly attracts serious mountaineers. There are many trails to the longhouses around the plateau area, however. Treks to Bario can be organized through travel agents in Miri, see page 110. Guides can also be hired in Bario and surrounding longhouses for RM100-120 per day and porters for around RM80-RM100 per day. It is best to go through the Penghulu, Ngiap Ayu, the Kelabit chief. He goes around visiting many of the longhouses in the area once a month. It is recommended that visitors to Bario bring sleeping bags and camping equipment if you plan to head off on treks. There aren't many restaurants in Bario so people usually eat at their guesthouse; ensure your guide has ample provisions for longer treks. Be aware that on certain treks, such as the one from Bario and Ba'kelalan you will pass through Indonesian territory. Though Indonesian immigration turn a blind eye to this temporary incursion, it would be prudent to carry your travel documents with you.

One of the most popular treks is the **Bario Loop**, which takes around five days to complete and is an exceptionally stunning walk with the opportunity to stay in some beautifully remote longhouses, most notably at **Long Dano**, **Pa Dilih** and **Pa Bareng**. The trail passes ancient megaliths, jungle and rushing streams. There are also stunning week-long treks to **Long Lellang** and a three day trek to the settlement of **Bakalalan** (Ba'kelalan)

Several of the surrounding mountains can be climbed from Bario, but they are, without exception, difficult climbs. Even on walks just around the Bario area, guides are essential as trails are poorly marked. The lower 'female' peak of **Bukit Batu Lawi** can be climbed without equipment, but the sheer-sided 'male' peak requires proper rock climbing equipment; it was first scaled in 1986. **Gunung Murudi** (2423 m) is the highest mountain in Sarawak and it is a very tough climb.

Essential Bario

Bario is accessible by air from Miri, Marudi and Ba'kelalan; a very bumpy five-hour drive from the coast on old logging roads; or via a seven-day trek from Marudi. The best time to visit the area is between March and October.

BACKGROUND

Bario

The local Kelabits' skill in harnessing water has allowed them to practise wet rice cultivation rather than the more common slash-and-burn hill rice techniques. Fragrant Bario rice is prized in Sarawak and commands a premium in the coastal markets. The more temperate climate of the Kelabit Highlands also allows the cultivation of a wide range of fruit and vegetables.

The plateau's near-impregnable ring of mountains effectively cut the Kelabit off from the outside world; it is the only area in Borneo which was never penetrated by Islam. In 1911 the Resident of Baram mounted an expedition which ventured into the mountains to ask the Kelabit to stop raiding the Brooke Government's subjects. It took the expedition 17 days to cross the Tamu Abu mountain range, to the west of Bario. The Kelabit were then brought under the control of the Sarawak government.

The most impressive mountain in the Bario area is the distinctive twin peak of the sheer-faced 2043 m **Bukit Batu Lawi** to the northwest of Bario. The Kelabit traditionally believed the mountain had an evil spirit and so never went near it. Today such superstitions are a thing of the past since locals are mostly evangelical Christians.

In 1945, the plateau was selected as the only possible parachute drop zone in North Borneo not captured by the Japanese. The Allied Special Forces that parachuted into Bario were led by Tom Harrisson, who later became curator of the Sarawak Museum and made the famous archaeological discoveries at Niah Caves (see page 97). His expedition formed an irregular tribal army against the Japanese, which gained control over large areas of North Borneo in the following months. You can see a stainless steel monument shaped like a sape (stinged instrument) built to commemorate this parachute drop and his success in recruiting local men for the fight against the Japanese. The memorial can be seen on the bridge outside the airport.

Listings Bario and the Kelabit Highlands

Where to stay

$$ The Ngimat Ayu House
Ulung Palang Bario, T013-840 6187.
Simple but exceptionally friendly homestay-style place with 8 rooms, limited electricity and no Wi-Fi, which provides plenty of opportunity to mingle with the people of Bario and try some local fare such as wild deer and boar. The owners can offer good advice about trekking and can put you in touch with decent guides.

$ Nancy Hariss Homestay
A short walk outside town, T013-8505 850.
A rustic place with plenty of communal spaces and gorgeous views of surrounding paddies and mountains. Hot water showers and electricity available in the evenings.

$ Tarawe
100 m north of the airfield.
A well-run place to stay with a good source of information. Simple rooms and a veranda overlooking a fish pond. Cable TV and electricity after dark. Recommended.

Transport

Air
Bario's airstrip is very small and, because of its position, flights are often cancelled due to mist. **MASwings** has daily connections with **Miri** (the flight on the prop plane takes 55 mins and is quite spectacular), **Marudi** and **Ba'kelalan**. Flights are always booked up well in advance.

Car
It's possible to charter a 4WD to drive you up to Bario from Miri on logging tracks. The journey can take up to 12 hrs and is bumpy and uncomfortable and will cost a wallet-stinging RM600. If you are desperate, ask around in travel agencies in Miri, but given the cheap cost of flying and the time it takes, flying is definitely the best option in this instance.

Walking
It is a 7-day trek between **Marudi** and Bario, sleeping in longhouses en route. This trip should be organized through a Miri travel agent (see page 110).

Limbang and around
administrative centre and starting point for the epic hike to Gunung Mulu

Limbang is the administrative centre for the Fifth Division and was ceded to the Brooke government by the Sultan of Brunei in 1890. The Trusan Valley, to the east of the wedge of Brunei, had been ceded to Sarawak in 1884. Very few tourists reach Limbang or Lawas but they are good stopping-off points for more adventurous routes to Sabah and Brunei. Limbang is the finger of Sarawak territory which splits Brunei in two.

Sights
Limbang's **Old Fort** was built in 1897, renovated in 1966, and was used as the administrative centre. During the Brooke era, half the ground floor was used as a jail. It is now a centre of religious instruction, Majlis Islam. Limbang is famous for its **Pasar Tamu** (market) every Friday, where jungle and native produce is sold. Limbang also has an attractive small museum, **Muzium Wilayah** ① *400 m south of the centre along Jln Kubu, Tue-Fri 0900-1645, Sat, Sun 1000-1600, free.* Housed in a wooden beige and white villa, the museum has a collection of ethnic artefacts from the region, including basketry, musical instruments and weapons. To the right of the museum, a small road climbs the hill to a park with a man-made lake.

Trekking
To trek to the **Gunung Mulu National Park** (see page 112), take a car south to Medamit; from there hire a longboat upriver to Mulu Madang, an Iban longhouse (three hours, depending on the water level). Alternatively, go further upriver to Kuala Terikan (six to seven hours when the water's low, four hours when it's high) where there is a simple zinc-roofed camp. From there take a longboat one hour up the Terikan River to Lubang China, which is the start of a two-hour trek along a well-used trail to Camp 5. There is a park rangers' camp about 20 minutes out of Kuala Terikan where it is possible to obtain permits and arrange for a guide to meet you at Camp 5. The longboats are cheaper to hire in the wet season.

Lawas

Lawas District was ceded to Sarawak in 1905. The Limbang River, which cuts through the town, is the main transport route. It is possible to travel from Miri to Bandar Seri Begawan (Brunei) by road, then on to Limbang and Lawas. From Lawas there are direct buses to Kota Kinabalu in Sabah.

Listings Limbang and around

Tourist information

Limbang

Residents' Office
T085-202105.

Where to stay

Limbang
Limbang has become a sex stop for Bruneians, whose government takes a more hard-line attitude to such moral transgressions, and consequently many hotels and guesthouses have a fair share of short-stay guests.

$$ Purnama Hotel
Jln Buangsiol, T085-216700, www.penviewhotel.com/purnama.
This 3-star hotel has selection of decidedly dated rooms, some of which are very garish but entirely serviceable. Views from the top floor over the river and surrounding countryside are glorious. There's Wi-Fi in the lobby and occasional live music in the bar.

$ Centre Point Hotel
Lot 1587 Jln Buangsiol, T085-212922.
A basic place with a/c rooms and a restaurant, situated along the river. Tops Limbang's limited bill of hotels.

$ Metro Hotel
Lot 781, Jln Bangkita, T085-211133.
Small, with fewer than 30 small but clean rooms, all with a/c, TV, fridge and good-quality beds. Recommended.

$ Muhibbah
Lot 790, Bank St, T085-213705.
Located in the town centre, this place has fairly clean but decidedly dated rooms with a/c, TV and bathroom.

Lawas

$$ Hotel Seri Malaysia Lawas
Jln Gaya, T085-283200, www.serimalaysia.com.my.
Fair-value mid-range hotel with comfortable rooms and efficient service. A fair bet if you are stuck in Lawas.

$ Lawas Federal
8 Jln Masjid Baru.
A/c and restaurant.

Restaurants

Limbang

$$ Tong Lok
Next to Purnama Hotel (see Where to stay).
Gruesome pink tablecloths and fluorescent lighting, but good Chinese food.

$ Hai Hong
1 block south of Maggie's Café.
Simple coffee shop. Good for breakfast, with fried egg and chips on the menu.

$ Maggie's Café
55A Jln Buangsiol.
Chinese coffee shop. Pleasant location for an evening meal or maybe even a bottle of 2 of icy beer with tables outside next to river in the evening. Braziers set up in evening for good grilled fish on banana leaf and dishes of spicy greens.

Festivals

Limbang

May The (movable) **Buffalo Racing Festival** marks the end of the harvesting season.

Transport

Limbang
Air

The airport is 5 km from town and taxis ferry passengers in. There are 2 daily connections with **Miri** and connections with **Lawas** and **KK** with MASwings.

Boat

Regular connections with **Lawas**, depart early in the morning (2 hrs, RM25). There is also an early-morning express departure to **Labuan** (RM20). Regular boat connections with **Bandar Seri Begawan**, Brunei (30 mins, RM25).

Lawas
Air

Frequent connections with **Miri**, connections to **KK** and **Limbang** and a twice-weekly flight to **Ba'kelalan** with MASwings.

Boat

Regular early morning connections to **Limbang** (2 hrs) and **Labuan** (2 hrs). Daily morning boat departures for **Muara** in Brunei at 1200 (RM25).

Bus

Connections with **Merapok** on the Sarawak/Sabah border (RM9). From here there are connections to **Beaufort** in Sabah (RM11, 2 hrs). Twice-daily connections with **KK** (RM30, 4 hrs).

Background

Sarawak earned its place in the archaeological textbooks when a 37,000-year-old human skull belonging to a boy of about 15 was unearthed in the Niah Caves in 1958 (see page 97), predating the earliest relics found on the Malay Peninsula by about 30,000 years. The caves were continuously inhabited for tens of thousands of years and many shards of palaeolithic and neolithic pottery, tools and jewellery as well as carved burial boats have been excavated at the site. There are also prehistoric cave paintings. In the first millennium AD, the Niah Caves were home to a prosperous community, which traded birds' nests, hornbill ivory, bezoar stones, rhinoceros horns and other jungle produce with Chinese traders in exchange for porcelain and beads.

Some of Sarawak's tribes may be descended from these cave people, although others, notably the Iban shifting cultivators, migrated from Kalimantan's Kapuas River valley from the 16th to 19th centuries. Malay Orang Laut, sea people, migrated to Sarawak's coasts and made a living from fishing, trading and piracy. At the height of Sumatra's Srivijayan Empire in the 11th and 12th centuries, many Sumatran Malays migrated to north Borneo. Chinese traders were active along the Sarawak coast from as early as the seventh century: Chinese coins and Han pottery have been discovered at the mouth of the Sarawak River.

From the 14th century right up to the 20th century, Sarawak's history was inextricably intertwined with that of the neighbouring Sultanate of Brunei, which, until the arrival of the White Rajahs of Sarawak, held sway over the coastal areas of north Borneo. For a more detailed account of how Sarawak's White Rajahs came to whittle away the sultan's territory and expand into the vacuum of his receding empire, see Robert Payne's *The White Rajahs of Sarawak*.

Enter James Brooke

As the Sultanate of Brunei began to decline around the beginning of the 18th century, the Malays of coastal Sarawak attempted to break free from their tributary overlord. They claimed an independent ancestry from Brunei and exercised firm control over the Dayak tribes inland and upriver. But in the early 19th century Brunei started to reassert its power over them, dispatching Pangiran Mahkota from the Brunei court in 1827 to govern Sarawak and supervise the mining of high-grade antimony ore, exported to Singapore to be used in medicine and as an alloy. The name 'Sarawak' is from the Malay word *serawak (antimony)*.

Mahkota founded Kuching, but relations with the local Malays became strained and Mahkota's problems were compounded by the marauding Ibans of the Saribas and Skrang rivers who raided coastal communities. In 1836 the local Malay chiefs, led by Datu Patinggi Ali, rebelled against Governor Mahkota, prompting the Sultan of Brunei to send his uncle, Rajah Muda Hashim to suppress the uprising. But Hashim failed to quell the disturbances and the situation deteriorated when the rebels approached the Sultan of Sambas, now in northwest Kalimantan, for help from the Dutch. Then, in 1839, James Brooke sailed up the Sarawak River to Kuching.

Hashim was desperate to regain control and Brooke, in the knowledge that the British would support any action that countered the threat of Dutch influence, struck a deal with him. He pressed Hashim to grant him the governorship of Sarawak in exchange for suppressing the rebellion, which he duly did. In 1842 Brooke became Rajah of Sarawak. Pangiran Mahkota – the now disenfranchised former governor of Sarawak – formed an alliance with an Iban pirate chief on the Skrang River, while another Brunei prince, Pangiran Usop, joined Illanun pirates. Malaysian historian J Kathirithamby-Wells wrote: "… piracy and politics became irrevocably linked and Brooke's battle against his political opponents became advertised as a morally justified war against the pirate communities of the coast."

The suppression of piracy in the 19th century became a full-time job for the Sarawak and Brunei rulers, although the court of Brunei was well known to have derived a large chunk of its income from piracy. Rajah James Brooke believed that as long as pirates were free to pillage the coast, commerce wouldn't grow and his kingdom would never develop; ridding Sarawak's estuaries of pirates – both Iban (Sea Dayaks) and Illanun – became an act of political survival. In *The White Rajahs of Sarawak*, Robert Payne wrote: "Nearly every day people came to Kuching with tales about the pirates: how they had landed in a small creek, made their way to a village, looted everything in sight, murdered everyone they could lay their hands on, and then vanished as swiftly as they came. The Sultan of Brunei was begging for help against them."

Anti-piracy missions afforded James Brooke an excuse to extend his kingdom, as he worked his way up the coasts, 'pacifying' the Sea Dayak pirates. Brooke declared war on them and with the help of Royal Naval Captain Henry Keppel (of latter-day Singapore's Keppel Shipyard fame), he led a number of punitive raids against the Iban Sea Dayaks in 1833, 1834 and 1849. "The assaults", wrote DJM Tate in *Rajah Brooke's Borneo*, "largely achieved their purpose and were applauded in the Straits, but the appalling loss of life incurred upset many drawing room humanitarians in Britain." There were an estimated 25,000 pirates living along the North Borneo coast when Brooke became Rajah. He led many expeditions against them, culminating in his notorious battle against the Saribas pirate fleet in 1849.

In that incident, Brooke ambushed and killed hundreds of Saribas Dayaks at Batang Maru. The barbarity of the ambush (which was reported in the *Illustrated London News*) outraged public opinion in Britain and in Singapore; a commission in Singapore acquitted Brooke, but badly damaged his prestige. In the British parliament, he was cast as a 'mad despot' who had to be prevented from committing further massacres. But the action led the Sultan of Brunei to grant him the Saribas and Skrang districts (now Sarawak's Second Division) in 1853, marking the beginning of the Brooke dynasty's relentless expansionist drive. Eight years later, James Brooke persuaded the sultan to give him what became Sarawak's Third Division, after he drove out the Illanun pirates who disrupted the sago trade from Mukah and Oya, around Bintulu.

In 1857, James Brooke ran into more trouble. Chinese Hakka goldminers, who had been in Bau (further up the Sarawak River) longer than he had been in Kuching, had grown resentful of his attempts to stamp out the opium trade and their secret societies. They attacked Kuching, set the Malay kampongs ablaze and killed several European officials; Brooke escaped by swimming across the river from his astana. His nephew, Charles, led a group of Skrang Dayaks in pursuit of the Hakka invaders, who fled across the border into Dutch Borneo; about 1000 were killed by the Ibans on the way; 2500 survived. Robert Payne writes: "The fighting lasted for more than a month. From time to time Dayaks would return with strings of heads, which they cleaned and smoked over slow fires, especially happy when they could do this in full view of the Chinese in the bazaars who sometimes recognized people they had known." Payne says Brooke was plagued by guilt over how he handled the Chinese rebellion, for so many deaths could not easily be explained away. Neither James nor Charles ever fully trusted the Chinese again, although the Teochew, Cantonese and Hokkien merchants in Kuching never caused them any trouble.

The second generation: Rajah Charles Brooke

Charles Johnson (who changed his name to Brooke after his elder brother, Brooke Johnson, had been disinherited by James for insubordination) became the second Rajah of Sarawak in 1863. He ruled for nearly 50 years. Charles did not have James Brooke's forceful personality, and was much more reclusive – probably as a result of working in remote jungle outposts for 10 years in government service. Robert Payne noted that "in James Brooke there was something of the knight errant at the mercy of his dream. Charles was the pure professional, a stern soldier who thought dreaming was the occupation of fools. There was no nonsense about him." Despite this he engendered great loyalty in his administrators, who worked hard for little reward.

Charles maintained his uncle's consultative system of government and formed a Council Negeri, or national council, of his top government officials, Malay leaders and tribal headmen, which met every few years to hammer out policy changes. His frugal financial management meant that by 1877 Sarawak was no longer in debt and the economy gradually expanded. But it was not wealthy, and had few natural resources; its soils proved unsuitable for agriculture. In the 1880s, Charles's faith in the Chinese community was sufficiently restored to allow Chinese immigration, and the government subsidized the new settlers. By using 'friendly' downriver Dayak groups to subdue belligerent tribes upriver, Charles managed to pacify the interior by 1880.

When Charles took over from his ailing uncle in 1863 he proved to be even more of an expansionist. In 1868 he tried to take control of the Baram River valley, but London did not approve secession of the territory until 1882, when it became the Fourth Division. In 1884, Charles acquired the Trusan Valley from the Sultan of Brunei, and in 1890, he annexed Limbang ending a six-year rebellion by local chiefs against the sultan. The two territories were united to form the Fifth Division, after which Sarawak completely surrounded Brunei. In 1905, the British North Borneo Chartered Company gave up the Lawas Valley to Sarawak too. "By 1890," writes Robert Payne, "Charles was ruling over a country as large as England and Scotland with the help of about 20 European officers." When the First World War broke out in 1914, Charles was in England and he ruled Sarawak from Cirencester.

The third generation: Charles Vyner Brooke

In 1916, at the age of 86, Charles handed power to his eldest son, Charles Vyner Brooke, and he died the following year. Vyner was 42 when he became Rajah and had already served his father's government for nearly 20 years. "Vyner was a man of peace, who took no delight in bloodshed and ruled with humanity and compassion," wrote Robert Payne. He was a delegator by nature, and under him the old paternalistic style of government gave way to a more professional bureaucracy. On the centenary of the Brooke administration in September 1941, Vyner promulgated a written constitution, and renounced his autocratic powers in favour of working in cooperation with a Supreme Council. This was opposed by his nephew and heir, Anthony Brooke, who saw it as a move to undermine his succession. To protest against this, and his uncle's decision to appoint a mentally deranged Muslim Englishman as his Chief Secretary, Anthony left for Singapore. The Rajah dismissed him from the service in September 1941. Three months later the Japanese Imperial Army invaded; Vyner Brooke was in Australia at the time, and his younger brother, Bertram, was ill in London.

BACKGROUND
Tom Harrisson: life in the fast lane

Reputed to be one of the most important figures in the development of archaeology in Southeast Asia, Tom Harrisson, the charismatic 'egomaniac', put Borneo and Sarawak on the map.

Tom Harrisson loved Sarawak and, it would seem, Sarawak loved him. He first visited Sarawak in 1932 as part of a Royal Geographical Expedition sent, along with around 150 kg of Cadbury's chocolate, to collect flora and fauna from one of the world's great natural treasure stores. Instead Harrisson found himself entranced by the territory's human populations and so the love affair began.

By all accounts, Harrisson was a difficult fellow – the sort that imperial Britain produced in very large numbers indeed. He was a womaniser with a particular penchant for other people's spouses, he could be horribly abusive to his fellow workers and he apparently revelled in putting down uppity academics. But he was also instrumental in putting Sarawak, and Borneo on the map and in raising awareness of the ways in which economic and social change was impacting on Sarawak's tribal peoples.

Before taking up the curatorship of the Sarawak Museum in 1947 Harrisson also distinguished himself as a war hero, parachuting into the jungle and organizing around 1000 headhunters to terrorize the Japanese. All in all, Tom Harrisson led life in the fast lane.

Those wanting to read a good biography of Harrisson should get hold of *The Most Offending Soul Alive* by Judith M Heimann, Honolulu, Hawaii University Press, 1998.

Japanese troops took Kuching on Christmas Day 1941 having captured the Miri oilfield a few days earlier. European administrators were interned and many later died. A Kuching-born Chinese, Albert Kwok, led an armed resistance against the Japanese in neighbouring British North Borneo (Sabah) – see page 296 – but in Sarawak, there was no organized guerrilla movement. Iban tribespeople instilled fear into the occupying forces, however, by roaming the jungle taking Japanese heads, which were proudly added to much older longhouse head galleries. Despite the Brooke regime's century-long effort to stamp out headhunting, the practice was encouraged by Tom Harrisson (see box, above) who parachuted into the Kelabit Highlands towards the end of the Second World War and put together an irregular army of upriver tribesmen to fight the Japanese. He offered them 'ten-bob-a-nob' for Japanese heads. Australian forces liberated Kuching on 11 September 1945 and Sarawak was placed under Australian military administration for seven months.

After the war, the Colonial Office in London decided the time had come to bring Sarawak into the modern era, replacing the anachronistic White Rajahs, introducing an education system and building a rudimentary infrastructure. The Brookes had become an embarrassment to the British government as they continued to squabble among themselves. Anthony Brooke desperately wanted to claim what he felt was his, while the Colonial Office wanted Sarawak to become a crown colony or revert to Malay rule. No one was sure whether Sarawak wanted the Brookes back or not.

The end of empire

In February 1946 the ageing Vyner shocked his brother Bertram and his nephew Anthony, the Rajah Muda (or heir apparent), by issuing a proclamation urging the people of Sarawak to accept the King of England as their ruler. In doing so he effectively handed the country over to Britain. Vyner thought the continued existence of Sarawak as the private domain of the Brooke family an anachronism; but Anthony thought it a betrayal. The British government sent a commission to Sarawak to ascertain what the people wanted. In May 1946, the Council Negeri agreed – by a 19-16 majority – to transfer power to Britain, provoking protests and demonstrations and resulting in the assassination of the British governor by a Malay in Sibu in 1949. He and three other anti-cessionists were sentenced to death. Two years later, Anthony Brooke, who remained deeply resentful about the demise of the Brooke Dynasty, abandoned his claim and urged his supporters to end their campaign.

As a British colony, Sarawak's economy expanded and oil and timber production increased, which funded the much-needed expansion of education and health services. As with British North Borneo (Sabah), Britain was keen to give Sarawak political independence and, following Malaysian independence in 1957, saw the best means to this end as being through the proposal of Malaysian Prime Minister Tunku Abdul Rahman. The prime minister suggested the formation of a federation to include Singapore, Sarawak, Sabah and Brunei as well as the Peninsula. In the end, Brunei opted out, Singapore left after two years, but Sarawak and Sabah joined the federation, having accepted the recommendations of the British government. Indonesia's President Sukarno denounced the move, claiming it was all part of a neo-colonialist conspiracy. He declared a policy of confrontation – **Konfrontasi**. A United Nations commission which was sent to ensure that the people of Sabah and Sarawak wanted to be part of Malaysia reported that Indonesia's objections were unfounded.

Communists had been active in Sarawak since the 1930s. The Konfrontasi afforded the Sarawak Communist Organization (SCO) Jakarta's support against the Malaysian government. The SCO joined forces with the North Kalimantan Communist Party (NKCP) and were trained and equipped by Indonesia's President Sukarno. But following Jakarta's brutal suppression of the Indonesian Communists, the Partai Komunis Indonesia (PKI), in the wake of the attempted coup in 1965, Sarawak's Communists fled back across the Indonesian border, along with their Kalimantan comrades. There they continued to wage guerrilla war against the Malaysian government throughout the 1970s. The Sarawak state government offered amnesties to guerrillas wanting to come out of hiding. In 1973 the NKCP leader surrendered along with 482 other guerrillas. A handful remained in the jungle, most of them in the hills around Kuching. The last surrendered in 1990.

Politics and modern Sarawak

In 1957 Kuala Lumpur was keen to have Sarawak and Sabah in the Federation of Malaysia and offered the two states a degree of autonomy, allowing their local governments control over state finances, agriculture and forestry. Sarawak's racial mix was reflected in its chaotic state politics. The Ibans dominated the Sarawak National Party (SNAP), which provided the first chief minister, Datuk Stephen Kalong Ningkan. He raised a storm over Kuala Lumpur's introduction of Bahasa Malaysia in schools and complained bitterly about the federal government's policy of filling the Sarawakian civil service with Malays from the Peninsula. An 'us' and 'them' mentality developed: in Sarawak, the Malay word *semenanjung* (Peninsula) was used to label the newcomers. To many, *semenanjung* was Malaysia, Sarawak was Sarawak.

In 1966 the federal government ousted the SNAP, and a new Muslim-dominated government led by the Sarawak Alliance took over in Kuching. But there was still strong political opposition to federal encroachment. Throughout the 1970s, as in Sabah, Sarawak's strongly Muslim government drew the state closer and closer to the Peninsula: it supported *Rukunegara* – the policy of Islamization – and promoted the use of Bahasa Malaysia. Muslims make up less than 30% of the population of Sarawak. The Malays, Melanaus and Chinese communities grew rich from the timber industry; the Ibans and the Orang Ulu (the upriver tribespeople) saw little in the way of development. They did not reap the benefits of the expansion of education and social services, they were unable to get public sector jobs and, to make matters worse, logging firms were encroaching on their native lands and threatening their traditional lifestyles.

It has only been in more recent years that the tribespeoples' political voice has been heard at all. In 1983, Iban members of SNAP – which was a part of former Prime Minister Dr Mahathir Mohamad's ruling Barisan Nasional (National Front) coalition – split to form the Party Bansa Dayak Sarawak (PBDS), which, although it initially remained in the coalition, became more outspoken on native affairs. At about the same time, international outrage was sparked over the exploitation of Sarawak's tribespeople by politicians and businessmen involved in the logging industry. The plight of the Penan hunter-gatherers came to world attention due to their blockades of logging roads and the resulting publicity highlighted the rampant corruption and greed that characterized modern Sarawak's political economy.

The National Front remains firmly in control in Sarawak. But unlike neighbouring Sabah, Sarawak's politicians are not dominated by the centre. The chief minister of Sarawak is Abduly Taib Mahmud, a Melanau, and his Parti Pesaka Bumiputra Bersatu is a member of the UMNO-dominated (United Malays National Organisation) National Front. But in Sarawak itself UMNO wields little power.

The ruling National Front easily won the 1999 election in Sarawak, successfully playing on voters' local concerns and grievances. The problem for the opposition is that local people think it is the state legislature that can help, not the federal parliament in KL, which seems distant and ineffective. So UMNO does not have a presence and it is the Parti Pesaka Bumiputra Bersatu which represents Sarawak in the National Front.

The challenge of getting the voters out in the most remote areas of the country was clearly shown in Long Lidom. There it cost the government RM65,000 to provide a helicopter to poll just seven Punan Busang in a longhouse on the Upper Kajang, close to the border with Indonesia. Datuk Omar of the Election Commission said that mounting the general election in Sarawak, with its 28 parliamentary seats, was a "logistical nightmare". Along with a small air force of helicopters, the Commission used 1032 long boats, 15 speed boats and 3054 land cruisers. The Commission's workforce numbered a cool 13,788 workers in a state with a population of just two million.

The 2006 state elections in Sarawak were won convincingly by the Barisan Nasional, which gained 62 out of the 71 contested seats. However, things look like they might be changing: the 2011 state election saw a much tighter victory for the BN, with them winning just 55 seats, and there were record gains for the Democratic Action Party (DAP). The next election is scheduled for the end of 2016 and is expected to be the closest election in Sarawak's history. What with disenfranchisement over Kuala Lumpur's rule growing, increasing financial woes affecting Malaysia, and the prime minister taken to court having being accused of pocketing US$681 million dollars of Saudi 'gift money', there is no doubt that people are considering political alternatives in the state.

Today there are many in Sarawak as well as in Sabah who wish their governments had opted out of the Federation, as did Brunei. Sarawak is of great economic importance to Malaysia, thanks to its oil, gas and timber. The state now accounts for more than one-third of Malaysia's petroleum production and more than half of its natural gas and accounted for 10.1 of the country's GDP in 2013m behind only Selangor and Kuala Lumpur. As with neighbouring Sabah however, almost all of Sarawak's oil and gas revenues go directly into the federal coffers.

Culture

People

About a third of the population is made up of Iban tribespeople who live in longhouses on the lower reaches of the rivers. Chinese immigrants, whose forebears arrived during the 19th century, make up around 30%. A fifth of the population is Malay; most are native Sarawakians, but some came from the Peninsula after the state joined the Malaysian Federation in 1963. The rest of Sarawak's inhabitants are indigenous tribal groups, of which the main ones are the Melanau, the Bidayuh and upriver Orang Ulu such as the Kenyah, Kayan and Kelabits; the Penan are among Southeast Asia's few remaining hunter-gatherers. The population of the state is almost 2.6 million. The people of the interior are classified as Proto-Malays and Deutero-Malays and are divided into at least 12 distinct tribal groups including Iban, Murut, Melanau, Bidayuh, Kenyah, Kayan, Kelabit and Penan.

Bidayuh In the 19th century, Sarawak's European community called the Bidayuh Land Dayaks, mainly to distinguish them from the Iban Sea Dayak pirates. The Bidayuh make up 8.4% of the population and are concentrated to the west of the Kuching area, towards the Kalimantan border. There are also related groups living in west Kalimantan. They were virtually saved from extinction by the White Rajahs, because the Bidayuh were quiet, mild-mannered people, they were at the mercy of the Iban headhunters and the Brunei Malays who taxed and enslaved them. The Brookes afforded them protection from both groups.

Most live in modern longhouses and are dry rice farmers. Their traditional long-houses are exactly like Iban ones, but without the tanju veranda. The Bidayuh tribe comprises five sub-groups: the Jagoi, Biatah, Bukar-Sadong, Selakau and Lara, all of whom live in far west Sarawak. They are the state's best traditional plumbers and are known for their ingenious gravity-fed bamboo water systems. They are bamboo specialists, making it into everything from cooking pots to finely carved musical instruments. Among other tribal groups, the Bidayuh are renowned for their rice wine and sugarcane toddy. Henry Keppel, who with Rajah James Brooke fought the Bidayuh's dreaded enemies, the Sea Dayaks, described an evening spent with the Land Dayaks thus: "They ate and drank, and asked for everything, but stole nothing."

Chinese Hakka goldminers had already settled at Bau, upriver from Kuching, long before James Brooke arrived in 1839. Cantonese, Teochew and Hokkien merchants also set up in Kuching, but the Brookes did not warm to the Chinese community, believing the traders would exploit the Dayak communities if they were allowed to venture upriver. In the 1880s, however, Rajah Charles Brooke allowed the immigration of large numbers of Chinese – mainly Foochow – who settled in coastal towns like Sibu. Many became farmers and ran rubber smallholdings. The Sarawak government subsidized the immigrants for the first year. During the Brooke era, the only government-funded schools were for Malays and few tribal people ever received a formal education. The Chinese, however, set up and funded their own private schools and many attended Christian missionary schools, leading to the formation of a relatively prosperous, educated elite. Today the Chinese comprise nearly a third of the state's population and are almost as numerous as the Iban; they are the middle-men, traders, shopkeepers, timber towkays (magnates) and express boat owners.

Iban Sarawak's best-known erstwhile headhunters make up nearly a third of the state's population and while some have moved to coastal towns for work, many remain in their traditional longhouses. But with Iban men now earning good money in the timber and oil industries, it is increasingly common to see longhouses bristling with TV aerials, equipped with fridges and flush toilets and Land Cruisers in the car park. Even modern longhouses retain the traditional features of gallery, veranda and doors.

The Iban are shifting cultivators who originated in the Kapuas River basin of west Kalimantan and migrated into Sarawak's Second Division in the early 16th century, settling along the Batang Lupar, Skrang and Saribas rivers. By the 1800s, they had begun to spill into the Rejang River valley. It was this growing pressure on land as more migrants settled in the river valleys that led to fighting and headhunting (see box, page 134).

The Iban joined local Malay chiefs and turned to piracy, which is how Europeans first came into contact with them. They were dubbed Sea Dayaks as a result, which is really a misnomer as they are an inland people. The name stuck, however, and in the eyes of Westerners, it distinguished them from Land Dayaks, who were Bidayuh people from the Sarawak River area. While Rajah James Brooke only won the Iban's loyalty after he had crushed them in battle (see page 175), he had great admiration for them and they bore

BACKGROUND
Skulls in the longhouse

Although headhunting has been largely stamped out in Borneo, there is still the odd reported case once every few years. But until the early 20th century, headhunting was commonplace among many Dayak tribes and the Iban were the most fearsome of all.

Following a headhunting trip, the freshly taken heads were skinned, placed in rattan nets and smoked over a fire, or sometimes boiled. The skulls were then hung from the rafters of the longhouse and they possessed the most powerful form of magic.

The skulls were considered trophies of manhood (they increased a young bachelor's eligibility) and symbols of bravery. They also testified to the unity of a longhouse. The longhouse had to hold festivals – or *gawai* – to appease the spirits of the skulls. Once placated, the heads were believed to bring great blessing – they could ward off evil spirits, save villages from epidemics, produce rain and increase the yield of rice harvests. Heads that were insulted or ignored were capable of wreaking havoc in the form of bad dreams, plagues, floods and fires. To keep the spirits of the skulls happy, they would be offered food and cigarettes and made to feel welcome in their new home. As the magical powers of a skull faded with time, fresh heads were always in demand. Tribes without heads were seen as spiritually weak.

Today, young Dayak men no longer have to take heads to gain respect. They are, however, expected to go on long journeys (the equivalent of the Australian aborigines' Walkabout), or *bejalai* in Iban. The one unspoken rule is that they should come back with plenty of good stories, and, these days, as most *bejalai* expeditions translate into stints at timber camps or on oil rigs, they are expected to come home bearing video recorders, TVs and motorbikes.

Many Dayak tribes continue to celebrate their headhunting ceremonies. In Kalimantan, for example, the Adat Ngayau ceremony uses coconut shells, wrapped in leaves, as substitutes for freshly cut heads.

no bitterness. He described them as "good-looking a set of men, or devils ... Their wiry and supple limbs might have been compared to the troops of wild horses that followed Mazeppa in his perilous flight."

Kelabit Tom Harrisson parachuted into Kelabit territory with the Allied Special Forces towards the end of the Second World War. The Kelabit Highlands around Bario were chosen because they were so remote. Of all the tribes in Sarawak, the Kelabit have the sturdiest, strongest builds, which is usually ascribed to the cool and invigorating mountain climate. Their fragrant Bario rice is prized throughout Sarawak. See also box, page 129.

Kenyah and Kayan These probably originally migrated into Sarawak from the Apo Kayan district in East Kalimantan. Kenyah and Kayan raids on downriver people were greatly feared, but their power was broken by Charles Brooke, just before he became the second White Rajah, in 1863. The Kayan had retreated upstream above the Pelagus Rapids on the Rejang River (see page 82), to an area they considered out of reach of their Iban enemies. In 1862 they killed two government officers at Kanowit and went on

BACKGROUND
The Kelabit in Borneo

The Kelabit, who live in the highlands at the headwaters of the Baram River, are closely related to the Murut (see page 302) and the Lun Dayeh and Lun Bawang of interior Kalimantan. They are skilled hill-rice farmers. The hill climate also allows vegetable cultivation. Kelabit parties are also famed as boisterous occasions, and large quantities of *borak* (rice beer) are consumed, despite the fact that the majority of Kelabit has converted to Christianity. They are also regarded as among the most hospitable people in Borneo.

a killing spree. Charles Brooke led 15,000 Iban past the Pelagus Rapids, beyond Belaga and attacked the Kayan in their heartland. Many hundreds were killed. In November 1924, Rajah Vyner Brooke presided over a peace-making ceremony between the Orang Ulu and the Iban in Kapit (there is a photograph of the ceremony on display in the Kapit Museum).

The Kenyah and Kayan in Sarawak live in pleasant upriver valleys and are settled rice farmers. Subgroups include the Kejaman, Skapan, Berawan and Sebop.

Malay About half of Sarawak's 300,000-strong Malay community lives around the state capital; most of the other half lives in the Limbang Division, near Brunei. The Malays traditionally live near the coast, although today there are small communities far upriver. There are some old wooden Malay houses with carved façades in the kampongs along the banks of the Sarawak River in Kuching. In all Malay communities, the mosque is the centre of the village, but while their faith is important to them, the strictures of Islam are generally less rigorously enforced in Sarawak than on the Peninsula. During the days of the White Rajahs, the Malays were recruited into government service, as they were on the Malay Peninsula. They were renowned as good administrators and the men were mostly literate in Jawi script. Over the years there has been much intermarriage between the Malay and Melanau communities. Traditionally, the Malays were fishermen and farmers.

Melanau The Melanau are a relaxed and humorous people. Rajah James Brooke, like generations of men before him and after him, thought the Melanau girls particularly pretty. He said that they had "agreeable countenances, with the dark, rolling, open eye of the Italians, and nearly as fair as most of that race". The Melanau live along the coast between the Baram and Rejang rivers; originally they lived in magnificent communal houses built high off the ground, like the one that has been reconstructed at the Sarawak Cultural Village in Kuching, but these have long since disappeared. The houses were designed to afford protection from incessant pirate raids (see page 126), for the Melanau were easy pickings, being coastal people. Their stilt-houses were often up to 12 m off the ground. Today most Melanau live in Malay-style pile-houses facing the river. Hedda Morrison, in her classic 1957 book *Sarawak*, wrote: "As a result of living along the rivers in swamp country, the Melanaus are an exceptionally amphibious people. The children learn to swim almost before they can walk. Nearly all progress is by canoe, sometimes even to visit the house next door."

The traditional Melanau fishing boat is called a *barong*. Melanau fishermen employed a unique fishing technique. They would anchor palm leaves at sea as they discovered that shoals of fish would seek refuge under them. After rowing out to the leaves, one fisherman would dive off his *barong* and chase the fish into the nets which his colleague

BACKGROUND

The Kenyah and Kayan in Borneo

These two closely related groups now live mainly in Sarawak and Kalimantan. They were the traditional rivals of the Iban and were notorious for their warlike ways. Historian Robert Payne, in his history *The White Rajahs of Sarawak*, described the Kayan of the upper Rejang as "a treacherous tribe, [who] like nothing better than putting out the eyes and cutting the throats of prisoners, or burning them alive".

They are very different from other tribal groups, have a completely different language (which has ancient Malayo-Polynesian roots) and are class conscious, with a well-defined social hierarchy. Traditionally their society was composed of aristocrats, nobles, commoners and slaves (who were snatched during raids on other tribes). One of the few things they have in common with other Dayak groups is the fact that they live in longhouses, although even these are of a different design, and are much more carefully constructed, in ironwood. Many have now been converted to Christianity (most are Protestant).

In contrast to their belligerent history, the Kenyahs and Kayans are much more introverted than the Ibans; they are slow and deliberate in their ways and are very artistic and musical. They are also renowned for their parties; visitors recovering from drinking *borak* rice beer have their faces covered in soot before being thrown in the river. This is to test the strength of the newly forged friendship with visitors, who are ill-advised to lose their sense of humour on such occasions.

Their artwork is made from wood, antlers, metal and beads. They use a lot of wooden statues and masks to scare evil spirits at the entrances to their homes.

hung over the side. The Melanaus were also noted for their production of sago, which they ate instead of rice. At Kuching's Cultural Village there is a demonstration of traditional sago production, showing how the starch-bearing pith is removed, mashed, dried and ground into flour. Most Melanau are now Muslim and have assimilated with the Malays through intermarriage. Originally, however, they were animists (animist Melanau are called Likaus) and were particularly famed for their elaborately carved 'sickness images', which represented the form of spirits which caused specific illnesses (see page 140).

Orang Ulu The jungle, or upriver, people comprise a range of different small tribal groups. Orang Ulu longhouses are usually made of *belian* (ironwood) and are built to last. They are well-known swordsmiths, forging lethal parangs from any piece of scrap metal they find. They are also very artistic people – skilled carvers and painters and famed for their beadwork – taking great care decorating even simple household utensils. Most Orang Ulu are decorated with traditional tattoos (see box, page 137).

Penan Perhaps Southeast Asia's only remaining true hunter-gatherers live mainly in the upper Rejang area and Limbang. They are nomads and are related, linguistically at least, to the Punan, former nomadic forest dwellers who are now settled in longhouses along the upper Rejang. The Malaysian government has long wanted the Penan to settle too, but has had limited success in attracting them to expensive new longhouses. Groups of

BACKGROUND

Tribal tattoos

Tattooing is practised by many indigenous groups in Borneo, but the most intricate designs are those of the upriver Orang Ulu tribes.

Designs vary from group to group and for different parts of the body. Circular designs are mostly used for the shoulder, chest or wrists, while stylized dragon-dogs (*aso*), scorpions and dragons are used on the thigh and, for the Iban, on the throat.

Tattoos can mean different things; for theman it is a symbol of bravery and for women, a good tattoo is a beauty feature. More elaborate designs often denote high social status in Orang Ulu communities – the Kayan, for example, reserved the *aso* design for the upper classes and slaves were barred from tattooing. In these Orang Ulu groups, the women have the most impressive tattoos; the headman's daughter has her hands, arms and legs completely covered in a finely patterned tattoo.

Designs are first carved on a block of wood, which is then smeared with ink. The design is printed on the body and then punctured into the skin with needles dipped in ink, usually made from a mixture of sugar, water and soot. Rice is smeared over the inflamed area to prevent infection, but it usually swells up for some time.

Penan hunter-gatherers still wander hunt wild pigs, birds and monkeys and search for sago palms to make their staple food, sago flour. The Penan are considered to be the jungle experts by all the other inland tribes. As they live in the shade of the forest, their skin is relatively fair. They have a great affection for the coolness of the forest and until the 1960s were rarely seen by the outside world. For them sunlight is extremely unpleasant. They are broad and more stocky than other river people and are extremely shy, having had little contact with the outside world. Most trade is conducted with remote Kayan, Kenyah and Kelabit longhouse communities on the edge of the forest.

In the eyes of the West, the Penan have emerged as the 'noble savages' of the late 20th century for their spirited defence of their lands against encroachment by logging companies. This spirited defence continues today. But it is not just recently that they have been cheated: they have long been the victims of other upriver tribes. A Penan, bringing baskets full of rotan to a Kenyah or Kayan longhouse to sell, may end up exchanging his produce for one bullet or shotgun cartridge. In his way of thinking, a bullet will kill one wild boar which will last his family 10 days. In turn, the buyer knows he can sell the same rotan downstream for RM50-100. Penan still use the blowpipe for small game, but shotguns for wild pig. If they buy the shotgun cartridges for themselves, they have to exchange empties first. Some of the Penan's shotguns date back to the Second World War, when the British supplied them to upriver tribespeople to fight the Japanese. During the Brooke era, a large annual market would be held which both Chinese traders and Orang Ulu (including Penan) used to attend; the district officer would have to act as judge to ensure the Penan did not get cheated.

Those wishing to learn more about the Penan should refer to Denis Lau's *The Vanishing Nomads of Borneo* (Interstate Publishing, 1987). Lau has lived among the Penan and has photographed them for many years; his photographs appear in *Malaysia – Heart of Southeast Asia* (Archipelago Press, 1991).

BACKGROUND

The palang

One of the more exotic features of upriver sexuality is the *palang* (penis pin), which is the versatile jungle version of the French tickler.

Traditionally, women suffer heavy weights being attached to their ear lobes to enhance their sex appeal. In turn, men are expected to enhance their physical attributes and entertain their womenfolk by drilling a hole in their organs, into which they insert a range of items, aimed at heightening their partner's pleasure.

Tom Harrisson, a former curator of the Sarawak Museum, was intrigued by the *palang*; some suspect his authority on the subject stemmed from first-hand experience. He wrote: "When the device is put into use, the owner adds whatever he prefers to elaborate and accentuate its intention. A lively range of objects can so be employed – from pigs' bristles and bamboo shavings to pieces of metal, seeds, beads and broken glass. The effect, of course, is to enlarge the diameter of the male organ inside the female."

It is said that many Dayakmen, even today, have the tattooman drill a hole in them. As the practice is now centuries old, one can only assume that its continued popularity proves it is worth the agony.

Dance

Dayak tribes are renowned for their singing and dancing, most famously for the hornbill dance. In her book *Sarawak*, Hedda Morrison wrote: "The Kayans are probably the originators of the stylized war dance now common among the Ibans but the girls are also extremely talented and graceful dancers. One of their most delightful dances is the hornbill dance, when they tie hornbill feathers to the ends of their fingers which accentuate their slow and graceful movements. For party purposes everyone in the longhouse joins in and parades up and down the communal room led by one or two musicians and a group of girls who sing." On these occasions, drink flows freely. With the Ibans, it is *tuak* (rice wine), with the Kayan and Kenyah it is *borak*, a bitter rice beer. After being entertained by dancers, a visitor must drink a large glassful, before bursting into song and doing a dance routine themselves. The best guideline for visitors on how to handle such occasions is provided by Redmond O'Hanlon in his book *Into the Heart of Borneo*. The general rule of thumb is to be prepared to make an absolute fool of yourself. This will immediately endear you to your hosts.

The following are the most common dances in Sarawak. **Kanjet Ngeleput** (Orang Ulu) dance is performed in full warrior regalia, traditionally celebrating the return of a hunter or headhunters. **Mengarang Menyak** (Melanau) dance depicts the processing of sago from the cutting of the tree to the production of the sago pearls or pellets. **Ngajat Bebunuh** (Iban) war dance is performed in full battledress, armed with sword and shield. **Ngajat Induk** (Iban) is performed as a welcome dance for those visiting longhouses. Ngajat Lesong (Iban) dance of the *lesong* or mortar is performed during *gawai*. **Tarian Kris** (Malay) dance is of the *kris*, the Malay dagger, which symbolizes power, courage and strength. **Tarian Rajang Beuh** (Bidayuh) dance is performed after the harvesting season as entertainment for guests to the longhouse. **Tarian Saga Lupa** (Orang Ulu) is performed by women to welcome guests to the longhouse, accompanied by the *sape* (see Music below). **Ule Nugan** (Orang Ulu) dance is to the sound of the *kerebo bulo*, or bamboo slates. The music is designed to inspire the spirit of the paddy seeds to flourish. The male dancers hold a dibbling stick used in the planting of hill rice.

Music

Gongs range from the single large gong, the *tawak*, to the *engkerumong*, a set of small gongs, arranged on a horizontal rack, with five players. An *engkerumong* ensemble usually involves five to seven drums, which include two suspended gongs (*tawak* and *bendai*) and five hour-glass drums (*ketebong*). They are used to celebrate victory in battle or to welcome home a successful headhunting expedition. Sarawak's Bidayuh also make a bamboo gong called a *pirunchong*. The *jatang uton* is a wooden xylophone which can be rolled up like a rope ladder; the keys are struck with hardwood sticks.

The Bidayuh, Sarawak's bamboo specialists, make two main stringed instruments: a three-stringed cylindrical bamboo harp called a *tinton* and the *rabup*, a rotan-stringed fiddle with a bamboo cup. The Orang Ulu (Kenyah and Kayan tribes) play a four-stringed guitar called a *sape*, which is also common on the Kalimantan side of the border. It is the most common and popular lute-type instrument, whose body, neck and board are cut from one piece of softwood. It is used in Orang Ulu dances and by witch doctors. It is usually played by two musicians, one keeping the rhythm, the other the melody. Traditional *sapes* had rotan strings; today they use wire guitar strings and electric pick-ups. Another stringed instrument, more usually found in Kalimantan, or deep in Sarawak's interior, is the *satang*, a bamboo tube with strings around the outside, cut from the bamboo and tightened with pegs.

One of the best-known instruments is the *engkerurai* (or *keluri*), the bagpipes of Borneo, which is usually linked with the Kenyah and Kayan, but is also found in Sabah (where it is called a *sompoton*). It is a hand-held organ in which four bamboo panpipes of different lengths are fixed to a gourd, which acts as the wind chamber. Simple *engkerurai* can only play one chord; more sophisticated ones allow the player to use two pipes for the melody, while the others provide a harmonic drone. The Bidayuh are specialists in bamboo instruments and make flutes of various sizes; big thick ones are called *branchi*, long ones with five holes are *kroto* and small ones are called *nchiyo*.

Arts and crafts

Bamboo carving   The Bidayuh (Land Dayaks) are best known for their bamboo carving. The bamboo is usually carved in shallow relief and then stained with dye, which leaves a pattern in the areas which have been scraped out. The Bidayuh carve utilitarian objects as well as ceremonial shields, musical instruments and spirit images used to guard the longhouse. The Cultural Village (Kampong Budaya) in Kuching is one of the best places to see demonstrations of Bidayuh carving.

Basketry   A wide variety of household items are woven from rotan, bamboo, bemban reed as well as nipah and pandanus palms. Malaysia supplies 30% of the world's demand for *manau rotan* (rattan). Basketry is practised by nearly all the ethnic groups in Sarawak and they are among the most popular handicrafts in Sarawak. A variety of baskets are made for harvesting, storing and winnowing paddy as well as for collecting and storing other items. The Penan are reputed to produce the finest rattan sleeping mats – closely plaited and pliable – as well as the *ajat* and *ambong* baskets (all-purpose jungle rucksacks, also produced by the Kayan and Kenyah). Many of the native patterns used in basketry are derived from Chinese patterns and take the form of geometrical shapes and stylized birds.

The Bidayuh also make baskets from either rotan or sago bark strips. The most common Bidayuh basket is the *tambok*, which is simply patterned and has bands of colour; it also has thin wooden supports on each side.

Beadwork Among many Kenyah, Kayan, Bidayuh, and Kelabit groups, beads have long been symbols of status and wealth; necklaces, skullcaps and girdles are handed down from generation to generation. Smaller glass or plastic beads, usually imported from Europe, are used to decorate baby carriers, baskets, headbands, jackets, hats, sheaths for knives, tobacco boxes and handbags. Beaded baby carriers are mainly used by the Kelabit, Kenyah and Kayan and often have shells and animals' teeth attached, which make a rattling sound to frighten away evil spirits. Rounded patterns require more skill than geometric ones; the quality of the pattern is used to reflect the status of the owner. Only upper classes are permitted to have beadwork depicting 'high-class' motifs such as human faces or figures. Early beads were made from clay, metal, glass, bone or shell (the earliest found in Niah Caves). Later on, many of the beads that found their way upriver were from Venice, Greece, India and China – even Roman and Alexandrian beads have made their way into Borneo's jungle. Orang Ulu traded them for jungle produce. Tribes attach different values to particular types of beads.

Blowpipes These are made by several Orang Ulu tribes in Sarawak and are usually carved from hardwood – normally *belian* (ironwood). The first step is to make a rough cylinder about 10 cm wide and 2.5 m long. This is tied to a platform, from which a hole is bored through the rod. The bore is skilfully chiselled by an iron rod with a pointed end. The rod is then sanded down to about 5 cm in diameter. Traditionally, the sanding was done using the rough underside of macaranga leaves. The darts are made from the nibong and wild sago palms and the poison itself is the sap of the upas (Ipoh) tree (*Antiaris toxicari*) into which the point is dipped.

Hats The Melanau people living around Bintulu make a big colourful conical hat from nipah leaves called a *terindak*. Orang Ulu hats are wide-brimmed and are often decorated with beadwork or cloth appliqué. Kelabit and Lun Bawan women wear skullcaps made entirely of beads, which are heavy and extremely valuable.

Pottery Malaysia's most distinctive ceramic designs are found in Sarawak where Iban potters reproduce shapes and patterns of Chinese porcelain which was originally brought to Borneo by traders centuries ago (see page 45). Copies of these old Chinese jars are mostly used for brewing *tuak* (rice wine).

Sickness images The coastal Melanau, who have now converted to Islam but used to be animists, have a tradition of carving sickness images (*blum*), usually from sago or other softwoods. The image is believed to take the form of the evil spirit causing a specific illness. They are carved in different forms according to the ailment. The Melanau developed elaborate healing ceremonies; if someone was struck down by a serious illness, the spirit medium would perform the berayun ceremony, using the *blum* to extract the illness from the victim's body. Usually, the image is in a half-seated position, with the hands crossed over the part of the body which is affected. During the ceremony, the medium tries to draw the spirit from the sick person into the image, after which it is set adrift on a river in a tiny purpose-made boat or hidden in the jungle. These images are roughly carved and can, from time to time, be found in antique shops.

Textiles The weaving of cotton *pua kumbu*, literally 'blanket' or 'cover', is one of the oldest Iban traditions. Iban legend recounts that 24 generations ago the God of War, Singalang Burong, taught his son how to weave the most precious of all *pua*, the *lebor api*. Dyed deep red, this cloth was traditionally used to wrap heads taken in battle.

The weaving of *pua kumbu* is done by the women and is a vital skill for a would-be bride to acquire. There are two main methods employed in making and decorating *pua kumbu*: the more common is the ikat tie-dyeing technique, known as *ngebat* by the Iban. The other method is the *pileh*, or floating weft. The Iban use a warp-beam loom which is tied to two posts, to which the threads are attached. There is a breast-beam at the weaving end, secured by a back strap to the weaver. A pedal, beneath the threads, lowers and raises the alternate threads which are separated by rods. The woven material is tightly packed by a beater. The material is tie-dyed in the warp.

Because the *pua kumbu* is made by the warp-tie-dyeing method, the number of colours is limited. The most common are a rich browny-brick-red colour and black, as well as the undyed white sections; blues and greens are used in more modern materials. Traditionally, *pua kumbu* were hung in longhouses during ceremonies and were used to cover images during rituals. Designs and patterns are representations of deities which figure in Iban myths and are believed to protect individuals from harm; they are passed down from generation to generation. Such designs, with deep spiritual significance, can only be woven by wives and daughters of chiefs. Other designs and patterns are representations of birds and animals, including hornbills, crocodiles, monitor lizards and shrimps, which are either associated with worship or are sources of food. Symbolic representations of trees, plants and fruits are also included. A typical example is the zigzag pattern which represents the act of crossing a river – the zigzag course is explained by the canoe's attempts to avoid strong currents. Many of the symbolic representations are highly stylized and can be difficult to pick out.

Malay women in Sarawak are traditionally renowned for their *kain songket*, sarongs woven with silver and gold thread.

Woodcarvings Groups are skilled carvers, producing everything from huge burial poles (like the Kejaman pole outside the Sarawak Museum in Kuching) to small statues and masks. Kenyah's traditional masks, used during festivals, are elaborately carved and often have large protruding eyes. Eyes are always emphasized, as they frighten the enemy. Other typical items include spoons, stools, doors, walking sticks, *sapes* (guitars), shields, tattoo plaques and the hilts of *parang ilang* (ceremonial knives). The most popular Iban motif is the hornbill, which holds an honoured place in Iban folklore, as the messenger for the sacred Brahminy kite, the ancestor of the Iban. Another famous carving is the sacred measuring stick, the *tuntun peti*, used to trap deer; it is carved to represent a forest spirit. The Kayan and Kenyah's most common motif is the *aso*, a dragon-like dog with a long snout. The Kenyah and Kayan carve huge burial structures (*salong*), as well as small ear pendants made of hornbill ivory. The elaborately carved masks used for their harvest ceremony are unique.

Brunei

gilded mosques, pristine rainforest and water villages

Brunei is a one-off; a tiny oil-rich sultanate on the north coast of Borneo, cornered and split in two by the Malaysian state of Sarawak.

Around 420,000 Bruneians are ruled over by one of the world's wealthiest men – the living link in a dynasty of sultans stretching back 600 years. At one time, Brunei was the driving seat of Borneo, but its territories were whittled away piece by piece, first by the Sulu kings, then by the British. Today, Brunei is a peculiar mix of material wealth and Malay tradition. Affluence has numbed Sultan Bolkiah's subjects into submission to the political system. Bruneians see no reason to complain: they pay no taxes and the purchase of cars and houses is heavily subsidized. Healthcare and education are free and trips to Mecca are a snip. Politics, it seems, is not their business. This climate of benign affluence, combined with the prohibition of alcohol and the complete lack of nightlife, makes Brunei's tagline – 'The Abode of Peace' – ring perfectly true.

Still, change is in the air. With oil and gas reserves expected to dry up in the next 20 to 40 years the economy needs to diversify. Fortunately Brunei holds a trump card for the future: ecotourism. One of the happy consequences of its dependence on oil is that three-quarters of its landmass is still covered by virgin rainforest, arguably the highest proportion of any country in the world. Brunei is the easy way into Borneo. You get kampong culture, pristine jungle, endangered wildlife and all the creature comforts you could hope for. Just don't expect to rough it.

Best for
River safaris ▪ Royal palaces ▪ Shopping ▪ Water villages

Bandar Seri Begawan 145
Around Brunei 162
Background 174

Footprint
picks

★ Kampong Ayer, page 147

Wander the endless boardwalks of Kampong Ayer, Brunei's huge water village; or take a tour on a lightning-fast water taxi.

★ Omar Ali Saifuddien Mosque, page 150

Brunei's definitive monument, an elegant lakeside mosque in the heart of the capital.

★ Nightmarket in Gadong, page 156

Taste the full range of local Malay food at this friendly night market on the outskirts of Bandar Seri Begawan.

★ Brunei River safari, page 159

Scream upriver in a *tambang* then paddle into the mangroves for a close encounter with rare proboscis monkeys.

★ Ulu Temburong National Park, page 166

Brave the canopy walkway for magnificent views over Brunei's interior rainforest.

★ Tasek Merimbun, page 170

Head inland to Brunei's largest lake, a magnificent peat-black body of water surrounded by dense jungle.

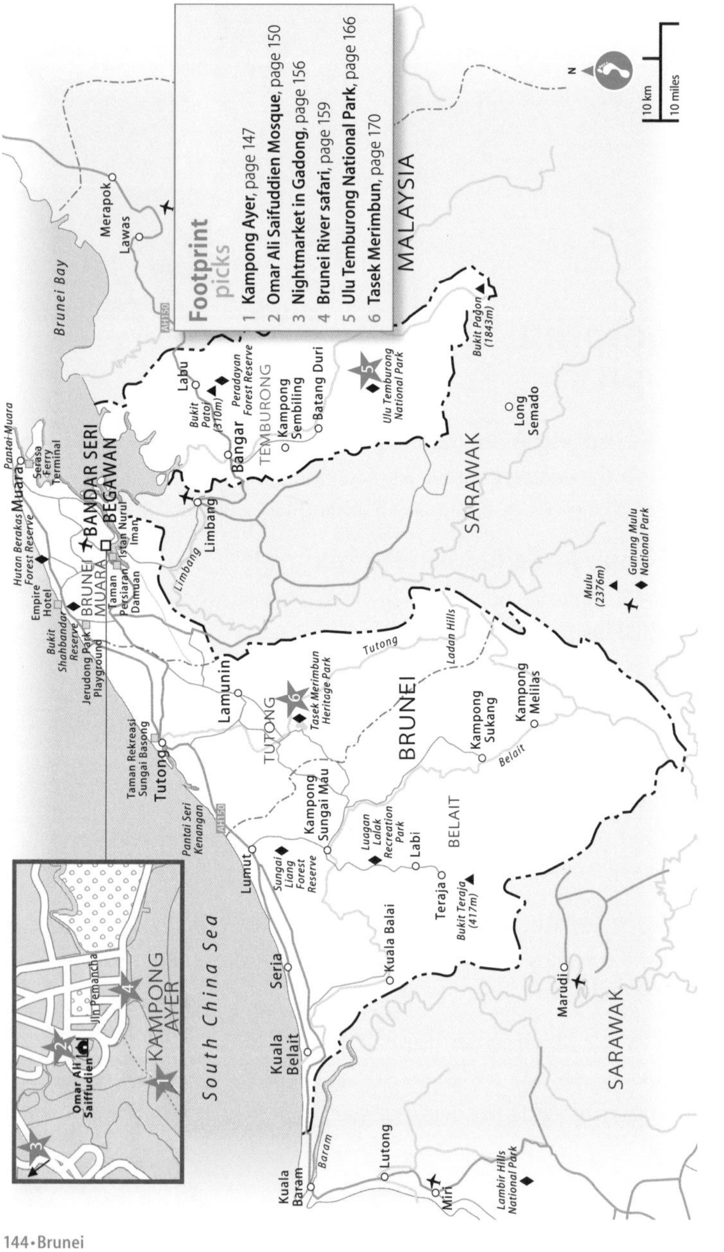
Footprint
picks
1 Kampong Ayer, page 147
2 Omar Ali Saifuddien Mosque, page 150
3 Nightmarket in Gadong, page 156
4 Brunei River safari, page 159
5 Ulu Temburong National Park, page 166
6 Tasek Merimbun, page 170
10 km
10 miles
N
MALAYSIA
SARAWAK
SARAWAK
BRUNEI
South China Sea
Brunei Bay
BANDAR SERI BEGAWAN
BRUNEI MUARA
TEMBURONG
TUTONG
BELAIT
Muara
Pantai Muara
Serasa Ferry Terminal
Hutan Berakas Forest Reserve
Empire Hotel
Bukit Shahbandar Reserve
Jerudong Park Playground
Taman Persiaran Damuan
Istana Nurul Iman
Limbang
Limbang
Bangar
Labu
Bukit Patoi (310m)
Peradayan Forest Reserve
Kampong Sembiling
Batang Duri
Ulu Temburong National Park
Bukit Pagon (1843m)
Long Semado
Lawas
Merapok
AH150
Gunung Mulu National Park
Mulu (2376m)
Ladan Hills
Tutong
Lamunin
Tasek Merimbun Heritage Park
Taman Rekreasi Sungai Basong
Tutong
Pantai Seri Kenangan
Kampong Sungai Mau
Kampong Sukang
Kampong Melilas
Belait
Luagan Lalak Recreation Park
Labi
Teraja
Bukit Teraja (417m)
Sungai Liang Forest Reserve
Lumut
Seria
Kuala Balai
Kuala Belait
Marudi
Kuala Baram
Baram
Lutong
Miri
Lambir Hills National Park
KAMPONG AYER
Omar Ali Saifudien
Jln Pemancha

Bandar Seri
Begawan

Bandar Seri Begawan, more commonly referred to simply as Bandar ('city' in Malay), is the capital of Brunei and the only place of any real size. Even so, Bandar's urban population is barely 50,000, and with most people living in the suburbs or among the stilted homes of the water village, downtown Bandar feels extraordinarily sleepy. This is no bad thing for the visitor; traffic and crowds are restricted to the suburbs, where most of the shops are located, leaving the centre in relative peace and quiet. The streets are clean and spacious, and the only persistent noise is the whirr of outboards, as water taxis (*tambang*) ferry people to and from the water village.

Bandar sits on a bend of the Sungai Brunei, with the stilted homes of Kampong Ayer (water village) reaching out across the river from the opposite bank. Back on dry land, the dominant feature is the impressive Omar Ali Saifuddien Mosque – though the primary point of reference nowadays seems to be the Yayasan Complex, a smart shopping mall whose two wings are aligned to provide a colonnaded vista of both the mosque and the river.

Essential Bandar Seri Begawan

Finding your feet

Brunei International Airport is 11 km south of Bandar Seri Begawan. There are regular buses from the airport to the bus station on Jalan Cator, in downtown BSB (0630-1800, B$2). Buses running this route include Nos 23, 26, and 38. Buses from Sarawak and other parts of Brunei also arrive here. A taxi from the airport costs about B$25, or B$30 after 1800. See Transport, page 160.

Getting around

Boat

Downtown BSB is tiny and easy to negotiate on foot. *Tambang* (water taxis) are the major form of public transport, with hundreds flying back and forth across the river, ferrying people to and from their stilted homes in Kampong Ayer. A short hop should cost around B$1, while a 45-minute tour of the water village will cost about B$20 (less if you barter hard).

Boats arriving from Sabah and Sarawak arrive at the Serasa Ferry Terminal in Muara, 20 km northeast of Bandar. Bus No 33 runs to the main bus station on Jalan Cator in the centre of BSB (30-45 minutes, B$2; taxi B$40).

Bus

The Brunei Museum, the Malay Technology Museum and the suburb of Gadong are all accessible on Central Line buses (daily 0630-1800), which pass through the main bus station on Jalan Cator.

Taxi

In theory, metered taxis operate in BSB and its suburbs: B$3 for the first kilometre (B$4.50 2100-0600) and B$1 for every subsequent kilometre. Often the driver will negotiate a fare rather than switch on the metre. Sample fares from downtown include B$15 to Gadong, B$35 to the Empire Hotel and B$40 to the Serasa Ferry Terminal in Muara. However, getting a cab isn't always easy as there is no centralized booking agency and they often zoom past when one tries to flag one down. Fares increase by 50% after 2200. For taxi companies, see Transport, page 160.

When to go

There are no real seasons to speak of as Bandar is consistently warm and receives plenty of rain year-round. On average, March is the driest month and October to December tend to be the wettest. The sultan's birthday is celebrated on 15 July with fireworks, processions and parades. See also www.bruneitourism.travel/events.

Weather Bandar Seri Begawan

January	February	March	April	May	June
31°C 24°C 207mm	31°C 24°C 128mm	32°C 24°C 127mm	32°C 24°C 211mm	33°C 24°C 234mm	32°C 24°C 193mm

July	August	September	October	November	December
32°C 24°C 192mm	33°C 24°C 223mm	32°C 24°C 240mm	32°C 24°C 297mm	31°C 24°C 243mm	31°C 24°C 259mm

take an exhilarating boat ride to the water village and soak up the city's laid-back charm

The main entry point to Bandar is via Jalan Tutong, which crosses the Sungai Kedayan tributary at Edinburgh Bridge, providing the first views of Kampong Ayer and the golden dome of the mosque. The road becomes Jalan Sultan, which cuts past a handful of museums and a small grid of shophouses, before hitting the waterfront. The city centre is bordered to the west by Sungai Kedayan, and, barely 500 m to the east, by the narrow Sungai Kianggeh tributary. Along its banks is the Tamu Kianggeh, an open-air market.

A number of the city's more interesting sights are located along the picturesque road which follows the course of the river east out of town. Jalan Residency runs past the Arts and Handicrafts Centre and the old British Residency itself, before becoming Jalan Kota Batu and bypassing the tombs of two sultans, the Brunei Museum and the Malay Technology Museum.

The suburbs of Kampong Kiarong and Gadong lie several kilometres to the northwest of the city centre. The former is a residential quarter, home to the enormous Kiarong Mosque, while Gadong is the main commercial centre, full of department stores and restaurants, and home, too, to an excellent *pasar malam* (night market). North of town, near the airport, are the government offices and the impressive but ghostly quiet National Stadium.

★ Kampong Ayer

When people think of Bandar Seri Begawan, they think of Kampong Ayer, the stretch of stilted homes extending over 3 km along the banks of Sungai Brunei. Officially, Kampong Ayer isn't part of the Bandar municipality; a reflection, perhaps, of the government's long-term aim to rehouse the villagers on dry land. It is merely a suburb. Not long ago, however, Kampong Ayer was all there was of Bandar; it was the British who began to develop the town on land, starting with construction of the Residency in 1906 (see Bubongan Dua Belas, page 152).

With its wonky walkways and ramshackle appearance, Kampong Ayer may look like a bit of a slum. Adventurer James Brooke got this false impression when he visited Brunei in the 1840s; he described Kampong Ayer as a "Venice of hovels, fit only for frogs". Antonio Pigafetta, the diarist on board the Magellan voyage of 1521, saw the village from a different perspective, describing it as the "Venice of the East".

The truth is that the architecture of Kampong Ayer is perfectly suited to the tropical environment, making use of local materials and allowing for excellent ventilation. The oldest houses stand on mangrove and ironwood posts, with walls of woven nipa palm. The modern buildings stand on reinforced concrete piles, which allow for double-storey structures to be built. Many of the houses are painted in a profusion of colours, with pot plants and bougainvillea spilling from covered verandas. It may look primitive, but take a closer look and you notice the trappings of wealth: all houses have electricity and a piped water supply; and many have satellite dishes and internet.

Records of Kampong Ayer go back 14 centuries. In its 16th-century heyday,

> **Tip...**
> Be extra careful when boarding a *tambang* at low tide as the steps can be very slippery. If you don't want to take a tour, hop on a *tambang* and ask to be dropped off somewhere in the water village (B$1-2). It's perfectly acceptable to have a walk around, though make sure you hold on tight to the rails of those rickety boardwalks and bridges.

the 'village' had a population of 100,000 and was the centre of an empire stretching across most of Borneo, Mindanao and the Sulu archipelago. Though it still claims to be the world's largest water village, today's population is a mere 39,000. The village is separated into 42 different units that can be considered as separate villages, each governed by a *tua kampong*

Bandar Seri Begawan

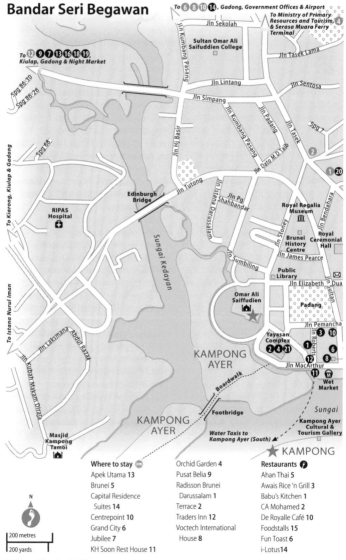

Where to stay
Apek Utama 13
Brunei 5
Capital Residence
  Suites 14
Centrepoint 10
Grand City 6
Jubilee 7
KH Soon Rest House 11

Orchid Garden 4
Pusat Belia 9
Radisson Brunei
  Darussalam 1
Terrace 2
Traders Inn 12
Voctech International
  House 8

Restaurants
Ahan Thai 5
Awais Rice 'n Grill 3
Babu's Kitchen 1
CA Mohamed 2
De Royalle Café 10
Foodstalls 15
Fun Toast 6
i-Lotus 14

(headman). These units are grouped into *mukims* (wards). The villages are connected by over 29,000 m of footbridges and over 36 km of boardwalks with the entire kampong containing more than 4200 buildings. The community is totally self-sufficient, with mosques, shops, schools, clinics and the odd karaoke lounge, even fire stations and floating petrol stations.

The future of Kampong Ayer looks somewhat uncertain. Many villagers have taken up the government's offer of free plots of land and subsidized housing and have moved on land. Meanwhile, the traditional cottage industries associated with each of the village units are giving way to new professions (today's young Bruneians aspire to become lawyers or computer programmers rather than blacksmiths or boat builders). Still, there are plenty of artisans left, and some will open their doors to passing visitors.

Visiting Kampong Ayer A good place to start is the **Kampong Ayer Cultural and Tourism Gallery** ① *south bank of the Sungei Brunei, Sat-Thu 0900-1130 and 1430-1700*. The gallery provides exhibits on the village's culture, community, history and crafts and has a viewing tower with sweeping views over the rooftops of the kampong.

To get to Kampong Ayer, jump aboard any of the water taxis (*tambang*) which race back and forth across the river. The main pick-up point is just south of the Yayasan Complex. The boatmen will compete raucously for your attention, then haggle with you over a price. The going rate is about B$20 for a very worthwhile one-hour tour. Most boatmen are happy to pass by the Istana (the best views are from the river); you may want to combine the tour with a trip downriver to spot proboscis monkeys, for an additional B$10 (see box, page 163).

It is also possible to access part of the water village by foot: set off along the boardwalk that runs along west from the Yayasan Complex and you soon come to a bridge across the Sungai Kedayan tributary. From here there are good views across the maze of stilted homes as far as the copper-domed Masjid Kampong Tamoi, an elegant mosque built on the water's edge.

Map labels:
Tasek Recreational Park
Lim Ah Siaw Pork Market 17
Jln Terala
Jln Berita
Jln Kampong Barangan
Spg 39
Spg 67
Spg 11
Sungai Kianggeh
14
9
Jln Kampong Kianggeh
7 5
Tamu Kianggeh
Bukit Subok Recreational Park
11
5
Jln Cator
US Embassy
Sungai Kianggeh
15
Jln Residency
Brunei
Temburong Jetty
Arts & Handicraft Centre
To ⑧ Bubongan Dua Belas, Brunei Museum & Malay Technology Museum

AYER

Kaizan Sushi **11**	Saffron **13**
Le Taj **16**	Seri Indah **8**
Lee Loi Fatt Foodstall **7**	Tasek Brasserie **20**
Lim Ah Siaw **17**	Zaika **21**
Piccolo Café **12**	
Pondok Sari Wangi **18**	
Pureland Vegetarian **9**	
Ricebowl **19**	
RMS Portview Seafood **4**	

★ Omar Ali Saifuddien Mosque

Jln McArthur. The compound is open daily 0830-2030; visiting hours for non-Muslims: Sat-Wed 0800-1730 (except prayer times); visitors must leave shoes outside and dress conservatively. Sometimes the lift that runs to the top of the 44-m minaret is in operation.

This mosque, built by and named after the 28th sultan (1950-1967), has become the symbol of Brunei, the nation's definitive monument. It is certainly one of Asia's finest-looking mosques, elegant and somehow modest, despite its great golden dome, its setting beside an artificial lake and its nightly illumination in unearthly green light.

Built in 1958 in classical Islamic style, the architecture is not overstated, although along with the sultan's hugely extravagant palace, the mosque was one of the first obvious signs of Brunei's oil wealth. When flakes of gold began falling from the central dome, due to contraction and expansion in the searing heat, the mosque quickly became something of a wonder to the villagers of Kampong Ayer (whose boardwalks run tight up to the edge of the mosque). Novelist Anthony Burgess' arrival as a teacher in Brunei coincided with the ceremonial opening of the mosque, and in his autobiography he recounts how this falling gold was "taken by the fisherfolk to be a gift from Allah".

The materials used to build and furnish the mosque came from right across the globe: carpets from Belgium and Arabia; chandeliers and stained glass from England; marble from Italy; granite from Shanghai; and, topping the central onion dome, a mosaic of more than three million pieces of gold-leafed Venetian glass. In the middle of the lake, which envelops the mosque on three sides, is a replica of a 16th-century *mahligai* (royal barge), used on special occasions and for Koran recital competitions.

Brunei Museum

About 4.5 km east of downtown Bandar along Jln Kota Batu, T224 4545, Sat-Thu 0900-1700, Fri 0900-1130 and 1430-1700, free. To get there, bus No 39 runs every 30 mins from the main bus terminal on Jln Cantor (or wait at the stop opposite the Arts and Handicraft Centre, see below).

Brunei's national museum holds a mixed bag of galleries, although it's certainly worth a visit. If you have limited time, head straight for the **Islamic Gallery**, an outstanding collection of artwork and artefacts from the sultan's personal collection. In pride of place on a marble pedestal in the centre of the gallery is a page of ornate calligraphy written by the sultan himself, in which he encourages his subjects to memorize the Koran. Around the pedestal, in Galleries 1 and 2, are the real McCoy: Korans and beautifully preserved pieces of calligraphy dating from as early as the ninth century. Across one wall is a talismanic banner from 18th-century India, on which the whole Koran is transcribed in tiny script. Further rooms hold collections of pottery and ceramics from the Islamic world; gold and silver jewellery and coins dating back to AD 661; delicate perfume bottles alongside a collection of Indian and Ottoman sabres; and several oddities, such as a decorative wooden boot with compass, inlaid with mother-of-pearl.

Also on the ground floor is the mediocre **Natural History Gallery** – full of awkward-looking stuffed animals, birds and insects – and the obligatory **Petroleum Gallery**, which charts the discovery and extraction methods of Brunei's black gold. Upstairs, in Gallery 4, is the **Traditional Culture Gallery**, with examples of *keris* (ceremonial daggers), *bedok* (call-to-prayer drums), *gasing* (spinning tops), traditional dress, hand-crafted kites and board games such as *congkak* and *pasang*. Traditional customs are explained, too (after birth, a date is placed on the tongue of a newborn and the placenta is either hung from

BACKGROUND
Bandar Seri Begawan

Bandar Seri Begawan's history can be traced back as far as the seventh century, by which time a water village was already well established on the banks of the Sungai Brunei. The original site of the village was Kota Batu, several kilometres to the east of today's capital (close to the Brunei Museum). Brunei's history is bound closely to the development of Kampong Ayer, which moved to its present-day location sometime before the 15th century.

By the time Portuguese explorer Ferdinand Magellan passed by on his round-the-world voyage in 1521, Kampong Ayer had developed from a small trading base and fishing settlement into a powerful entrepôt. The Spanish crew were astounded to find a sprawling water village of some 100,000 people – much larger than today's capital – complete with the trappings of great wealth. The settlement flourished as a collecting point for much-coveted jungle products such as sandalwood, beeswax, birds' nests, turtle shells, sago and camphor. Along with the trade in commodities came the blending of cultures and ideologies, with Islam first establishing a foothold in the late 14th century. Kampong Ayer went on to become the centre of a small empire whose sphere of influence extended across much of Borneo and the Philippines.

Bandar Seri Begawan – known as Brunei Town until 1970 – only established itself as a land-based settlement under the influence of the British. It was in 1904 that Stewart McArthur, the first British Resident, encouraged inhabitants to move onto reclaimed land beside the water village. One of the first buildings to appear was the British Residency, set in the wooden building known now as Bubongan Dua Belas (see page 152). The sultan himself followed in 1909, moving the *istana* (palace) onto land for the first time in 500 years.

It was not until the discovery of oil in 1929 that Brunei Town really began to develop, with the first grid of shophouses appearing and a new set of government buildings. The capital's modern landmarks – the Omar Ali Saifuddien Mosque and the Istana Nurul Iman – were built in the 1950s, after exports of oil and natural gas had begun to take off. But the capital never expanded beyond the dimensions of a small town. In 2007, Sultan Bolkiah gave permission for an expansion of the city from 4.97 square miles to 38.75 square miles indicating that ambitious development plans are afoot.

The centre of Bandar has remained a quiet, almost sleepy, place with development limited mainly to the suburbs. Kampong Ayer, meanwhile, is gradually dwindling in size, thanks to government initiatives to encourage its inhabitants to move inland. The water village, it seems, doesn't fit with the sultan's progressive vision of a modern Brunei. However, in 2013, Sultan Bolkiah made concessions to those Bruneians who wished to stay in the water village yet have a better standard of living by decreeing that two-storey concrete stilt houses were to be built in the centre of Kampong Ayer.

a tree, buried or floated downriver). Next door, the **Archaeology and History Gallery** (Gallery 5) provides a thorough introduction to the history of the region from neolithic times. Gallery 6 is for temporary exhibitions.

Malay Technology Museum
Behind the Brunei Museum, Sun-Thu 0900-1700, Fri 0900-1130 and 1430-1700, Sat 0945-1700.

A staircase leads down the hill from the back of the Brunei Museum to the Malay Technology Museum, where a series of dioramas explain the development of fishing techniques, boatmaking, stilt house construction, metalwork and *songkok* (hats worn by Muslim men) weaving. The top floor of the museum includes examples of indigenous dwellings (from the Murut, Kedayan and Dusun tribes of the interior), along with tools such as blowpipes and fishing traps.

Along the road, between the museum and the centre of town, look out for the tombs of two of Brunei's greatest sultans. **Sultan Syarif Ali** (1426-1432) was the founder of Islamic rule in Brunei, while **Sultan Bolkiah** (1485-1524) presided over the 'golden age' of Brunei, conquering Sulu and the Philippines.

Bubongan Dua Belas
Jln Residency, 1 km east of the town centre, T224 4545, Mon-Thu 0900-1630, Fri 1430-1630, Sat 0900-1130, free.

Bubongan Dua Belas, which means Twelve Roofs, served as the British Residency until Brunei's Independence in 1984. It was built on the side of a hill overlooking Kampong Ayer in 1906 and is one of Brunei's oldest surviving buildings, with traditional wood shingle roofing and hardwood floors. The building now hosts a small **Relationship Exhibition**, celebrating the ties between Brunei and the UK. There are charts and maps of the Kampong Ayer area dating from the time of the first British contact in 1764. There is also a fascinating report on Brunei, penned by Acting Consul Stewart McArthur, which led to the appointment of the first British Resident in 1904. He describes the "strange and picturesque" ceremony of the *mengalei padi* harvest festival: "Everyone was feasting and I regret to say that, when I left, nearly everyone was overcome by *borak*, an extremely nauseous drink made locally from *padi* and of which I was forced to partake."

Arts and Handicraft Centre
Jln Residency, T224 0676, daily 0800-1700, free.

The Arts and Handicraft Centre was established as a means of preserving traditional skills, such as weaving, brass casting and *keris* making. The centre is focused more on workshops for young Bruneians than attracting tourists, though there is a handicraft shop selling hand-crafted jewellery, basketry, *keris* (ceremonial daggers), *songket* (traditional fabric woven with gold thread), *songkok* (hats worn by Muslim men) and other gifts.

Round the other side of the handicraft centre, past one of the most enormous strangler figs you're ever likely to see, is the **Ratna Dina Arif Gallery** ① *T866 6934, Mon 1400-1600, Tue, Thu, Sat 1000-1630, Fri, Sun 1000-1700*, with exhibits by local artists.

Royal Regalia Museum
Jln Sultan, T223 8358, Sun-Thu 0900-1700, Fri 0900-1130, 1430-1700, Sat 0945-1700, free (shoes have to be removed before entering).

Dedicated almost exclusively to the present sultan's life, this is (predictably) the flashiest of all Brunei's museums, set in an extravagant domed building in the centre of town. Bring an extra top – the main galleries are air conditioned to fridge temperatures – and try not to take too much notice of the guards, who are armed to the hilt (literally), each with truncheon, dagger and gun.

The museum's opening in 1992 coincided with the sultan's Silver Jubilee celebrations, and many of the exhibits relate to this event. The Royal Chariot – an enormous gold-winged thing that looks like a movie prop – is the largest exhibit, while the strangest is probably the creepy golden hand and forearm, used to support the chin of the sultan during the coronation. There are hundreds of photos, too, and a mass of ceremonial costumes, armoury and other regalia items. The **Constitutional Gallery** charts Brunei's recent history.

Next door is the **Brunei History Centre** ⓘ *Sat-Thu 0745-1215 and 1330-1630, free*, which serves as a centre of research for documenting the history and genealogy of the royal family. The centre is open to the public, but there's not much to see.

The enormous building across the road is the **Lapau Di Raja (Royal Ceremonial Hall)**, site of the 1968 coronation ceremony. The hall is closed to the public.

Parks and green spaces

For the best vantage points above Bandar and Kampong Ayer, head for the **Bukit Subok Recreational Park**, which rises steeply off Jalan Residency. The entrance to the park is just before Bubongan Dua Belas (the old Residency building). A boardwalk loops through the forest between a series of viewing towers. The going is steep, so avoid visiting during the middle part of the day.

The **Tasek Lama Recreational Park** is a more sedate option, with a picnic area, a small waterfall and a reservoir. It is situated about 1 km north of the centre. To get there, head north along Jalan Tasek Lama and turn right opposite the Sultan Omar Ali Saifuddien College. From the park gates, it's another 500 m or so to the waterfall.

Bandar's suburbs

bustling night markets and stunning mosques

The increasingly busy suburbs of Bandar lie a few kilometres to the northwest of the centre, across Edinburgh Bridge. Gadong is the commercial centre and primary suburb of Bandar Seri Begawan. It's not pretty on the eyes in the way that Bandar is (Gadong is a traffic-clogged grid of modern shophouses and department stores), but this is the modern-day heart and soul of the capital. It is where Bruneians come to shop and to eat, either in local restaurants and international franchises or at the foodstalls of the excellent *pasar malam* (night market), which serves up (mainly) Malay food seven days a week. Kiulap, a little closer to the city centre, is really an extension of Gadong, with more shops and offices. These two places act as a foil to the strangely quiet city centre and offer a refreshing glimpse into modern Brunei.

Just south of Kiulap is **Kampong Kiarong**, home to the stunning Masjid Jame'Asr Hassanil Bolkiah also known as **Kiarong Mosque** ⓘ *Sat-Wed 0800-1200, 1400-1500, 1700-1800, shoes must be removed before entering; sometimes closed to the public on Sat*. The mosque was built in 1992 to commemorate the sultan's Silver Jubilee. Though it supplanted Masjid Omar Ali Saifuddien (see page 150) as Brunei's national mosque, there seem to be mixed opinions as to which is superior. The older mosque conforms more to classical convention and forms the focal point of Bandar itself. The Kiarong Mosque, meanwhile, is bigger and brasher, set in landscaped gardens and immense in size, with a quartet of intricate minarets and 29 gilded cupolas. Around 5 km north of the city centre are the government offices, scattered widely around a leafy grid of streets near Brunei International Airport.

Tourist information

Brunei Tourism
Has a branch in the Arrivals area of the airport, and at the Ministry of Primary Resources and Tourism (see below), www.bruneitourism.travel.
This government-run tourist office offers the useful *Explore Brunei* visitor guide with a detailed map of the local bus routes.

Kampong Ayer Cultural and Tourism Gallery
South bank, Kampong Ayer (see page 147). Mon-Thu and Sat 0900-1215, 1330-1630, Fri 1130-1400.
Information about Brunei and free maps.

Ministry of Primary Resources and Tourism
Out of town on Jln Menteri Besar, T238 2822, www.mprt.gov.bn.
The place to obtain permits for visiting Ulu Temburong National Park.

Where to stay

Large discounts are often available if you book in advance through hotel websites.

$$$ The Brunei Hotel
95 Jln Pemancha, T224 4828, www.thebruneihotel.com.
In the heart of town, this recently upgraded hotel has got it right with its warm and friendly atmosphere. There are 65 comfortable modern rooms with cable TV and fast internet, and a good café, **Choices**, which is popular with workers in the nearby banks and offices. Free airport pick-up.

$$$ The Capital Residence Suites
Simpang 2, Lot 20127, T222 0067, www.capitalresidencesuites.com.
Smart, elegant rooms with excellent service and lots of friendly, useful advice offered to first time visitors to BSB. This hotel is short walk from the sights in the town centre and has free pick-up/drop-off to the airport and the port at Muara. Room sizes vary so ask to see a few. Excellent value.

$$$ Jubilee
Down a side road, 10 mins' walk from the waterfront, Jubilee Plaza, Jln Kampong Kiangngeh, T222 8070, www.jubileehotel brunei.com.
Popular with business people on a budget, this place has spacious carpeted rooms with cable TV, internet access and large bathroom. More expensive rooms have a kitchenette and lounge area. Airport transfers are included in the rate. They also offer one complimentary return trip to a host of destinations in BSB. Good promotional rates offered.

$$$ Radisson Brunei Darussalam
Jln Tasek Lama, T622 4272, www.radisson.com.
The city's best business hotel with over 140 spacious, bright and comfortable modern rooms with cable TV and fast internet access throughout. Rooms at the back face lush greenery. There are 2 notable restaurants, a pool and a fitness centre. Staff can provide a good map for walkers/joggers with routes as far as Tasek Waterfall. The entire hotel has been spruced up recently and is looking fresh and inviting. It's a pleasant 10-min walk from the hotel to downtown, though a free shuttle bus service is offered.

$$ Terrace
Jln Tasek Lama, T224 3554, www.terracebrunei.com.
There is plenty of retro charm at this solidly 1980s hotel which has a lift with chunky buttons, dark corridors and rooms that are well past their prime. All rooms have fridge and cable TV and are fair value. There's a small pool, fitness centre with ancient machines and internet access in the lobby. Though the hotel is old, it's not without charm and staff are friendly.

$ APEK Utama Hotel

Simpang 2, Kampong Pintu Malim, Jln Kota Batu, T872 1222, www.apekutamahotel.com.
Though this place is a *tad ulu* (far from anything), its homely vibes, fast Wi-Fi and intensely patterned bed sheets are guaranteed to provide a comfortable stay. Staff are friendly and recommend hopping on a water taxi to get into town; the 5-min journey is exciting and mitigates the Brunei 'bus waiting' game. A fair budget option.

$ KH Soon Rest House

140 Jln Pemancha, T222 2052, www.khsoon-resthouse.tripod.com.
BSB's most renowned backpacker haunt. This sprawling hostel, slap bang in the middle of the city centre, has large somewhat dirty rooms slap bang in the middle of the city centre. All rooms have a/c and more expensive ones have attached bathroom (with broken toilets, electricity sockets next to the shower, etc). The friendly staff can arrange tours and can offer good local information. As a rule of thumb for budget travellers, use this place as an option if you can't get a room at the **Pusat Belia** and **APEK Utama**, which are both significantly more wholesome and better value.

$ Pusat Belia

Jln Sungai Kianggeh, T222 2900, jbsbelia@brunet.bn.
Possibly the best budget place in the country with spotless 4- and 10-bed dorms and friendly staff. It's not a busy place and the chances are that you'll get an entire room to yourself. There is also one room available for married couples, with a double bed. Pool (B$1) and internet café. On the down side, staff have a tendency to disappear for long periods which is profoundly frustrating when attempting to check in or out. Also, there's no Wi-Fi. The hostel also closes for long breaks throughout the year, so whilst it's a good budget option, it's not the most reliable. For those who want to explore the country in depth, it's worth enquiring to see if staff will arrange stays in Brunei's other youth hostels in Temburong and Tutong.

Bandar's suburbs

$$$$ The Centrepoint

Abdul Razak Complex, Gadong BE3519, T243 0430, www.thecentrepointhotel.com.
A large, opulent hotel with plenty of marble and Malay-style Islamic touches. There are 216 rooms, from the comfortable and spacious 'deluxe' to the gargantuan 'presidential suite' (a whopping B$1700 a night). There are a number of restaurants, a pool, gym, squash and tennis courts and a ballroom. Good location next to a shopping mall, though a bit of a trek from all the major tourist sights. Significant discounts available through online hotel agencies.

$$$ Grand City

Lot 25115, Block G, Kampong Pengkalan Gadong, BE3719, T245 2188, grandcity@ brunei.net.
A fair mid-range option, popular with people on stopovers. It's okay providing you don't mind staying out of town (in Gadong suburb). Rooms are comfortable and have a/c, TV and tea and coffee facilities though are a bit starved of light. The price includes airport transfer and breakfast. There's a handy shuttle bus service to the nearby commercial areas. Free Wi-Fi in the lobby.

$$$ Orchid Garden

Lot 31954, Simpang 9, Kampong Anggerek Desa, Jln Berakas, T233 5544, www. orchidgardenbrunei.com.
Slightly dated 4-star hotel next to the National Stadium (between the airport and the government complex), a few kilometres from Bandar centre. Spacious and comfortable rooms with internet access, cable TV and bathroom with bathtub. There are a couple of good places to eat here including **Vanda** Chinese restaurant. Also has a pool, gym and spa. This is the closest hotel to the airport, so is handy for stopovers. Free shuttle bus into town.

$$ Traders Inn
Block D, Lot 11620, Jln Gadong, T244 28228, www.tradersinn-bn.com.
Excellent value hotel with 84 clean, comfortable a/c rooms with TV, attached bathroom and Wi-Fi. Though it's within easy walking distance of eateries and shops in Gadong, it is a little far out for those who need to be in the city centre.

$$ Voctech International House
Jln Pasar Baharu, Gadong BE1318, T244 7992, www.voctech.org.bn.
Owned by SEAMEO (Southeast Asian Ministers of Education Organisation), this place has 26 rooms used by visiting international guests. It is close to the eateries of Gadong and its renowned *pasar malam*. Rooms are simple and clean and have private balcony, a/c attached bathroom and TV. There is also an airport shuttle service. Recommended.

Restaurants

★ The *pasar malam* (night market) in the suburb of **Gadong** is probably the best place to sample local fare. Every evening from about 1700, hundreds of stalls turn out seemingly endless varieties of satay, curries, grilled meats and Malay coconut-based sweets. The same sort of food is available on a smaller scale at the **Tamu Kianggeh** (open-air market) in downtown Bandar.

Also worth trying are the foodstalls on the waterfront near the Temburong jetty for *nasi campur* and *teh tarik*. The **Padian Foodcourt** (1st floor, Yayasan Complex, daily 0900-2200) is great for cheap local food and drink, as well as Thai and Indonesian staples. There is a good food court on the 3rd floor of Wisma Setia, Jln Pemancha with lashings of good-value Thai food. There are also larger food courts in **Gadong**, including one on the top floor of The Mall, which serves the full range of Asian cuisines: try Malay *nasi lemak* and beef *rendang*.
You'll find yourself drinking vast amounts of fruit juice in Brunei (it's served in place of alcohol). However, if you have brought in your allowance of alcohol (and declared it at customs), top-end restaurants will often allow you to drink it with your meal.
Restaurants come and go with great frequency in Bandar Seri Begawan. A selection of the current favourites is listed below.

$$$ Kaizen Sushi
Waterfront, T222 6336.
With fantastic views across the river to Kampong Ayer, this place offers gorgeous Japanese fare with top service. The restaurant is one of the top choices for lunch and dinner in the downtown area. If you don't want to wait, it's best to make a reservation.

$$$ Tasek Brasserie
Radisson Brunei Darussalam hotel (see Where to stay), T224 4272. Open 0630-2400.
The ideal spot to indulge in a waistline expanding buffet extravaganza. The spit roast lamb buffet on Fri and Sat evenings is recommended. The menu also has a variety of safe Western and Asian bets for those in need of some creature comforts.

$$$ Zaika
G24, Block C, Yayasan Complex, T223 0817. Daily 1130-1430 and 1800-2000.
Excellent North Indian cuisine in pleasing wood-panelled surroundings (*zaika* means fine dining in Urdu). Try tandoori chicken or lamb (straight from an authentic oven) and Kashmiri *rogan josh*. Classical Indian lamps hang overhead, old Indian paintings adorn the walls, and gentle Indian music tinkles in the background. The menu is vast.

$$ Ahan Thai
Ground floor, Jubilee Plaza, Jln Kampong Kianggeh, T223 9599. Daily 1000-2345.
Friendly place with a huge menu of Thai dishes including good seafood and some tasty Thai salads. The juices here are enormous. There's a huge TV and Wi-Fi access. Excellent value for money.

$$ Awais Rice n' Grill
144A ground floor, BA2110, Jln Pemancha, T222 5397.

Don't be put off by the name – this Pakistani restaurant has fine grilled kebabs, freshly baked naans and a good selection of juices. The atmosphere isn't exactly classy but it's a good place for an honest meaty feed.

$$ Babu's Kitchen
Jln Roberts. Daily 0600-1800.
Spotless place doling out large plates of Chinese and Thai food to hungry office workers.

$$ De Royalle Café
38 Jln Sultan, T222 0257. 24 hrs.
This smart café offers simple Western meals, large filled baguettes and plenty of coffee and cakes. There's outdoor seating, newspapers to browse and Wi-Fi access. You can also buy bus tickets from here.

$$ Piccolo Café
Lot 11, Jln MacArthur, T224 1558.
Pleasant little café with quality coffee and teas, and tasty cakes and sandwiches. There's mellow background music, and a selection of magazines to browse. Very contemporary for BSB and a good escape from the afternoon heat.

$$ RMS Portview Seafood
1st floor, Yayasan Complex, T223 1466. Daily 1000-2300.
Popular place that pulls in the punters with its variety of Thai, Japanese and Chinese dishes. A cheery and good-value dining option, popular with families. Excellent steamboats.

$ CA Mohamed
Unit 202, Yayasan Complex, T223 2999. Daily 0700-2100.
Speak to any local about their top city dining choice and this one invariably crops up. There's a solid selection of *mamak* (Indian Muslim) dishes such as *mee mamak* and *murtabak* – not good for the heart, but delightful for the belly.

$ Fun Toast
Jln Sultan. Daily 0600-0700.
A smart bakery with excellent set breakfasts with chunky toast. There is also a daily set lunch. It's a good place to fill up before heading out on a trip.

$ Seri Indah
Opposite the waterfront wet market, Jln MacArthur, T224 3567.
A simple *mamak* (Indian Muslim) restaurant serving delicious *roti kosong* and *teh tarik*.

Bandar's suburbs

$$$ Saffron
Unit 8, ground floor, Seri Kiulap Complex, T223 5888. Open 0830-2300.
Take your wallet out for a thrashing at this place, which has a selection of heady flavours covering the east from the souqs of Lebanon to the humid climes of the Malay archipelago. They have recently started offering some fine desserts, including delicious chocolate eclairs. It's a very popular choice.

$$ i-Lotus
Simpang 12-26, off Jln Tungku Link, T242 2466.
Top-notch Chinese cuisine served in a relaxing environment. Though the menu is dominated by Chinese dishes, there are a few with a distinct nod to Thai fare and even a couple of sultry equatorial additions, such as coconut prawns and tapioca cake. The pumpkin soup, served in a hollowed out pumpkin, is a good conversation piece. Jump in a cab to get here.

$$ Lee Loi Fatt Foodstall
4 Bgn Haji Abdul Rahman, Kiulap, T223 6432. Open 1000-1800.
Famed for its *laksa* and delicious *cucur udang* (fried prawns with battered yam served with peanut sauce) this place offers some intriguing Malay/Chinese fusion flavours.

$$ Le Taj
Seri Kiulap Complex, 2d Floor, Jln Kiulap.
North Indian food with the noticeable influence of a British curry house, with thick rich sauces, fluffy naans and light biryani. The lamb masala is this place's standout dish.

$$ Lim Ah Siew
Bekas Bangunan Pasar Babi, Jln Teraja, T222 3963.
If you thought you time in Brunei would be a pigless experience, think again. This

unassuming eatery offers all manner of porky cuts, though the winning dishes must be the dim sum, which change daily.

$$ Pondok Sari Wangi
Unit 12-13, Abdul Razak Complex, Gadong, T244 5045. Daily 1000-2200.
Excellent spot for authentic Indonesian cuisine, including delicious *ikan pannggang, ayam penyet,* and well-known Javanese dishes such as *nasi timbel.* Seafood enthusiasts will enjoy the selection of cooked softshell crabs.

$ Pureland Vegetarian
Unit 15, Bangunan Awang Ahmand bin Haji Hassan, Kiulap. Mon-Sat 0800-1400 and 1730-2100.
Operating on a pay-what-you-want idea, customers can choose from a buffet of over 30 Chinese vegetarian dishes, drinks, soups and desserts. There is no cashier, only a donation box that diners put in what they feel the meal was worth. The food is tasty, healthy and the atmosphere highly convivial.

$ Ricebowl Restaurant,
72 Jln Batu Bersurat, T863 0665. Daily 0800-1800.
A popular place, perfect for a good economical breakfast or lunch. The truly ravenous will appreciate the restaurant's '3 egg combo', for breakfast, though there are also other intriguing options such as 'volcano mash' to keep one's calorie intake towards the roof. Asian rice and noodle dishes in cheery surrounds.

Festivals

Check www.bruneitourism.travel/events for a detailed overview of Brunei's major events.

Jan-Feb Chinese New Year. A 2-week celebration beginning with a family reunion dinner on New Year's Eve.
23 Feb National Day Celebrations. Celebration of Independence at the Hassanal Bolkiah National Stadium.
1 Jun Royal Brunei Armed Forces Day. Celebrates the creation of the Royal Brunei Armed Forces, with military parades.

Jun (changeable) Ramadan. The holy month, when Muslims abstain from eating and drinking between dawn and dusk. During fasting hours it is considered ill-mannered to eat, drink or smoke openly in public. The end of Ramadan is marked by the **Hari Raya Puasa** celebration, when families gather for a feast.
15 Jul The Sultan's Birthday. One of the biggest events in the national calendar and the only time when the grounds of the Istana Nural Iman are open to the public. Royal address and an investiture ceremony.
Dec (changeable) The Prophet's Birthday. As well as religious functions, there's a procession through the streets of Bandar Seri Begawan.

Entertainment

Brunei is a 'dry' country and Bandar Seri Begawan is virtually deserted in the evening, except for the suburb of Gadong with its lively *pasar malam.* This is open until late and is busy with Bruneians buying the local food on sale.

Obviously, there is no bar scene here; the closest you get are the mocktail lounges in the top hotels where you can listen to sedate local bands and twinkling pianos. The Jerudong Park Playground (see page 163) is about as lively as it gets when it comes to entertainment and even that is deadly quiet by Western standards.

Out of town, however, is a different story. Stumble across a remote longhouse, and you enter another world. Guests are entertained with gusto and will almost certainly be offered traditional rice wine (*tuak* in Iban), a drink so ingrained in indigenous heritage that the sultan has exempted it from the ban on alcohol. Certainly, in the towns of Brunei, entertainment is something that happens – if at all – behind closed doors.

Cinema
Citizens of Brunei take their cinema pretty seriously. To catch the latest blockbuster head to **Seri Qlap Cineplex** (Level 2, Seri

Q-Lap Mall, T223 2277, www.tsqbrunei.com), or **The Mall Cineplex** (3rd floor, The Mall, Gadong, T242 2455). Francophiles will enjoy a visit to the Cine Club at the **Alliance Francaise** (1A Simpang 68, Jln Batu Bersurat, T265 4245, every Thu at 2000).

Shopping

Brunei's main shopping district is centred on the suburb of Gadong, 4 km from the centre of Bandar Seri Begawan. The principal shopping malls here are **Gadong Centrepoint** and **The Mall**, both on the main thoroughfare.

In Bandar itself, shopping is focused on the elegant **Yayasan Complex**, which has everything from small boutiques and restaurants to a supermarket and an upmarket department store, **Hua Ho**.

Crafts

Traditional handicrafts include brassware, silverware, *keris* (ornate ceremonial daggers) and a type of *songket* known as *jong sarat* (a traditional cloth, hand woven with gold and silver thread). Bandar's **Arts and Handicraft Centre** (see page 152) sells all these, though the choice is limited. Each of the major shopping malls has one or 2 gift shops selling Southeast Asian crafts (again, prices are much higher than in Malaysia). The **Radisson** hotel has upmarket gift and antiques shops.

Occasionally there are handicrafts for sale at the **Tamu Kianggeh** in Bandar Seri Begawan, though this is predominantly a food market. **Kampong Ayer** is another place where it is possible to find crafts and antiques (at one time, the water village thrived as a centre for cottage industries, with silversmiths, brass casters, blacksmiths, boat builders and *songket* weavers). You won't find anything on your own; ask the boatmen.

Markets

See also Gadong night market, under Restaurants, above.

Rimba Horicultural Centre, *Rimba. Daily 0800-1800*. This is a popular spot for plant lovers, with a colourful array of indoor and outdoor plants and gardening equipment.

Tamu Kianggeh, *right in the heart of town, on the bank of the Kianggeh River*. This buzzing market sells handicrafts, medicinal herbs, cheap local fruit and vegetables and some interesting delicacies.

Weekend Market (24-hr), *Jln Sultan. Sat and Sun from 1800*. The whole street comes alive at weekends with stalls selling tasty food, clothes and accessories. It's a popular place for an evening stroll and a spot of people watching.

What to do

Jungle trekking

Jungle trekking is one of the main attractions for visitors. The best place is the **Ulu Temburong National Park** (see page 166), but there are plenty of other opportunities in each of Brunei's districts. The easiest (and often the cheapest) way of organizing a trip into the rainforest is through one of the Bandar-based tour operators (see below).

★ River trips

No trip to Brunei is complete without a *tambang* ride along the Brunei River (Sungai Brunei). These trips can combine tours of the water village with a water safari in search of proboscis monkeys. Any of the tour operators listed below can arrange a river trip and most operators guarantee sightings of proboscis monkeys. Once the location has been reached, the boatman will cut the engine and paddle quietly into the mangroves to allow for a close encounter with the monkeys. A 2-hr monkey-spotting trip starts at B$65 (minimum 2 people). It is cheaper to head to the river and hire a boatman to take you down river to spot the monkeys (B$30 for a 1½-hr trip). However, the boatmen won't guarantee a sighting.

Sailing

The Royal Brunei Yacht Club, *Serasa, T277 2011, www.royalbruneiyachtclub.com*. The yacht club offers sailing courses from their clubhouses in Serasa and Kota Batu. There are also kayaks and canoes for rent. Visitors who are members of other sailing clubs can use the facilities here if their club has a reciprocal relationship. The clubhouse in Kota Batu is a sociable spot to spend an evening and has a pool and restaurant, popular with expats.

Sports

There's a stunning 18-hole floodlit golf course, designed by Jack Nicklaus, at the **Empire Hotel & Country Club** (see page 164). The club also has facilities for tennis, squash, badminton, 10-pin bowling and snooker. The **Royal Brunei Golf Club** (T261 1582), though less exclusive than the Empire, is an excellent course and claimed by its designer, Ron Freams, to be the Augusta of Asia.

As far as leisure centres go, you won't beat the **Hassanal Bolkiah National Stadium** (close to the government offices, between the airport and the centre of Bandar Seri Begawan). Built to Olympic specifications, it has a track-and-field complex, tennis centre, squash courts and a pool. As you might imagine, you'll have the place to yourself. There are plenty of private sports clubs catering to the large expat population, but visitors are limited to hotel facilities.

Tour operators

Independent travel in Brunei is a little more complicated than it is in Malaysia. That's not to say that it is impossible – anyone can visit Ulu Temburong independently, for example, but it works out cheaper to go as part of an organized tour. Plus, it saves the hassle of applying for permits and organizing transport. Because Brunei is still in its infancy as a tourist destination, you're very unlikely to find yourself in a large tour group (more often than not, you'll have a guide to yourself; many of them are indigenous to the region and hugely knowledgeable). The major tour operators based in Bandar Seri Begawan are listed below. **Borneo Guide**, *Unit 204, 1st floor, Kiaw Lian Building 104, Jln Pemancha, BSB, T242 6923,*

www.borneoguide.com. Well-organized company offering city tours and good array of activities in Ulu Temburong.
Century Travel Centre, *1st floor, Darussalam Complex, Jln Sultan, BSB, T222 1747, www.centurytravelcentre.com.*
Freme Travel Services, *Wisma Jaya, Jln Pemancha, BSB, T333 5025, www.freme.com.*
Intrepid Tours, *Unit G4, 1st floor, Bangunan Sungai Akar Central Simpang 158, Jln Sungai Akar, T222 1685, www.bruneibay.net/ intrepidtours.* Specializes in adventure and wildlife trips to Selirong Island, Ulu Temburong and even to see the oilfields out at Seria.
Mas Sugara Travel Services, *1st floor, Complex Warisan, Mata Simpang 322, Jln Gadong, T242 3963, www.massugara.com.* A range of city and oilfield tours.
Pan Bright Travel Services, *Haji Ahmad Laksamana Building, 38-39 Jln Sultan, T224 0980, www.panbright.com.*
Sunshine Borneo Tours, *No 2, Simpang 146, Jln Kiarong, T244 6812, www.exploreborneo. com.* Well regarded for their birdwatching trips and firefly spotting cruises.

Water sports

Poni Divers, *Seri Qlap Mall, Unit L3/12, T223 3655, www.ponidivers.com.* Offers a variety of dive courses.

Transport

Air

Royal Brunei Airlines (RBA Plaza, Jln Sultan BS 8671, T222 5931, www.bruneiair.com) connects BSB with the following cities: **Bangkok** (Suvarnabhumi), **Denpasar** (Bali), **Dubai, Ho Chi Minh City, Hong Kong, Jakarta, Kota Kinabalu, Kuala Lumpur, London, Manila, Melbourne, Singapore, Shanghai** (Pudong) and **Surabaya**.

AirAsia and **MAS** (mezzanine floor, Bangunan Hj Ahmad Laksamana Othman, Lot 38-39, Jln Sultan, T22 41689) fly to **Kuala Lumpur**.

Silk Air and **Singapore Airlines** (5th floor Bangunan Hj Ahmad Laksamana Othman 38-39 Jln Sultan, T224 4902) fly to **Singapore**.

Boat

Boats, of course, are the main form of transport around **Kampong Ayer**. Small, speedy *tambang* depart from the jetty behind the **Yayasan Complex** from dawn until late at night. A short journey across to the water village should cost B$1 though expect to pay more for longer journeys.

Regular speedboats leave from the **Temburong Jetty** on Jln Residency in Bandar Seri Begawan to **Bangar**, the main town in Temburong District (hourly 0745-1630; B$15 return). Access upriver to the interior of Brunei is by indigenous longboat. Journeys need to be pre-arranged (best to speak to a tour operator, see above).

To Malaysia Boats leave from the **Serasa Ferry Terminal** (known as **Serasa Muara**), at Muara, 20 km northeast of Bandar, (Express bus No 33 runs from Jln Cator to Serasa Muara, 30-45 mins, B$2; taxi B$40). From Serasa Muara there are 6 daily boats to **Labuan** from 0730-1330 (B$15 plus a B$2 tax) with connecting departures to **Kota Kinabalu** (RM34). Travellers wishing to go all the way through to KK in one day are advised to catch an early boat from Serasa Muara to ensure they are able to get the 1300 ferry from Labuan to KK. Speedboats also depart from the main jetty to **Labuan**, **Lawas** and **Limbang**.

Bus

Buses serve Bandar Seri Begawan and the surrounding Brunei Muara district fairly regularly during daylight hours. There are 6 bus routes: the Eastern, Western, Northern, Southern, Central and Circle Lines, each of which run buses every 15-20 mins, 0630-1800. The handiest route is probably the **Central Line**, which links the main bus station in Bandar Seri Begawan (on Jln Cator) with **Gadong** and the Brunei Museum (B$1). Buses for **Muara** (B$3), **Tutong** (B$4), **Seria** (B$6) and **Kuala Belait** (B$7.50) leave less regularly from the **Jln Cator** bus station. **International** There are numerous international options from BSB.

To Indonesia There is a daily bus departing for **Pontianak** at 0900 (at least 24 hrs, B$90). Enquire at the bus station on Jln Cator.

To Malaysia The easiest option is to use the bus service provided by **PHLS Express**. You can purchase tickets from **De Royalle Café** on Jln Sultan, T223 2519 or online at www.easybook.com. There is a daily morning bus to **Kota Kinabalu** (8 hrs, B$45), **Limbang** (B$10), **Lawas** (B$25), **Beaufort** (B$40) and **Sipitang** (B$30).

There are also 2 daily departures to **Miri** in Sarawak at 0700 and 1300 (B$15, 4 hrs). The alternative well-trodden path to Miri is convoluted but interesting. Take one of the large blue or white buses to **Seria** (2 hrs, B$6) which leave every hour from Jln Cator. At Seria transfer to a minibus bound for the border at **Kuala Belait** (30 mins, B$1) from where there are buses on to Miri (2 hrs).

Car

To make the most of a trip to Brunei, it's best to hire a car. The major car hire firms operate out of the airport or in Bandar Seri Begawan, and there are plenty of cheaper local firms to choose from, too.

Car hire **Avis**, Radisson Brunei Darussalam (see Where to stay), Jln Tasek, T222 7100; **Hertz**, Lot Q33, West Berakas Link, T239 0300 (airport T245 2244), www.hertz.com; and **Qawi Enterprise**, Lot 38554 Jln Penghubong Berakas Lambak Kanan, T234 0380.

Taxi

Metered taxis are a rare find in Brunei. Fares are set at B$3 for the first kilometre (B$4.50, 2100-0600) and B$1 for every subsequent kilometre. However, you'll generally have to negotiate. Note that taxis are thin on the ground here so expect to wait for some time. For longer journeys, it makes more sense to hire a car. Taxis can be waved down. Otherwise call T222 2214 (**Bandar Seri Begawan**); T333 4581 (**Kuala Belait**); T322 2030 (**Seria**); T234 3671 (**airport**).

Around
Brunei

The capital, Bandar Seri Begawan, makes the ideal base for forays deeper into Brunei. Most of the following sights can be visited on day trips from the capital, either on guided tours or with a hire car. Of Brunei's four districts, Temburong is the least populated and, for many people, the most appealing, thanks to the Ulu Temburong National Park. Each of the remaining districts offers its own diversions, with the interior of Belait providing the most challenging itineraries.

Brunei Muara District
go mountain biking at Bukit Shahbandar or visit Jerudong, Brunei's strangely quiet theme park

Brunei Muara is the smallest of Brunei's four districts, with Bandar Seri Begawan at its heart. As well as several notable sights on the outskirts of Bandar, there are a few minor sights further afield, including sandy beaches, forest reserves and a theme park.

Several kilometres upstream from the capital is the official residence of the sultan, the **Istana Nurul Iman** (www.istananuruliman.org), its twin gold cupolas clearly visible from the river. It is the largest residential palace in the world and must surely count as one of the most extravagant, too. Beneath the curving Minangkabau-style roofs lie a staggering 1778 rooms (including 257 bathrooms), which makes the istana bigger than the Vatican and on a par with Versailles. The banquet hall seats 5000 and there's an underground car park to house the sultan's extensive collection of cars (which runs into three figures). The palace is open to the public for three days a year and welcomes around 200,000 people. Visitors need to go through a medical screening before being led to shake the hand of the sultan or his wife. After this, there is a free meal and

Essential Around Brunei

Finding your feet

To explore Brunei in any depth, you really need to hire a car. Thanks to subsidized vehicles and cheap petrol, most Bruneians drive; as a result of this, the public transport system is far from comprehensive. There are no internal flights within Brunei (it's so small that flying would be impractical).

WILDLIFE
Proboscis monkeys

Proboscis monkeys are not pretty to look at. At least, they're an acquired taste. With their pendulous noses, pot bellies and hooded eyes, they look more like caricatures than bona fide monkeys. The Indonesians had a special name for them; not orang-utan (man of the forest), but *orang belanda*, meaning Dutchman (more a snipe at their would-be oppressors than a simian insult). In Borneo they also have other local names including *bekantan, bekara, kahau, rasong, pika* and *batangan*.

It is one of Brunei's great secrets that it holds the world's largest population of proboscis monkeys. With an estimated 10,000 of them living along the banks of Sungai Brunei, this is more than the rest of their scattered populations put together. The Kinabatangan Wetlands of Sabah are widely thought to be the best place to spot proboscis monkeys. Not so; just minutes from Brunei's capital, by *tambang*, plentiful troops of proboscis monkeys feed peacefully among the mangrove trees.

Proboscis monkeys are unique to Borneo. They are, with the Tibetan macaque, the world's largest monkeys, with adult males often exceeding 25 kg. Sexual dimorphism is pronounced in the species with males having a significantly greater body mas than females as well as noses that frequently reach 10 cm or more in length, drooping well below the mouth. They are great swimmers, with their long noses serving well as snorkels. Scientists, however, point to sex rather than swimming as the reason for the unusual hooter. Having a big nose is a matter of pride for a male proboscis (who, incidentally, sports a permanent erection). It's all to do with Darwinian sexual selection: the bigger the nose, the bigger the harem (proboscis monkeys live in troops of 10-28 animals with a single adult male at the helm). In common with most of larger mammals in Borneo, the proboscis monkey is a seriously threatened species – though you might not think so from their numbers on the Brunei River. It is thought that no more than 20,000 proboscis monkeys survive in the wild and population numbers are thought to have plummeted by more than 50% in the past four decades.

children are presented with a small green bag containing money. This unique experience is worthwhile, though the time spent in queues is epic. For the best views, catch a water taxi from Bandar Seri Begawan. You'll pass by the royal helipad and the royal jetty, where the sultan's guests (including Queen Elizabeth II on her last visit) are welcomed.

Alternatively, make your way to the **Taman Persiaran Damuan**, a 1-km-long park that runs along the riverside just beyond the palace. Within the park are sculptures from each of the six original ASEAN nations. If you're lucky, and you visit the park at dusk, you may spot proboscis monkeys (see box, above) on **Pulau Ranggu**, the small island opposite the park. Proboscis monkeys are an endangered species endemic to Borneo. To guarantee sightings, take a proboscis tour by *tambang* along the Sungai Damuan tributary; it's one of the highlights of a trip to Brunei for any nature enthusiast. Look out for monkeys crossing the river (they swim doggy style, their bulbous noses raised above the water like snorkels). See What to do, page 165.

Jerudong Park Playground ① *Kampong Jerudong (along the Muara–Tutong Highway northwest of Bandar Seri Begawan), T261 1777, www.jerudongpark.com.bn, Wed 1600-2300, Fri 1500-2330, Sat and Sun 1000-2330, shorter hours during Ramadan so check the website,*

B$10, children (under 1.4 m) B$8, is a peculiar theme park that opened in 1994 to coincide with the sultan's 48th birthday. By Western standards, it's nothing special and has a slightly jaded feel, the highlight being the log flume. Thanks to Brunei's tiny population, it is probably the quietest theme park in the world; on some days you'll have the park more or less to yourself. Beware, many of the rides are often out of action due to a lack of spare parts (ask before handing over the entry fee). There has been significant investment to reinvigorate the park in recent years including the addition of a water park, which seems to be the most popular attraction and makes for a cool outing for kids.

Just along the coast from Jerudong Park is the extravagant **Empire Hotel & Country Club** (see page 164), which is worth a look for its towering, 80-m gold-adorned atrium – said to be the tallest in the world. Both the hotel and theme park were built by Prince Jefri, brother to the sultan and an endless source of scandal (see box, page 180).

Muara and around

At Brunei's northeast tip is the port of Muara, a nondescript place with a single sleepy grid of shophouses and nothing much to draw visitors. There are several nearby beaches that are pleasant enough, if you can bear the heat. **Pantai Muara** is a 4-km stretch of sand north of Muara, with a kids' playground and picnic shelters among the casuarinas, while to the south, at the end of a road lined with mansions, is a sandy spit known as **Pantai Serasa**, home to a fleet of traditional fishing boats and the **Serasa Watersports Complex**. Boats from Sarawak arrive at the port in Serasa Muara (see Transport, below).

There are two forest reserves worth visiting along the main Muara–Tutong highway, which runs beside Brunei's north-facing coastline. **Bukit Shahbandar Reserve** ⓘ *just east of Kampong Jerudong, take bus No 55, and alight at the bridge before Pantai Jerutong, from there it is a hairy 15-min walk along the highway to the park entrance*, is a popular spot with joggers and walkers, with some fairly demanding trails running up and down seven hills. At the highest point, there's a wooden observation tower. The park was used for the mountain biking event when Brunei hosted the Southeast Asian Games and a network of tough tracks criss-cross the hilly forest. At the time of writing, there were no bikes for rent at the park.

The **Hutan Berakas Forest Reserve** ⓘ *directly north of the airport*, is wilder, with trails weaving through casuarina forests and *kerangas* (heath forest), the favoured habitat of carnivorous pitcher plants. There are paved trails here, a popular picnic area and a lovely long beach used by Bruneians for swimming.

Out in Brunei Bay itself is Brunei's largest island, the mangrove-covered **Pulau Selirong** ⓘ *45-min boat ride from the mainland; tours can be arranged with many of the Bandar-based operators and start at B$70 (see page 160)*. The island is uninhabited has been designated as a forest reserve; 2 km of elevated walkways have been installed. Monitor lizards, crabs, mud skippers and wading birds can be viewed, along with the occasional mangrove snake and saltwater crocodile. Keep an eye out for flying lemurs.

Listings Brunei Muara District

Where to stay

$$$$ **Empire Hotel & Country Club**
Jerudong BG3122, T241 8888,
www.theempirehotel.com.

If you are the mood for a bit of glamour and luxury, then the Empire is Brunei's No 1 choice. Set along the beach, this resort is a monument to the extravagance of the sultan's brother, Prince Jefri (see box, page 180).

No expense was spared in the construction of this 6-star hotel, which centres around an 80-m-high, marble-pillared atrium. The 400-plus rooms all have large balconies and huge marble-clad bathrooms, with walk-in showers and vast bathtubs. The 'presidential suite' covers more than 650 sq m and has its own lavish indoor pool, with attached sauna, steam room and jacuzzi. With the click of a button, a cinema screen descends from the ceiling above the pool. There are antiques aplenty and swathes of gold leaf. Facilities include an 18-hole Jack Nicklaus golf course, sports club, cinema and numerous pools, including a meandering 11,000-sq-m lagoon pool with fake, sandy beach (great for kids), kids' club, 7 dining outlets, water sports including scuba-diving, sailing, jet skiing, kayaking and parasailing. There's a free shuttle to Bandar Seri Begawan, 4 times daily. Check for special discounts; low occupancy means that rooms are often excellent value.

Restaurants

$$$ Li Gong
Empire Hotel & Country Club (see Where to stay), T241 8888, ext 7329. Thu-Mon 1830-2200, and Sun buffet brunch 1130-1500.
Excellent Chinese cuisine, set in a pavilion surrounded by koi ponds. The menu covers specialities from every province in China. The buffet brunch on Sun is a luxurious way to stuff yourself on oriental goodies.

$$$ Spaghettini
Empire Hotel & Country Club (see Where to stay), T241 8888, ext 7368. Tue-Sat 1830-2230.
Italian-style trattoria, with its own authentic, wood-fired oven and dough-flinging chefs. Perched at the top of the towering atrium at the **Empire Hotel**.

What to do

Water sports
Oceanic Quest, *No 6, Simpang 46, Jln Perusahaan, Kampong Serasa, Muara, T277 1190, www.oceanicquest.com.* Daily dive trips, muck diving, wreck diving and reef-diving trips.

Transport

Boat
The **Serasa Ferry Terminal** at Muara has connections with Labuan, KK, Lawas and Limbang. See Bandar transport, page 161, for details.

Temburong District

stunning forest treks at Ulu Temburong National Park

Temburong is the forested finger of land set adrift from the rest of Brunei by the Malaysian district of Limbang, which was snatched from Brunei's control in 1890 by Raja Brooke of Sarawak. The population of Temburong is just under 10,000, with Malays living alongside a scattered population of Iban, Murut and Kadazan tribespeople. The whole district has something of a village atmosphere; wherever you go in Temburong, it seems that everybody knows one another.

Bangar
Bangar (not to be confused with Bandar) is a quiet place with a single row of shophouses and a sultry, sleepy air. There's a mosque, a few government offices, a resthouse and a few coffee shops, otherwise there's no particular reason to linger. Most people carry straight on in the direction of the Ulu Temburong National Park, the principal attraction for visitors to the district.

Essential Temburong District

Speedboats for Temburong leave regularly from the Temburong Jetty on Jalan Residency in Bandar Seri Begawan. They roar downriver, passing briefly into Brunei Bay, before weaving through the mangrove channels as far as Bangar, Temburong's main town. The journey is an adventure in itself: look out for proboscis monkeys swimming doggy style across the narrow channels.

★ Ulu Temburong National Park

The 50,000-ha Ulu Temburong National Park is the jewel in the crown of Brunei's ecotourism push. It sits in the remote southern portion of Temburong, in the heart of the **Batu Apoi Forest Reserve**. The region has never been settled or logged, so there are no roads, and access to the park is by *temuai* (traditional longboat). The fact that few people visit is part of the appeal; the park remains unscathed by tourism, despite being easily accessible. There can't be many places in the world where you can leave the city mid-morning, have a picnic lunch deep in pristine rainforest and be back at your hotel by late afternoon.

Despite being relatively unknown, Ulu Temburong compares favourably with the jungle reserves of neighbouring Sarawak and Sabah. Work carried out at the **Belalong Rainforest Field Studies Centre** confirms the unusual biodiversity of Ulu Temburong; many species new to science have been found here and one scientist was reported to have identified more than 400 separate species of beetle on a single tree. The main attraction for visitors, however, is the towering **canopy walkway**, which stands 50 m tall and provides unbeatable views of the surrounding forest. Being on the walkway at sunrise as the jungle comes alive is a magnificent experience.

Flora and fauna Borneo's rainforests are among the most biodiverse places on Earth and Ulu Temburong is no exception. More species of tree can be found in a single hectare here than in the entirety of North America. Animal life is abundant too, though hard to spot. Some of the more conspicuous creatures include flying lizards, Wallace's flying frog, pygmy squirrels, wild boar, mousedeer, gibbons (more often heard than seen), various species of hornbill (the biggest being the majestic rhinoceros hornbill, frequently seen gliding across the river) and of course myriad weird and wonderful insects, from the peculiar lantern beetle to the Rajah Brooke birdwing butterfly. The canopy walkway provides the opportunity to look directly down upon the jungle canopy, home to the greatest density of life. Notice the abundance of epiphytes, plants that survive at this height by clinging on to host trees. From the walkway, it is sometimes possible to see tiger orchids, one of the largest of their species.

Trekking With 7 km of wooden walkways, few visitors stray off the main trail, though there is unlimited scope for serious trekking in the vicinity (either using Park HQ as a base, or camping out in the forest). The terrain here is steep and rugged and not suited to those without a moderate level of fitness. Wherever you go, take plenty of water. Falling trees and landslides often lay waste to sections of the boardwalk, making it unlikely that the whole trail will be open at any one time.

The boardwalk begins at Park HQ and leads across the Sungai Temburong via a footbridge to the foot of a towering hill, upon which stands the canopy walkway. The climb is steep and sweaty, with almost 1000 steps. Once you've conquered the hill, reaching the canopy walkway itself is no easy matter either: the walkway is suspended in sections between 50-m-tall aluminium towers built around a seemingly endless series of step ladders. The views from the top of the jungle canopy are truly magnificent, with the confluence of Sungai Temburong and Sungai Belalong at your feet. Gaze for long enough and you'll probably spot the black and white backs of hornbills as they glide from tree to tree along the riverbank.

From the walkway, the trail continues for several kilometres along a steeply descending boardwalk in the direction of a second suspension bridge across Sungai Temburong. The boardwalk ends at Sungai Apan, a narrow stream. By following the course of the stream upriver, you soon come to a picturesque waterfall, with a plunge pool deep enough for swimming (outside dry season). A steep trail traverses the hillside with the aid of ropes to a second waterfall.

Most people make their way back to Park HQ by longboat from the confluence of Sungai Apan and Sungai Temburong (returning on foot would mean retracing your steps along the boardwalk). You may cross tracks with local Iban, who fish this stretch of the river with traps and nets. They'll probably wave you over and offer you a swig of *tuak* (rice wine), or more likely, Bacardi rum.

Those looking for the chance to explore largely uncharted rainforest may be interested in tackling the strenuous week-long trek to the summit of **Bukit Pagon** (1843 m), which is situated near the border with Sarawak in the southernmost corner of Temburong. Contact the tourist office, or one of the Bandar-based tour operators, for help with arrangements.

Essential Ulu Temburong National Park

Finding your feet

The journey to Ulu Temburong is half the fun and involves two boat journeys and a taxi ride. Bangar-bound speedboats (known as 'flying coffins') leave regularly from the jetty on Jalan Residency in Bandar Seri Begawan (daily every 30 minutes 0745-1600, 45 minutes, B$6 one-way; visitors are advised to carry their passport and ensure it is inside something waterproof).

From Bangar jetty, there are taxis to take visitors south along a sealed road to Batang Duri (literally 'spiky hamlet'), a small settlement on the banks of Sungai Temburong. From here, visitors need to charter a longboat for the final leg of the journey upriver to Park HQ (90 minutes, around B$50 per boat), with towering dipterocarps climbing the river banks. In the dry season (July and August) water levels can be low and passengers may have to get out and help push the boat.

Though it is possible to visit Ulu Temburong independently, most people find it simpler to use one of the Bandar-based tour operators (see page 160); they'll make all travel arrangements and provide guides and entry permits (an all-inclusive day trip costs around B$163). It is perfectly possible to visit the park as a day trip, though there is accommodation available for longer stays (see Where to stay, page 168).

Park information

Entry fee B$5. If you are travelling independently, be sure to get hold of an entry permit in advance from the **Ministry of Primary Resources and Tourism**, Jalan Menteri Besar, Bandar Seri Begawan BB3910, T238 2822, www.mprt.gov.bn (see page 154).

At Park HQ, visitors need to sign a register and pay the entry fee before heading into the park proper. There's a small information centre here with displays, and a series of chalets and dormitories, linked by plankwalks.

Peradayan Forest Reserve
20 mins east of Bangar by road; taxis cost around B$15 one-way or B30 return including a reasonable amount of waiting time.

If time is very limited, you may consider skipping Ulu Temburong and heading instead for the Peradayan Forest Reserve. Within the reserve is a small forest recreation park with picnic tables and trails, one of which climbs to the summit of **Bukit Patoi** (310 m), passing caves along the way. The summit of the hill is a bare patch of stone, allowing wide views across the forest north to Brunei Bay and east to Sarawak. A tougher and less distinct trail continues from here to the summit of **Bukit Peradayan** (410 m).

Longhouses
Though the majority of Temburong's indigenous inhabitants have moved into detached homes, plenty still live in longhouses. If you are visiting a remote longhouse, you may be welcome to turn up unannounced (see Where to stay, below) but some have more formal arrangements with tour operators for receiving guests. The largest is a 16-door Iban longhouse (home to 16 families) situated along the road to Batang Duri, at **Kampong Sembiling**. Various guides and tour operators will stop off here, allowing visitors to meet the inhabitants and try a glass or two of *tuak* (rice wine). If it's daytime, there won't be many people around, but you'll get a chance to see inside a modern Iban longhouse, complete with satellite TV and parking bays for cars.

Another longhouse offering homestays is the curiously named five-door **Amo C**, located just north of **Batang Duri** itself. Overnight guests are set up with mattresses on the *ruai* (communal veranda) and guided treks along hunting trails can be arranged for a fee.

Listings Temburong District

Where to stay

\$\$\$ Sumbiling Eco Village
204 Kiaw Lian Building, 1st floor, Jln Pemancha, www.borneoguide.com/ecovillage for enquiries and bookings.
This ecotourism project is managed by **Borneo Guide** in conjunction with the local villagers and offers rustic tented accommodation and simple fan rooms. Packages are all-inclusive and include night treks, jungle camping and the ascent of Bukit Lutut. There are lots of opportunities for river swimming and communing with the marvellous nature of Temburong. Packages include pick-up from the jetty in Bandar Seri Begawan.

\$\$\$ Ulu Ulu Temburong Resort
PO Box 2612, BSB, T244 1791, www.uluuluresort.com.
If you want to visit Ulu Temburong independently there is a wide range of simple yet comfortable accommodation available here. Some rooms have verandas with day beds –perfect for an afternoon nap. There are also some deckchairs laid out along the riverside and a delightful lounge built in traditional kampong style with lots of comfy chairs and a simple café offering good food. The resort can organize a number of packages for trips around the park, including kayaking, trekking, tubing and more. Recommended.

\$\$ Government Resthouse
Jln Batang Duri, Bangar, T522 1239.
A short walk from the jetty along the road to Batang Duri, the resthouse offers simple, functional rooms.

\$ Pusat Belia (youth hostel)
100 m from the jetty, T522 1694.
A clean and wholesome hostel with segregated a/c dorms. Good value if you fancy lingering in Bangar.

$ Longhouses

Visitors to Temburong District can stay at various longhouses either informally or as part of an organized tour. Those most commonly visited are **Amo C** and the main longhouse at **Kampong Sembiling**, both along the Batang Duri road. **Amo C** longhouse has an informal homestay arrangement with guests: for a small amount (no more than B$20), they will feed you and set you up with mattresses on the *ruai* (common veranda).

Hospitality is an important part of indigenous culture and, in theory, any longhouse will put you up for the night. In practice, this is only the case with the more traditional or remote longhouses (see Ulu Belait, page 173). If you turn up at a longhouse unannounced, be sure to follow the correct etiquette. Always ask the permission of the headman, or Tuai Rumah, before heading inside. Remove shoes before entering a family room (*bilik*), or an area of the *ruai* laid with mats. More often than not, shoes are not worn at all in a longhouse and are left at the entrance to the *ruai*.

Tutong District

the weekly market draws ethnic minorities from around the region

The central district of Tutong is wedged between Belait District to the west and Limbang (Malaysia) to the east, following the flood plain of Sungai Tutong. Recent growth in agriculture has seen the introduction of small-scale plantations in areas of Tutong, though most of the district is sparsely populated and covered with rainforest.

Tutong town and around

The coastal highway passes by the district capital, Tutong, a small and pleasant town on the banks of the river. There's nothing much for the visitor to do here, other than stop by the small wet market or the nearby *tamu* (the regional open-air market, held every Thursday afternoon through to Friday morning). The *tamu* draws Tutong's indigenous inhabitants – Kedayan, Dusun and Iban tribespeople – who come down from the interior to sell their produce. It is mainly a food market, though there are handicrafts on sale, too.

A kilometre to the north of Tutong is the **Taman Rekreasi Sungai Basong**, a small recreation park with a pond, a stream and picnic tables. Meanwhile, just west of town is **Pantai Seri Kenangan** ('Unforgettable Beach'), a largely forgettable spit of sand dividing Sungai Tutong from the sea. Still, the beach is kept clean and the sea here is calm. Every July a local festival is held on the beach, with Malay games such as top spinning and kite flying.

Kampong Kuala Tutong

The road continues along the spit as far as Kampong Kuala Tutong, a sleepy place set among coconut palms. There's a small boatyard here called **Marine Yard**, where river trips can sometimes be organized. The arrangement is pretty informal, and you'll have to just turn up and hope there's someone around. The boat weaves upriver through mangrove-lined swampland, past Dusun and Malay kampongs. Look out for monkeys and estuarine crocodiles, which can sometimes be seen basking on the sandbanks. River tours along Sungai Tutong can be arranged locally.

★ Tasek Merimbun Heritage Park

No public transport. If you've rented a car, head west from Bandar Seri Begawan on the old Tutong Rd (rather than the coastal highway). At Mile 18, take the left fork for Lamunin. Beyond Kampong Lamunin itself, follow signs for Tasek Merimbun. The journey takes up to 1½ hrs.

Brunei's largest lake, Tasek Merimbun, is becoming increasingly popular as a weekend escape from the city. The setting is magnificent: an S-shaped, peat-black body of water surrounded by wetlands, peat-swamp forest and lowland dipterocarp rainforest.

In the centre of the lake is tiny island, accessible by boardwalk. On the banks of the lake is a small visitor centre with a few fish tanks, plus chalets for accommodation. Local Dusun have kayaks for rent, too. Opposite the chalets is a 2-km botanical trail through the rainforest. Guides can be hired for longer treks in the area.

The park is rich in wildlife including crocodile and clouded leopard (Borneo's biggest cat). The most important scientific discovery has been the white-collared fruit bat, which appears to be unique to Tasek Merimbun.

The area is also home to Dusun tribespeople, who for many centuries took advantage of the abundance of fish and wildlife. Now that the lake has been set aside as a nature reserve only a handful of Dusun people remain.

Listings Tutong District

Where to stay

$$ Halim Plaza
Lot No 9003, Kampong Petani, Tutong TA1141, T426 0588.
Located inside a small shopping mall, this place offers a range of comfortable rooms with TV and attached bathroom and is mainly patronized by Malaysians or Bruneians on business. Great value for those stopping over in Tutong.

$ Researchers' Quarter
Tasek Merimbun Heritage Park, c/o Director of Brunei Museum, T222 2713, bmdir@bunet.bn.
If available, the Researchers' Quarter (a new wooden chalet) at Tasek Merimbun can be used by the public. Contact the Brunei Museum in advance.

Shopping

For indigenous handicrafts that are better priced than those in Bandar Seri Begawan, you could try the weekly tamu (open-air market) in **Tutong**, which starts Thu afternoon and finishes late morning on Fri.

Belait District

large numbers of expats; oil wells dominate the landscape

Belait wears two faces. On the one hand it is oil country, the driving force behind Brunei's economy and home to a large population of British and Dutch expats. On the other, it is the best example of 'old' Brunei – Brunei before oil.

When oil was first discovered at Seria in 1929, the whole region was largely uninhabited, the lowlands dominated by peat swamps, mangroves and rainforest, with indigenous Iban and Dusun tribespeople sticking largely to the valley of Sungai Belait. Though the coastal strip has developed beyond recognition, the interior remains largely unscathed.

Aside from Temburong, Belait District is the best place to explore Brunei's rainforest and visit indigenous longhouses. Most visitors are unaware of this: the tourism infrastructure here remains underdeveloped, so few people visit – apart from British Army recruits undergoing a round of brutal jungle training. Nevertheless, the interior of Belait is earmarked as an important ecotourism destination for the future, and tour operators are beginning to put together itineraries into the region.

Seria

Seria is a surreal place. Once open swampland, Seria is now dominated by level fields full of lawn-mowing tractors, egrets and nodding donkeys – small land-based oil wells that nod back and forth as they pump oil to the surface. There is no real centre of town to speak of; row upon row of neat bungalows line the roads – home, presumably to Chinese and expat oil workers, whose wives ride about town in Land Cruisers. It is a strange, functional place with an odd mix of inhabitants that includes indigenous tribespeople and a garrison of Gurkhas.

The town straggles along the coastal strip between Seria and Kuala Belait, which serves as the centre of Brunei's oil production. On the edge of Seria is the Billionth Barrel Monument, commemorating the obscene productivity of Brunei's first oil field. For those who want to delve deeper into the history and technicalities of oil production, there is the **Oil & Gas Discovery Centre (OGDC)** ⓘ *F20 Jln Tengah, Seria, T337 7200, www.ogdcbrunei. com, Mon-Sat 0830-1700, Sun 0930-1800, B$5, B$1 child*, set in a building that resembles an oil drum. It's a fun place for kids, with a gyroscope, a bed of nails and a fish pond.

Kuala Belait

Though it all started at Seria, Kuala Belait (known locally as KB) is the district's principal town. It also serves as the border town with nearby Sarawak. Like Seria, Kuala Belait is a purely functional place that has developed over time to serve the needs of the oil workers. The centre of town comprises a large grid of streets with Chinese shophouses alongside multinational outlets such as the **Body Shop** and **KFC**.

Kuala Belait sits on the east bank of the Sungai Belait and it's possible to hire a boat upriver as far as Kuala Balai (see below). Boats leave from behind the market building on Jalan Pasar, at the southern end of Jalan McKerron (sometimes spelt Mackeron).

Listings Belait District

Where to stay

$$$ Brunei Sentosa
92-93 Jln McKerron, PO Box 252, Kuala Belait KA1131, T333 4341, www.bruneisentosahotel.com.
In the heart of town and handy for the bus station for connections to Seria or Miri. With oil workers pouring out during the day, and a fairly grim façade, this place is not the most elegant of places to stay, Nevertheless, rooms are fairly comfortable (though some could use a clean) and have cable TV, a/c and attached bathroom.

$$$ Plaza Sutera Biru
Lot 73, Jln Sungai, KA2331, www.psb.com.bn.
This is probably the top hotel in town with friendly staff used to dealing with the requests of international guests. Rooms are comfortable and though slightly dim are filled with pleasantly ostentatious touches making for a pleasant stay.

$$$ Riviera

Lot 106, Jln Sungai, Kuala Belait KA2331,
T333 5252, www.rivierahotelkb.webs.com.
Located on the riverfront in the town centre,
this hotel has 30 comfortable and modern
rooms and suites. All rooms have a minibar,
cable TV and a large marble bathtub.
Frequent promotions make this hotel good
value. Good restaurant mainly offering Malay
cuisine, and special promotions offered at
the gym over the road.

Belait Interior

swamps, forest and trips to interior longhouses

The people from these parts are known as the Belait Malays and they have a lot in common with the Melanau people of coastal Sarawak, including their Muslim faith, their traditional reliance on sago processing and their stilted longhouses.

Kuala Balai

Before the oil boom, the main settlement in this part of Brunei was the riverine village of Kuala Balai, situated about an hour upriver from Kuala Belait. Between 1930 and 1980 the population slowly dwindled, until the village virtually ceased to exist. Today just a handful of permanent inhabitants remain.

Despite the fact that Kuala Balai is now little more than a ghost town, it is still possible to get a sense of how things once looked; the old longhouse, which deteriorated many years ago, has been rebuilt as part of a Raleigh International project. And there are still one or two old sago processors around, though they use light machinery now, rather than trampling the sago scrapings underfoot, as was once the way. Just downriver from the longhouse is a small wooden box on stilts by the riverside. Inside are 20 human skulls, victims of headhunters from as long ago as the 17th century.

As elsewhere in Belait District, tourism hasn't yet taken off and few people visit the longhouse, but at the time of writing there were plans to market Kuala Balai more actively as a tourist destination.

Jalan Labi

The other route into the interior of Belait is via Jalan Labi, a decent road which turns south off the coastal highway at Kampong Lumut, near the border with Tutong District. A little way along the road is Brunei's oldest forest reserve, the **Sungai Liang Forest Reserve**, with ponds, picnic shelters and various well-maintained paths into the surrounding forest. One path climbs a steep hill as far as a treehouse (closed for renovation at the time of writing). Close by is the **Forestry Department** building, set back from the road, with a small *palmetum* (palm garden) leading up to the offices. There's also a tiny forestry museum here, **Muzium Perhutanan** ⓘ *Mon-Thu and Sat 0800-1215 and 1330-1630*, with two rooms of displays that aren't worth going out of your way for.

The Labi road continues south through undulating rainforest as far as the village of Kampong Labi itself, passing the **Labi Hills Forest Reserve** along the way. Within the reserve's boundary is the 270-ha **Luagan Lalak Recreation Park**, covering an area of alluvial swampland, which floods to become a lake during the monsoon. The lake (or swamp, depending on the season) is accessible via a 200-m-long boardwalk.

Kampong Labi, some 40 km south of the coastal highway, is a small settlement that has served for years as a base for speculative (and unsuccessful) oil drilling in the surrounding hills. Tropical fruits, such as rambutan, durian, cempedak and jackfruit, are grown in the area. Beyond Labi, the road turns into a dirt track which serves as an access route to a number of Iban longhouses. The largest of these is the 12-door **Rumah Panjang Mendaram Besar**, home to 100 or so people. Like most of the longhouses in Brunei, this one has piped water and electricity, with the men commuting to the towns to work for either Shell or the government. A nearby trail leads to the **Wasai Mendaram**, a large waterfall with plunge pool for bathing.

At the end of the 12-km track is **Rumah Panjang Teraja**. The inhabitants of this six-door longhouse cultivate paddy, rear pigs and chickens, and grow their own fruit and vegetables. From the longhouse, a well-marked trail leads to the summit of **Bukit Teraja**, from where there are magnificent views as far as Gunung Mulu (see page 112) in Sarawak. Walking the trail to the summit takes about 1½ hours. Reported wildlife sightings along the way include orang-utans, Borneo bearded pigs, barking deer, macaques and hornbills.

Ulu Belait

Further longhouses can be found deep in the interior, along the upper reaches of Sungai Belait. These are accessible by longboat from Kampong Sungai Mau, which is situated halfway along the Jalan Labi. Of course, it is possible to begin the journey in Kuala Belait, passing Kuala Balai along the way, but this route takes many hours.

The journey upriver into Ulu Belait ('Upriver Belait') depends on the level of the water; in the dry season its upper reaches are barely navigable. **Kampong Sukang**, some two hours from Kampong Sungai Mau by longboat, is a community of Dusun and Punan tribespeople, with two longhouses and a hamlet of family homes. The Punan are nomadic hunter-gatherers by tradition, though the inhabitants of Kampong Sukang were persuaded to settle here back in the 1970s. They now farm paddy rather than relying on the old staple diet of wild sago, but they still hunt in the traditional manner using blowpipes and poison darts.

If you're feeling still more intrepid, there is another hamlet of longhouses at **Kampong Melilas**, located one to three hours – depending on the water level – upriver from Kampong Sukang. These are home to Iban people and, like the Labi longhouses, they are upgraded versions of the traditional longhouse, though this community supports a thriving cottage industry in traditional basketry and weaving. Beyond Kampong Melilas, there are hot springs and plenty of waterfalls; a guide can be arranged at the village.

Background

Brunei's early history is obscure, but although precise dates have been muddied by time, there is no doubt that the sultanate's early prosperity was rooted in trade. As far back as the seventh century, China was importing birds' nests from Brunei, and Arab, Indian, Chinese and other Southeast Asian traders were regularly passing through. Links with Chinese merchants were strongest: they traded silk, metals, stoneware and porcelain for Brunei's jungle produce: bezoar stones, hornbill ivory, timber and birds' nests. Chinese coins dating from the eighth century have been unearthed at Kota Batu, 3 km from Bandar Seri Begawan. Large quantities of Chinese porcelain dating from the Tang, Sung and Ming dynasties have also been found. The sultanate was on the main trade route between China and the western reaches of the Malayan archipelago and by the 10th to the 13th centuries trade was booming. By the turn of the 15th century there was a sizeable Chinese population settled in Brunei.

It is thought that in around 1370 Sultan Mohammad became first Sultan. In the mid-1400s, Sultan Awang Alak ber Tabar married a Melakan princess and converted to Islam. Brunei already had trade links with Melaka and exported camphor, rice, gold and sago in exchange for Indian textiles. But it was not until an Arab, Sharif Ali, married Sultan Awang Alak's niece that Islam spread beyond the confines of the royal court. Sharif Ali – who is said to have descended from the Prophet Mohammad – became Sultan Berkat. He consolidated Islam, converted the townspeople, built mosques and set up a legal system based on Islamic sharia law. Trade flourished and Brunei assumed the epithet Darussalam (the abode of peace).

The golden years

The coastal Melanaus quickly embraced the Muslim faith, but tribal groups in the interior were largely unaffected by the spread of Islam and retained their animist beliefs. As Islam spread along the coasts of north and west Borneo, the sultanate expanded its political and commercial sphere of influence. By the 16th century, communities all along the coasts of present-day Sabah and Sarawak were paying tribute to the Sultan. The sultanate became the centre of a minor empire whose influence stretched beyond the coasts of Borneo to many surrounding islands, including the Sulu archipelago and Mindanao in the Philippines. Even Manila had to pay tribute to the Sultan's court.

On 8 July 1521 Antonio Pigafetta, an Italian historian on Portuguese explorer Ferdinand Magellan's expedition, visited the Sultanate of Brunei and described it as a rich, hospitable and powerful kingdom with an established Islamic monarchy and strong regional influence. Pigafetta published his experiences in his book, *The First Voyage Around the World*. He writes about a sophisticated royal court and the lavishly decorated Sultan's palace. Brunei Town was reported to be a large, wealthy city of 25,000 households. The townspeople lived in houses built on stilts over the water.

In 1526 the Portuguese set up a trading post in Brunei and from there conducted trade with the Moluccas – the famed Spice Islands – via Brunei. At the same time, more Chinese traders immigrated to Brunei to service the booming trade between Melaka and Macau and to trade with Pattani on the South Thai isthmus.

But relations with the Spaniards were not so warm; the King of Spain and the Sultan of Brunei had mutually exclusive interests in the Philippines. In the 1570s Spaniards attacked several important Muslim centres and in March 1578, the captain-general of the Philippines, Francesco de Sande, led a naval expedition to Brunei, demanding the Sultan pay tribute to Spain and allow Roman Catholic missionaries to proselytize. The Sultan would have none of it and a battle ensued off Muara, which the Spaniards won. They captured the city, but within days the victors were stopped in their tracks by a cholera epidemic and had to withdraw. In 1579 they returned and once again did battle off Muara, but this time they were defeated.

The sun sets on an empire

Portugal came under Spanish rule in 1580 and Brunei lost a valuable European ally: the sultanate was raided by the Spanish again in 1588 and 1645. But by then Brunei's golden age was history and the Sultan's grip on his further-flung dependencies had begun to slip.

In the 1660s civil war erupted in Brunei due to feuding between princes and, together with additional external pressures of European expansionism, the once-mighty sultanate all but collapsed. Only a handful of foreign merchants dealt with the sultanate and Chinese traders passed it by. Balanini pirates from Sulu and Illanun pirates from Mindanao posed a constant threat to the Sultan and any European traders or adventurers foolhardy enough to take them on. In return for protection from these sea-borne terrorists, the Sultan offered the British East India Company a base on the island of Labuan in Brunei Bay in the late 1600s, although the trading post failed to take off.

For 150 years, Brunei languished in obscurity. By the early 1800s, Brunei's territory did not extend much beyond the town boundaries, although the Sarawak River and the west coastal strip of North Borneo officially remained under the Sultan's sway.

James Brooke – the man who would be king

The collection of mini-river states that made up what was left of the Sultanate were ruled by the *pangeran*, the lesser nobles of the Brunei court. In the 1830s Brunei chiefs had gone to the Sarawak valley to organize the mining and trade in the high-grade antimony ore, which had been discovered there in 1824. They recruited Dayaks as workers and founded Kuching. But, with the support of local Malay chiefs, the Dayaks rebelled against one of the Brunei noblemen, the corrupt, Pangeran Makota, one of the Rajah's 14 brothers. By all accounts, Makota was a nasty piece of work, known for his exquisite charm and diabolical cunning.

It was into this troubled riverine mini-state, in armed rebellion against Makota, that the English adventurer James Brooke sailed in 1839. Robert Payne, in *The White Rajahs of Sarawak*, describes Makota as a "princely racketeer" and "a man of satanic gifts, who practised crimes for pleasure". Makota confided to Brooke: "I was brought up to plunder the Dayaks, and it makes me laugh to think that I have fleeced a tribe down to its cooking pots." With Brooke's arrival, Makota realized his days were numbered.

In 1837, the Sultan of Brunei, Omar Ali Saifuddien Mosque, had dispatched his uncle, Pengiran Muda Hashim, to contain the rebellion. He failed, and turned to Brooke for help. In return for his services, Brooke demanded to be made governor of Sarawak.

After he had been formally installed in his new role by Sultan Omar, Brooke set about building his own empire. Brooke exploited rivalries between various aristocratic factions of Brunei's royal court which climaxed in the murder of Pengiran Muda Hashim and his family.

No longer required in Sarawak, Hashim had returned to Brunei to become chief minister and heir apparent. He was murdered – along with 11 other princes and their families – by Sultan Omar. The Sultan and his advisers had felt threatened by their presence, so they disposed of Hashim to prevent a coup. The massacre incensed Brooke. In June 1846 his British ally, Admiral Sir Thomas Cochrane, bombarded Brunei Town, set it ablaze and chased the Sultan into the jungle.

Cochrane wanted to proclaim Brooke the sultan of Brunei, but decided, in the end, to offer Sultan Omar protection if he cleaned up his act and demonstrated his loyalty to Queen Victoria. After several weeks, the humiliated Sultan emerged from the jungle and swore undying loyalty to the Queen. As penance, Sultan Omar formally ceded the island of Labuan to the British crown on 18 December 1846. Although Brunei forfeited more territory in handing Labuan to the British, the Sultan calculated that he would benefit from a direct relationship with Whitehall. It seemed that London was becoming almost as concerned as he was about Brooke's expansionist instincts. A Treaty of Friendship and Commerce was signed between Britain and Brunei in 1847 in which the Sultan agreed not to cede any more territory to any power, except with the consent of the British government.

The Sultan's shrinking shadow

The treaty did not stop Brooke. His mission, since arriving in Sarawak, had been the destruction of the pirates who specialized in terrorizing Borneo's coastal communities. Because he knew the Sultan of Brunei was powerless to contain them, he calculated that their liquidation would be his best bargaining chip with the Sultan, and would enable him to prise yet more territory from the Sultan's grasp. Over the years he engaged the dreaded Balanini and Illanun pirates from Sulu and Mindanao as well as the so-called Sea-Dayaks and Brunei Malays, who regularly attacked Chinese, Bugis and other Asian trading ships off the Borneo coast. As a result, Sultan Abdul Mumin of Brunei ceded to Brooke the Saribas and Skrang districts, which became the Second Division of Sarawak in 1853 and, eight years later, he handed over the region that was to became the Third Division of Sarawak.

But by now the Sultan was as worried about territorial encroachment by the British as he was about Brooke and as a counterweight to both, granted a 10-year concession to much of what is modern-day Sabah to the American consul in Brunei. This 72,500 sq km tract of North Borneo later became British North Borneo and is now the state of Sabah.

With the emergence of British North Borneo, the British reneged on their agreement with the Sultan of Brunei again and the following year approved Brooke's annexation of the Baram river basin by Sarawak, which became its Fourth Division. The Sarawak frontier was advancing ever northwards.

In 1884 a rebellion broke out in Limbang and Rajah Charles Brooke refused to help the Sultan restore order. Sultan Hashim Jalilul Alam Aqamaddin, who acceded to the throne in 1885, wrote to Queen Victoria complaining that the British had not kept their word. Sir Frederick Weld was dispatched to mediate and his visit resulted in the Protectorate Agreement of 1888 between Brunei and Britain, which gave London full control of the Sultanate's external affairs. When Brooke annexed Limbang in 1890 and united it with the Trusan Valley to form the Fifth Division of Sarawak, while the Queen's men looked on, the Sultan was reduced to a state of disbelief. His sultanate had now been completely surrounded by Brooke's Sarawak.

From sultanate to oilfield

In 1906 a British Resident was appointed to the Sultan's court to advise on all aspects of government except traditional customs and religion. In his book *By God's Will*, Lord Chalfont suggests that the British government's enthusiastic recommitment to the Sultanate through the treaty may have been motivated by Machiavellian desires. "More cynical observers have suggested that the new-found enthusiasm of the British government may not have been entirely unconnected with the discovery of oil ... around the turn of the century." Oil exploration started in 1899, although it was not until the discovery of the Seria oilfield in 1929 that it merited commercial exploitation. Historian Mary Turnbull notes the quirk of destiny that ensured the survival of the micro-sultanate: "It was ironic that the small area left unswallowed by Sarawak and North Borneo should prove to be the most richly endowed part of the old sultanate."

The Brunei oilfield fell to the Japanese on 18 December 1942. Allied bombing and Japanese sabotage prior to the sultanate's liberation caused considerable damage to oil and port installations and urban areas, necessitating a long period of reconstruction in the late 1940s and early 1950s. Australian forces landed at Muara Beach on 10 July 1945. A British Military Administration ruled the country for a year, before Sultan Sir Ahmad Tajuddin took over.

In 1948 the governor of Sarawak, which was by then a British crown colony, was appointed high commissioner for Brunei, but the Sultanate remained what one commentator describes as "a constitutional anachronism". In September 1959 the UK resolved this by withdrawing the Resident and signing an agreement with the Sultan giving Whitehall responsibility for Brunei's defence and foreign affairs.

Because of his post-war influence on the development of Brunei, Sultan Omar was variously referred to as the father and the architect of modern Brunei. He shaped his sultanate into the anti-Communist, non-democratic state it is today and, being an Anglophile, held out against independence from Britain. By the early 1960s, Whitehall was enthusiastically promoting the idea of a North Borneo Federation, encompassing Sarawak, Brunei and British North Borneo. But Sultan Omar did not want anything to do with the neighbouring territories as he felt Brunei's interests were more in keeping with those of peninsular Malaysia. The proposed federation would have been heavily dependent on Brunei's oil wealth. Kuala Lumpur did not need much persuasion that Brunei's joining the Federation of Malaysia was an excellent idea.

Democrats versus autocrat

In Brunei's first general election in 1962, the left-wing Brunei People's Party (known by its Malay acronym, PRB) swept the polls. The party's election ticket had marked an end to the Sultan's autocratic rule, the formation of a democratic government and immediate independence. Aware that there was a lot at stake, the Sultan refused to let the PRB form a government. The Sultan's emergency powers, under which he banned the PRB, which were passed in 1962, remain in force, enabling him to rule by decree.

On 8 December 1962, the PRB – backed by the Communist North Kalimantan National Army, effectively its military wing – launched a revolt. The Sultan's insistence on British military protection paid off as the disorganized rebellion was quickly put down with the help of a Gurkha infantry brigade and other British troops. Within four days the British troops had pushed the rebels into Limbang, where the hard core holed up. By 12 December the revolt had been crushed and the vast majority of the rebels disappeared into the interior, pursued by the 7th Gurkha Rifles and Kelabit tribesmen.

Early in 1963, negotiations over Brunei joining the Malaysian Federation ran into trouble, to the disappointment of the British. The Malaysian prime minister, the late Tunku Abdul Rahman, wanted the Sultanate's oil and gas revenues to feed the federal treasury in Kuala Lumpur and made the mistake of making his intentions too obvious. The Tunku envisaged central government exercising absolute control over oil revenues – in the way it controls the oil wealth of Sabah and Sarawak today. Unhappy with this proposal and unwilling to become 'just another Malaysian sultan', Omar abandoned his intention to join the Federation.

Meanwhile, Indonesia's Sukarno was resolute in his objective of crushing the new Federation of Malaysia and launched his *Konfrontasi* between 1963 and 1966. Brunei offered itself as an operational base for the British army. But while Brunei supported Malaysia against Indonesia, relations between them became very strained following the declaration of the Federation in September 1963.

In 1975 Kuala Lumpur sponsored the visit of a PRB delegation to the UN, to propose a resolution calling on Brunei to hold elections, abolish restrictions on political parties and allow political exiles to return. In 1976 Bruneian government supporters protested against Malaysian 'interference' in Bruneian affairs. Nonetheless, the resolution was adopted by the UN in November 1977, receiving 117 votes in favour and none against. Britain abstained. Relations with Malaysia warmed after the death of Prime Minister Tun Abdul Razak in 1976, leaving the PRB weak and isolated. The party still operates in exile, although it is a spent force. Throughout the difficult years, the Sultan had used his favourite sport to conduct what was dubbed 'polo diplomacy', fostering links with like-minded Malaysian royalty despite the tensions in official bilateral relations.

By 1967, Britain's Labour government was pushing Sultan Omar to introduce a democratic system of government. Instead, the Sultan opted to abdicate in favour of his 21-year-old son, Hassanal Bolkiah. In November 1971, a new treaty was signed with Britain. London retained its responsibility for Brunei's external affairs, but its advisory role applied only to defence. The Sultan was given full control of all internal matters. Under a separate agreement, a battalion of British Gurkhas was stationed in the Sultanate. As Bruneians grew richer, the likelihood of another revolt receded.

Independence

Britain was keen to disentangle itself from the 1971 agreement: maintaining the protectorate relationship was expensive and left London open to criticism that it was maintaining an anachronistic colonial relationship. Brunei did not particularly relish the prospect of independence as, without British protection, it would be at the mercy of its more powerful neighbours. But in January 1979, having secured Malaysian and Indonesian assurances that they would respect its independence, the government signed another agreement with London, allowing for the Sultanate to become independent from midnight on 31 December 1983 after 150 years of close involvement with Britain and 96 years as a protectorate.

Politics

In January 1984, Sultan Hassanal Bolkiah declared Brunei a 'democratic' monarchy. Three years later, he told his official biographer Lord Chalfont: "I do not believe that the time is ripe for elections ... When I see some genuine interest among the citizenry, we may move towards elections." Independence changed little: absolute power is still vested in the Sultan, who mostly relies on his close family for advice. Following Independence, the Sultan took up the offices of prime minister, finance minister and minister of home affairs. In 1986, he relinquished the latter two, but appointed himself defence minister. He also took over responsibility for finance on the resignation of his brother, Prince Jefri (see box, page 180).

In May 1985 the Brunei National Democratic Party (BNDP) was officially registered. Its aim was to introduce a parliamentary democracy under the Sultan. But just before the Malays-only party came into being, the government announced that its employees would not be allowed to join any other party. In one stroke, the BNDP's potential membership was halved.

In early 1986, the Brunei United National Party, an offshoot of the BNDP, was formed. Unlike its parent, its manifesto was multi-racial. The Sultan allowed these parties to exist until 1988 when he proscribed all parties and imprisoned, without trial, two of BNDP leaders.

In the early 1990s, the Sultan was reported to have become increasingly worried about internal security and about Brunei's image abroad. Eight long-term political detainees, in prison since the abortive 1962 coup, were released in 1990. The last political detainee, the former deputy leader of the Brunei People's Party (PRB), Zaini Ahmad, is said to have written to the Sultan from prison following the releases. He apparently apologized for the 1962 revolt and called for the democratically elected Legislative Council – as outlined in the 1959 constitution – to be reconvened. To coincide with the Sultan's 50th birthday in 1996, Zaini Ahmad was released from prison. The exiled PRB has been greatly weakened and increasingly isolated since Brunei's relations with Malaysia became more cordial following the sultanate's accession to the Association of Southeast Asian Nations (ASEAN) in 1984 and clearly the Sultan and his adviser no longer feel threatened by the party.

Foreign relations

Brunei joined ASEAN on Independence in 1984. Prince Mohammed, the foreign affairs minister, is said to be one of the brightest, more thoughtful members of the royal family, but in foreign policy, Brunei is timid and goes quietly along with its ASEAN partners. Relations with Malaysia are greatly improved, but the sultanate's closest ties in the region, especially in fiscal and economic matters, are with Singapore. Their relationship was initially founded on their mutual distrust of the Malaysian Federation, which Brunei never joined and Singapore left two years after its inception in 1965. Singapore provides assistance in the training of Brunei's public servants and their currencies are linked.

As an ASEAN member, on good terms with its neighbours, Brunei doesn't have many enemies. But if its Scorpion tanks, ground-to-air missiles and helicopter gunships seem a little redundant, consider the experience of another oil-rich Islamic mini-state: Kuwait.

Modern Brunei

The last years of the 20th century saw Brunei's waning fortunes come to a head. By 2001, the country's per capita GDP was down almost 50% on what it had been at the time of Brunei's Independence. The troubles began with the Asian economic crisis of 1997 and were further compounded by falling oil prices and by the collapse of the country's biggest non-oil company, Amedeo Development Corporation, which had run up debts of US$3.5 billion. Amedeo had been owned and run by the sultan's brother and finance minister, Prince Jefri, a man of excessive extravagance and little business acumen (see box, page 180). The prince resigned from his position as finance minister, and a national scandal followed, with the sultan eventually suing his brother for siphoning billions of dollars from the Brunei Investment Agency, for which the prince had served as chairman. The brothers eventually settled out of court, but the publicity has had lasting consequences, damaging Brunei's credibility with foreign investors. Brunei's shaken economy has now stabilized, but the whole episode has served to highlight just how over-dependent Brunei is on oil (at present Brunei's economy relies almost exclusively on exports of oil and LNG – liquefied natural gas with 96% of the nation's exports being oil and gas related, significantly more than Saudi Arabia, the UAE or Kuwait). As oil prices peak and trough, so do Brunei's fortunes. More worryingly, the nation's oil and gas reserves are expected to dry up in 2037 and 2033 respectively. This vulnerability has prompted the sultan to initiate reforms – both economic

BACKGROUND
Estranged brothers

Prince Jefri's playboy lifestyle and his embezzlement of government funds would cause a scandal in any country. In the context of Brunei's modesty, the prince's behaviour stands out as plain shocking. He is the thorn in the side of his more conservative brother, the Sultan of Brunei.

In 1997 – year of the Asian Economic Crisis – Prince Jefri's company, the Amedeo Development Corporation, collapsed under the weight of US$3.5 billion of debts. Its legacy is the area around Jerudong, where the prince built the world's most extravagant polo ground, the theme park and the Empire Hotel & Country Club (complete with a Jack Nicklaus golf course). The hotel alone was said to have cost an astonishing US$800 million.

Surprisingly, Bruneians seem to have a soft spot for Prince Jefri. Over the years, his ambitious projects have provided many jobs. But this doesn't hide his playboy tendencies and when you have billions to play with, the sky is the limit. The name of his 165-ft yacht? *Tits*. And its two tenders? *Nipple 1* and *Nipple 2*. Why ever not? Prince Jefri has three wives, two ex-wives, 18 (official) children and a penchant for Filipino and American beauty queens, who he used to fly in for his own pleasure – until one of them tried to sue him in the US, claiming she had been lured to Brunei to become a sex slave.

In 2001, the sultan himself sued his brother for embezzling some US$20 billion from the Brunei Investment Agency (BIA), for which the prince had served as chairman. The brothers eventually settled the case out of court. The greatest publicity surrounded the auction in August 2001 of Prince Jefri's personal items, removed from his palaces by Amedeo's liquidator to appease creditors, including a set of gold-plated toilet brushes and an F1 racing-car simulator.

and political. Diversification of the economy has now become a priority and the sultan has curbed government spending while encouraging the growth of privatization.

One of his primary visions was to transform Brunei into an Offshore Financial Haven (in the vein of Bermuda or the Isle of Man) and the government has now achieved this. So-called Islamic Finance is also being targeted. In 2000, the BIFC (Brunei International Finance Centre) began trading successfully.

Ecotourism, meanwhile, is another of Brunei's trump cards for the future (more than 70% of the land mass remains cloaked in virgin rainforest). Still, many commentators point out that visitor figures are likely to remain low until the government eases laws on the prohibition of alcohol. Perhaps more significant has been the political fallout of Brunei's economic problems. The new-found desire to attract investors and tourists has forced the sultan to reconsider Brunei's international image. There has been a shift away from the Islamic conservatism of the 1990s – a fact underlined by the dismissal in 2005 of the education minister, a conservative Islamist whose introduction of a strict religious education had become increasingly unpopular. Prior to this, the first tentative move towards 21st-century democracy was instigated, with the appointment of a new legislative council. In September 2004, the country's parliament reopened for the first time since Independence. Though no political parties are allowed, a new 45-seat council was called for, with 15 elected members. To all intents and purposes, the sultan still retains authoritarian control over his kingdom – just as his ancestors

The sultan subsequently brought further cases against his brother, to try and force Prince Jefri to reveal his remaining sources of income and to get back some properties claimed by Prince Jefri as part of his lifestyle expenses. The BIA reopened litigation proceedings against Prince Jefri in 2006 using the High Court of England to freeze the prince's assets.

In the meantime, the prince started legal proceedings against his former barrister, Thomas Derbyshire, and his wife, both in the UK and US. The pair were accused of stealing assets during the time that they had worked for him, as they had been given power of attorney over several of the prince's companies and were accused of using funds from property sales for themselves. They contended the case, claiming all money used had been for the prince and his family and they subsequently counter-sued for the US$12 million they stated they were owed. This legal case is thought to have cost the State of Brunei over US$60 million to litigate despite the value of the case being significantly less. The court eventually ruled in Thomas Derbyshire's favour and the prince was obliged to pay US$21 million.

In 2008 Prince Jefri was summoned to London for contempt of court, after it was claimed he had made a number of misstatements at a previous hearing. The prince declined to show his face at the hearing and the judge issued a warrant for his arrest. Prince Jefri has been back in Brunei since late 2009 and has been seen with members of the royal family.

Controversy seems to follow the prince wherever he goes. In 2010, pictures of a statue purporting to show Prince Jefri and his ex-fiancée Micha Raines engaging in sexual intercourse were leaked to the press, ensuring the prince's extravagant lifestyle never remains far from the front pages.

have for 600 years. Nevertheless, the pending elections are being viewed as the first step towards a modern Brunei – a Brunei without oil, but with a new politics of consensus. This 45-seat council has been whittled down to a proposed 20 seats, including 15 elected members and the remainder chosen by the Sultan. However, as of 2016, no election has been called. In the well-planned comfort of Brunei, democracy doesn't seem to be something citizens are clamouring for.

Sharia law

Whilst ecotourism may be an alternative source of revenue, much of the world was incensed by the sultan's 2014 decision to impose sharia law in Brunei. The law is to be implemented in three phases and has prompted an outcry from well-known figures such as Richard Branson and Jay Leno, with celebrities calling for a ban on the sultan's many well-known hotels around the world and human rights advocates calling the decision mediaeval and draconian. The first phase of the law, currently in action, is for fines and jail time for those caught not attending Friday prayers and pregnancy outside marriage. The second and third phases, to be implemented in 2016, will include execution, by stoning, for blasphemy, homosexuality and adultery. Parts of sharia law will be imposed on the non-Muslim population of Brunei, including expatriate workers and visitors to the country. The sultan brushed off any criticism levelled at him for his decision, declaring that "it was not for fun, but to obey Allah's command as written in the Quran".

It is believed that part of the reason for the sultan's imposition of sharia law is related to Brunei's reliance on oil and gas and the inevitable challenges faced by the country once the oil and gas has run out. In 2008, the Sultan launched Wawasan Brunei 2035, a plan to transform his nation into a kind of Islamic Singapore, and for Brunei to have a "dynamic and sustainable economy". However, with 93% of government revenues dependent on oil and gas Brunei and its population face an extraordinary set of challenges. Whilst the plans to increase tourist arrivals into the country have been implemented, Brunei was the only Southeast Asian country not to see any growth in its tourism industry from 2002-2013. To further complicate matters, several prominent US politicians are trying to get rid of Brunei from its list of members of the Trans-Pacific Partnership free trade agreement as a result of the imposition of sharia. The economic future of Brunei remains far from secure though it seems much of the population remains unfazed and there have been responses claiming the foreign media is sensationalizing the issue unnecessarily.

Population

In the days of Charles Brooke, the sultanate had a population of about 20,000. It now stands at 415,717 (July 2014 estimate). The city-state of Singapore has more than 12 times as many people. Today 60% of the country's population lives in towns; more than half is aged under 20 and a third is under 14. At 2.2% a year, Brunei has one of the fastest growing populations in the region; it also has the region's lowest death rate and second lowest infant mortality rate after Singapore; Bruneians' average life expectancy is 77. About 66% of the population is Malay, 10% Chinese, 3% indigenous tribal groups and 21% other (see People, page 185); there are also some 100,000 expatriate workers – both professionals and labourers. The average density of population is low: about 67 people per sq km; most are concentrated along the narrow coastal belt.

Land and environment

Geography and geology

Brunei Darussalam lies about 400 km north of the equator, between four degrees and five degrees north, on the northwest coast of Borneo. The sultanate has a 160 km-long coastline, facing the South China Sea. The country is divided into four districts: Brunei/Muara, Tutong, Belait and Temburong.

Territorially, modern Brunei is the rump of what was once a sprawling empire. Today the sultanate has a land area of 5769 sq km, a pinprick on the map, about twice the size of Luxembourg. In 1981 the government bought a cattle ranch at Willeroo, in Australia's Northern Territory, which is larger than the whole of Brunei. As a country, it is a geographical absurdity; its two wedges of territory are separated by Limbang, ceded to the expansionist Charles Brooke, Rajah of Sarawak in 1890. Bruneians commute between the Temburong district and Bandar Seri Begawan in speedboats nicknamed 'flying coffins'.

Most of Brunei occupies a low alluvial coastal plain. There are four main rivers, flowing north into the South China Sea. The coastal lowlands and river valleys are characterized by a flat or gently undulating landscape, rarely rising more than 15 m above sea level. The coastline is mainly sandy except for a stretch of rocky headlands between Muara and Pekan Tutong. These cliffs rise to a height of about 30 m, where the north coastal hills meet the South China Sea. Further west, the Andulau Hills stand at the north end of a watershed that separates the drainage basins of the Belait and Tutong.

Towards the interior of West Brunei, along the border with Sarawak and in South Temburong district, it gets much hillier. In West Brunei there are two upland areas, comprised of sandstones and shale: the Ladan Hills run north to south between the Tutong and Limbang basins. Bukit Bedawan is the highest of these, at 529 m. In Belait district, near the border with Sarawak, are the Labi Hills – the highest being Bukit Teraja at 417 m. The south half of Temburong district is much more mountainous, with deep, narrow valleys and several hills of over 600 m. The highest of these is Bukit Pagon at 1850 m, although the summit itself is actually outside Brunei.

The Seria oilfield, the source of Brunei's liquidity, lies on a narrow anticline, a quarter of which is submerged by the sea. All the oil comes from a strip just 13 km long and 2.5 km wide. The oil is in fractured blocks of sandstone between 240 m and 3000 m below the surface. Some of the oil under the sea is accessed by wells drilled from the shore which reach more than 1.5 km out to sea.

Climate

Brunei is only five degrees north of the equator and so is characterized, like the rest of North and West Borneo, by consistently hot and sticky weather: uniform temperature, high humidity (average 82%) and regular rainfall.

Daily temperatures average at 28°C. Midday temperatures rarely exceed 35°C; at night it is unusual for the temperature to dip below 21°C. The average daily minimum temperature is 23°C, the maximum 32°C.

Rainfall is well distributed throughout the year but there are two distinct seasons: there is less rainfall between February and August, and the rainy season sets in during September and runs through to the end of January. The northeast monsoon peaks in December and January and is characterized by short-lived violent downpours. Even during the monsoon season, though, there is a 50% chance of it not raining each day and a daily average of seven hours of sunshine. The annual average rainfall is over 2500 mm a year, nearly five times that of London or more than double New York's annual rainfall. The south interior region, including Temburong district, is wetter, with up to 4060 mm a year. The west coast areas get between 2540 and 3300 mm of rainfall a year. In Bandar Seri Begawan, the average annual rainfall is 2921 mm.

Flora and fauna

Like much of the neighbouring Malaysian state of Sarawak, the low-lying areas of Brunei are characterized by peat swamp forest which is unsuited to agriculture. In parts the peat is up to 9 m thick and cannot support permanent agriculture. About 70% of Brunei is still covered in lush virgin jungle. If secondary forest – known as *belukar* – is included, about 80% of Brunei's land area is still forested.

Apart from the peat swamp forest, Brunei has areas of heath forest (*kerangas*) on sandy soils near the coast, and mangrove, which grows on the tidal mudflats around Brunei Bay and in the Belait and Tutong estuaries. The most common mangrove tree is the bakau, which grows to a height of about 9 m and has stilt roots to trap sediment. The *bakau* was the source of *cutch* – a dye made from boiling its bark, and used in leather tanning, which was produced at Brunei Bay until the 1950s. Bakau wood also made useful piles for stilt houses in Bandar Seri Begawan's Kampong Ayer as it is resistant to rotting, and excellent charcoal. Also on the coast, between Kuala Belait and Muara, are stretches of casuarina forest.

Away from the coastal plain and the river valleys, the forest changes to lowland rainforest – or mixed dipterocarp forest – which supports at least eight commercial hardwood species. The *Dipterocarpacae* family forms the jungle canopy, 30-50 m above the ground. Timber from Brunei's jungle is used locally – none is exported. By 1990, logging firms were required to use sustainable management techniques and within a year, felling was cut to half the 1989 level. Forest reserves have been expanded and cover 320,000 ha. Indeed, Brunei has some of Southeast Asia finest forests – despite its small size when compared with the neighbouring Malaysian states of Sabah and Sarawak and with Indonesian Borneo (Kalimantan).

Wildlife

Brunei's jungle has been left largely intact; thanks to its oil wealth there is no need to exploit the forest. Loggers and shifting cultivators have been less active than they have in neighbouring territories and the forest fauna have been less disturbed. Their only disruptions come from a few upriver tribespeople, a handful of wandering Penan hunter-gatherers, the odd scientist and the occasional platoon of muddied soldiers on jungle warfare training exercises.

Relatively few tourists venture into Brunei's jungle as Sarawak's nearby national parks are much more accessible and better known. The year of 1996, however, marked the opening of the Ulu Temburong National Park with its network of wooden walkways and a fantastic canopy walkway. What's more, Brunei is the best place for spotting the rare proboscis monkey (see box, page 163). For those who have access to a car, there are also several jungle trails on Brunei's doorstep.

Brunei boasts much of Borneo's jungle exotica. For oil explorers and their families in the early 1900s, some local residents proved more daunting than others. Up until the 1960s, encounters with large crocodiles were commonplace in Brunei, and in the oil town of Seria they posed a constant menace to the local community. In August 1959 Brunei Shell Petroleum was forced to recruit a professional crocodile catcher. Mat Yassin bin Hussin claimed to have caught and destroyed more than 700 crocodiles in a career spanning 40 years, the largest being a highly unlikely 8.5-m-long man-eater that had devoured 12 Ibans south of Kuala Belait.

Mat Yassin's technique was to sprinkle gold dust into the river as part of a magic ritual, then to dangle chickens over bridges on baited rattan hooks. According to GC Harper, a Seria oilfield historian, Mat Yassin would wait until a crocodile jumped for the bait and then he would "blow down its snout with the aid of a blowpipe to make the strong reptile weak. It could then be dragged up the riverbank and its jaws tied before it was destroyed." Mat Yassin silenced cynics when he landed two man-eaters in as many days and said he had come across an old white crocodile which was considered sacred; he refused to touch it because it "could never be destroyed either by bullets or by magic".

Culture

Arts and crafts

Brass is said to have been introduced into Brunei in the late 15th century, when the Sultanate became particularly famous for its brass cannon, which were used in battle and to convey messages between villages about deaths, births and festivities, such as the beginning and end of Ramadan. The 500 cannon and guns in the Brunei Museum are largely of local manufacture. Brass cannon and gongs were items of currency and barter and were often used in dowries, particularly among the tribal Belaits and Dusuns. Brassware is a prized family heirloom, and was the basis of fines in the traditional legal system. In 1908 there were more than 200 brass workers in Brunei, but by the mid-1970s their numbers had reportedly fallen to fewer than 10. Today, traditional casting by the 'lost wax' technique is being revived. Brunei's **silversmiths** have a good reputation for their intricate designs, betelnut boxes being a speciality. **Gold jewellery**, mostly 22 and 24 carat is also reasonable.

The best known local **textile** is *Kain Jong Sarat*, a cotton sarong, usually about 2 m in length, woven with more than 1000 gold threads on a handloom. Today Jong Sarat are only used on ceremonial occasions. The *Sukma-Indera* is distinguished by its multi-coloured floral patterns, while the *Tenunan* is woven with gold thread and worn by men round the waist on Hari Raya Aidil Adha; it can cost up to B$1000.

People

Brunei 'Malays', who make up 66% of the sultanate's population, are mostly Kedayans or Melanaus, indigenous to north Borneo. There was no great migration of Malays from the peninsula. Similarly, few Iban migrated into what is modern Brunei, although in the 19th century, they pushed up to the middle reaches of Sarawak's rivers, which in those days came under the sultanate's ambit. Ibans, Muruts, Kedayans, Dayaks and even Dusuns are all represented in the 3% of the population labelled 'indigenous tribal groups'.

Today, most Bruneian Malays are well off and well educated; more than half of them have secure government jobs. Car ownership in Brunei is a telling indicator of Bruneians' affluence: the country has one of the highest car population ratios in the world. Recognizing that things might get out of hand, in 1995 the authorities introduced a new car tax to try and curb Brunei's love affair with the automobile. The standard of living is high by Southeast Asian standards although there are poorer communities living in Kampong Ayer and Kampong Kianggeh (near the open market). Many of these are recent immigrants – there is a high level of illegal immigration from the neighbouring states of Sabah and Sarawak as well as from Kalimantan.

The government policy of 'Bruneization' discriminates positively in favour of the Malays and against the Chinese, who make up 10% of the population. Most of the Chinese are fairly wealthy as they account for the vast majority of Brunei's private sector businesspeople. Unlike the Malays, the Chinese did not automatically become citizens of Brunei at Independence, even if they could trace their ancestry back several generations. The question of citizenship is very important as only Bruneian citizens can enjoy the benefits of the welfare state: free education, health care, subsidized housing and government jobs.

Religion

Brunei is a Sunni Muslim monarchy; the state motto, 'Always render service by God's guidance', is emblazoned on the crescent on Brunei's national flag. Islam appears to have been firmly established in the Sultanate by the mid-15th century. Today it is the official religion and a religious council advises the Sultan, who is head of the Islamic faith in Brunei, on all Islamic matters.

Sabah

soaring mountains, underwater adventures and rainforest

Sabah may not have the colourful history of neighbouring Sarawak, but there is still a great deal to entice the visitor.

It is the second largest Malaysian state after Sarawak, covering 73,500 sq km, making it about the size of Scotland. Occupying the northeast corner of Borneo, Sabah is shaped like a dog's head, the jaws reaching out in the Sulu and Celebes seas, and the back of the head facing onto the South China Sea.

The highlights of Sabah are abundant and accessible. The state is blessed with stunning (yet rapidly diminishing) wildlife and natural wonders including caves, reefs, forests and mountains. The Gunung Kinabulu National Park is named after Sabah's (and Malaysia's) highest peak and is one of the state's most visited destinations. Also popular is the Sepilok Orang-Utan Rehabilitation Sanctuary outside Sandakan. Marine sights include the Turtle Islands National Park, the Danum Valley Conservation Area and Sipadan Island, one of Asia's finest dive sites.

While Sabah's indigenous groups were not cherished as they were in Sarawak by the White Rajahs, areas around towns such as Kudat, Tenom, Keningau and Kota Belud still provide memorable insights into the peoples of the region.

Best for
Diving ▪ Jungle treks ▪ Wildlife spotting

Kota Kinabalu 190
Off the coast & south of
   Kota Kinabalu. 213
North of Kota Kinabalu. 235
Gunung Kinabalu
   National Park 241
East coast 254
Background 294

Footprint
picks

★ **Manukan Island**, page 215

Snorkel among the coral or soak up laid-back beach vibes.

★ **Crocker Range National Park**, page 228

Enjoy great hiking trails and hair-raising adventures down the Padas River.

★ **Sabah's *tamu* and Murut villages**, page 230

Bargain for local delicacies and watch blowpipes being made.

★ **Gunung Kinabalu**, page 246

Catch sunrise on the summit of Malaysia's tallest peak.

★ **Sepilok Orang-Utan Rehabilitation Centre**, page 266

Get up close to orang-utans at this world famous rehabilitation centre.

★ **Sungai Kinabatangan**, page 270

A guided river cruise is your best chance to spot orang-utans in the wild.

★ **Danum Valley Conservation Area**, page 276

Trek deep into the rainforest to spot pygmy elephants and hornbills.

★ **Sipadan Island Marine Reserve**, page 282

Swim with turtles at this world-class diving site.

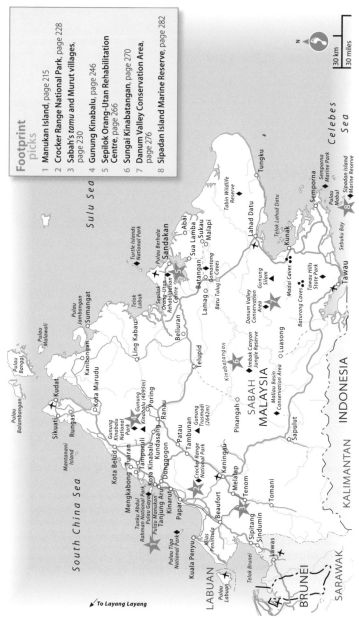

Footprint picks

1 **Manukan Island**, page 215
2 **Crocker Range National Park**, page 228
3 **Sabah's *tamu* and Murut villages**, page 230
4 **Gunung Kinabalu**, page 246
5 **Sepilok Orang-Utan Rehabilitation Centre**, page 266
6 **Sungai Kinabatangan**, page 270
7 **Danum Valley Conservation Area**, page 276
8 **Sipadan Island Marine Reserve**, page 282

30 km
30 miles

N

Celebes Sea

Sulu Sea

Tungku

Semporna Marine Park
Pulau
Mabul

Sipadan Island
Marine Reserve

Tabin Wildlife
Reserve

Telok Lahud Datu

Semporna

Kunak

Tawau

Sebuku Bay

Lahad Datu

Gunung Silam

Madai Caves

Tawau Hills
State Park

Baturong Caves

Pulau
Malawali

Pulau
Banggi

Turtle Islands
National Park

Pulau Berhala
Sandakan
Abai

Sua Lamba
Malapi
Sukau

Batangan
Gomantong
Caves

Sepilok
Orang-Utan
Rehabilitation
Centre

Lamag
Batu Tulug

Danum Valley
Conservation
Area

Pulau
Jambongan
Sumangat

Kanibongan

Telok
Labuk

Ling Kabau

Beluran

Telupid

Kinabatangan

Imbak Canyon
Jungle Reserve

Luasong

INDONESIA

KALIMANTAN

South China Sea

Pulau
Balambangan

Mantanani
Island

Sikuati
Kudat
Rungas

Kota Marudu

Gunung
Kinabalu
National
Park

Gunung
Kinabalu (4095m)
Poring

Ranau

Tambunan

Pinangah

SABAH
MALAYSIA

Malau Basin
Conservation Area

Sapulut

Mengkabong
Tunku Abdul
Rahman National Park
Pulau Gaya
Pulau Manukan
Tanjung Aru
Kinarut

Kota Belud
Tuaran
Tamparuli
Kota Kinabalu
Donggogon
Kundasang
Patau

Gunung
Trusmadi
(2642m)

Crocker Range
National Park

Keningau

Melalap

Tomani

Papar

Kuala Penyu

Pulau Tiga
National Park

Klias
Peninsula

Beaufort
Tenom

Sipitang
Sindumin

Lawas

SARAWAK

Telok Brunei

BRUNEI

LABUAN

Pulau
Labuan

To Layang Layang

Essential Sabah

Getting around

Air Kota Kinabalu is the main transport hub with air links to much of east Asia and Australia, including daily flights from Kuala Lumpur. Most major towns in Sabah have airports for domestic flights, including Sandakan, Labuan, Miri, Mulu, Sibu, Kudat, Kuching, Tawau and Lahad Datu. Tawau is the nearest airport to the Sipadan Island Marine Resort.

Boat Sabah has international ferry connections with Brunei via Pulau Labuan (from KK), Indonesia (from Tawau) and the Philippines (from Sandakan).

Car Car hire is good value though not all roads are paved and 4WD is recommended.

Minibus Shared minibuses run between towns and go to most places, providing a cheap and efficient service. They leave when full and you can get off wherever you like. It's possible to charter the whole minibus if you don't want to wait.

Taxi Taxis are the quickest way to get around town and can be chartered for longer trips. Taxi stands can generally be found next to large hotels, shopping malls and bus terminals.

Train Sabah has one main train line, the Sabah State Railway, which runs from KK to Papar via Kudat and Beaufort. The *North Borneo Express* is a restored steam train that runs to Kinarut and Papar but is more of a tourist experience.

When to go

Sabah's equatorial climate means that temperatures rarely exceed 32°C or fall below 21°C, making it fairly pleasant all year. However, October to December is the rainy season, which spoils plans for the beach and makes climbing Mount Kinabalu or trekking in Sabah's national parks an unpleasant and slippery experience. For spotting turtles on the east coast islands, your best chance is between May and September. The best period for birdwatching is October to March when migratory species visit the area.

Time required

A couple of days could be spent doing day trips in and around KK, such as the Gaya market, Tunku Abhul Rahman Marine Park or Mari Mari cultural village. Allow three days to visit Sepilok and the Kinabatangan River; two to three days to hike up Mount Kinabalu including half a day for a soak in the Poring Hot Springs afterwards; three to four days for a diving trip out to Sipadan or Kapalai, or to go trekking in the Danum Valley. For Maliau Basin it's best to allow five days. If short on time, consider taking an organized tour and some internal flights.

Useful websites

www.borneo360.com Sabah travel guide
www.sabahhomestay.my Sabah Homestay Association
www.tourism.gov.my Tourism Malaysia

National parks information

All accommodation and trekking at Mount Kinabalu and Poring Hot Springs is organized through **Sutera Sanctuary Lodges**, www.suterasanctuarylodges.com (see page 250). **Mount Kinabalu Booking Office**, www.mountkinabalu.com (see page 205), is worth a look for its wealth of up-to-date information and variety of interesting packages. **Borneo Nature Tours**, www.borneonaturetours.com (see page 205) deals with the majority of tourism-related activity in Danum Valley and Maliau Basin and is perhaps the easiest first point of contact. You can also contact **Sabah Parks**, www.sabahparks.org.my (see page 197). The official body that regulates the parks is the **Sabah Foundation** (Yayasan Sabah Group), www.ysnet.org.my (see page 194).

Kota
Kinabalu

KK (population 452,000) is most people's introduction to Sabah for the simple reason that it is the only city with extensive air links to other parts of the country as well as a handful of regional destinations. KK is a modern state capital with little that can be dated back more than 50 years. Highlights include the State Museum and the town's markets. Out of town, within a day's excursion, are beaches such as Tanjung Aru and those near Tuaran, as well as a number of Kadazan and Bajau districts, with their distinctive markets. While it is necessary to go further afield to get a real view of tribal life, this is better than nothing.

The city is strung out along the coast, with jungle-clad hills as a backdrop. Two-thirds of the town is built on land reclaimed from the shallow Gaya Bay and at spring tides it is possible to walk across to Gaya Island. Jalan Pantai, or Beach Road, is now in the centre of town. Successive land reclamation projects have meant that many of the original stilt villages, such as Kampong Ayer, have been cut off from the sea and developed. The government is cleaning up these areas and the inhabitants of the water villages have been rehoused.

Essential Kota Kinabalu

Finding your feet

Kota Kinabalu International Airport, T088-325555, is 7 km south of town in Tanjung Aru. There are two terminals, one on either side of the runway. Most airlines, including **Malaysian Airlines**, use Terminal 1, while Terminal 2 is used by budget airlines such as **Air Asia**. It is a long walk (one hour) between the two terminals, so take advantage of the hourly shuttle service (RM5) which connects them; look for signs in the Arrivals halls of the terminals.

To get into town, airport shuttle buses run 0800-1900 starting at Terminal 1, and heading to Terminal 2 before terminating at Padang Merdeka station (RM5/RM3) in the centre. There is also a bus stop outside Terminal 2 where the local 16c minibus service runs hourly (RM1.50) to Terminal Wawasan in the south of town. The local 17 minibus service heads into town from Terminal 1 five minutes' walk from the airport (RM1.50). Taxis from the airport cost RM30 to the city centre; buy coupons in advance from the booths outside the Arrivals hall. The journey takes 20-40 minutes, depending on the traffic.

Jessleton Point Ferry Terminal in KK has boat connections with Pulau Labuan (see page 218) and Tunku Abdul Rahmen National Park (see page 214).

Getting around

The city sprawls for several kilometres from the airport to Likas Bay, however the centre is quite small and easy to walk around. There is no central bus station but buses and minibuses run from several terminals around the city providing a service around town and to destinations further afield. All minibuses have their destinations on the windscreen and leave when full; you can get off wherever you like. Most rides in town cost RM0.50-2. Red taxis are unmetered, dark blue taxis metered. Taxi rides around town should cost RM10-20. There are also plenty of car hire firms. See Transport, page 205.

Best experiences

The golden domes and Islamic architecture of the Masjid Sabah, page 192
Sabah State Museum, an introduction to the state's indigenous culture and environment, page 192
Waterfront Esplanade; enjoy fresh seafood as the sun sets over the South China Sea, page 200
Tanjung Aru Beach; spend a day relaxing or flying a kite, page 208
Monsopiad Cultural Village or Mari Mari Cultural Village will give you an insight into Sabah's ethnic groups, pages 208 and 210
Explore one of the nearby islands in Gaya Bay from Jessleton Point Jetty, page 214

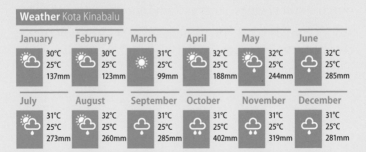

Weather Kota Kinabalu

January	February	March	April	May	June
30°C 25°C 137mm	30°C 25°C 123mm	31°C 25°C 99mm	32°C 25°C 188mm	32°C 25°C 244mm	32°C 25°C 285mm

July	August	September	October	November	December
31°C 25°C 273mm	32°C 25°C 260mm	31°C 25°C 285mm	31°C 25°C 402mm	31°C 25°C 319mm	31°C 25°C 281mm

stunning sunsets, a weekly market and the starting point for most trips

Only three buildings remain of the old town: the old General Post Office on Jalan Gaya, Atkinson's Clocktower (built in 1905 and named after Jesselton's first district officer) and the old red-roofed Lands and Surveys building. The renovated post office now houses the Sabah Tourism Board.

Masjid Sabah and Sabah State Museum

To get to Masjid Sabah and the Sabah State Museum complex there are minibuses that stop near Wisma Kewangan on the KK–Tanjung Aru road, and near Queen Elizabeth Hospital on the KK–Penampang road.

The golden dome of **Masjid Sabah** ① *Jln Tunku Abdul Rahman, Sat-Thu daily 0800-1200 and 1400-1700, Fri 1400-1700, regular minibuses from the city centre,* is visible from most areas of the city, although it is actually about 3 km away. Completed in 1975, it is one of the biggest mosques in Malaysia and, like the Federal Mosque in Kuala Lumpur, a fine example of contemporary Islamic architecture. It can accommodate 12,000 worshippers.

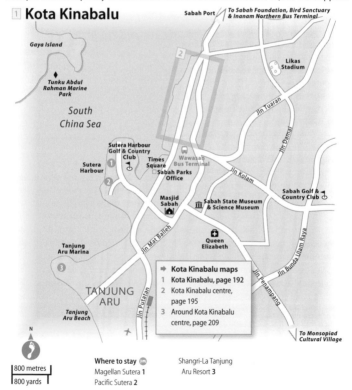

1 Kota Kinabalu

⇒ **Kota Kinabalu maps**
1 Kota Kinabalu, page 192
2 Kota Kinabalu centre, page 195
3 Around Kota Kinabalu centre, page 209

800 metres
800 yards

Where to stay 🛏
Magellan Sutera **1**
Pacific Sutera **2**

Shangri-La Tanjung
Aru Resort **3**

BACKGROUND
Mat Salleh: fort builder and folk hero

Mat Salleh was a Bajau, and son of a Sulu chief, born in the court of the Sultan of Sulu. He was the only native leader to stand up against the increasingly autocratic whims of the North Borneo government as it sequestrated land traditionally belonging to tribal chiefs. Under the British North Borneo Chartered Company and the subsequent colonial administration, generations of schoolchildren were taught that Mat Salleh was a rabble-rouser and troublemaker. Now Sabahans regard him as a nationalist hero.

In the *British North Borneo Herald* of 16 February 1899, it was reported that when he spoke, flames leapt from his mouth; lightning flashed with each stroke of his *parang* (cutlass) and when he scattered rice, the grains became wasps. He was said to have been endowed with 'special knowledge' by the spirits of his ancestors and was also reported to have been able to throw a buffalo by its horns.

In 1897 Mat Salleh raided and set fire to the first British settlement on Pulau Gaya (off modern day Kota Kinabalu). For this, and other acts of sabotage, he was declared an outlaw by the governor. A price tag of 700 Straits dollars was put on his head and an administrative officer, Raffles Flint, was assigned the unenviable task of tracking him down. Flint failed to catch him and Mat Salleh gained a reputation as a military genius.

Finally, the managing director of the Chartered Company, Scottish adventurer and former gunrunner, William C Cowie, struck a deal with Mat Salleh and promised that his people would be allowed to settle peacefully in Tambunan, which at that time was not under Chartered Company control.

Half the North Borneo administration resigned as they considered Cowie's concessions outrageous. With it looking increasingly unlikely that the terms of his agreement with Cowie would be respected, Mat Salleh retreated to Tambunan where he started building his fort; he had already gained a fearsome reputation for these stockades. West coast resident G Hewett described it as "the most extraordinary place and without [our] guns it would have been absolutely impregnable". Rifle fire could not penetrate it and Hewett blasted 200 shells into the fort with no noticeable effect. The stone walls were 2.5 m thick and were surrounded by three bamboo fences, the ground in front of which was studded with row upon row of sharpened bamboo spikes. Hewett's party retreated, having suffered four dead and nine wounded.

Mat Salleh had built similar forts all over Sabah and the hearts of the protectorate's administrators must have sunk when they heard he was building one at Tambunan. A government expedition arrived in the Tambunan Valley on the last day of 1899. There was intensive fighting throughout January, with the government taking village after village, until at last the North Borneo Constabulary came within 50 m of Mat Salleh's fort. Its water supply had been cut off and the fort had been shelled incessantly for 10 days. Mat Salleh was trapped. On 31 January 1900 he was killed by a stray bullet which hit him in the left temple.

Perched on a small hill overlooking the mosque is the relatively new purpose-built **Sabah Museum and Heritage Village** ⓘ *Jln Muzium, T088-253199, www.museum.sabah. gov.my, daily 0900-1700, RM15, also guided tours, take bus 13 (RM) from town heading to*

Penampang, which is designed like a Rungus longhouse. It is divided into ethnography, natural history, ceramics, history and archaeology. The ethnographic section includes an excellent display on the uses of bamboo. There is also tribal brassware, silverware, musical instruments, basketry and pottery, as well as a collection of costumes and artefacts from Sabah tribes such as the Kadazan/Dusun, Bajau, Murut and Rungus.

One of the most interesting items in this collection is a *sininggazanak,* a wooden statue, like a totem pole, supposedly resembling the deceased. If a Kadazan man died without an heir, it was the custom to erect a *sininggazanak* on his land. There is also a collection of *bangkaran* (human skulls) which, before the tribe's wholesale conversion to Christianity, would have been suspended from the rafters of Kadazan longhouses. Every five years a *magang* feast was held to appease the spirits of the skulls.

The museum's archaeological section contains a magnificently carved coffin found in a limestone cave in the Madai area. Upstairs, the natural history section provides a good introduction to Sabah's flora and fauna. Next door is a collection of jars, called *pusaka*, which are tribal heirlooms. They were originally exchanged by the Chinese for jungle produce, such as beeswax, camphor and birds' nests.

Next door to the State Museum is the **Science Museum**, containing an exhibition on Shell's offshore activities. The **Art Gallery and Multivision Theatre**, within the same complex, is also worth a browse. The art gallery is small and mainly exhibits works by local artists. Among the more interesting items on display are those of Suzie Mojikol, a Kadazan artist; Bakri Dani, who adapts Bajau designs; and Philip Biji, who specializes in burning Murut designs onto chunks of wood with a soldering iron. The ethnobotanical gardens are on the hillside below the museum. There is a cafeteria in the main building. Occasional cultural performances are held in the museum.

Sabah has a large Christian population and the **Sacred Heart Cathedral** has a striking pyramidal roof that is clearly visible from the Sabah State Museum complex.

Signal Hill viewpoint

Signal Hill (Bukit Bendera), just southeast of the central area, gives a panoramic view of the town and islands and is a great spot for taking in the spectacular sunsets. In the past, the hill was used as a vantage point for signalling to ships approaching the harbour.

Likas Bay

There is an even better view of the coastline from the top of the **Sabah Foundation (Yayasan Sabah) Complex** ⓘ *4 km northeast of town, overlooking Likas Bay*. This surreal glass sculpture houses the chief minister's office. The Sabah Foundation was set up in 1966 to help improve Sabahans' quality of life. The foundation has a 972,800-ha timber concession, which it claims to manage on a sustainable-yield basis (achievement of a high-level annual output without impairing the long-term productivity of the land). More than two-thirds of this concession has already been logged. Profits from the timber go towards loans and scholarships for Sabahan students, funding the construction of hospitals and schools and supplying milk, textbooks and uniforms to school children. The foundation also operates a 24-hour flying ambulance service to remote parts of the interior. In recent years the foundation has begun to invest more directly in conservation, seeing potential financial returns from ecotourism and rainforest-derived medicines amongst others. The major pristine areas that haven't been logged within the concession are Danum Valley, the Maliau Basin conservation area and the Imbak Canyon.

Between the Yayasan Sabah and the city centre is one of Borneo's largest squatter communities, visibly demonstrating that not all share equally in the timber boom.

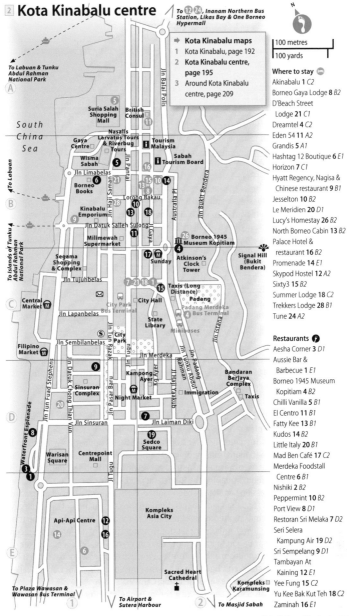

2 Kota Kinabalu centre

To ⑫ ㉔ *Inanam Northern Bus Station, Likas Bay & One Borneo Hypermall*

To Labuan & Tunku Abdul Rahman National Park

➜ Kota Kinabalu maps
1 Kota Kinabalu, page 192
2 Kota Kinabalu centre, page 195
3 Around Kota Kinabalu centre, page 209

100 metres
100 yards

Where to stay
Akinabalu **1** C2
Borneo Gaya Lodge **8** B2
D'Beach Street
Lodge **21** C1
Dreamtel **4** C2
Eden 54 **11** A2
Grandis **5** A1
Hashtag 12 Boutique **6** E1
Horizon **7** C1
Hyatt Regency, Nagisa & Chinese restaurant **9** B1
Jesselton **10** B2
Le Meridien **20** D1
Lucy's Homestay **26** B2
North Borneo Cabin **13** B2
Palace Hotel & restaurant **16** B2
Promenade **14** E1
Skypod Hostel **12** A2
Sixty3 **15** B2
Summer Lodge **18** C2
Trekkers Lodge **28** B1
Tune **24** A2

Restaurants
Aesha Corner **3** D1
Aussie Bar & Barbecue **1** E1
Borneo 1945 Museum Kopitiam **4** B2
Chilli Vanilla **5** B1
El Centro **1** B1
Fatty Kee **13** B1
Kudos **14** B2
Little Italy **20** B1
Mad Ben Café **17** C2
Merdeka Foodstall Centre **6** B1
Nishiki **2** B2
Peppermint **10** B2
Port View **8** D1
Restoran Sri Melaka **7** D2
Seri Selera Kampung Air **19** D2
Sri Sempelang **9** D1
Tambayan At Kaining **12** E1
Yee Fung **15** C2
Yu Kee Bak Kut Teh **18** C2
Zaminah **16** E1

South China Sea

To Labuan

To Islands of Tunku Abdul Rahman National Park

Suria Salah Shopping Mall
British Consul
Gaya Centre
Nasalis Larvatus Tours & Riverbug Tours
Tourism Malaysia
Sabah Tourism Board
Wisma Sabah
Borneo Books
Kinabalu Emporium
Lorong Bakau
Milimewah Supermarket
Segama Shopping & Complex
Borneo 1945 Museum Kopitiam
Atkinson's Clock Tower
Sunday
Signal Hill (Bukit Bendera)
Central Market
City Park Bus Terminal
City Hall
Padang Merdeka Bus Terminal
Taxis (Long Distance)
Filipino Market
State Library
Minibuses
City Park
City Park
City Hall
Kampong Ayer
Sinsuran Complex
Night Market
Bandaran Berjaya Complex
Immigration
Taxis
Warisan Square
Centrepoint Mall
Sedco Square
Api-Api Centre
Kompleks Asia City
Kompleks Karamunsing
Sacred Heart Cathedral

Jln Balai Polis
Jln Bukit Bendera
Australia Pl
Jln Pantai
Jln Haji Saman
Jln Datuk Salleh Sulong
Jln Gaya
Jln Tujuhbelas
Jln Lapanbelas
Jln Sembilanbelas
Jln Tun Fuad Stephens
Jln Pasar Baru
Jln Merdeka
Jln Tuku Abdul Rahman
Jln Padang
Jln Istana
Jln Haji Yakub
Jln Tun Razak
Jln Sinsuran
Jln Laiman Diki
Jln Tun Razak
Waterfront Esplanade

To Plaza Wawasan & Wawasan Bus Terminal
To Airport & Sutera Harbour
To Masjid Sabah

BACKGROUND
Kota Kinabalu

Kota Kinabalu started life as a trading post, established in 1881 by the British North Borneo Chartered Company under the directorship of William C Cowie (see page 295); not on the mainland, but on Gaya Island, opposite the present town, where a Filipino shanty town is today. On 9 July 1897 rebel leader Mat Salleh (see box, page 193), who engaged in a series of hit-and-run raids against the British North Borneo Chartered Company's administration, landed on Pulau Gaya. His men looted and sacked the settlement and Gaya township was abandoned.

Two years later the Europeans established another township but this time located on the mainland, opposite Pulau Gaya, adjacent to a Bajau stilt village. The kampong was called 'Api Api' ('Fire! Fire!') because it had been repeatedly torched by pirates over the years. After the Gaya experience, it was an inauspicious name. The Chartered Company renamed it Jesselton, after Sir Charles Jessel, one of the company directors. However, for years, only the Europeans called it Jesselton; locals preferred the old name, and even today Sabahans, especially those from the Chinese dialect groups, sometimes refer to their state capital as Api.

Jesselton owed its raison d'être to a plan that backfired. William C Cowie, a former gun-runner for the Sultan of Sulu, became managing director of the Chartered Company in 1894. He wanted to build a trans-Borneo railway and the narrow strip of land just north of Tanjung Aru and opposite Pulau Gaya, with its sheltered anchorage, was chosen as the terminus.

Photographs in the Sabah State Museum chart the town's development from 1899, when work on the North Borneo Railway terminus began in earnest. By 1905, Jesselton was linked to Beaufort by a 92-km narrow gauge track. By 1911 it had a population of 2686, half of whom were Chinese and the remainder Kadazans and Dusuns; there were 33 European residents. Jesselton was of little importance in comparison to Sandakan, the capital of north Borneo.

When the Japanese Imperial Army invaded Borneo in 1942, Jesselton's harbour gave the town strategic significance and it was consequently completely flattened by the Allies during the Second World War. Jesselton followed Kudat and Sandakan as the administrative centre of north Borneo at the end of the Second World War, and the city was rebuilt from scratch. In September 1967 Jesselton was renamed Kota Kinabalu after the mountain; its name is usually shortened to KK. Kota Kinabalu was awarded city status in 2000 and is now the sixth largest city in Malaysia.

Over in Likas Bay is **Kota Kinabalu City Bird Sanctuary** ⓘ *www.sabahwetlands.org, Tue-Sun 0800-1800, RM15, children RM10*, a 24-ha mangrove forest with a 1.5-km boardwalk. Possible sightings include egrets, kingfishers, green pigeons, purple herons, plover and redshanks. A pair of binoculars is recommended.

Markets

Gaya street market ⓘ *Jln Gaya, Sun 0600-1300*, sells a vast range of goods from jungle produce and handicrafts to pots and pans. The **KK Handicraft Centre (Pasar Kraftangan)** ⓘ *almost opposite the main minibus station on Jln Tun Fuad Stephens*, was formerly known as the **Filipino market** as most of the stalls are run by Filipino immigrants. Filipino and local handicrafts are sold in the hundreds of cramped stalls along winding alleyways that are strung with low-slung curtains of shells, baskets and bags. The Filipino market is a good place to buy cultured pearls and has everything from fake gems to camagong-wood salad bowls, fibre shirts and traditional Indonesian medicines alongside the usual tourist knick-knacks. Further into town, on the waterfront, is the **central market** selling mainly fish, fruit and vegetables. There is also raw honey for sale. The rough and ready hawker centre upstairs has wonderful views over the sea towards Pulau Gaya. The daily fishing catch is unloaded on the wharf near the central market. There is a lively **evening market** selling cheap T-shirts and jewellery in front of the City Park.

Listings Kota Kinabalu *maps pages 192 and 195.*

Tourist information

Sabah Parks Office
Block H, Level 1-5, Lot 45 & 46, KK Times Square, Coastal Highway, T088-523300, www.sabahparks.org.my.

Sabah Tourism Board
51 Jln Gaya, T088-212121, www.sabah tourism.com. Mon-Fri 0800-1700, Sat-Sun and public holidays 0900-1600.
A great first point for help when arriving in KK. The office is well stocked with leaflets and information and has courteous, helpful staff.

Tourism Malaysia
Lot 1-0-7, Tingkat Bawah, Blok 1 Lorong Api-Api 1, Api Api Centre, T088-211732, www.tourism.gov.my.
Not as useful for Sabah as for Sarawak, but still does its best.

Where to stay

Well-heeled tourists will seek the more refined out-of-town resorts (see page 211); but in KK itself, mid-range hotels have improved immeasurably in recent years. The increased number of budget airlines flying into KK has also prompted the opening of a number of decent budget guesthouses.

$$$$ Sutera Harbour Resort
1 Sutera Harbour Blvd, T088-318888, www.suteraharbour.com.

South of the city centre, this resort was created from reclaimed land covering 156 ha that was previously the South China Sea. The Harbour consists of 2 hotels (1000 rooms in total): the **Magellan Sutera**, and the **Pacific Sutera**. The former is more relaxed, with many sports activities, including 27 holes of golf and a spa. The latter is a business hotel, with superb conference facilities.

$$$ Hotel Grandis
Suria Sabah Shopping Mall, 1 Jln Tun Fuad Stephens, T088-522888, www. hotelgrandis.com.
Comfortable new hotel near the boat jetties with sea views from some rooms. Rooms are spacious and well appointed with good facilities for families including pool and a rooftop bar for parents in need of sunset refreshments.

$$$ Hotel Sixty3
63 Jln Gaya, T088-212663, www.hotelsixty3.com.
This central place is well located for the Sun market and gets bonus points for the spacious rooms and bathrooms. Rooms are calmly decorated in soothing neutral tones and come with fast Wi-Fi. Staff are friendly and helpful.

$$$ Hyatt Regency
Jln Datuk Salleh Sulong, T088-221234, www.kinabalu.regency.hyatt.com.
Central location with 288 a/c rooms and 3 restaurants. There's also a pool and kids'

pool. There's live entertainment at the **Shenanigan's Fun Pub**, while **Avantang Spa** is a massage and fitness centre with views over the bay from the treadmills. Tours and treks organized. Good value.

$$$ Le Meridien
Jln Tun Fuad Stephens, Sinsuran, T088-322222, www.lemeridien.com/kotakinabalu.
A popular hotel for the well-heeled, with 306 smart, modern rooms, some with superb views over the bay. There's a pool, gym and excellent restaurant and club. For the best prices, book online well in advance.

$$$ The Palace Hotel
1 Jln Tangki, Karamunsing, T088-217222, www.thepalacehotel-sabah.com.
This distinctive castellated hotel, with 160 rooms, stands on a hill south of KK. Facilities include a pool, sauna, spa, gym and conference rooms.

$$$ Promenade
4 Lorong Api-Api 3, Api-Api Centre, T088-265555, www.promenade.com.my.
Recently renovated, this 4-star hotel on the seafront is popular with domestic and international Chinese business travellers. Sea view rooms are only a fraction more expensive than the city view rooms and worth every ringgit for the sunset. There are 4 dining outlets, a large pool and a gym.

$$ Courtyard
Unit G–800, 1Borneo Hypermall (see Shopping, below), Jln Sulaiman, T088-528228, www.courtyardhotel1borneo.com.
Super-slick rooms with gargantuan flatscreen TV. There's Wi-Fi in the bar and lobby, as well as a café with panoramic rooftop terrace.

$$ Dreamtel
5 Jln Padang, T088-240333, www.dreamtel.my.
Fair-value lodgings a short stroll from the town centre. This business hotel may not be the most inspiring choice in town, but it has clean, functional rooms and friendly staff. The Airport Bus Terminal is just outside

making this handy for those with an early morning flight. Rooms on the upper floors have excellent sunset views over the city. Limited facilities for those with children.

$$ Eden 54
54 Jln Gaya, T088-266054, www.eden54.com.
Excellent value in the heart of the city. The 39 rooms are modern, kept spotlessly clean and have TV and Wi-Fi, though some are windowless. There's a social area with plenty of cosy seats for travellers to exchange tales.

$$ Hashtag 12 Boutique Hotel
Block 3, 1st floor, Api-Api Commercial Centre, T088-313007.
Friendly new place near with a selection of tidy rooms and dorms. Gets rave reviews for its cleanliness and helpful staff.

$$ Horizon Hotel
Jln Pantai, T088-518000, www.horizonhotelsabah.com.
Popular hotel in the city centre with well-furnished and comfortable rooms, big TVs and decent Wi-Fi. Psychedelic carpets and a horse sculpture in the minimalist reception give this place a unique sense of identity. Pool, gym and decent breakfast.

$$ Jesselton
69 Jln Gaya, T088-223333, www.jesseltonhotel.com.
The first to open in KK, this classic hotel dates from 1954. With just 32 rooms, it is considered KK's premier boutique-style hotel. It's an old establishment, with everything from a shiny red London cab to shoe shining at your service. There's an Italian restaurant on the ground floor and all rooms have Wi-Fi.

$$ Tune Hotel
Unit G 803, 1Borneo Hypermall (see Shopping complexes, below), Jln Sulaiman, T03-7962 5888, www.tunehotels.com.
A new hotel in the **1Borneo** shopping mall, 7 km from the city. This chain is the latest venture of **AirAsia** supreme, Tony Fernandez, and is run using the same model as a budget airline: book early, pay less. Rooms are

comfortable and have attached bath but are plastered with advertisements. TV, a/c and Wi-Fi costs extra.

$$-$ D'Beach Street Lodge
Jln Pantai, Lot 48, T088-258228, www.dbeachstreet.com.
Newly refurbished hotel, well situated for those that enjoy live music (there's a bar just downstairs – bring ear plugs). Rooms are functional and many have a balcony facing the street. Staff can be a tad laid back and uninterested, but this place is all about location and value (dorms cost RM35).

$ Akinabalu
Lot 133, Jln Gaya, T088-272188, www.akinabaluyh.com.
Popular backpacker haunt with a massive communal space with plenty of books and free internet access. Rooms are a bit gloomy, with windows onto a corridor only, but it's a good spot to meet other travellers.

$ Borneo Backpackers
24 Lorong Dewan, at the foot of Signal Hill on the corner with the roundabout, T088-234009, www.borneobackpackers.com.
In a renovated 1950s printing works, this backpacker hostel has 50 beds, internet, laundry, lounge, roof garden, and tourist information. The ground floor houses a post war-era coffee shop stacked with wartime photos and antique-style furniture. There's a variety of rooms, plus dorms with fan (RM20 per person) or a/c (RM25 per person).

$ Borneo Gaya Lodge
78 Jln Gaya, T088-242477, www.borneogayalodge.com.
A quiet and relaxed hotel with a selection of clean and comfortable a/c rooms with TV and Wi-Fi, and an a/c dorm. Breakfast is included. Many rooms are windowless. Tour information available.

$ Lucy's Homestay (Backpacker Lodge)
Australia Pl, 25 Lorong Dewan (by the Atkinson clock tower), T088-261495, welcome.to/backpackerkk.

Owned by the genial Lucy, who gets rave reviews from her guests, this sociable spot is one of the better budget options in town, although when lots of guests are staying, it can feel a bit cramped. Accommodation is mainly in dorms, although there are also 3 private rooms. Simple kitchen, excellent library and small balcony. Due to its popularity it's a good idea to book several days in advance.

$ North Borneo Cabin
74 Jln Gaya, T088-272800, www.northborneocabin.com.
A collection of spacious, spartan rooms and dorms (RM23) with shared bathroom, free breakfast and Wi-Fi. Friendly staff.

$ SKYPOD
Wisma 1 Sulaman, Jln Sulaman, T018-667 8055, www.skypod.my.
Though this place is located 10 km from the city centre, it is spotlessly clean and offers the chance to sleep in excellent-value pods, or tiny little niches. The contemporary design and fast Wi-Fi make this a popular flashpacker hangout. There's a free daily shuttle bus into town.

$ Summer Lodge
2nd/3rd and 4th floor, Lot 120 Gaya St, T088-244499, www.summerlodge.com.my.
Spacious and popular hotel in the centre, near a few good eating and drinking spots. Rooms are simple, cleanish and have high ceilings and a/c. There's a rooftop garden for the smokers on the 4th floor and plenty of bathrooms scattered about the place, although more expensive rooms are en suite. There are often DVDs playing in the reception, and the nearby Beach St market kicks off in a colourful style on weekends.

$ Trekkers Lodge
30 Jln Haji Saman, T088-252263, www.trekkerslodge.com.
Very busy place, so book ahead by several days if you want a double room. Well set up for travellers, with helpful staff, sitting-out area, library and tour information (good deals

with **Borneo Divers**). Due to its popularity, however, it feels cramped and can get a bit grubby, particularly the dorms. The en suite rooms are not good value.

Homestays

Homestays in Sabah are organized through the **Sabah Homestay Association** (7th floor Wisma Tun Fuad Stephen, T013-872 1765, www.sabahhomestay.my).

Restaurants

The waterfront has a range of restaurants with outdoor seating facing the South China Sea. Befitting Kota Kinabalu's status as the great melting pot of Borneo, here one can dine on the freshest seafood, get stuck into a fragrant bowl of Vietnamese *pho bo* or enjoy a crisp southern Indian *thosai* alongside more standard archipelago fare.

$$$ Aussie Bar and Barbecue
Waterfront Esplanade, Jln Tun Fuad Stephens.
Simple no-frills Australian bar-cum-steakhouse, with a bright green and yellow frontage. This is a good spot for carnivores on the hunt for steaks, but it also has fusion dishes and salads.

$$$ Chilli Vanilla
Jln Haji Samin, T088-238098. Open 1000-2230.
A snug place with good vibes and a cosmopolitan crowd of travellers and locals. The theme in distinctly Mediterranean though those with a hankering for hearty goulash will come away feeling chuffed. Service can be slow and it might be worth booking ahead, but those in need of high-quality Western food at reasonable prices will be more than satisfied

$$$ Kudos
Jesselton Hotel (see Where to stay), T088-532166. Open 0700-2230.
European bistro offerings with a menu stretching from fish n' chips to squid ink pasta and handsome looking burgers. Famed for its breakfasts which, though not cheap, will keep you going for hours.

$$$ Little Italy
Ground floor, Hotel Capital, 23 Jln Haji Saman, T088-232231. Lunch and dinner.
Visitors rightly rave about this award-winning pizza and pasta place with Italian chef. Recommended.

$$$ Nagisa
Hyatt Regency Hotel (see Where to stay).
Fancy place with tables facing the South China Sea serving up some of the most delectable Japanese fare in town. There's an open kitchen, sushi bar, *teppanyaki* counters and a private *tatami* room for the wealthy.

$$ Chinese Restaurant
Hyatt Regency Hotel (see Where to stay).
Broad menu of good Chinese cuisine including Shanghainese, Sichuan and Cantonese, although its signature dish, the delicious Peking duck, hails from the north. A popular place for Sunday dim sum and gets packed on weekend evenings. Recommended.

$$ El Centro
Lot 32, Jln Haji Salman.
Excellent Mexican fare served up in cheery surroundings with consistently excellent vegetarian options, live music and well-priced cocktails and beers. This place turns into a popular expat watering hole after 2200. Recommended.

$$ Mad Ben Café
Lot 121, Jln Gaya, T016-845 0073. Open 1100-2300.
Family-friendly place with a good-value Western menu and cheerful ambience. Generous portions. Busy in the evenings.

$$ Nishiki
Jln Gaya, opposite the Wing On Life Building.
Good-sized portions of Japanese food, friendly staff.

$$ Port View
Waterfront, T088-221753.
A garish Chinese seafood palace with a gigantic bank of aquariums featuring the catch of the day including lobster, grouper,

crab and more. The chilli crab is renowned. Very popular at weekends. Recommended.

$$ Restoran Sri Melaka
9 Jln Laiman Diki, Kampong Ayer (Sedco Complex, near Shiraz).
Popular with the fashionable KK set, serves great Malay and Nyonya food.

$$ Seri Selera Kampung Air
Sedco Sq, Kampung Air, T088-210400. Open 1500-0200.
Fun tourist-orientated place with 7 different seafood eateries, street stalls and nightly cultural shows.

$ Aesha Corner
Waterfront, Anjung Perdana.
Cheap Malay canteen facing the sea. Good place to splash out on a variety of spicy halal dishes, including a Thai *tom yam*.

$ Borneo 1945 Museum Kopitiam
23 Jln Dewan, T019-883 3829. Open 0900-2300.
Interesting coffee shop serving fine ice coffees and cold beer to go with local staples set in spacious cool environment with decor commemorating the Australian involvement in Borneo in the Second World War and the Sandakan Death March.

$ Fatty Kee
8 Lorong Bakau, Jln Pantai.
Be prepared to queue at this legendary Chinese chicken wing house. Wings here are served with a variety of sauces, with locals claiming garlic to be the best. Steamed vegetable dishes ease the conscience a tad and those without a hankering for wings can take heart in the fantastic seafood curry. Recommended.

$ Peppermint
Lot 25, G/F, Jln Pantai.
Hugely popular at lunchtime with local workers; arrive after 1200 and you'll have to join the queue. There's a simple but effective menu of *pho* (noodle soup), beef stew, spicy chicken rice and spring rolls.

$ Sri Sempelang
Sinsuran 2, on the corner with Jln Pasar Baru.
Great Malay canteen with enormous fruit juices and tables outside. Locals recommend it and it's a decent place to catch a bit of late-night footie with a *teh tarik* and a *roti prata*.

$ Tambayan At Kaining
G/F Api Api Centre, T016-818 5311.
Outrageously authentic Filipino restaurant with lots of rattan furniture and leafy plants. Popular with overseas Filipinos, the menu includes *sinagang*, garlic rice, and *calderata*. Recommended.

$ Yee Fung
127 Jln Gaya. Open 0630-1700.
Local Chinese residents rave about this simple eatery, which gets packed out at lunch with hungry punters wanting their signature *yee fung laksa*, fragrant claypot chicken rice and – for those with a stomach for organs – the *ngau chap*. Recommended.

$ Yu Kee Bak Kut Teh
74 Jln Gaya. Open from 1600.
Family-run affair serving up delectable bowls of *bak kut teh* (aromatic herbal pork rib soup). Order with salted vegetables, tofu skin and deep fried doughsticks for a truly fantastic dining experience. Recommended.

$ Zaminah
Api-Api Centre. Open 1000-2200.
Fairly standard Malaysian Indian Muslim restaurant with the usual *rotis* and curries.

Foodstalls
There are foodstalls above the **central market**; the **night market** on Jln Tugu; on the waterfront at the **Sinsuran Food Centre**; and at **Merdeka Foodstall Centre**, Wisma Merdeka. **Sedco Square**, Kampong Ayer, is a large square filled with stalls serving ubiquitous *ikan panggang* and satay; there's a great atmosphere in the evenings.

Bars and clubs

Bars

Many popular bars are along the **Waterfront Esplanade**. Notable drinking venues along this stretch include the **Cock and Bull**, an English-style pub; **Shamrock's Irish Bar**, with Kilkenny and Guiness; and **Hito** with excellent happy hour prices and outdoor seating good for sundowners. All are in a strip and make a colourful short pub crawl. Bars and restaurants, all with outdoor seating, are strung along **Beach St**, a pedestrianized lane between Jln Pantai and Jln Gaya.

Upperstar

Segama Complex, opposite the Hyatt Regency hotel (see Where to stay).
Sandwiches and fried food. Jugs of Long Island iced tea and good beer promotions.

Clubs

Shenanigan's at the Hyatt Regency hotel and **Rumba** at Le Meridien are also good late-night venues (see Where to stay).
KK Times Square is a short cab ride out of town and is an office complex by day, but comes alive at night. **Sully's** is a jazz bar with good selection of whiskies and wines. **Firefly** is popular with cool young things and has good happy hour prices and DJs, and for those looking for a long night out, **White Room** offers plenty of space for dancing and chatting over bottles of spirits well into the early hours.

Bed

At the end of Waterfront Esplanade.
Popular late-night club with a big dance floor, live music, DJs and lounge area. This is the closest KK has to a conventional nightclub and gets pleasantly raucous as the hours tick by.

Entertainment

Cinemas

There's a **Growball Cinemax** cinema in the Centre Point Mall (see shopping complexes, below); and **Golden Screen Cinemas** in the Suria Sabah shopping mall in town on Jln Haji Saman, and at the 1Borneo mall on Jln Sulaiman.

Cultural shows

Kadazan-Dusun Cultural Centre (Hongkod Koisaan), *KDCA Bldg, Mile 4.5, Jln Penampang, to get there, take a green and white bus from the MPKK Building, next to the state library.* The restaurant is open all year, but in late May, during the harvest festival, the cultural association comes into its own (see Festivals, below).
Kampong Nelayan, *Taman Tun Fuad, Bukit Padang, www.kampungnelayan.com.* A floating seafood market restaurant with dance shows during dinner.
Mari Mari Cultural Village, *see page 210.* Daily cultural performances with food and transport included in the tour price.

Festivals

May Sabah Fest, www.sabahfest.com. A big carnival of dancing, music and cow races, takes place at the Kompleks JKKN Sabah in early May, when the Kadazun/Dusun celebrate their harvest festival.
May Magavau, a post-harvest celebration, is carried out at Kadazan-Dusun Cultural Centre (see Entertainment, above), with dancing, feasts, shows and lots of *tapai*.

Shopping

Antiques

There are good antiques shop at the bottom of the Chun Eng Bldg on Jln Tun Razak, and a couple on Jln Gaya. The **Merdeka Complex** and **Wisma Wawasan 2020** are also home to a number of antiques shops. You need an export licence from Sabah State Museum to export rare antiques.

Books

Borneo Books, *BG26 Phase 2, Wisma Merdeka, ground floor, T088-241050, www.borneo books.com.* Eco-friendly books about Borneo, plus a travellers' book exchange and large collection of classic National Geographic magazines. This should be the first port of call for nature lovers, amateur ethnographers and twitchers.

Popular, *1Borneo Hypermall, Jln Sulaiman*. Wide selection of fiction, non-fiction and general interest books in English.

Times Books, *Suriah Sabah Shopping Mall*. Good selection of books, with fiction, magazines, and local interest.

Zenithway, *29 Jln Pantai*. English books and magazines, also Penguin books.

Clothes

For branded clothing head to the shopping malls of **Centre Point** and **1Borneo** (see Shopping complexes, below), which have all the usual brands and are easy places to blow some some cash on some threads.

Electronic goods

VCDs, DVDs and stereo equipment are considered the cheapest in the country here. Try **Karamunsing Kompleks** and the **Centre Point Mall**.

Handicrafts

Handicrafts consist mainly of baskets, mats, tribal clothing, beadwork and pottery. There is also a handicraft shop at the airport.

Api Tours, *Lot 49, Bandaran Berjaya*. Small selection of handicrafts.

Borneo Gifts, *ground floor, Wisma Sabah*.

Borneo Handicraft, *1st floor, Wisma Merdeka*. Local pottery and material made into clothes.

Elegance Souvenir, *1st floor, Wisma Merdeka*. Lots of beads of local interest (another branch on ground floor of Centrepoint).

Kraftangan Kompleks, *Jln Tun Fuad Stephens*. With good crafts from around the region.

Malaysian Handicraft, *Cawangan Sabah, No 1, Lorong 14, Kg Sembulau, T088-234471, Mon-Sat 0815-1230, Fri 0815-1600*.

Sabah Art and Handicraft Centre, *1st floor, Block B, Segama Complex (opposite New Sabah Hotel)*.

Sabah Handicraft Centre, *Lot 49 Bandaran Berjaya (next to Shangri-La)*. Good selection (also has branches at the museum and the airport).

The Crafts, *Lot AG10, ground floor, Wisma Merdeka, T088-252413*.

Jewellery

Most shops in Wisma Merdeka.

Shopping complexes

1Borneo Hypermall, *Jln Sulaiman (7 km outside the city, jump on a city bus heading to Sepangar, RM2), www.1borneo.net*. The largest shopping mall in Borneo, this large complex has it all – designer boutiques, generic chain stores, coffee shops, bookshops, bowling lanes, hotels, a cineplex and some good eateries – making it ideal for people who want a day of hedonistic consumerism.

Centre Point Mall, *1 Jln Centre Point, www.centrepointsabah.com*.

Kompleks Karamunsing, *Jln Karamunsing*.

Likas Square, *north of Likas Sports Complex*. Pink shopping complex with recreation club.

Segama Complex, *Jln Tun Fuad Stephens, between Jln Segama and Jln Segama II*.

Suriah Sabah Shopping Mall, *1 Jln Tun Fuad Stephens, www.suriasabah.com.my*.

Warisan Square, *A-G-18, Jln Tun Fuad Stephens*. A relatively new complex with eateries, boutiques and swimwear outlets.

Wisma Merdeka, *J ln Tun Razak, www.wismamerdeka.com*.

Wisma Sabah, *Jln Haji Saman*.

What to do

Bowling

There are bowling alleys in the **Centre Point Mall** and at **1Borneo Hypermall** (see Shopping complexes, above).

Diving

Do not believe dive shops if they tell you that you must book through their offices in KK – it's often cheaper to book through local offices in the area where you want to dive. One exception to this rule is Sipadan Island. Only limited numbers of divers are allowed to dive in the area per day due to conservation concerns. Diver limits only apply to Sipadan. Mabul and other islands have yet to impose restrictions. To obtain permits in advance, contact Sipadan tour operators (see page 286).

Borneo Divers, *9th floor Wisma Jubili, 53 Jln Gaya, T088-222226, www.borneodivers.info; also has an office in Tawau, T089-761214.* Operates exotic scuba-diving trips all over Borneo including Sipadan and Mabul, and has accommodation on Mamutik Island (Tunku Abdul Rahman). Dive trips are well organized. Offers a wide selection of training courses.

Dive Down Below Marine and Wildlife Adventures, *KK Times Square, Lot 33G, Block F, T088-488997, www.divedownbelow.com.* Run by a friendly British couple, this outfit has received plaudits for their dive and snorkel trips out to Pulau Gaya (where they have a Five-Star PADI Dive Station), Pulau Tiga and the Usukan Bay Second World War wrecks. They can also arrange land tours to Kinabatangan and Gomantong. Recommended.

Seaventures, *G23B ground floor, Wisma Sabah, Jln Tun Fuad Stephens, T088-251669, www.seaventuresdive.com.* Offers dive packages off a former working oil rig off Mabul Island near Sipadan.

Golf

Green fees are considerably higher over the weekend, up to double the weekday rate. Fees range from RM250-450. Prices drop slightly for night golf after 1700 (available at Sutera Harbour). It's possible to book in for 9 holes starting at RM120.

Sabah Golf and Country Club, *Bukit Padang, T088-247533, www.sgccsabah.com.* The oldest course in the state, this 18-hole championship course affords magnificent views of Mt Kinabalu.

Sutera Harbour Golf and Country Club, *on reclaimed land just to south of the city, www.suteraharbour.com.* A 27-hole layout

with great views across to the islands of Tunku Abdul Rahman Park.

Spas

The big name hotels have their own spas, see Where to stay.

Gaya Reflexology, *114 Jln Gaya.* Offers good-value massage and other treatments. Helpful for those who have stiff legs after a Kinabalu climb.

Sports complexes

The sports complex at Likas is open to the general public. It has volleyball, tennis, basketball, gym, badminton, squash, aerobics and a pool. To get there take a Likas-bound minibus from Plaza Wawasan.

Likas Square (see shopping complexes, above), has a recreation club with tennis, squash, jogging, golf, driving range, pool and children's playground.

Tour operators

The **Sabah Tourism Board** (see page 197, www.sabahtourism.com), has a full list of tour agents. Tours that are widely available include: Kota Belud *tamu* (Sunday market), Gunung Kinabalu Park (including Poring Hot Springs), Sandakan's Sepilok Orang-Utan Rehabilitation Centre, train trips to Tenom through the Padas Gorge and tours of the islands in the Tunku Abdul Rahman National Park. Several companies specialize in scuba-diving tours.

Best Borneo, *Lot 3B20, Level 3, Central Shopping Plaza, Kepayan Ridge, Jln Banjaran, T088-262780, www.bestborneo.com.my.* Good for tours into the interior around Sapulut and Batu Punngul with nights spent at jungle camps or in Murut longhouses.

Borneo Eco Tours, *Lot 1, Pusat Perindustrian, Kolombong Jaya, 88450, T088-438300, www.borneoecotours.com.* Award-winning operator that specializes in environmentally aware tours. Their **Sukau Rainforest Lodge** (www.sukau.com) on the Kinabatangan River is highly recommended.

Borneo Nature Tours, *ground floor, Lot 10, Block D, Sadong Jaya Complex, T088-267637, www.borneonaturetours.com.* Official agent operating within the excellent Danum Valley Conservation Area, including **Borneo Rainforest Lodge** (see page 279), and the Maliau Basin (see page 290).

Borneo Ultimate, *Lot G29 ground floor, Wisma Sabah, T088-225188, www.ultimate borneo.com.* Adventure tours including whitewater rafting, mountain biking, jungle trekking, and sea kayaking. Also facilitates volunteers on local community projects.

Borneo Wildlife Adventures, *Lot F, 1st floor, General Post Office building, T088-213668, www.borneo-wildlife.com.* Specializing in nature tours, wildlife and cultural activities.

Diethelm Borneo Expeditions, *Suite 303, 2nd floor, Menara MBF, 1 Jln Sagunting, T088-266353, www.diethelmtravel.com.* Well-respected operator offering a variety of tours including cycling, diving, whitewater rafting and wildlife spotting.

Exotic Borneo, *Likas Post Office, Likas, T088-245920, www.exborneo.com.* Well-run but fairly pricey themed tours including culture, adventure and nature.

Mount Kinabalu Booking Office, *Lot 1-37, Star City North Complex, 1st floor, Jln Asia City, T088-448709, www.mountkinabalu.com.* Slick operation offering a wide range of Mount Kinabalu activities and all-inclusive packages including summit treks and Via Ferrata tours.

Mountain Torq, *Suite 01-03/04, Level 2 Menara MAA, 6 Lorong Api Api 1 T088-268126, www.mountaintorq.com.* Organizes Via Ferrata treks on the north face of Gunung Kinabalu alongside a range of other mountain climbing activities.

Nasalis Larvatus Tours, *Lot 226, 2nd floor, Wisma Sabah, Jln Tun Abdul Razak, T088-230534, www.nasalislarvatustours.com.* Runs **Nature Lodge Kinabatangan** (www.naturelodgekinabatangan.com), an excellent mid-range lodge about 1 hr upriver from Sukau. More luxurious accommodation is in the process of being built and recent upgrades include hot showers. It's currently a fairly quiet part of the river with a wide range of activities including kayaking, nature walks and boat trips. At least 2-3 nights are needed to get the most from the area. There's great wildlife viewing, with elephants, many bird species, crocodiles, orang-utans and other primates often spotted.

Whitewater rafting

Rafting is available on the Papar River (grades I and II), Kiulu River (grades II-III), Kadamaian River (grade II-III) and Padas River (grade III-IV). Trips usually require a minimum of 3 people. See also **Diethelm Borneo Expeditions** (see Tour operators, above).

Riverbug/Traverse Tours, *Lot 227-229, 2nd floor, Wisma Sabah, Jln Tun Fuad Stephen, T088-260501, www.traversetours.com.* Whitewater rafting specialist. Well-organized 1-day rafting trips on the Padas River (grade III-IV) run from KK. Prices include experienced guides, transport and safety equipment, plus a post-river barbecue. No terrifying rapids, but big waves, warm water and the spectacular scenery of the Crocker Range make this a fun day out for everyone. The smaller Kiulu River (grades II-III) is just as picturesque, but with smaller rapids and occasional slow moving sections interspersed with deep pools, good for learning basic kayaking skills or for a first whitewater descent. They also run a proboscis monkey wetland tour, climbing Mount Trusmadi and trekking, biking and camping tours across Sabah.

Air

To get to the airport take the airport shuttle (RM5/children RM3) from Padang Merdeka station hourly 0730-2015, which run first to Terminal 2, then to Terminal 1. A taxi from the city centre to the airport should not be more than RM40 (20-40 mins).

There are no direct connections between KK and Europe, North America or Australia. Instead, travellers must transit on the way.

The most usual points of transit are KL, Bandar Seri Begawan or Singapore, though Hong Kong and Shanghai are also well connected to the city. KK is well connected with the major towns in Sabah. For airport information, see page 191.

MASwings (ground floor, MAS/MASwings Administration Building, off Jln Petagas, Kota Kinabalu International Airport, T1300-883000) connects KK with **Sandakan, Labuan, Miri, Mulu, Sibu, Kudat, Kuching, Tawau** and **Lahad Datu** and it's cheap. There are also regular connections with **KL** and other cities in peninsular Malaysia.

International connections include: **Air Asia** (Lot G24, ground floor, Wisma Sabah) and **Silk Air** (Tg Aru Plaza, 1st floor, Block B, Jln Mat Salleh, T088-485450) to **Singapore; Air Asia** to **Jakarta** and **Hong Kong; Royal Brunei** (Bangunan Kswp, Lot BG-3B, ground floor, Mail No 30, Jln Karamunsing Jt Bypass, Karamunsing, T088-242193) to **Bandar Seri Begawan; Korean Air** (Lot 2B, Airport, T088-251152) and **Asiana** (Suite 7-7E, 7th floor, Menara MAA, 6 Lorong Api Api, T088-268677) to **Seoul; Cebu Pacific** (c/o Skyzone Tours, Suite G-02, Menara MAA, 6 Lorong Api Api, T088-448871) to **Manila** and **Cebu;** and **Dragonair** (E-30-3 Signature Office Block E, Lot 30, 3rd floor, KK Times Square, T088-254 733) to various cities in China including **Shenzhen, Shanghai, Guangzhou** and **Taipei** (Taiwan).

Boat

Getting to Brunei overland takes 6 hrs including 2 ferries: the first from KK to the island of **Labuan;** then from Labuan to **Muara** in Brunei. Or it's a 45-min flight.

Ferries run from KK's Jessleton Point Ferry Pier (10 mins' walk north of the centre) to **Labuan** twice daily at 0800 and 1330; the journey takes 3 hrs (RM39.60 one way). From Labuan's jetty, there are 6 daily ferries to the Serasa Ferry Terminal in **Muara** (**Brunei**) between 1000 and 1730 (1 hr, RM38). For travellers heading through to Brunei from KK, there is a package including both ferry

tickets for RM60/children RM38 (plus RM3 departure tax). This does not include the RM10 departure tax payable in Labuan. It's essential to catch the first departure if you want to make it one day. From the Serasa Ferry Terminal, minibuses run to **Bandar Seri Begawan** (45 mins, B$2).

Boats also run from Jessleton Point Ferry Pier to the **Tunku Abdul Rahman National Park** (see page 214).

Bus/minibus

There's no central bus station in KK. Instead there are 4 bus stations and terminals serving the city and state.

The **Northern Bus Terminal** is in Inanam, 10 km from the city centre. This terminal offers long-distance express coaches to **Sandakan, Semporna, Lahad Datu** and **Tawau.** To get there from KK, hop on local bus No 4 or 8 (RM2), or take a taxi (RM20). Express coaches are efficient and good value. Coaches depart from Inanam between 0600 and 2030. Sample fares include **Tawau** (0730, 0745, 1400, 2000, RM70, 9 hrs), **Sandakan** (0730, 0800, 0930, 1130, 1200, 1400, RM43, 6 hrs), **Semporna** (0730, 0830, 0900, 2000, RM75, 9 hrs), **Lahad Datu** (0700, 0830, 0900, 2000, RM52, 8 hrs).

The **Padang Merdeka** bus station is at Merdeka Square in the centre of town and has buses heading to destinations in the interior and to the west of the city including **Sipitang, Beaufort, Lawas, Tenom, Ranau** (for Kinabalu National Park), **Kota Belud, Papar, Tambunan** and **Keningan.**

The **City Park Bus Terminal,** Beach St, next to the Court House, is where city minibuses leave from. There are lots of bus companies and when you arrive at the bus station touts will try to get you to use their company. It's advisable to buy your ticket the day before. The time on the ticket is a rough guide only. Get there 10 mins before to guarantee your seat, but you may have to wait until the bus is full. Buses to **Tenom** (0800, 1200, 1600, RM17, 3 hrs), **Keningau** (8 daily, RM15, 2½ hrs), **Beaufort** (more than 10 daily, RM12, 2 hrs).

Minibuses run throughout the day to **Ranau** (RM20). Daily buses leave at 0800 from here to **Bandar Seri Begawan** (RM100, 7 hrs) and **Miri** (RM90, 10 hrs). The boat trip package to Brunei via Labuan is far more interesting than the direct bus and much better value (see Boat, above).

The **Wawasan Bus Terminal**, on Jln Kemajuan in the south of town, has buses and minibuses serving KK and the surrounding towns, such as **Penampang**, **Likas** and **Tuaran**. All buses and minibuses have their destinations on the windscreen and most rides in town cost RM0.50-RM2 and leave when full. You can get off wherever you like.

Car
Not all roads in the interior of Sabah are paved and a 4WD vehicle is advisable for some journeys. Car hire is not expensive with rates starting at RM110 for the day. All vehicles have to be returned to KK as there are no agency offices outside KK (it may be possible to leave a vehicle elsewhere and pay a surcharge for it to be picked up and returned on your behalf), although local car hire is usually available. Drivers must be between the ages of 21 and 60 and have an international driving licence. **ABAN-D Rent a Car**, Lot 22, 1st floor, Taman Victory, Mile 4.5, Jln Penampang, T088-722300. **Adaras Rent-a-Car**, Lot G03, ground floor, Wisma Sabah, T088-216 6671. **Borneo Express Car Rental**, G25 Wisma Sabah, T016-886 0780, www.borneocar.com. **Hertz**, Level 1, Lot 39, Kota Kinabalu Airport, T088-317740. **Elegant Tours and Rent a Car**, G25, ground floor, Wisma Sabah, T088-232602, www. visitmalaysiasabah.com.

Taxi
There are taxi stands outside most of the bigger hotels and outside the General Post Office, the Segama complex, the Sinsuran complex, next to the DPKK building, the Milemewah supermarket, the Capitol cinema and in front of the clocktower (for taxis to **Ranau**, **Keningau** and **Kudat**). Approximate fares from town: RM20 to **Tanjung Aru Resort**, RM20 to the **Sabah Foundation**, RM12-15 to the museum, RM20 to the airport. Minibuses can also be privately chartered.

Train
The station is 5 km out of town in Tanjung Aru. There is only 1 train line in Sabah, known as the **Sabah State Railway**, www.railway. sabah.gov.my. The single-line track travels 134 km from Tanjung Aru to **Tenom** in the interior and stops at 14 places along the way including **Kudat**, **Beaufort** and **Papar**. The journey to Tenom takes around 6 hrs. Fares are very good value with a one-way ticket to Papar costing RM.1.85. Check the website for the latest prices and timetables.

Railway enthusiasts will enjoy the restored **North Borneo Railway**, with rolling stock dating from the colonial era. The twice-weekly service (Weds, Sat) is particularly popular with foreign tourists. The steam train departs at 0930 from Tanjung Aru and stops at **Kinarut** and **Papar** with time allocated for a quick wander around the towns. Breakfast and a tiffin lunch are served on board. The train returns to Tanjung Aru at 1340. Tickets cost RM318/children RM159 and must be booked at least 1 day in advance through **Sutera Harbour Resort**, T088-318888, www. suteraharbour.com/north-borneo-railway.

In the countryside surrounding Kota Kinabalu are a number of interesting towns that make for great day trips from KK. Penampang District is home to the Kadazan community and includes settlements including Donggongon Township and Penampang New Town where you can get a glimpse of traditional Kadazan life. Further to the north lie the Bajau village of Mengkabong and the charming town of Tuaran with its famed nine-storey pagoda.

Tanjung Aru Beach
5 km south of KK. Take the Tanjung Aru (beach) bus from the Wawasan Bus Terminal.

This is the best beach near KK, after those in Tunku Abdul Rahman National Park, and is close to **Shangri-La Tanjung Aru Resort**, 5 km south of KK (see Where to stay, page 211). It is particularly popular at weekends with kiteflyers, swimmers and joggers, and there is a good open-air food court that looks onto the beach.

Penampang District
To get to Penampang, take bus No 13 from Wawasan bus station (RM1.80, 30 mins) or jump in a taxi for around RM20 one way.

The old town of Donggongon, 13 km southeast of KK, was demolished in the early 1980s and the new township was built in 1982. The population is mainly Kadazan or Sino-Kadazan and about 90% Christian. On a steep hill on the far side of the new town is the Roman Catholic **St Michael's Church** ① *a 20-min walk; turn left just before the bridge – and after the turn-off to the new town – through the kampong and turn left again after the school,* the oldest church in town. A granite building with a red roof, it was originally built in 1897 but is not dramatic to look at and has been renovated over the years. Services are in Kadazan but are fascinating, and visitors are warmly welcomed; hymns are sung in Kadazan and Malay.

The social focus of the week is the **market** which takes place on Thursdays and Fridays from 0600-1400. Look out for the *tapai* (rice wine) and jars of *bambangan* (lightly pickled wild mangoes).

There are many **megaliths** in the Penampang area that are thought to be associated with property claims, particularly when a landowner died without a direct heir. Some solitary stones standing in the middle of paddy fields are more than 2 m tall. The age of the megaliths has not been determined. Wooden figures called *sininggazanak* can also be seen in rice fields (see page 194).

Monsopiad Cultural Village
5 km along the Ramaya–Putaton road, Penampang, T088-761336, www.monsopiad.com. Daily 0900-1700; cultural shows at 0900, 1100, 1400 and 1600; guided tours at 1000, 1200 and 1500. RM55, children aged 7-12 RM25. From KK, take No 13 bus from Wawasan bus station to Donggongon town (RM1.50). At Donggongon, take a minibus to Terawi (RM1) and tell the driver you want to go to Monsopiad Cultural Village. If driving, the house is hard to find; from Donggongon new town take the main road east past the Shell station and turn right at sign to Jabatan Air; past St Aloysus Church, the house is on the left about 1.5 km from the turn-off. A taxi from KK costs RM35 one way. Shuttle buses are available from hotels in town at RM65, children RM45. Or contact Monsopiad to arrange a pick-up.

This privately owned cultural village is named after a fearsome Kadazan warrior-cum-headhunter: Siou do Mohoing, the so-called Hercules of Sabah. Inside the house are 42 fragile human skulls, some of which are said to be 300 years old and possess spiritual powers. They are laced together with leaves of the hisad palm, representing the victims' hair. For those who have already visited longhouses in Sarawak, this collection of skulls, in the rafters of an ordinary little kampong house overlooking the village and the Penampang River, is a bit of an anticlimax. But Dousia Moujing and his son Wennedy are very hospitable and know much about local history and culture. They preside over their ancestor's dreaded sword (although Wennedy reckons it's not the original, even though there are strands of human hair hanging off it). A three-day, three-night feast is held in May, in the run-up to the harvest festival. Visitors should remove footwear and not touch the skulls or disturb the rituals or ceremonies in progress. A reconstruction of the original Monsopiad main house gives an insight into the life and times of the warrior and

③ Around Kota Kinabalu

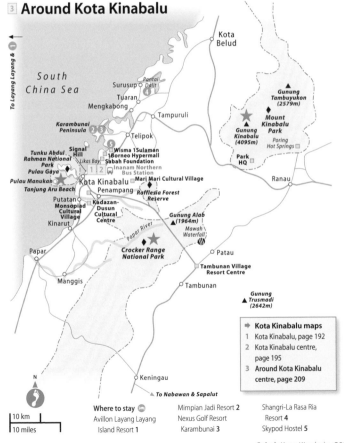

Where to stay 😴
Avillon Layang Layang
Island Resort 1

Mimpian Jadi Resort 2
Nexus Golf Resort
Karambunai 3

Shangri-La Rasa Ria
Resort 4
Skypod Hostel 5

➡ Kota Kinabalu maps
1 Kota Kinabalu, page 192
2 Kota Kinabalu centre, page 195
3 Around Kota Kinabalu centre, page 209

his descendants. There is a good restaurant serving traditional dishes; the *kadazandusun hinara* is recommended. It consists of fresh sliced raw fish marinated in lime juice, mixed with chilli, garlic and shallots. Visitors can also take part in cooking classes.

Mari Mari Cultural Village

25 km east of KK, Kionsom, Inanam, T013-881 4921, www.marimariculturalvillage.com. Tours daily at 1000, 1400 and 1800. Traverse Tours (see page 205) runs return trips from KK for RM160, children RM140.

In a rural forest setting, the cultural village offers the chance to get familiar with five of Sabah's ethnic groups; Bajau, Murut, Rungus, Dusun and Lundayeh. Members of each community have built replicas of their respective traditional homes and give visitors demonstrations of blow pipe making, fire starting with bamboo and samples of traditional food. Presented as a kind of living museum (you don't see many Murut dressed in loincloths and hunting with blow pipes nowadays), the tour makes for a good half-day outing for families. There is also a waterfall around 400 m from the village which is great for a dip after a hot morning tramping around the houses.

Tamparuli

42 km north of KK at the junction of the roads north and east. Buses marked 'Tamparuli' leave from the Padang Merdeka Bus Station at the bottom of Signal Hill in KK, RM3, 40 mins.

A popular stop for tour buses, Tamparuli has a suspension bridge straddling the Tuaran River, which was built by the British Army in 1922. The bridge is immortalized as the 'Jambatan Tamparuli' ('jambatan' means bridge) in a Kadazandusun folk song, describing the plight of a young girl who lost a shoe whilst crossing the bridge. There is a good handicraft shopping centre here. The best day to visit is Wednesday for the weekly *tamu* (market).

A slightly offbeat attraction just outside Tamparuli is **Rumah Terbalik (Upside-down House)** ① *Batu 21, Jln Telibong, T088-260263, www.upsidedownhouse.com.my, RM18, children RM5.* One of only five 'upside-down' houses in the world, everything inside has been flipped. Appliances are stuck to the ceiling and even the car hangs from its driveway above visitors' heads. It is a tad disorientating but makes for a fun detour. There's a decent café attached and a 3D museum where you can be photographed stepping out of a gigantic rafflesia.

Mengkabong Water Village and Tuaran

Take a Tuaran bus from Wawasan Bus Terminal in KK (RM3) then change to a local minibus to Mengkabong Water Village. Taxis charge about RM50, or you can take a tour.

The Bajau (sea nomad) fishing stilt village of **Mengkabong** is within easy reach of KK and is likened to an Asian Venice. The village is particularly photogenic in the early morning, before Mount Kinabalu – which serves as a dramatic backdrop – is obscured by cloud. The fishermen leave Mengkabong at high tide and arrive back with their catch at the next high tide. They use sampan canoes, hollowed out of a single tree trunk, which are crafted in huts around the village. Some of the waterways and fields around Mengkabong are choked by water hyacinth, an ornamental plant that was originally introduced by Chinese farmers as pig fodder from South America.

For visitors wanting to escape the popular beaches close to KK, **Tuaran**, 45 minutes north of KK, offers a quieter alternative and is a good access point for several different destinations including Mengkabong. There is a weekly *tamu* here on Sunday mornings, known for its local cakes and pastries. The *kueh lapis* (layer cake) from Tuaran is renowned. Also, keep an eye out for the colourful nine-storey Ling Sang pagoda.

The nearby **Karambunai Beach** has a good picnic area, clean beach and sea. Close by is the **Mimpian Jadi Resort** (see page 212).

Karambunai Peninsula

This scenic peninsula, 30 km north of KK, has been transformed by a sprawling multimillion-dollar **Nexus Golf Resort** (see page 212). There is a golf course open to the public and a number of expensive spas and restaurants, but no public access to the beach.

Layang Layang

Some 300 km northwest of KK in the South China Sea, Layang Layang (Swallow Reef) is a tiny man-made atoll originally built for the Malaysian navy. It is part of the Spratly Archipelago claimed by China, Vietnam, Taiwan and the Philippines. It has become a famous, albeit expensive, dive site. There is one resort on the island that caters solely to divers. You need to book a flight through the resort; there are usually at least four flights a week to the island, but details need to be confirmed in advance, with plenty of notice. See also colour section, page 15.

Listings Around Kota Kinabalu *map page 209.*

Where to stay

$$$$ Avillon Layang Layang Island Resort
300 km off the coast of KK, T603-2170 2185 (booking office in KL), www.avillionlayang layang.com. Or book through the office in KK: Unit 4-1, 1st floor, Block A, Lintas Sq, Jln Lintas.
This 3-star resort has 76 rather plain rooms and 10 suites, movie room, pool, restaurant and bar. Apart from the resort the atoll is rather bleak with only an airstrip. Most reservations are part of a dive package. A 6-day/5-night package in hammerhead season costs US$1780 inclusive of all meals, 3 boat dives a day and equipment. Return flights are not included and cost US$408 return from KK. In 2015, in an effort to strengthen Malaysia's sovereignty over the islands, POS Malaysia placed a postbox under water so divers can send postcards on their way to dive the hammerheads and manta rays. The postbox even has its own exclusive postcode of 88005. You have to enjoy diving to make the visit worthwhile, but the underwater world is spectacular.

$$$$ Shangri-La Rasa Ria Resort
12 km north of KK, overlooking Pantai Dalit Beach, near Tuaran (local buses run to Tuaran), T088-792888, www.shangri-la.com.
A top-class resort with 330 rooms, a free-form pool, water sports, an 18-hole golf course, a driving range, spacious gardens, horse riding, cultural events, several restaurants including a Japanese and a seafood beachfront one and 30 ha of forest nature reserve with semi-tame orang-utans. There have been some complaints about the integrity of an orang-utan fostering programme run by the resort and the cleanliness of the beach away from the resort. The resort is popular with families and has a good kids' club with wide selection of activities for children. Recommended.

$$$$ Shangri-La Tanjung Aru Resort
5 km south of KK, 20 Jln Aru, Tanjung Aru Beach, T088-225800, www.shangri-la.com.
This hotel, with 500 rooms and a pool, is a veritable institution for the well-heeled and is one of the best hotels in Sabah, along with its sister hotel, the **Rasa Ria** at Tuaran. The hotel is noticeably on the honeymoon circuit for Europeans and its gardens have won

awards. The hotel's **STAR Marina** offers a wide selection of water-based activities from PADI courses to cruises. Recommended.

$$$$ Sinurambi Bed and Breakfast
22 km southeast of KK, Km5 Inobong–Teriang road, T019-860 4730, www.borneocountrystay.com.
Stunning B&B located at the top of a mountain top only 500 m from the Crocker Range National Park. This is a great place for families with a lovely swimming pool and a snooker room. There are 5 rooms, some with a balcony offering spectacular views over the hills. Book in advance.

$$$ Mimpian Jadi Resort
No 1 Kuala Matinggi, Kampong Pulau, Simpangan, Karambunai Beach, T088-787799. To get there, take a bus to Menggatal, then a bus to Karambunai.
Popular with domestic tourists and busy at weekend, this place has chalets, a private beach, water sports, fishing, mini zoo, karaoke bar, horse riding, volleyball, children's playground, and restaurants serving Malay/Chinese and Western food. From the resort, it's possible to charter a boat to a small Bajau fishing village, Kampong Penambawan, on the north bank of the river. Nearby there is a suspension bridge and rapids where it is possible to swim.

$$$ Nexus Golf Resort Karambunai
30 km northeast of KK, Menggatal, Karambunai Peninsula, T088-411222, www.nexusresort.com.
This sprawling 13.5-sq-km resort built along the coast has 485 ocean-view rooms and a full range of facilities including 18-hole golf course, 3 pools and sports activities. It's popular with business guests and has conference facilities. The resort is a bit tired but is in an excellent location.

Restaurants

There are mainly seafood foodstalls in Tanjung Aru Beach – recommended for *ikan panggang* – and satay stalls. It's very busy at weekends, but on weekdays it is rather quiet, with only a few stalls to choose from.

$$$ Peppino
20 Jln Aru, Tanjung Aru Beach, T088-327888. Open 1800-2230.
Award-winning restaurant inside the **Shangri-La Hotel** serving up possibly the most refined grub in town, topped with a dollop of superlative service. The food is certainly not cheap, but foodies will rejoice in the melt-in-the mouth veal cheek, risottos and ravioli. Worth a splurge.

$$ Seafood Market Restaurant
Tanjung Aru Beach, T088-238313.
Pick your own fresh seafood and get advice on how to have it cooked.

Shopping

The **Kaandaman Handicraft Centre** (below the Seafood Market Restaurant at Tanjung Aru Beach), sells local handicrafts. **Tanjung Aru Resort** has a few handicraft shops in the arcade.

What to do

Sailing and water sports
STAR Marina, *Tanjung Aru, next to the hotel.* Snorkelling packages start at around RM100 per day, windsurfing, kayaking and paddleboarding at RM80 per hr and fishing RM300 per hr. Tours to various offshore islands can be arranged.

Off the coast
& south of
Kota Kinabalu

West of KK is the Tunku Abdul Rahman Park, a reef and coral marine park. Travelling south from KK, the route crosses the Crocker Range to Tambunan. Continuing south the road passes through the logging town of Keningau and on to Tenom, where the Sabah State Railway runs, snaking down the Padas Gorge to Beaufort. The Padas River is the best place to go whitewater rafting in Sabah. Few towns are worth staying in for long on this route, but it is a scenic journey. Pulau Tiga National Park is a forest reserve where the pied hornbill can be spotted and Pulau Labuan is a tax-free haven off the coast.

The five islands in Gaya Bay, which make up Tunku Abdul Rahman Park (TAR), lie 3-8 km offshore. Coral reefs fringe all the islands in the park. The best reefs are between Pulau Sapi and Pulau Gaya, although there is also reasonable coral around Manukan, Mamutik and Sulug. Named after Malaysia's first prime minister, they became Sabah's first national park in 1923 and were gazetted in 1974 in an effort to protect their coral reefs and sandy beaches. Geologically, the islands are part of the Crocker Range formation, but as sea levels rose after the last ice age, they became isolated from the massif.

Flora and fauna

Pulau Gaya has some of Sabah's only undisturbed coastal dipterocarp forest. On the other islands most of the original vegetation has been destroyed and secondary vegetation predominates, such as ferns, orchids, palms, casuarina, coconut trees and tropical fruit trees. Mangrove forests can be found at two locations on Pulau Gaya. Animal and birdlife includes the long-tailed macaque, bearded pig, pangolin (on Pulau Gaya), white-bellied sea eagle, pied hornbill, green heron, sandpiper, flycatcher and sunbird.

There is a magnificent range of marine life because of the variety of the reefs surrounding the islands. The coral teems with exotica such as butterfly fish, Moorish idols, parrot fish, bat fish, razor fish, lion fish and stone fish, in stark contrast to the areas that have been depth-charged by Gaya's notorious dynamite fishermen.

The islands

Pulau Gaya By far the largest island, Pulau Gaya was the site of the first British North Borneo Chartered Company settlement in the area in 1881; the settlement lasted only 15 years before being destroyed in a pirate attack. There is still a large community on the island on the promontory facing KK, but today it is a shanty town of stilt houses built haphazardly over the sea. Known as **Kampong Lok Urai**, this community is home to 6000 Filipinos, Suluk and Bajau who often work as labourers in KK. The kampong is considered by the inhabitants of KK to be a dangerous, crime-ridden place and in 2014 a fire wiped out a sizeable chunk of the village prompting the local government to suggest moving the inhabitants into better, permanent housing in Kinarut. This was met with huge opposition from the local Sabahan community and the issue is yet to be resolved. On Pulau Gaya there are 20 km of marked trails including a plankwalk across a mangrove swamp and many beautiful little secluded bays. **Police Bay** is a popular, shaded beach. **Gayana Island EcoResort** is a large chalet development on the island with its own ferry from the KK jetty. **Gaya Island Resort** also pulls in well-heeled punters seeking a bit of seclusion from city life. There is a 250-m zipline connecting Pulau Gaya to Pulau Sapi, which hurls wide-eyed tourists between the islands (book through travel agents in KK as part of a Pulau Gaya nature trek).

Pulau Sapi The most popular of the islands for weekenders, Pulau Sapi also has good beaches and trails. It is connected to Pulau Gaya at low tide by a sandbar, and that wickedly fast zipline. There are good day-use facilities but no accommodation except camping.

Pulau Mamutik Closer to the mainland, Pulau Mamutik is the smallest island but has a well-preserved reef off the northeast tip.

★**Pulau Manukan** Pulau Manukan is the site of the Park HQ and most of the park accommodation. It has good snorkelling to the south and east and a particularly good beach on the east tip. It is probably the best of all the islands to visit but is heavily frequented by day trippers and rubbish is sometimes a problem. There is accommodation here; the **Manukan Island Resort** (www.manukan.com). Marine sports facilities stretch to the hire of mask, snorkel and fins (RM15, plus RM50 deposit for the day), and diving equipment. There's a swimming pool, water sports sailing centre, banana boat trips, glass-bottom boat trips and windsurfing. Fish feeding off the jetty attracts large shoals of fish, making it a good place for snorkelling.

Pulau Sulag Pulau Sulag is further away than the other islands and less developed, but it has the best reefs. This small island has a sand spit, making it good for swimming. There are dive facilities and a restaurant. You can also camp here.

Listings Tunku Abdul Rahman Park

Where to stay

Significant discounts are available Mon-Fri.

$$$$ Gaya Island Resort
Maholom Bay, Pulau Gaya, T03-2783 1000, www.gayaislandresort.com.
Luxurious island retreat offering modern 47-sq-m villas with gigantic bathubs and views over the South China Sea or Mount Kinabalu. There's a good library here with a selection of Borneo-related titles and a 40-m pool. Jungle hikes, spa treatments and a range of water sports available.

$$$$ Gayana Island EcoResort
East coast of Pulau Gaya, www.gayana-eco-resort.com. Reservations: Lot 6, Tanjung Lipat, Jln Gaya, KK, T088-380390.
Upmarket resort with a range of chalets. Recommended are the **Palm Villas** which jut out over the sea and have a glass-bottomed reception room. Decent snorkelling is just a short leap from your bed. Noted for its good service, this resort also has a reef rehabilitation research centre with some interactive programmes available for interested visitors. Activities include diving, snorkelling, fishing windsurfing, jungle

trekking and yachting. There are 6 ferries from KK Ferry Terminal to the resort daily. The sister resort $$$$ **Bunga Raya Resort** (www.bungarayaresort.com), also on Pulau Gaya, offers well-furnished wooden chalets, and plenty of green space for children to run wild in.

$$$$ Manukan Island Resort
Pulau Manukan, www.manukan.com.
Surrounded by a protected coral reef, Manukan Island is blanketed in rainforest and has gorgeous white sandy beaches. This slightly pricey resort offers plush hillside and beachside chalets, fresh seafood and a range of water sports. There's even a 1500-m jogging track for those like can't bear to leave their running shoes at home.

Camping
It's possible to camp on any of the islands (RM5 per day). Obtain permission from the **Sabah Parks Office** (Lot 45 & 46, Block H, Level 1-5, Times Square, KK, T088-523500 www.sabahparks.org.my). The island gets packed with tourists during the day, but if you camp you can enjoy a near-deserted island after 1700 when the rabble departs. Beware of leaving your clothing unattended at the edge of the forest, as monkeys have been known to run off with it!

Restaurants

There's an excellent restaurant on Pulau Manukan. Pulau Mamutik and Pulau Sapi each have a small shop selling limited and expensive food and drink, and Sapi has some hawker-style food. For Pulau Sulug, Sapi and Mamutik take all the water you need – there is no drinkable water supply here. Shower and toilet water is only provided if there has been sufficient rain.

What to do

Diving
There are at least 10 popular dive sites around the TAR islands, with reef depths of 3-21 m, providing a variety of experiences. It's possible to dive all year with an average visibility of about 12 m. The water is cooler Nov-Feb, when visibility is not as good. For extensive information on the various coral/fish/dive sites, contact **Borneo Divers** (www.borneodivers.info), or **Dive Down Below** (www.divedownbelow.com).

Snorkelling
Snorkel, mask and fins can be rented from boatmen at the Jesselton Point Ferry Terminal in KK. Snorkelling equipment is also available for hire on Sapi and Manukan.

Transport

From Jesselton Point Ferry Terminal, small boats carry 6 people and will leave for any of the islands (RM23 per person fixed price) when full, but everyone needs to agree a destination and a return time. For 2 island hops it costs RM33, for 3 hops, RM43. It's possible to charter a boat for RM204, for visits to **Police Beach**, **Malahom Bay** or any of the islands. Trips can also be negotiated with local fishermen.

This park is 48 km off the coast of KK. Declared a forest reserve in 1933, the 15,864-ha park is made up of three islands: Pulau Tiga, Kalampunian Damit and Kalampunian Besar.

The islands

Pulau Tiga achieved global fame as the location for the first season of American reality TV series *Survivor*, chosen for its unspoilt natural landscape. It is still a draw for fans of the show, though sadly the setting for the show's Tribal Council was destroyed by a fire. The three islands that make up the park came into existence in 1897, the result of an earthquake in Mindanao. Pulau Tiga's three low hills were all formed by mud volcanoes. The last big eruption, in 1941, was heard 160 km away and covered the island in a layer of boiling mud. The bubbling mud pools that remain at three points across the island are a slightly bizarre but interesting bathing experience and something that distinguishes the island from others in the area. The dipterocarp forests on the islands are virtually untouched and they contain species not found on other west coast islands, such as a poisonous amphibious sea snake (*Laticauda colubrina*), also known as the banded sea krait, which comes ashore on Pulau Kalampunian Damit to lay its eggs. Rare birds such as the pied hornbill (*Anthracoceros convexus*) and the megapode (*Megapodus freycinet*) are found here, as well as flying foxes, monitor lizards, wild fruit trees and mangrove forest. A network of trails, marked at 50-m intervals, leads to various points of interest.

Underwater the island offers good diving at a diverse range of sites. There's excellent coral growth mid-channel and plenty of smaller marine life and fish making this a colourful spot. It's variable after storms and strong winds. The small offshore house reef is good, with lots of anemones, clown fish and the occasional turtle. As long as you're

Essential Pulau Tiga National Park

Finding your feet

To get to Pulau Tiga, take a bus from KK to Kuala Penyu, a small settlement at the tip of the Klias Peninsula (140 km, two hours, RM18). From Kuala Penyu, it's a 30-minute boat ride (departures at 1000 and 1500; the boat can only be booked as part of a tour package) to the island. If you have booked to stay at the **Survivor Lodge**, you can arrange a bus and boat package transport from KK departing KK at 0800 and 1230. Transport can also be arranged through **Sipadan Dive Centre**, www.pulautiga.com.my (see page 286), which runs the island's resort, or **Dive Down Below**, www.divedownbelow.com (see page 204). The latter can arrange a speedboat direct to the islands from KK (one hour), though this is only really worth the money if you're just going for a day trip. See http://www.sabahtourism.com/destination/pulau-tiga-survivor-island.

Park information

The Park HQ, on the south side of Pulau Tiga, is mainly used as a botanical and marine research centre and tourism is not vigorously promoted. As a result there are no special facilities for tourists.

When to go

The best time to visit is between February and April, when it is slightly drier and the seas are calmer.

not expecting the vast underwater cliffs and crystal-clear conditions of the Sipadan area, Pulau Tiga has plenty to keep you entertained on the marine front.

Listings Pulau Tiga National Park

Where to stay

As well as the lodge, below, there is also a hostel that can hold up to 32 people. Book in advance through the Sabah Parks Office in KK (see page 197); there is also an attached canteen. It is possible to camp.

$$$ Pulau Tiga Survivor Lodge
T088-218710, www.sdclodges.com.
Owned by **Sipadan Dive Centre** (see page 286). Standard chalets and a/c superior rooms with comfortable king-sized beds and drink-making facilities. The resort also organizes water sports, treks and trips to nearby islands, including Kalampunian Damit Island (also known as Snake Island) where visitors can learn more about the highly venomous banded sea kraits that congregate there (you can even have one around your neck!). There are a number of jungle activities offered including palm frond weaving and splashing about in the nearby mud baths. It's a bit overpriced and looks somewhat tired in places. Fans of the TV show *Survivor* flock here as this was the setting for the first ever season of the programme.

Pulau Labuan

an island territory with good diving and duty-free shopping

Labuan is one of the historically stranger pieces of the Bornean jigsaw. Originally part of the Sultanate of Brunei, the 92-sq-km island, 8 km off the coast of Sabah, was ceded in 1846 to the British who were enticed to take it on by the discovery of rich coal deposits. It joined the Malaysian Federation in 1963, along with Sabah and Sarawak. In 1984 it was declared a tax-free haven – or an 'International offshore financial centre' – and hence this small tropical island with just 87,000-odd inhabitants has a plethora of name-plate banks and investment companies. For the casual visitor it offers some attractions, but not many. There are good hotels, lots of duty-free shopping, a golf course, sport fishing and diving, plus a handful of historic and cultural sights. Labuan has an unusual atmosphere with a distinct frontier edge. The island's duty-free booze and cigarette prices, cosmopolitan population and seedy nightlife combine to make this city feel pleasantly edgy.

Essential Pulau Labuan

Finding your feet

The airport is 5 km from town. There is a reasonable island bus network, a few car hire firms and a small number of taxis. There are regular connections to Brunei and Sabah by boat from the harbour. See Transport, page 225.

Sights

Away from the busy barter jetty, Labuan Town, a name largely superseded by its name of **Port Victoria**, is a dozy, seedy and unremarkable Chinese-Malaysian mix of shophouses, coffee shops, sleazy karaoke bars and cheap booze shops. The **Labuan An'Nur Jamek State Mosque** is an impressive site, whilst the manicured **golf course** is popular with businessmen. Illegal cockfights are staged every Sunday afternoon. There is an old brick **chimney** at Tanjung Kubong, believed to have been built as a ventilation shaft for the short-lived coal-mining industry established by the British in 1947 to provide fuel for their steamships on the Far Eastern trade route. Remnants of the industry, which had petered out by 1911, are to be found in a maze of **tunnels** in this area. Near Tanjung Kubong is a **Bird Park**.

On the west coast there are pleasant beaches, mostly lined with kampongs. There is a large **Japanese war memorial** on the east coast and a vast, well-tended, **Allied war cemetery** between the town and the airport with over 3000 graves, most of which are unknown soldiers. The **Peace Park** at Layang Layangan marks the Japanese surrender point on 9 September 1945, which brought the Second World War to an end in Borneo.

Boat trips can be made to the small islands around Labuan, although only by chartering a fishing vessel. The main islands are **Pulau Papan** (an uninspiring island between Labuan and the mainland), **Pulau Kuraman**, **Pulau Rusukan Kecil** (known locally as the floating lady) and **Pulau Rusukan Besar** (floating man). These last three have good beaches and coral reefs but none have any facilities.

Off the south coast of the island is the **Marine Park**; a great place to dive, especially as there are four shipwrecks scattered in these waters. The park has 20 dive sites. See What to do, page 225.

Listings Pulau Labuan *map page 222.*

Tourist information

Tourist Information Office
Lot 4260, Jln Dewan/Jln Berjaya,
T087-423445.
See also www.labuantourism.com.my.

Where to stay

Hotels in Labuan are generally poor value and rather uninspiring compared to towns in Sabah and Sarawak. Prices at more expensive places drop during the week. There is little accommodation catering for budget travellers, and what there is tends to be drab.

$$$ Billion Waterfront
1 Jln Wawasan, T087-418111.
Overlooking the yacht marina (and also an industrial seascape), this place has a marina-look combined with the atmosphere of being on a cruise. It's a popular alternative to the **Dorsett** for business types, though it is in need of some attention to bring it back to its sleek former glory. The rooms are nice enough, fairly modern and come with

cable TV and minibar. The highlight is the large pool. The hotel manages the 50-berth marina with internationally rated facilities. The harbourmaster organizes yacht charters and luxury cruises.

$$$ Grand Dorsett
462 Jln Merdeka, T087-422000,
www.dorsetthotels.com/labuan.
This award-winning hotel is Labuan's most upmarket offering, with a huge sparkling lobby, pool, fitness centre and an array of food and beverage outlets including **Victoria's Brasserie** with superb seafood and daily themed buffet dinners. The **Fun Pub** has live music and nightly drinks specials. Rooms are comfortable and some have excellent views over the port.

$$$ Lazenda Hotel
Block C&D, Lazenda Centre, Jln Okk Abdullah,
T087-580 800, www.lazendahotel.com.
A new hotel in the centre of town with modern rooms, spacious bathrooms and a decent restaurant serving local favourites. A fair option in this price bracket.

BACKGROUND
Pulau Labuan

With a superb deep-water harbour (the name Labuan comes from the Brunei Malay dialect word labohan meaning anchorage), Labuan promised an excellent location from which the British could engage the pirates who were terrorizing the northwest Borneo coast. Labuan also had coal, which could be used to service steamships. Sarawak's Rajah James Brooke became the island's first governor in 1846 and two years later it was declared a free port. It also became a penal colony: long-sentence convicts from Hong Kong were put to work on the coal face and in the jungle, clearing roads. The island was little more than a malarial swamp and its inept colonial administration was perpetually plagued by fever and liver disorders. Its nine drunken civil servants provided a gold mine of eccentricity for novelists Joseph Conrad and Somerset Maugham. In *The Outstation*, Maugham describes the desperate attempt by Resident Mr Warburton to keep a grip on civilization in the wilds of Malaysia: "The only concession he made to the climate was to wear a white dinner jacket; but otherwise, in a boiled shirt and high collar, silk socks and patent leather shoes, he dressed as formally as though he was dining at his club in Pall Mall..."

By the 1880s ships were already bypassing the island and the tiny colony began to disintegrate. In 1881 William Hood Treacher moved the capital of the new territory of British North Borneo from Labuan to Kudat and eight years later the Chartered Company was asked to take over the administration of the island. In 1907 it became part of the Straits Settlements, along with Singapore, Malacca (Melaka) and Penang.

Labuan was occupied by the Japanese from 1941 until 1945 and renamed Maida Island. The island and its airstrip was a key priority for the Allied forces and after a four day offensive starting on 10 June 1945 most of the island was under Allied control. Japanese General Masao Baba surrendered on 9 September at Surrender Point on Layang-Layang Beach.

$$$ Palm Beach Resort and Spa
Jln Batu Manikar, T087-418700, www.palmbeachresortspa.com.
On the northwest tip of Labuan, 20 mins from town centre by free shuttle. The resort, built with polished wood (the owner is a timber tycoon), is set in 15 ha of gardens dotted with tall palms that reach down to the beach. The 250 rooms, all sea-facing with generous balconies, are very spacious. There's a large pool at sea level with swim-up bar and a separate children's pool, fitness centre, tennis, playroom, business centre and duty-free shop. The beach is regularly cleaned and

sprayed for sandflies, but the sea is not recommended for swimming due to jellyfish. The hotel is in need of a bit of touching up and is somewhat run down in areas. It's a fair bet for families and is popular with expats on weekend getaways from Brunei.

$$$ Tiara Labuan
Jln Tanjung Batu, T087-414300, www.tiaralabuan.com.
On the west coast next to the golf course, a 5-min taxi ride from the town centre. This well-established hotel gets good reviews for its buffets and proximity to the beach. Though not the most contemporary of

Modern Labuan

In 1946 Labuan became a part of British North Borneo and was later incorporated into Sabah as part of the Federation of Malaysia in 1963. Datuk Harris is thought to own half the island (including the Hotel Labuan). As chief minister, he offered the island as a gift to the federal government in 1984 in exchange for a government undertaking to bail out his industrial projects and build up the island's flagging economy. The election of a Christian government in Sabah in 1986, making it Malaysia's only non-Muslim-ruled state, proved an embarrassment to the then prime minister Doctor Mahathir Mohamad. Labuan has strategic importance as a federal territory, wedged between Sabah and Sarawak. It is used by garrisons of the Malaysian army, navy and air force.

In declaring Labuan a tax haven the Malaysian government set out its vision of Labuan becoming the Bermuda of the Asia-Pacific for the 21st century; and in 2000, the Labuan International Financial Exchange (LFX), a wholly owned subsidiary of the Kuala Lumpur Stock Exchange, was established on the island. Some 6500 offshore firms had set up on the island by the end of 2014 including 300 licensed financial institutions and major global banks. This, together with several five-star hotels, makes it seem that Labuan's days of being a sleepy rural backwater are over. Since 2008 under the auspices of the Labuan International Business and Financial Centre (IBFC), Labuan has been aggressively pursuing an agenda to become one of Asia's leading financial centres.

Included in the island's population of about 87,000 are 10,000 Filipino refugees, with about 21 different ethnic groups. The island is the centre of a booming 'barter' trade with the southern Philippines; Labuan is home to a clutch of so-called string vest millionaires, who have grown rich on the trade. In Labuan, 'barter' is the name given to smuggling. The Filipino traders leaving the Philippines simply over-declare their exports (usually copra, hardwood, rotan and San Miguel beer) and under-declare the imports (Shogun jeeps, Japanese hi-fi and motorbikes), all ordered through duty-free Labuan. With such valuable cargoes, the traders are at the mercy of pirates in the South China Sea. To get round this, they arm themselves with M-16s, bazookas and shoulder-launched missiles. This ammunition is confiscated on their arrival in Labuan, stored in a marine police warehouse, and given back to them for the return trip.

hotels, it has plenty of tropical charm and surrounds a large lotus pond and deep-blue pool complete with jacuzzi. Built onto Adnan Kashoggi's old mansion, it has an Italian feel with terracotta tiles, putty pink stone, a glorious gilt fountain and long shady arcades. Tanjung Batu Beach across the road is rather muddy, but good for walks when the tide is out. **Labuan Beach Restaurant** is here too.

$$ Ambassador 2
Lot 1 & 2 Jln Bunga Kesuma, T087-581242.
Chinese-run hotel with a range of clean rooms, unfortunately reeking of cigarettes. The small single rooms are tiny and an

extra RM10 will get a much more spacious 'superior' room. All rooms have TV, a/c and attached bath.

$$ Global Hotel
Lot U0017, Jln OKK Awang Besar (near the market), T087-425201.
Smallish rooms with cable TV, tatty carpets and attached hot water bathroom. Many rooms are windowless. Staff are friendly enough, but this place is overpriced for what is on offer.

$$ Hotel Aifa
Lot UO217 Jln Tun Mustapha, T087-424888, www.hoteaifa.com.

A large place in the heart of town with a range of comfortable, well-decorated rooms with questionable colour schemes and psychedelic carpets (making a welcome change from Labuan's drab offerings) and huge TV. Facilities include café, bar and Wi-Fi throughout.

$$ Mariner
Jln Tg Purun (on the crossroads opposite the police HQ), T087-418822, mhlabuan@ streamyx.net.
A clean hotel with 60 recently renovated a/c rooms with attached bathroom and TV with in-house movies. Friendly staff. This is one of the better options in town in this price bracket.

$$ Pantai View
Lot U0068, Jln OKK Awang Besar, T087-411339.
This place is one of the better hotels in town with simple clean rooms, friendly staff and spacious rooms with Wi-Fi, cable TV, marble floor and attached hot water bathroom. There are a couple of good Indian restaurants downstairs for late-night snacks. Free tea, coffee and mineral water. Recommended.

$ Labuan Avenue Hotel
Lot UO157, Jln Okk Awang Besar, T087-427157.
The best budget option in town with cheery staff and functional, clean rooms, communal kitchen area and a small smoking terrace outside. Fair value.

$ Pulau Labuan
27-28 Jln Muhibbah, T087-416288.
Fair-value old school hotel with limited character but clean a/c rooms with TV and attached bathroom. A coffee shop downstairs serves Western food and cold beer. There's no lift, so if you have heavy bags ask for a room on a lower floor.

Labuan Town/Bandar Labuan

South China Sea

Where to stay
Aifa 9
Ambassador 2 13
Billion Waterfront 4
Global 3
Grand Dorsett hotel & Victoria's Brasserie 10
Labuan Avenue 11
Lazenda 12
Mariner 5
Palm Beach Resort 1
Pantai View 6

To Menumbok, Kota Kinabalu, Limbang, Lawas & Brunei

100 metres
100 yards

$ Sara
Jln Dewan, T087-417811, saratel@tm.net.my.
Smart hotel popular with families and
business folk without the seedy undertones
of many other city hotels. Rooms have cable
TV and attached bathroom and there is
Wi-Fi on the 1st floor and lobby. There's an
excellent Malay eatery, **Seri Malindo**.

Homestays

The local government offers a variety of
homestay packages with local families in
traditional Malay kampongs, which is a great
way to see the island and learn about Malay
life. On offer is a stay at the water village
opposite Port Victoria, a night at Sungai Labu
village on the coast 12 km from the town
and a 2-night stay at Bukit Kuda. Various
activities can be arranged from joining a
gotong royong (communal clean-up), cooking
lessons, fishing trips and Kedayan cultural

performances. Prices start at RM65 a night
including all meals. Highly recommended.
Contact **Labuan Tourism Action Council**,
Labuan Sea Port Complex, T087-422622,
www.labuantourism.com.my.

Restaurants

Several basic Chinese places to be found
along Jln Merdeka and Jln OKK Awang Besar.

$$ Fratini's
Jln Bunga Kesuma, T087-417555.
A hidden gem of an Italian restaurant serving
authentic handmade pizzas and good salads
(wine is a bit pricey) in a relaxed setting.
Good place to take a break from Asian fare.

$$ Fisherman's Wharf
Jln Kemajuan.
Delectable seafood offerings make this one
of the most popular places to eat in town.

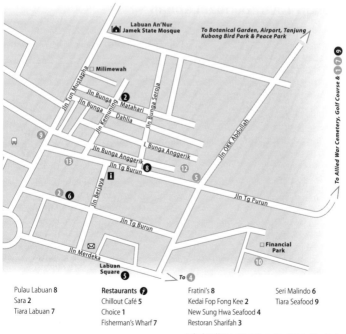

Labuan An'Nur
Jamek State Mosque

To Botanical Garden, Airport, Tanjung
Kubong Bird Park & Peace Park

To Allied War Cemetery, Golf Course & ❶ ❼ ❾

Milimewah

Jln Tun Mustapha
Jln Bunga ❷ Matahari
Jln Kemuning
Jln Bunga
Dahlia
Jln Bunga Seroja
Jln Bunga Anggerik
Jln Bunga Anggerik
Jln Tg Burun ❽ ❶❷
Jln OKK Abdullah
❺
Jln Berjaya
❷ ❻
Jln Tg Purun
Jln Tg Burun
Jln Merdeka
Labuan
Square ❺
To ❹
Financial
Park
❶⓪

Pulau Labuan 8
Sara 2
Tiara Labuan 7

Restaurants ❼
Chillout Café 5
Choice 1
Fisherman's Wharf 7

Fratini's 8
Kedai Fop Fong Kee 2
New Sung Hwa Seafood 4
Restoran Sharifah 3

Seri Malindo 6
Tiara Seafood 9

Getting a table at the weekend can be a challenge but worthwhile once presented with huge garlic prawns, steamed fish dishes and lobster.

$$ Tiara Seafood Restaurant
Jln Tanjung Batu.
Another fantastic seafood offering with famed dishes including salt and pepper squid, prawns and fresh fish. Recommended.

$$ Victoria's Brasserie
Grand Dorsett Hotel (see Where to stay)
Changing daily theme buffet selection that includes Penang street food, barbecue nights and, perhaps most popular of all, the seafood buffet. This is the place for gluttons in need of a stuffing.

$$-$ Chillout Café
Unit 2-6 Level 2, Labuan Times Square.
Well-made coffees and a wide selection of teas with good burgers, sandwiches and freshly baked bread and cakes in a smart contemporary setting.

$ Choice
Jln Okk Awang Besar.
The town's best selection selection of north and south Indian dishes from *dosai* to naan, and biryani to tender tandoori. The fish biryani is particularly good. Recommended.

$ Kedai Kop Fong Kee
Lot 5 and 6, Jln Kemuning.
While this place certainly won't win any awards for cleanliness, it's buzzing at lunchtimes as punters get stuck into generous plates of chicken rice, steaming bowls of delicious prawn *mee* and a daily dim sum selection.

$ New Sung Hwa Seafood
Jln Ujong Pasir, PCK Building.
Amongst the best-value seafood restaurants in Malaysia, chilli prawns, superb grilled stingray steak with wickedly spicy *sambal*. It's not all about the seafood as the Chinese style vegetable dishes are also superb. No menu. Recommended.

$ Restoran Sharifah
Jln Merdeka.
Just opposite the ferry terminal, this busy place has a good choice of Malay and Indian Muslim dishes. The *roti prata* here fly out the kitchen at an alarming rate.

$ Seri Malindo
Lot U0358 Jln Dewan.
Spotless a/c restaurant offering good *nasi campur.*

Foodstalls
There are foodstalls above the wet market and at other end of town, along the beach next to the **Island Club**. There are also stalls on Jln Muhibbah opposite the end of Jln Bahasa, west of the cinema, and a few hawker stalls behind **Hotel Pulau Labuan**.

Shopping

Duty free
If you plan to take duty-free goods into Sabah or Sarawak, you have to stay on Labuan for a minimum of 72 hrs. **Labuan Duty Free** (Bangunan Terminal, Jln Merdeka, T087-411573). Opened in Oct 1990, 142 years after Rajah James Brooke first declared Labuan a free port. The island's original duty-free concession did not include alcohol or cigarettes, but the new shop was given special dispensation to sell them. 2 months later the government extended the privilege to all shops on the island, which explains the absurd existence of a duty-free shop on a duty-free island. The shop claims to be the cheapest duty free in the world; however, you will find competitively priced shops in town too. **Monegain** (U0178, BA, Jln Merdeka, T087-416326) eg can undercut most other outlets on the island due to the volume of merchandise it turns over: worth more than RM1 million a month. The shop owes its success to Filipino 'barter traders' who place bulk purchase orders for electronic goods or cigarettes. These are smuggled back to Zamboanga and Jolo and find their way onto Manila's streets within a week.

Brunei's alcohol-free citizens also keep the shop in business; they brought liquor worth nearly RM2 million from Labuan into Brunei within the 1st 3 months of trading. Duty-free shopping is such a big deal in Labuan that they have an annual carnival at the end of the year with live music and dancing to add to the hedonistic consumerism.

Handicrafts
Behind Jln Merdeka and before the fish market, there is a congregation of tin-roofed shacks housing a Filipino handicrafts and textile market and an interesting wet market.

Supermarkets
Financial Park, *Jln Merdeka*. A shopping complex with Milimewah supermarket. Duty-free shopping, stuffed turtles and restaurants. One of the more popular shopping hangouts in town.
Labuan Farmer's Market, *along Jln Okk Awang Besar*. Fantastic array of local foodstuffs, well worth a look. Look for the blue tents. There's a weekend *tamu* near here selling touristy nicknacks.
Milimewah, *Lot 22-27, Lazenda Commercial Centre, Phase II, Jln Tun Mustapha*. Department store with a supermarket on the ground floor.
Thye Ann Supermarket, *central position below Sri Mutiara*.

What to do

Diving
Boasting 4 major wrecks off the island's coast, Labuan claims to be Southeast Asia's premier destination for wreck diving. Second World War buffs will enjoy diving at the 2 war wrecks. The wrecks lie at depths of 30-35 m with visibility ranging from 6 m to 20 m. Entering the wrecks is best left to those with experience, but novices can still enjoy the amazing sanctuaries for life they provide.
Absolute Air Scuba, *www.absoluteairscuba. com*. A new company offering a range of diving courses and trips around the island.

Borneo Divers, *1 Jln Wawasan, Waterfront Labuan Financial hotel, T087-415867, www. borneodivers.info*. This outfit specializes in 2-day packages diving on shipwrecks off Labuan for certified scuba-divers.

Fishing
Fishing with a hook and line is permitted but the use of spearguns and nets is not. Permits are not necessary.

Golf
Labuan International Golf Club, *Jln Sungai Papar, T087 468468, www.ligc.com.my*. Set in 81 ha of lush greenery, this is a magnificent spot for a bit of tropical golfing. The 72-par 18-hole course is gaining a solid reputation among the Borneo golfers and those in the know. Fees start at RM170 for a weekday round. Half price for 9 holes.

Horse riding
Labuan Horse Riding Centre, *T087-466828*. For a different way to go sightseeing. It offers beach and paddock rides plus lessons.

Transport

Air
There are daily flights to **KK** and **KL** (MAS and Air Asia) and to **Miri** with MAS Wings.

Boat
Ferries depart and arrive at **Bangunan Terminal Feri Penumpang**, next to the duty-free shop on Jln Merdeka. All times are subject to change. Tickets are sold at arrival points at the ferry terminal, but can be bought in town at **Duta Muhibbah Agency**, T087-413827. There are 2 connections a day with **Menumbok** (RM15, the nearest mainland point) by speedboat (20 mins) or car ferry, from where it's a 2-hr bus ride to **KK**. Currently there are 2 boats a day to **Kota Kinabalu** (2½ hrs, RM34, 0800-1300). There are 2 daily boats to **Limbang** at 1230 and 1400 (1½ hrs, RM23) and one to **Lawas** (both in Sarawak), at 1230 (1½ hrs, RM23).

On weekends and public holidays in **Brunei** the ferries are packed and it's a scramble to get a ticket. You can reserve tickets at the ticket office at the ferry terminal. Boats leave Labuan for Brunei's **Serasa Muara Terminal** 6 times daily (0830-1630, RM38, 1½ hrs).

Bus

Local buses around the island leave from Jln Bunga Raya. Bus services cease running after

1900. Fares cost RM1-3 depending on the distance covered.

Car

Adaras Rent-a-Car, T087-421590. **Travel Rent-a-Car**, T087-423600.

Taxi

Taxis are easy enough to get at the airport, ferry terminal and around hotels. Make sure to agree on a fare before embarking.

South of Kota Kinabalu

take the steam train to agricultural towns and traditional markets

To the south of Kota Kinabalu lie the market towns of Papar, Keningau, Tenom and Beaufort all of which can be accessed by car or by train. A short drive up into the mountains from Tambunan is the beautiful Crocker Range National Park, the largest single protected area in Sabah and paradise for hikers and birdwatchers.

Papar

Formerly a sleepy Kadazan village, 38 km south of KK, Papar is developing fast. In *bandar lama* (the old town) there are rows of quaint wooden shophouses, painted blue and set along spacious boulevards lined with palms. There is a large market in the centre. The Papar area is famous for its fruit and there is a good *tamu* every Sunday.

Nearby, **Pantai Manis**, a 3-km stretch of golden sand with a deep lagoon good for swimming, can be reached easily from Papar. It is also possible to make boat trips up the Papar River, which offers gentle rapids for less energetic whitewater rafters. Rafting trips can be organized through tour agents in KK (see page 204).

The **Klias Wetlands** is a new destination promoted by **Sabah Tourism**, popular with visitors who do not have time to visit the east coast of Sabah. Boat trips operate through a mangrove swamp and the Klias River, with the chance to spot proboscis monkeys, long-tailed macaques, silver langur monkeys and an abundance of birdlife. The Klias Peninsula lies 120 km south of KK; trips down the Klias River depart from the Kota Klias jetty. Booking via a tour operator in KK is recommended (see page 204).

Tambunan

The twisting mountain road that cuts across the Crocker Range National Park (see page 228) and over the **Sinsuran Pass** at 1649 m is very beautiful. There are dramatic views down over Kota Kinabalu and the islands beyond and glimpses of Mount Kinabalu to the northeast. The road itself, from KK to Tambunan, was the old bridleway that linked the west coast to the interior. Inland communities traded their tobacco, rattan and other jungle produce for salt and iron at the coastal markets. The road passes through Penampang (see page 208). Scattered farming communities grow hill rice, pineapples, bananas, mushrooms and other vegetables that are sold at roadside stalls, where wild and cultivated orchids can also be found. After descending from the hills the road enters the sprawling flood plain of Tambunan – the **Pegalam River** runs through the plain – which, at the height of the paddy season, is a magnificent patchwork of greens.

ON THE ROAD
Rafflesia: the world's largest flower

The rafflesia (*Rafflesia arnoldi*), named after Stamford Raffles, the founder of modern Singapore, is the largest flower in the world. The Swedish naturalist Eric Mjoberg wrote in 1930 on seeing the flower: "The whole phenomenon seems so amazing, so unfamiliar, so fantastic, that we are tempted to explain: such flowers cannot be real!"

Stamford Raffles, who discovered the flower for Western science 100 years earlier during his first sojourn at Bengkulu on the west coast of Sumatra, noted that it was "a full yard across, weighs 15 pounds, and contains in the nectary no less than eight pints [of nectar]...".

The problem is that the rafflesia does not flower for very long – only for a couple of weeks, usually between August and December. At other times of the year there is usually nothing to see. The plant is in fact parasitic, so appropriately its scent is more akin to rotting meat than any perfume. Its natural habitat is moist, shaded areas.

Tambunan District covers an area of 134,540 ha. At 650 m to 900 m, it enjoys a spring-like climate during much of the year. The area is largely Kadazan/Dusun, Sabah's largest ethnic group, and the whole area explodes into life each May during the harvest festival when copious quantities of *lihing*, the famed local rice wine, are consumed and *Bobolians* (high priestesses) still conduct various rituals. There is a *lihing* brewery inside the **Tambunan Village Resort Centre**. The Tambunan (Valley of the Bamboo), so-called as there are at least 12 varieties of bamboo to be found here, also lays claim to the Kitingan family. Joseph was Sabah's first Christian chief minister until he was deposed in March 1994. His brother, Jeffrey, was formerly head of the Sabah Foundation. He entered politics in 1994 on his release from detention on the Malaysian Peninsula. He had been charged under Malaysia's internal security act of being a secessionist conspirator.

A concrete structure at **Tibabar**, just outside Tambunan, situated amongst the rice fields and surrounded by peaceful kampong houses, commemorates the site of **Mat Salleh's Fort** ① *daily 0900-1700, free*, and the place of his death. Mat Salleh, now a nationalist folk hero, led a rebellion for six years against the **Chartered Company** administration until he was killed in 1900 (see box, page 193). The memorial has been set up by the Sabah State Museum and houses some exhibits including weapons, Salleh paraphernalia and a photo of the man himself.

Tambunan Rafflesia Information Centre ① *On the KK–Tambunan road, T087-899589, daily 0800-1500.* The centre is located at the roadside on the edge of a forest reserve that has been set aside to conserve this remarkable flower (see box, above). The information centre has a comprehensive and attractive display on the rafflesia and its habitat and information on flowers in bloom. If trail maps are temporarily unavailable, ask the ranger to point out the sites where blooms can be seen on the large relief model of the forest reserve at the back of the information centre. The blooming period of the flower is very short so, to avoid disappointment, it's worth phoning the centre first. Ranger guides are available at the centre and cost RM100 for a group of six or less.

Ahir Terjan Sensuron This waterfall is 4 km from the Rafflesia Information Centre on the Tambunan–KK road (heading towards KK). From the road, it is a 45-minute walk. Every

Thursday morning a large market is held here, selling tobacco, local musical instruments, clothing, strange edible jungle ferns and yeast used to make fermented rice wine. There are also bundles of a fragrant herb known as *tuhau*, a member of the ginger family that is made into a spicy condiment or *sambal* redolent of the jungle. A smaller market is held on Sunday in **Kampong Toboh**, north of Tambunan.

★**Crocker Range National Park** ① *Contact Head Station Keningau T087-220924, daily 0800-1700, RM10, take a taxi from Keningau taxi station for around RM40; there are 6-7 daily departures to Keningau from KK (RM16).* The Crocker Range was recognized as a Biosphere Reserve by UNESCO in 2014. The park incorporates 139,919 ha of hill and montane forest, which includes many species endemic to Borneo. It is the largest single totally protected area in Sabah. There is good accommodation provided in the park at **Manis Manis**, www.manismanisresort.com.my (see page 232), with chalets, dorms and camping facilities offering spectacular views over the hills. The **Mawah Waterfall** is reached by following the road north towards Ranau to Kampong Patau, where a sign beside the school on the left indicates a gravel road leading almost to the waterfall (Mawah Airterjun). It is 15 minutes down the road by car and between five and 10 minutes' walk along the trail.

Gunung Trusmadi Gunung Trusmadi (2642 m), 70 km southeast of Kota Kinabalu, is the second highest mountain in Malaysia, but very few people climb it: the route is difficult and facilities, compared with Gunung Kinabalu, are few. There are two main routes to the top: the north route, which takes four days to the summit (and three days down) and the south route, which is harder but shorter taking two days to the summit. Trusmadi is famous for its huge, and very rare, pitcher plant *Nepethes trusmadiensis*, found only on one spot on the summit ridge. It is also known for its fantastic view north, towards Gunung Kinabalu, which rises above the Tambunan Valley. There is a wide variety of vegetation on the mountain as it rises from dipterocarp primary jungle through oak montane forest with mossy forest near the summit and heath-like vegetation on top. An expedition to Trusmadi requires careful planning and should not be undertaken casually. A more detailed account of the two routes is in *Mountains of Malaysia – A Practical Guide and Manual*, by John Briggs.

Keningau

The Japanese built fortifications around their base in Keningau during the Second World War. It is now rather a depressing, shabby lumber town, smothered in smoke from the sawmills. The timber business in this area turned Keningau into a boom town in the 1980s and the population virtually doubled within a decade. The felling continues, but there is not much primary forest left these days. There are huge logging camps all around the town and the hills to the west. Logging roads lead into these hills off the Keningau–Tenom road, which are accessible by 4WD vehicles. It is just possible to drive across them to Papar, which is a magnificent route. If you do attempt the drive, steer well clear of log-laden trucks on their way down the mountain. There are two weekly markets held here. One is at **Bingkor** on Thursdays and the other at **Pekan** on Sunday mornings. Both are principally noted for their Kadazan handicrafts. The one held at Pekan is more convenient for visitors as it is right in the centre of town.

Batu Punggul and Batu Tinahas **Sapulut** is deep in Murut country and is accessible from Keningau by a rough road via Kampong Nabawan (4WD required). At Sapulut, follow the river of the same name east through Bigor and Kampong Labang to Kampong Batu

Punggul at the confluence of Sungai Palangan, a 2½-hour journey. **Batu Punggul** is a limestone outcrop protruding 200 m above the surrounding forest, about 30 minutes' walk from the kampong; it can be climbed without any equipment, but with care. It is quite a dangerous climb, but there are plenty of handholds and the view of the surrounding forest from the top is spectacular. Both the forest and the caves in and around Batu Punggul are worth exploring. Nearby is the less impressive limestone outcrop, **Batu Tinahas**, with huge caves and many unexplored passages. It is thought to have at least three levels of caves and tunnels. Some tour operators in KK offer trips here.

Longhouse visits There is a short stretch of road leading from Sapulut to Agis, just a four-hour boat ride from the Kalimantan border. There is even an immigration checkpoint at Pegalungan, which is a settlement en route. (**Note** It's not possible to cross into Indonesia from here.) There are many rivers and longhouses worth exploring here. One particular longhouse is **Kampong Selungai**, only 30 minutes from Pegalungan. Here it is possible to see traditional boatbuilders at work, as well as weaving, mat making and beadwork. Given the luxury of time, it is a fascinating area where traditional lifestyles have not changed much. It is possible to charter a minibus along the Nabawan road to **Sapulut**, where you can hire boats upriver. At Sapulut, ask for the the headman, or *kepala*. He should be able to arrange the trip upriver, which could take up to two days, with accommodation in Murut longhouses. As in neighbouring Sarawak, these long upriver trips can be prohibitively expensive unless you are in a decent-sized group. Alternatively, book at tour through **Best Borneo**, www.bestborneo.com.my (see page 204), in KK, which offers reasonably priced trips into the interior around Sapulut with longhouse accommodation.

Tenom

Situated at the end of the Sabah State Railway, southwest of Keningau on the banks of the Sungei Lapas, Tenom is a hilly inland town, with a population of 55,000, predominantly Murut (60%) with a sizeable population of Hakka Chinese (20%) whose ancestors came from Longchuan in Guangdong, attracted by the rich soil around the town. Although it was the centre of an administrative district under the Chartered Company from the turn of the century, known as Fort Birch, most of the modern town was built during the Japanese occupation in the Second World War. It is in the heart of Murut country, but don't expect to see longhouses and Murut in traditional costume; many Murut have moved into individual houses, except in the more remote parts of the interior, and their modernized bamboo homes are often well equipped.

Note the **statue of Ontoros Antorom** in the town centre. Ontoros was a Murut who led a rebellion against British colonists in 1915 in an incident known as the Rundum Revolt. Fed up with taxation on goods such as rice and the British policy forcing every Murut couple with more than one child to give one of their children away for forced labour, Ontoros led the rebellion of 1000 Murut warriors from Tenom and Keningau. The Murut, fighting with only blow pipes, spears and Ontoros' alleged supernatural powers, held off a heavy British counter attack of well-armed imperial soldiers. On the way to peace talks, the Murut delegation was surrounded by British soldiers and Ontoros was executed

The surrounding area is very fertile and the main crops are soya beans, maize and a variety of vegetables. Cocoa is also widely grown. The cocoa trees are often obscured under shade trees called *pokok belindujan*, with bright pink flowers. The durians from Tenom (and Beaufort) are thought to be the best in Sabah. *Tamu* (market) is on Sunday.

BACKGROUND
★ Sabah's markets and trade fairs

In Sabah, an open trade fair is called a *tamu*. Locals gather to buy and sell jungle produce, handicrafts and traditional wares. *Tamu* comes from the Malay word *tetamu*, to meet, and the biggest and most famous is held at Kota Belud, north of Kota Kinabalu in Bajau country.

Tamus were fostered by the pre-war British North Borneo Chartered Company, when district officers would encourage villagers from miles around to trade among themselves. It was also a convenient opportunity for officials to meet with village headmen. They used to be strictly Kadazan affairs, but today *tamus* are multicultural events. Sometimes public auctions of water buffalo and cattle are held. Some of the biggest *tamus* around the state are:

Monday: Tandek, Tuaran
Tuesday: Kiulu, Kuala Penyu, Topokan, Kudat
Wednesday: Tamparuli, Kudat
Thursday: Keningau (Bingkor), Tambunan, Sipitang, Telipok, Simpangan
Friday: Sinsuran, Weston
Saturday: Penampang, Beaufort, Sindumin, Matunggong, Kinarut
Sunday: Tambunan, Tenom, Kota Belud, Papar, Gaya Street (KK) Keningau (Pekan Keningau)

★ **Murut villages** There are many Murut villages surrounding Tenom, all with their own churches. In some villages there is also an oversized mosque or *surau*. The **Murut Cultural Centre** ① *T087-302421, daily 0900-1700, free*, is 10 km out of town. Run by the Sabah Museum, this 13-ha site is next to the Pegalan River and displays the material culture of the Murut people including basketry, cloth and the famous Murut trampolines of *lansaran*. The **Pesta Kalimaran** festival is held for two days each year at the centre at the start of April and showcases the culture of the Murut through music, dance and art. It's very touristy but well worth a visit. The best longhouses are along the Padas River towards Sarawak at Kampong Marais and Kampong Kalibatang where blowpipes are still made. At **Kemabong**, 25 km south of Tenom, the Murut, who are keen dancers, have a *lansaran* dancing trampoline; a wooden platform sprung with bamboo which can support ten Murut doing a jig.

Sabah Agricultural Park ① *15 km northeast of Tenom, T087-737952, www.sabah.net. my/agripark, Tue-Sun 0900-1630, RM25, children RM10; take a taxi or minibus from Tenom to get here (RM30/RM20 per person)*. This research initiative developed by the Sabah State Government is also the site of Tenom's **orchid farm**, which has been developed into an agro-tourism park. One of the more celebrated aspects of the park is the **Bee Centre**, highlighted in a Sir David Attenborough BBC documentary. Five of the world's honeybee species can be seen here. Bikes are available for rental (RM3 per hour) and it's possible to camp (RM10). The park makes for a good family day out with plenty of space to run around and enough natural diversions to keep young minds occupied for a few hours.

Beaufort

This small, sleepy, unexciting town is named after British Governor Leicester P Beaufort of the North Borneo Company, who was a lawyer and was appointed to the post despite having no experience of the East or of administration. He was savaged by Sabahan historian KG Tregonning as "the most impotent governor North Borneo ever acquired and who, in the manner of nonentities, had a town named after him."

Beaufort is a quaint town, with riverside houses built on stilts to escape the constant flooding of the Padas River. The *tamu* (market) is on Saturday. War buffs will want to make their way to the **Starcevich Monument** on the edge of town. The monument was erected to commemorate the actions of Leslie Starcevich from the Australian 9th Division Army. In June 1945, the Australians, on their way to Labuan found their way blocked by a Japanese garrison at Beaufort. In fierce fighting on the edge of town, Starcevich led two counter attacks with his Bren gun, destroying Japanese positions. He was subsequently awarded the Victoria Cross and went on to live out his days as a farmer in Western Australia. The population of Beaufort erected the memorial to commemorate the liberation of the town from Japanese occupation.

The **Garama Wetlands**, 1 km from Beaufort, are popular for the 1½-hour dusk river cruises where flying foxes, proboscis monkeys and silver leaf monkeys can be spotted. There are a number of restaurants along the river and a boardwalk for gentle stroll. River cruises can be booked through **Riverbug Tours**, www.riverbug.asia, in KK (see page 205).

Sipitang

South of Beaufort, Sipitang is a sleepy coastal town with little to offer the traveller apart from a supermarket and a few hotels (see page 233). It's the closest town in Sabah to the Sarawak border and minibuses run from Beaufort to Sipitang and on to Sindumin, where you can connect with buses bound for Lawas in Sarawak by walking across the border to Merapok. There is an immigration checkpoint here and month-long permits are given for visitors to Sarawak.

Listings South of Kota Kinabalu

Where to stay

Papar

$$$ Beringgis Beach Resort
Km 26, Jln Papar, Kampong Beringgis, Kinarut, T088-752333, www.beringgis.com.
A sprawling resort on the beach with spotless a/c rooms with TV and Wi-Fi. There's a pool, restaurant, lots of Southeast Asian games, such as *carom* and *congkak*, all of which make this a popular spot for families and city dwellers on weekend getaways.

$$$ Sunborneo Resort
Km 22, Jln Papar, Laut Kinarut, T019-817 7888, www.sunborneo.com.my.
A wonderful island resort with a variety of chalets offered in a secluded cove or jungle-covered hillside. Rooms are basic but comfortable and packages include all

meals and snorkelling equipment as well as boat transfer from the mainland. Activities include birdwatching, diving and various other water sports.

$$ Langkah Syabas Beach Resort
21 km south of KK, Jln Papar Baru, Kinarut, T088-752000, www.langkahsyabas.com.my.
25 spacious chalets of varying size with huge verandas set around the pool. Ask for one of the newer room with a sea view. A/c, fans, TV, tennis and riding centre close by, attractive tropical garden. 100 m to the beach.

$$-$ Seaside Travellers Inn
Km 20, Papar–KK Highway, Kinarut, T088-750555, www.seasidetravellersinn.com.my.
Fairly unexciting place with a/c rooms set in a pleasant location off the beach. Free Wi-Fi and variety of water sports on offer.

Tambunan

The area is renowned for its *lihing* (rice wine); see it being brewed at the TVRC factory.

$ Borneo Heritage Village Resort
Also known as Tambunan Village Resort Centre (TVRC). Signposted off the main road before town, on both sides of the Pegalam River, T088-774076.

Accommodation is in chalets and a 'longhouse' dorm made of split bamboo. There's a restaurant, motel and entertainment centre (with karaoke and slot machines), hall and sports field. There are also a couple of retreat centres located about 10 mins' walk away. Staff can help arrange guides for treks up Gunung Trus Madi.

$ Tambunan Inn
Lot E, Blok E-7, Sudc Tambunan New Shophouses, T087-771240.

Located in a newish Chinese shophouse in town, this place is the only genuine budget option in Tambunan. Rooms are spacious and clean, though not overly exciting. The owner, Yabin, is a good source of local information. Wi-Fi available in the lobby.

Keningau

$$ Juta
Jln Milimewa, T087-337888, www.hoteljuta.com.

The tallest building in town, with recently refurbished rooms which have cable TV and weak Wi-Fi. Café and restaurants, which are popular with the local Chinese community. Do not be surprised to hear the hallways shudder to the sound of karaoke renditions of Hokkien or Cantonese classics.

$$ Perkasa
Jln Kampong Keningau, T088-331045, www.perkasahotel.com.my.

Somewhat retro business hotel, often used by visiting European tour groups with comfortable a/c rooms on the edge of town. Rooms on the higher floors offer good views of the surrounding hills. There's a Chinese restaurant, coffee house and health centre.

$$-$ Manis Manis Rooftop of Borneo Resort
Mile 8, Kimanis–Keningau Highway, Crocker Range National Park, T088-719 900, www.manismanisresort.com.my.

Excellent resort perched on the hillsides of the Crocker Range and inside the actual park. Accommodation is inside a variety of new, large and spacious chalets and lodges. There are abundant opportunities for hiking and birdwatching in the park. The **Cinnamon Café** serves good local food and their evening barbecue is worth a try.

$ Hillview Garden Resort
1 Jln Menawo, T087-338500, www.hillviewgardens.co.nr

Cheery family-orientated place away from town with 25 rooms and a pool. Occasional live music, dancing and opportunities to down a few glasses of local *tapai* rice wine.

Tenom

$$ Perkasa
On top of the hill above town, T087-735811, www.perkasahotel.com.my.

A large hotel with superb views over Tenom and the surrounding countryside. Rooms are spacious and decidedly retro, with TV, a/c and en suite bathroom. As guests are few and far between, the restaurant, **Tenom Perkasa**, has a limited but well-priced range of Chinese and Western dishes. A fair option though in need of a serious face lift.

$ Orchid
Block K, Jln Tun Mustapha, T087-737600.

Within walking distance of the bus stop. Small and slightly run down but friendly with clean, well-maintained rooms. A bit noisy at weekends

$ Rumah Rehat Lagud Sebren
Agricultural Research Station Resthouse, located in the heart of the agricultural park, agripark@sabah.net.my.

Dorms (RM25) and camping (RM10 per person). Dorms are packed during the school holidays, so book in advance.

Beaufort

A distinctly average selection of hotels, all roughly the same and slightly overpriced. Rooms have a/c and bathrooms.

$ Mandarin Inn
Lot 38, Jln Beaufort Jaya, T087-212800.
A/c rooms.

$ River Park Hotel
AH150, Pekan Beaufort, T087-223 333.
A short stroll from the bridge and the railway station, this place has fairly clean rooms and cheerful staff.

Sipitang

$ Asanol
T087-821506.
Good-value rooms with bathrooms.

$ SFI Motel
SFI Housing Complex, 10 Jln Jeti, T087-802097.
Clean place with a selection of a/c rooms with attached hot water bathroom.

$ Shangsan
T088-821800.
Comfortable rooms with a/c and TV.

Restaurants

Papar

There are several run-of-the-mill coffee shops and restaurants in the old town.

$ D'Soka Restaurant
Km 17, Papar Highway, T013-860 7352.
Located along the KK–Papar highway, this place serves highly commended local fare including a sumptuous red velvet cake and even runs a cooking school. Phone for details.

$ Seri Takis
New Town (below the lodging house).
Serves *padang* food.

Keningau

There are a number of new pseudo-Western joints in town. Those who have missed chips will find solace here.

$ Afterwork Café
Lot 11, Adnan Shopping Complex.
Pizza, pasta, salmon and chips with an Asian twist. Friendly and good value.

$ Permata Café,
Jln Okk Sodomon
Styled as a bistro and serving Chinese standards and a few Western dishes such as steak and lamb chops, this place is a decent bet.

$ Seri Wah Coffee Shop
On the corner of the central square and near some foodstalls.
Simple but well-cooked Chinese fare. Try the *ngau chap* (beef noodles).

Tenom

$ Curry Emas
Specializes in monitor lizard claypot curries, dog meat and wild cat.

$ Restoran Chi Hin
Jln Tapikong Cina Bypass.
Chinese coffee shop.

$ Sapong
Perkasa Hotel (see Where to stay).
Serves local and Western dishes.

$ Y&L (Young & Lovely) Food & Entertainment
Jln Sapong (2 km out of town).
Noisy, but easily the best restaurant in Tenom. Mainly Chinese food: freshwater fish (steamed *sun hok*, also known as *ikan hantu*) and venison; washed down with the local version of *air limau* (or *kitchai*) which comes with dried plums. Giant TV screen.

$ Yong Lee
Town centre.
Coffee shop serving cheap Chinese fare.

Beaufort

$ Brunei Satay House
Lot 110 Jln Chung.
Busy place serving up big plates of satay. There's an a/c room upstairs. English is

limited here so practise your Bahasa Melayu on the friendly waiters.

$ Little Town Seafood
Jln Stesen 1.
Popular Chinese seafood. Good variety of dishes and busy at weekends.

$ Restoran Alif
Lot 8, Kampung Bingkul.
Get your *roti canai* and *teh tarik* cravings sorted here.

Shopping

Tambunan
Handicrafts
There is a *tamu* (market) on Thu. The **Handicraft Centre**, just before the Shell petrol station, sells traditional local weaving and basketry.

Transport

Papar
Minibus
Minibuses leave from the Bandar Lama area. There are regular connections with **KK** (1 hr) and **Beaufort** (1 hr).

Train
Daily departures to **Beaufort** (1 hr) and **Tanjung Aru** (1 hr).

Tambunan
Minibus
Buses marked for Tambunan go from the Padang Merdeka Bus Station at the bottom of Signal Hill in **KK** (1½ hrs).

Taxi
To **KK** for RM120 or shared taxi for around RM16 per passenger.

Keningau
Minibus
These leave from the centre, by the market. Regular buses to **KK** and **Tenom**.

Taxi
A taxi to **KK** costs around RM200 or RM30 per passenger in a shared taxi.

Tenom
Minibus
Minibuses leave from centre of town on Jln Padas. Regular connections with **Keningau** (45) mins and **KK** (3 hrs).

Taxi
To **KK** costs around RM220 or shared taxis are available for a fraction of the price (RM35); they leave from the main street (Jln Padas).

Train
Daily departures for **Tanjung Aru** (6 hrs) and **Papar** (5 hrs).

Beaufort
Minibus
Minibuses leave from centre of town. Regular connections with **KK** (2 hrs RM12).

Train
Daily departures to **Tanjung Aru** (2 hrs) and **Tenom** (4 hrs).

Sipitang
There is a line of minibuses and taxis along the waterfront. The jetty for ferries to **Labuan** (daily departures) is a 10-min walk from the centre.

North of
Kota Kinabalu

From KK, the route heads north to the sleepy Bajau town of Kota Belud which wakes up on Sundays for its colourful *tamu* (market). Near the northernmost tip of the state is Kudat, the former state capital. The region northeast of KK is more interesting, with Gunung Kinabalu always in sight. From Kota Belud, the mountain looks completely different. It is possible to see its tail, sweeping away to the east, and its western flanks, which rise out of the rolling coastal lowlands.

Kota Belud

come on a Sunday for Sabah's largest traditional market

This busy little town is in a beautiful location, nestled in the foothills of Mount Kinabalu on the banks of the Tempasuk River, but doesn't have much going on except for its market. It is the heart of Bajau country, the so-called 'cowboys of the East'; the whole area is generally lacking in sights.

Sabah's largest **market**, or *tamu*, is held every Sunday from 0600, behind the mosque in Kota Belud. A mix of people – Bajau, Kadazan/Dusun, Rungus, Chinese, Indian and Malay – come to sell their goods and it is a social occasion as much as a market. Aside from the wide variety of food and fresh produce on sale, there is a weekly water buffalo auction at the entrance. Visitors are strongly recommended to get there early, but don't expect to find souvenirs. However, the *tamu besar* (big market) held in November has cultural performances and handicrafts on sale.

This is an account of the market by a civil servant, posted to the Kota Belud district office in 1915: "The *tamu* itself is a babel and buzz of excitement; in little groups the natives sit and spread their wares out on the ground before them; bananas, *langsats*, pines and bread-fruit; and, in season, that much beloved but foul-smelling fruit, the durian. Mats and straw-hats and ropes; fowls, goats and buffaloes; pepper, *gambia sirih* and vegetables; rice (*padi*), sweet potatoes and *ubi kayu*; *dastars* and handkerchiefs, silver and brassware. In little booths, made of wood, with open sides and floors of split bamboos and roofs of *atap* (sago palm-leaf) squat the Chinese traders along one side of the *tamu*. For cash or barter they will sell; and many a wrangle, haggle and bargain is driven and fought before the goods change hands, or money parted with."

BACKGROUND

Kota Belud

The first Bajau to migrate to Sabah were pushed into the interior, around Kota Belud. They were originally a seafaring people but then settled as farmers in this area. The famed Bajau horsemen wear jewelled costumes, carry spears and ride bareback on ceremonial occasions. The ceremonial headdresses worn by the horsemen, called dastars, are woven on backstrap looms by the womenfolk of Kota Belud. Each piece takes four to six weeks to complete. Traditionally, the points of the headdress were stiffened using wax; these days, strips of cardboard are inserted into the points.

The **Tempasuk River** has a wide variety of migrating birds and is a proposed conservation area. More than 127 species have been recorded along this area of the coastal plain and over 500,000 birds flock here every year, many migrating from northern latitudes in winter. These include 300,000 swallows, 50,000 yellow longtails and 5000 water birds. The best period for birdwatching is October to March. Between Kota Belud and the sea are mangrove swamps with colonies of proboscis monkeys. You can hire small fishing boats in town to go down the Tempasuk River or join a sunset tour from operators in Kota Belud (around RM180).

Listings Kota Belud

Where to stay

$ Kota Belud Travellers Lodge
Lot 6, Plaza Kong Guan, T088-977228.
Simple place with a variety of clean rooms.

$ Mynopungguk Homestay
Outside town, T016-837 9681,
http://mynopungguk.blogspot.sg.
Friendly homestay with 3 large en suite rooms. Live with and be treated as part of the family, getting invited to local celebrations such as weddings. Offers good tours, local information and fantastic local Sabahan dishes. Activities include buffalo riding, jungle trekking, river swimming, cultural dancing and visits to local *tamus*.

$ TD Lodge
Block D, Lot D20-D24, Kompleks Alapbana, T088-975111, www.hoteltangdynasty.com/ kotabelud.
Comfortable, spacious rooms with friendly staff in the heart of town.

Restaurants

There are several Indian coffee shops around the main square.

$ Bismillah Restoran
35 Jln Keruak (main square).
Excellent *roti telur*.

$ Indonesia Restoran
Next to the car park behind the Kota Belud Hotel.
Indonesian favourites including satay, *soto ayam* (chicken noodle soup) and *bakso* (meat balls in noodles).

Festivals

Nov Tamu Besar. The annual market is a very colourful event and includes a parade and equestrian games by the Bajau horsemen. Contact **Sabah Tourism** (www.sabahtourism.com, see page 197), for more information.

Shopping

Markets

There's a daily market in the main square and a fish market south of the main market. The large *tamu* is held every Sun, and the annual *tamu besar* in Nov with a wide variety of local handicrafts for sale.

The following are the main markets in the Kota Belud District. **Mon and Sat**: Kota Belud. Market time is 0600-1200. All *tamus* provide many places to eat. **Tue**: Pandasan (along the Kota Belud–Kudat road). **Wed**: Keelawat (along the Kota Belud–KK road). **Thu**: Pekan Nabalu (along the Kota Belud–Ranau road). **Fri**: Taginambur (along the Kota Belud–Ranau road, 16 km from Kota Belud).

Transport

Minibus

Minibuses run from main square. There are regular connections with **KK**, **Kudat** and **Ranau**. Kota Belud is a good place to stop off if travelling between **KK** and **Kudat** (3½ hrs), with easy transport connections.

Kudat

visit Rungus longhouses and stay on the stunning Tip of Borneo

Kudat town, surrounded by coconut groves, is right on the northern tip of Sabah, 160 km from KK. The local people here are the Rungus, members of the Kadazan tribe. Gentle, warm and friendly, the Rungus have clung to their traditions more than other Sabahan tribes and some still live in longhouses, although many are now building their own houses. Rungus longhouses are built in a distinctive style with outward-leaning walls; the Sabah State Museum (see page 193) incorporates many of the design features of a Rungus longhouse. The Rungus used to wear coils of copper and brass round their arms and legs and today the older generation still dress in black. They are renowned for their fine beadwork and weaving. A handful of Rungus longhouses are dotted around the peninsula, away from Kudat town.

Sights

Kudat is dotted with family farms cultivating coconut trees, maize and groundnuts, and keeping bees. Seafood is also an important industry and features heavily in the local diet. Kudat is inhabited by many other ethnic groups: Bonggi, Bajau, Bugis, Kadazandusun, Obian, Orang Sungai and Suluk. The *tamu* (market) is on Mondays.

There are some beautiful unspoilt white-sand beaches north of town; the best known is **Bak-Bak**, 11 km north of Kudat, though it can get crowded at weekends. The beach is signposted off the Kota Belud–Kudat road; take a minibus (irregular), or a taxi.

Sikuati, 23 km west of Kudat on the northwest side of the Kudat Peninsula, has a good beach. Every Sunday, at 0800, the Rungus come to the market in this village. Local handicrafts are sold. You can get there by minibus.

Between Kota Belud and Kudat there is a marsh and coastal area with an abundance of birds. Costumed Bajau horsemen can sometimes be seen here.

The **Longhouse Experience** ① *tour companies organize trips; contact Sabah Tourism, T088-212121, www.sabahtourism.com,* is possibly the most memorable thing to do in Kudat. A stay at a longhouse enables visitors to observe, enjoy and take part in the Rungus' unique lifestyle. There are two Bavanggazo longhouses with 10 units. Nearby are the village's only modern amenities, toilets and showers. During the day, the longhouse corridor is busy with Rungus womenfolk at work stringing elaborate beadworks and

BACKGROUND

Kudat

The East India Company first realized the potential of the Kudat Peninsula and set up a trading station on Balambangganan Island, to the north of Kudat. The settlement was finally abandoned after countless pirate raids. Kudat became the first administrative capital of Sabah in 1881, when it was founded by a Briton, AH Everett. William Hood Fletcher, the protectorate's first governor, first tried to administer the territory from Labuan, which proved impossible, so he moved to the newly founded town of Kudat which was nothing more than a handful of *atap* houses built out into the sea on stilts. It was a promising location, however, situated on an inlet of Marudu Bay, and it had a good harbour. Kudat's glory years were shortlived; it was displaced as the capital of North Borneo by Sandakan in 1883.

Today it is a busy town dominated by Chinese and Filipino traders (legal and illegal) on the coast and prostitutes trading downtown. Kudat was one of the main centres of Chinese and European migration in the late 19th century. Most of the Chinese who came to Kudat were Christian Hakka vegetable farmers: 96 of them arrived in April 1883 and they were followed by others, given free passages by the Chartered Company. More Europeans, especially the British, began to arrive on Kudat's shores with the discovery of oil in 1880. Frequent pirate attacks and an inadequate supply of drinking water forced the British to move their main administrative offices to Sandakan in 1883.

weaving baskets and their traditional cloth. Visitors can experience and participate in these activities. Longhouse meals are homegrown; fish and seafood come from nearby fishing villages, drinks include young coconuts and local rice wine. Evening festivities consist of the playing of gongs with dancers dressed in traditional Rungus costume. See box, page 72, for advice on visiting longhouses.

Matunggong, 43 km south of Kudat, is a less touristy area best known for its longhouses, though they are rather dilapidated now.

At **Gombizau Honey Bee Farm** ⓘ *T013-548 1885, RM5,* visitors get to learn about bee-keeping and the harvesting of beeswax, honey and royal jelly.

Kampong Sumangkap is an enterprising little village where you can learn about traditional gong- and handicraft-making (RM5). Contact the **factory** ⓘ *T019-535 9943, www.sabahtourism.com/destination/kampung-sumangkap-gong-factory, RM5,* to arrange a tour. Visitors in large groups will often be taken to the town hall for a performance.

Where to stay

$$$$ Hibiscus Beach Retreat
A short distance from the
Tip of Borneo, T019-850704,
www.hibiscusbeachretreat.com.
Beautifully furnished 1-bedroom chalet,
with decking offering stunning views and
refreshing sea breezes. This is a great option
for people looking for peace and quiet
and long beach walks. Daily maid service
included and a range of dining and activities
can be pre-arranged.

$$ Kudat Golf and Marina Resort
Off Jln Urus Setia, T088-611211,
www.kudatgolfmarinaresort.com.
A large orange monster next to a marina
surrounded by a huge and unsightly car park.
Rooms are spacious and many have superb
sea views. The main attraction is the 18-hole
championship golf course.

$ North Borneo Biostation
Kampung Bak Bak, Mile 7, T010-803 7310,
www.borneobiostation.com.
A selection of simple high-ceilinged
A-frame chalets on the beach at Bak Bak,
a short drive from Kudat. Friendly vibes
and a range of activities including trekking,
diving and fishing.

$ Ria Hotel
Jln Marudu, Lot 3, T088-622226,
riahotel2002@hotmail.com.
Simple, functional and good-value place
in the centre of town with sea views and a
reasonable dining option downstairs. Good
option for a budget stay.

Transport

Minibus
Minibuses leave from Jln Lo Thien Hock.
Regular connections with **KK** (3½ hrs).

Pulau Mantanini

idyllic island with accommodation to suit all budgets

One hour by speedboat from Kota Belud off Sabah's northwestern coast is Pulau
Mantanani. The island and its surrounding islets offer a more rugged, unrestrained
vibe than the sanitized upmarket resorts around Sabah's coastline. There are a
number of decent places to stay, offering a good chance to relax and get away from
it all – just don't expect the island to be manicured exclusively for all your needs.
You might well find yourself sharing a stunning sunset with a dairy cow and her calf
wandering along the beach. The island has a couple of local fishing communities in
addition to a diverse range of wildlife.

Mantanani is all about location. Get yourself out of bed just before sunrise on a clear
day and you'll be treated with a breathtakingly vast silhouette of Mount Kinabalu rising
more than 4 km into the morning sky, framed in golden light as the sun rises behind it.
Whilst daylight has already reached most of Sabah, a huge triangular shadow, tens of
kilometres across, holds Mantanani and the nearby coast in darkness for a just a few
minutes longer – a truly spectacular way to begin your day on the island. On the not
uncommon overcast days, dark storm clouds laced with lightning around the mountains
summit can also be quite beautiful.

Diving

The surrounding waters can't always be described as crystal clear, but they're renowned in the scuba community for their muck-diving opportunities, different species of nudibranch and diverse underwater life, as well as several interesting wrecks.

Listings Pulau Mantanani

Where to stay

Accommodation can be arranged through **Mantanani Island Booking Centre**, Lot 1-39 Asia City Complex, 1st floor, Jln Asia City, KK, T088-448409, www.mantanani.com. Diving tours and other activities are also offered. There are a few places to choose from on this undoubtedly beautiful island.

$$$ Bembaran Beach Resort
Located on Dugong Beach, a beautiful beach that was previously well known for its dugong (seemingly a less frequent visitor nowadays), the resort offers chalets on full board basis. Electricity available in the evenings and early mornings.

$$$ Mantanani Dream Resort
Newly built and offering well-furnished rooms including the plush sea accented VIP Honeymoon room. All meals are included and electricity is available around the clock.

$$-$ Mari-Mari Backpackers Lodge
Simple somewhat spartan accommodation in huts with hammocks or dorms. Limited electricity. Meals are not provided but can be booked in advance.

Gunung Kinabalu
National Park

Gunung Kinabalu is the pride of Sabah, the focal point of the national park and probably the most magnificent sight in Borneo. In recognition of this, the park was declared a World Heritage Site by UNESCO in 2000 – a first for Malaysia. The mountain made international headlines in June 2015 when it was hit by a powerful earthquake, killing 18 trekkers and forcing the six-month closure of the mountain to visitors.

Although Gunung Kinabalu has foothills, its dramatic rockfaces, with cloud swirling around them, loom starkly out of the jungle. The view from the top is unsurpassed and on a clear day you can see the shadow of the mountain in the South China Sea, over 50 km away – Mantanani Island (page 239) is a great spot to see the mountain and its shadow from a different perspective. Even if you're not planning on climbing Gunung Kinabalu itself, it's well worth spending a few days exploring the park, one of the most biodiverse areas in Borneo.

Essential Gunung Kinabalu National Park

Finding your feet

From KK, take any minibus or bus heading to Ranau from the City Park Bus Terminal or Padang Merdeka and ask the driver to drop you at the park entrance. The journey costs around RM20 one-way and takes about 90 minutes.

Park HQ

Park HQ is a short walk from the main Ranau–KK road, and all the accommodation and restaurants are within 15 minutes' walk of the main compound. There is a shop next to Park HQ which has trekking supplies, and good books on the mountain and its flora and fauna. Slide and film shows are held in the mini-theatre in the administration building at 1400 during the week and at 1930 on weekends and public holidays (RM2). The museum displays information on local flora and fauna, beetles and foot-long stick insects. There is a daily guided trail walk at 1100 from the park administration building. This is a gentle walk with a knowledgeable guide, although the number of participants tends to be large.

Tip...

A small colour pamphlet, *Mount Kinabalu/A Guide to the Summit Trail*, published by Sabah Parks, is a good guide to the wildlife and the trail itself.

Accommodation

The park is run by **Sutera Sanctuary Lodges**, ground floor of Wisma Sabah, KK, T088-243629, www.suterasanctuarylodges,com, Monday-Friday 0900-1830, Saturday 0900-1630, Sunday 0900-1500. All accommodation in the park must be booked in advance through its office, unless you are on an all-inclusive tour (see below).

Permits and entrance fees

It costs RM200 per person (RM80 per child) to climb Gunung Kinabalu; a RM15 (RM10 per child) entry fee must be paid on arrival by all park visitors and compulsory insurance costs RM7. The climb has become extremely popular in the last few years and it is crucial to book a slot as early as possible, up to six months in advance. Since the 2015 earthquake, the number of people being issued permits to climb to the peak is limited to 135 per day.

Guides and porters

Hiring a **guide** is compulsory: it costs RM230 for a group of up to five. If you have any children in the group, a separate guide needs to be hired (RM230). This guide will be dedicated to the children and can manage up to two children at a time. Therefore if your group is comprised of two adults and two children you'll need to hire two guides: one for the adult group and one for the children – a total of RM460. This might some unreasonably expensive for some but the extra cost for guides has been implemented since the 2015 earthquake, when a number of children died and groups of climbers were left stranded on the mountain.

Porters are available for between RM65 (one way from Timpohon to Laban Rata) to RM80 (one way from Timpohon to the summit) and will carry a maximum load of 10 kg. Guides and porters should be reserved at least a day in advance at the Park HQ or at **Sutera Sanctuary Lodges**. On the morning of your climb, go to the HQ and a guide will be assigned to you.

Tours

Numerous agencies offer all-inclusive climbing packages including accommodation, transport, fees, guides and porters; see www.mountkinabalu.com. Tours cost in the region of RM1730-2000 per person. See also Where to stay, page 250.

Independent visits

A group of you can share a taxi, book dorm accommodation and hire a guide for the climb for slightly less than a tour, including all the fees, at around RM1400 per person. If you are doing it by yourselves it is best to get to the park a day in advance, and stay at Park HQ to get up early for the first part of the climb to Laban Rata. Alternatively, you can get up at 0600 in KK and try to arrive at the Park HQ before 0900 to be sure of finding a guide that day. You may still be able to pick up a guide if you are there before 1000, although you will be unlikely to find anyone else to share with; the climb should begin no later 1100, allowing enough time to reach Laban Rata.

If you are desperate to go, short of time and have been informed that there are no rooms or permits available for the next few days, it might still be worth turning up in person to enquire. However, with only 135 permits issued daily, it could be a long wait.

Reports suggest that beds/mattresses up the mountain can sometimes be found if someone turns up in person. This method should be an absolute last resort, and it is by no means guaranteed to work. If things don't work out, accommodation will probably be available at Park HQ, or there are a number of good places within 2 km of the park.

When to go

The average rainfall is 400 cm a year, with an average temperature of 20°C at Park HQ but at Panar Laban it can drop below freezing at night. With the wind chill factor on the summit, it feels very cold. The best time to climb Gunung Kinabalu is in the dry season between March and April when views are clearest. The worst time has traditionally been November to December during the monsoon, although wet or dry periods can occur at any time of the year. Avoid weekends, school and public holidays if possible.

The park is occasionally closed to climbers. Check with the Mount Kinabalu Booking Office (www.mountkinabalu.com) or contact the **Sutera Sanctuary Lodges**, see below, to check the mountain is open for climbing when you intend to visit.

Equipment

It gets very cold at the summit, especially before sunrise. A thick jacket is recommended, but at the very least you should have a light waterproof and thick sweater to beat the wind chill on the summit. You can hire jackets from Laban Rata but you need to book ahead as there are limited numbers. Carry a dry sweater and socks in your backpack and change just before you get to the peak – if it's raining the damp chill is worse than the actual cold. There are small shops at Park HQ and Laban Rata that sell gloves, hats, raincoats, torches and food for the climb (but it's cheaper if you stock up in KK). It is also best to bring a sweater or thick shirts; the shops in Wisma Merdeka (see page 203) sell cheap woollies. Walking boots are recommended, but not essential; many people climb the mountain in trainers. Stock up on food, chocolate and drinking water in KK the day before. Essential items include a torch, toilet paper, water bottle, plasters, headache pills and suntan lotion. A hat is good for guarding against the sun and the cold. Lockers are available, RM10 per item, at the Park HQ reception office. Sleeping bags are provided free of charge in the **Laban Rata Resthouse**; essential for a good night's sleep. The resthouse also has hot water showers, but soap and towels are not provided. Some of the rooms are well heated; cheaper ones are very cold.

BACKGROUND

Gunung Kinabalu National Park

In the first written mention of the mountain, in 1769, Captain Alexander Dalrymple of the East India Company, wrote from his ship in the South China Sea: "Though perhaps not the highest mountain in the world, it is of immense height." During the Second World War Kinabalu was used as a navigational aid by Allied bombers – one of whom was quoted as saying "That thing must be near as high as Mount Everest". It's not, but at 4095 m, Gunung Kinabalu is the highest peak between the Himalayas and New Guinea. It is not the highest mountain in Southeast Asia: peaks in northern Myanmar (Hkakabo Razi) and the Indonesian province of Papua (Puncak Jaya, Gunung Trikora and Gunung Mandala) are all higher, placing Kinabalu fifth on the list – a fact rarely reflected in the Malaysian school geography syllabus.

There are a number of theories about the derivation of its name. The most convincing is the corruption of the Kadazan Aki Nabulu, 'the revered place of the spirits'. For the Kadazan, the mountain is sacred as they consider it to be the last resting place of the dead and the summit was believed to be inhabited by their ghosts. In the past the Kadazan are said to have carried out human sacrifices on Mount Kinabalu, carrying their captives to the summit in bamboo cages, where they would be speared to death. The Kadazan guides still perform an annual sacrifice to appease the spirits. Today they make do with chickens, eggs, cigars, betel nuts and rice on the rock plateau below the Panar Laban rockface.

The Chinese also lay claim to a theory. According to this legend, a Chinese prince arrived on the shores of northern Borneo and went in search of a huge pearl on the top of the mountain, which was guarded by a dragon. He duly slew the dragon, grabbed the pearl and married a beautiful Kadazan girl. After a while he grew homesick and took the boat back to China, promising his wife that he would return. She climbed the mountain every day for years on end to watch for her husband's boat. He never came and in desperation and depression, she lay down and died and was turned to stone. The mountain was then christened China Balu, or Chinaman's widow.

In 1851, Sir Hugh Low, the British colonial secretary in Labuan, made the first unsuccessful attempt at the summit. Seven years later he returned with Spencer

Flora and fauna

The range of climatic zones on the mountain has led to the incredible diversity of plant and animal life. Kinabalu Park is the meeting point of plants from Asia and Australasia. There are thought to be more than 1200 species of orchid alone and this does not include the innumerable mosses, ferns and fungi. These flowering plants of Kinabalu are said to represent more than half the families of flowering plants in the world. Within the space of 3 km, the vegetation changes from lowland tropical rainforest to alpine meadow and cloud forest. The jungle reaches up to 1300 m; above that, to a height of 1800 m, is the lower montane zone, dominated by 60 species of oak and chestnut; above 2000 m is the upper montane zone with true cloud forest, orchids, rhododendrons and pitcher plants. Above 2600 m, growing among the crags and crevices of the summit rock plateau are gnarled tea trees (*Leptospermums*) and stunted rhododendrons. Above 3300 m, the soil

St John, the British consul in Brunei. Low's feet were in bad shape after the long walk to the base of the mountain, so St John went on without him, with a handful of reluctant Kadazan porters. He made it to the top of the conical southern peak, but was "mortified to find that the most westerly [peak] and another to the east appeared higher than where I sat." He retreated and returned three months later with Low, but again failed to reach the summit, now called Low's Peak (standing at 4095 m above sea level). From Low's Peak, the eastern peaks, just 1.5 km away, look within easy reach. As John Briggs points out in his book *Mountains of Malaysia*, "It seems so close, yet it is one of the most difficult places to get to in the whole of Borneo".

Kinabalu remained unconquered for another 30 years. The first to reach the summit was John Whitehead, a zoologist, in 1888. Whitehead spent several months on the mountain collecting birds and mammals and many of the more spectacular species bear either Low's or Whitehead's name. More scientists followed and then a trickle of tourists, but it was not until 1964, when Kinabalu Park (encompassing 75,000 ha) was gazetted, that the 8.5-km trail to the summit was opened.

In recent times the mountain has attracted around 200,000 visitors a year, with at least 30,000 attempting the summit. In June 2015 the mountain was struck by a 6.0 magnitude earthquake whose tremors could be felt as far away as Miri and Bandar Seri Begawan. The quake lasted around 30 seconds and led to the deaths of 18 climbers including a group of Singaporean primary school children and one of their teachers. As the epicentre of the earthquake was so near to Gunung Kinabalu it led to massive landslides and caused significant damage to the mountain itself, including breaking off one of the distinctive peaks, Donkey Peak, at the top of the mountain. The mountain was closed to climbers until December 2015. When it reopened, the number of climbing permits was reduced to 135 per day and a new and safer trail was created.

Some of the ethnic groups living around the mountain believed the earthquake was a direct result of the "Aki" (mountain spirit) being angered by the behaviour of 10 foreign tourists who had stripped naked and urinated on the peak on 30 May, six days before the earthquake struck. The tourists were detained under threat of imprisonment, but were later released without charge. The furious local Kadazan-Dusun community performed rituals to appease the angered mountain spirit.

disappears, leaving only club mosses, sedges and Low's buttercups (*Ranunculus lowii*), which are alpine meadow flowers.

Among the most unusual of Kinabalu's flora is the world's largest flower, the rust-coloured rafflesia (see box, page 227). It can usually only be found in the section of the park closest to Poring Hot Springs. Rafflesia are hard to find as they only flower for a couple of weeks between August and December.

Kinabalu is also famous for the carnivorous pitcher plants, which grow to varying sizes on the mountain. A detailed guide to the pitcher plants of Kinabalu can be bought in the shop at Park HQ. Nine different species have been recorded on Kinabalu. The largest is the giant Rajah Brooke's pitcher plant; Spencer St John claimed to have found one of these containing a drowned rat floating in four litres of water. Insects are attracted by the scent and, when they settle on the lip of the plant, they cannot maintain a foothold on the waxy, ribbed surface. At the base of the pitcher is an enzymic fluid which digests the 'catch'.

Rhododendrons line the trail throughout the mossy forest (there are 29 species in the park), especially above the Paka Cave area. One of the most beautiful is the copper-leafed rhododendron, with orange flowers and leaves with coppery scales underneath. There are an estimated 1000 species of orchid in the park, along with 621 species of fern and 52 palm species.

It is difficult to see wildlife on the climb to the summit as the trail is well used, although tree shrews and squirrels are common on the lower trails. There are, however, more than 100 species of mammal living in the park. The Kinabalu summit rats, which are always on cue to welcome climbers to Low's Peak at dawn, and nocturnal ferret badgers are the only true montane mammals in Sabah. As the trees thin with altitude, it is often possible to see tree shrews and squirrels, of which there are more than 28 species in the park. Large mammals, such as flying lemurs, red-leaf monkeys, wild pigs, orang-utan and deer, are lowland forest dwellers. Nocturnal species include the slow loris (*Nycticebus coucang*) and the mischievous-looking bug-eyed tarsier (*Tarsius bancanus*). If heading to Kinabalu specifically to spot wildlife, then the longer, less visited Mesilau Trail is almost certainly a more productive option.

More than half of Borneo's 518 species of bird have also been recorded in Kinabalu Park, but the variety of species decreases with height. Two of the species living above 2500 m are endemic to the mountain: the Kinabalu friendly warbler and the Kinabalu mountain blackbird.

More than 61 species of frog and toad and 100 species of reptile live here. Perhaps the most interesting frog in residence is the horned frog, which can be impossible to spot thanks to its mastery of camouflage. The giant toad is common at lower altitudes; it's covered with warts, which are poisonous glands. When disturbed, these squirt a stinking, toxic liquid. Other frogs found in the park include the big-headed leaf-litter frog, whose head is bigger than the rest of its body, and the green stream shrub frog, which has a magnificent metallic green body, but is deadly if swallowed by any predator.

The famous flying tree snake has been seen in the park. It spreads its skin flaps, which act as a parachute when the snake leaps blindly from one tree to another.

There are nearly 30 species of fish in the park's rivers, including the unusual Borneo sucker fish (*Gastomyzon borneensis*), which attaches itself to rocks in fast-flowing streams. One Sabah Parks publication likens them to 'underwater cows', grazing on algae as they move slowly over the rocks.

Walkers and climbers are more likely to come across the park's abundant insect life than anything else. Examples include pill millipedes, rhinoceros beetles, the emerald green and turquoise jewel beetles, stick insects, 'flying peapods', cicadas, and a vast array of moths (including the giant atlas moth) and butterflies (including the magnificent emerald green and black Rajah Brooke's birdwing).

★ Gunung Kinabalu

The climb to the summit of Mount Kinabalu is not something that should be undertaken lightly. It can be punishingly cold at the top and altitude sickness can be a problem. Some points of the trail are steep and require adequate footware. Changeable weather conditions add to the hazards.

Following the earthquake in 2015, the **Mesilau Trail** remains closed. The **Timpohon Trail** is still open, and a new and safer trail, the **Ranau Trail**, from Laban Rata to the summit, has been created. Most treks are well used and are easy walks, but the **Liwagu Trail** is a good three- to four-hour trek up to where it joins the summit trail and is very steep and slippery in places; not advised as a solo trip.

The climb to the summit and back should take two days; four to six hours from Park HQ at 1585 m to the Panar Laban huts on the first day. On the second day, it is a further three hours from the huts to the summit. Most people set off before dawn to arrive at the peak for sunrise, before descending to Park HQ by around midday.

Gurkha soldiers and others have made it to the summit and back in well under three hours. For the really keen, or foolhardy, depending on your perspective, there is

Gunung Kinabalu Trail

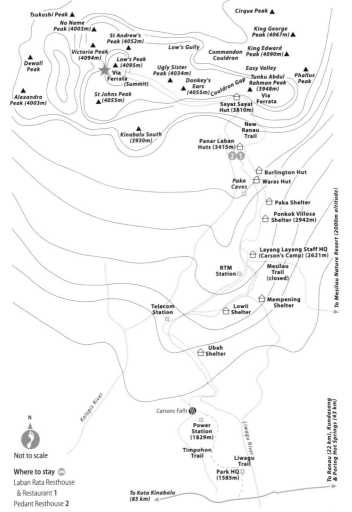

Tsukushi Peak ▲

No Name Peak (4052m) ▲

Cirque Peak ▲

St Andrew's Peak (4052m) ▲

King George Peak (4067m) ▲

Victoria Peak (4094m) ▲

Low's Gully

Commandon Couldron

King Edward Peak (4090m) ▲

▲ **Dewall Peak**

Low's Peak (4095m) ▲ **Via Ferrata (Summit)**

Ugly Sister Peak (4034m) ▲

Easy Valley

Tunku Abdul Rahman Peak (3948m) ▲ **Via Ferrata**

▲ **Phallus Peak**

Donkey's Ears (4055m) ▲

Cauldron Gap

▲ **Alexandra Peak (4003m)**

St Johns Peak (4055m) ▲

Sayat Sayat Hut (3810m) 🏠

Kinabalu South (3930m) ▲

New Ranau Trail

Panar Laban Huts (3415m) 🏠
2 **1**

Burlington Hut 🏠

Paka Caves

Waras Hut 🏠

Paka Shelter 🏠

Ponkok Villosa Shelter (2942m) 🏠

To Mesilau Nature Resort (2000m altitude) ►

Layang Layang Staff HQ (Carson's Camp) (2621m) 🏠

RTM Station 🏢

Mesilau Trail (closed)

Mempening Shelter 🏠

Telecom Station 🏢

Lowii Shelter 🏠

Ubah Shelter 🏠

Kolopis River

Carsons Falls ⛰️

Power Station (1829m)

Timpohon Trail

Liwagu Trail

Liwagu River

Park HQ (1585m) 🏢

To Ranau (22 km), Kundasang & Poring Hot Springs (43 km) ►

N
🧭
Not to scale

To Kota Kinabalu (85 km) ◄

Where to stay 🛏️
Laban Rata Resthouse & Restaurant **1**
Pedant Resthouse **2**

also the annual **Kinabalu Climbathon** (see page 253). The climb to the top requires no special skills, however deaths have occurred due to the hazards of climbing an unfamiliar mountain where changes in the weather can be sudden and dramatic. Keep to the trails and keep your group together.

The trail   The trail starts at the power station (1829 m), from where it is a 25-minute walk to the first shelter. Soon afterwards, the trail splits in two: the left goes to the radio station and the helipad and the right towards the summit. The next stop is **Layang Layang staff headquarters** (with drinking water, cooking facilities and accommodation), also known as **Carson's Camp** (2621 m). There is one more shelter, **Ponkok Villosa** at 2942 m, about 45 minutes from Carson's Camp, before the stop at the path to **Paka Caves**, which is really just an overhanging rock by a stream. Paka is a 10-minute detour to the left, where Low and St John made their camps.

From the cave/fifth shelter the vegetation thins out and it is a steep climb to **Panar Laban huts** – which includes the well-equipped **Laban Rata Resthouse** (3550 m) and the **Pendant Resthouse** (3289 m – prioritized for Via Ferrata users) – affording magnificent views at sunset and sunrise. The name Panar Laban is derived from Kadazan words meaning Place of Sacrifice: early explorers had to make a sacrifice here to appease the spirits and this ritual is still performed by the Kadazan once a year. **Sayat Sayat hut** (3810 m) – named after the ubiquitous shrubby tea tree – is an hour further on, above the Panar Laban rockface. Most climbers reach Panar Laban (or the other huts) in the early afternoon in order to rest up for a 0300 start the next morning to reach the summit by sunrise.

This second part of the trail – 3 km long – is more demanding technically, but the trail is well laid out with regular resting points every 500 m. Ladders, handrails and ropes are provided for the steeper parts (essential in the wet, as the granite slabs can be very slippery). The final kilometre has no hand rails or ropes but is less steep. The first two hours after dawn are the most likely to be cloud free. For enthusiasts interested in alternative routes to the summit, John Briggs's *Mountains of Malaysia* provides a detailed guide to the climb.

Via Ferrata ⓘ *www.mountaintorq.com*. Asia's first Via Ferrata (iron road) opened in 2007 and is the also world's highest. It is still relatively quiet with three possible routes taking between two to five hours to complete. The trail uses fixed rungs, rails, cables and stemples wrapped around the north face of the mountain. This slightly hair-raising adventure provides an experience akin to mountain climbing and a chance to see parts of the mountain usually never experienced by most visitors. The trail starts at Panar Laban Rock Face (3300 m) and reaches its highest point at 3776 m.

Mountain Garden
Tours leave at 0900, 1200, 1500; the garden is closed at other times, RM5.

Situated behind the park administration building, this landscaped garden has species from the mid-levels of the mountain, which have been planted in natural surroundings.

Mesilau Nature Resort and Park
Daily 0900-1600, RM15 conservation fee plus RM10 for guided nature walk.

This rainforest resort nestles at the foot of Mount Kinabalu at 2000 m. The main attractions are the cool climate and the superb views up the mountain and across the plains toward Ranau and the sea. A trail from the resort joins the main trail at Layang

Layang. Alternatively, there are a number of walks to be made around the reserve in this secluded location.

Poring

T088-878801, if you've already paid the entrance fee to the national park, keep your ticket for entrance to the hot springs; if staying at Poring there is no charge and the baths can be used all day; permits are not necessary. Minibuses to the springs leave Park HQ at 0900, 1300, 1600; alternatively, flag down a bus/minibus to Ranau on the main road, a 2-min walk from HQ and take a taxi from there to Poring.

Poring lies 43 km from Gunung Kinabalu Park HQ and is part of the national park. The **hot sulphur baths** ⓘ *RM15 per hr; sulphur bath and jacuzzi, RM20 per hr*, were installed during the Japanese occupation of the Second World War for the jungle-weary Japanese troops. There are individual concrete pools that can fit two people, with taps for hot- and cold-spring mineral water; once in your bath you are in complete privacy. However, many visitors now complain that the water is no longer hot, more like lukewarm. The springs are on the other side of the Mamut River from the entrance, over a suspension bridge. They are a fantastic antidote to tiredness after a tough climb up Gunung Kinabalu. There is also a cold water rock pool. The pools are in a beautiful garden setting of hibiscus and other tropical flowers, trees and thousands of butterflies. There are some quite luxurious private cabin baths available and also large baths which hold up to eight people. The deluxe cabins have lounge areas and jacuzzis. The Kadazans named the area Poring after the towering bamboos of that name nearby.

The **jungle canopy walk** ⓘ *daily 0900-1600, RM5, camera RM5, video RM30, guides available*, at Poring is a rope walkway 35 m above the ground, which provides a monkey's-eye view of the jungle; springy but quite safe. The entrance is five minutes' walk from the hot springs and the canopy walkway is 15 minutes' walk from the entrance. The canopy walkway at Danum Valley is far more exciting. If the weather is clear at Ranau, it is generally safe to assume that the canopy walk will also be clear.

Kipungit Falls are only about 10 minutes' walk from Poring and swimming is possible here. Follow the trail further up the hill and after 15 minutes you come to bat caves; a large overhanging boulder provides shelter and a home for the bats.

The **Langanan Waterfall Trail** takes 90 minutes one way, is uphill, but worth it. There is another hard, 90-minute trail to **Bat Cave** (inhabited by what seems to be a truly stupendous number of bats) and a waterfall. The **Butterfly Farm** ⓘ *Tue-Sun 0900-1600, RM4*, was established close to the springs by a Japanese-backed firm in 1992 and is very educational in the descriptions of butterflies and other insects.

There is also an information centre, a rafflesia centre, orchid centre, aviary and tropical garden at Poring. It is better not to visit the hot springs at the weekend or on public holidays if you want to relax in a peaceful atmosphere.

Ranau and Kundasang

The Ranau plateau, surrounding the Kinabalu massif, is one of the richest farming areas in Sabah and much of the forest not in the park has now been devastated by market gardeners. Even within the national park's boundaries, on the lower slopes of Mount Kinabalu itself, shifting cultivators have clear-felled tracts of jungle and planted their patches. More than 1000 ha are now planted out with spinach, cabbage, cauliflower, asparagus, broccoli and tomatoes, supplying much of Borneo.

Kundasang and Ranau are unremarkable towns a few kilometres apart; the latter is bigger. The **war memorial**, behind Kundasang, which unfortunately looks like Colditz, is in memory of those who died in the death march in the Second World War (see page 296). The walled gardens represent the national gardens of Borneo, Australia and the UK.

Mentapok and **Monkobo** are southwest of Ranau. Both are rarely climbed. Mentapok (1581 m), can be reached in 1½ days from Kampong Mireru, a village at the base of the mountain. A logging track provides easy access halfway up the south side of the mountain. Monkobo is most easily climbed from the northwest, a logging track from Telupid goes up to 900 m and from here it is a two-hour trek to the top. It is advisable to take guides, organized from Ranau or one of the nearby villages.

Some 17 km on the road to Sandakan is the **Sabah Tea Garden** ① *Km 17, Ranau–Sandakan road, Kampung Nalapak, T088-440882, www.sabahtea.net; factory tours RM12; factory tour plus set lunch RM34,* the only organic tea farm in Borneo and offering a range of activities other than just sitting back with a cuppa and admiring the views. They offer a variety of packages including a rainforest adventure, where tourists sleep in a bamboo forest and swim in the Sapayon River before learning some survival cooking techniques. More genteel activities include tea tree planting and an informative factory tour. There are also some good accommodation options available here.

Listings Gunung Kinabalu National Park *map page 247.*

Where to stay

Management of the park is privatized. All accommodation must be booked in advance through **Sutera Sanctuary Lodges** (ground floor, Wisma Sabah, KK, T088-243629, www.suterasanctuary lodges.com, Mon-Fri 0900-1830, Sat 0900-1630, Sun 0900-1500). Compared to elsewhere in Sabah, Kinabalu accommodation is expensive.

Park HQ
Each cabin has a fireplace, kitchen, shower, gas cooker, fridge, and cooking and eating utensils. Electricity, water and firewood are provided free of charge. The rates quoted below are reduced on weekdays. The most expensive option at the Park HQ is the **Rajah Lodge**, sleeping 6 people, RM8000 for the whole lodge with all meals and a personal butler; very comfortable. **Kinabalu Lodge**, 6 people, RM3500 per night, all meals, cable TV, also very comfortable. The **Summit Lodge**, 4 people, RM2820 per night, and the **Garden Lodge**, 4 people, RM2820 per night, are both very comfortable and meals

are included; also cable TV; nice and toasty inside. **Nepenthes Lodge**, 4 people, RM800 per night. **Peak Lodge**, 4 people, RM1250 per night. **Ligawu Suite**, 2 people, RM950 per night, cable TV, breakfast and hot showers. **Hill Lodge**, 2 people, RM850 per night. **Rock Twin Share**, 2 people, RM350 per night, has a shared bathroom and common area with fireplace. **Grace Hostel**, unheated dorms with shared bathroom for RM250 per bed, includes breakfast. The **Rock Hostel** offers much of the same for the same price. Note that the prices given here are rack rates. A shop around various tour company websites and package deals can reveal discounts of 30-40%.

The following are close to Park HQ:

$$ Haleluyah Retreat Centre
Jln Linouh, Km 61, Tuaran–Ranau road, T088-423993, kandiu@tm.net.my.
This Christian centre is open to all. Located at 1500 m, close to the foot of Mount Kinabalu, it makes a good stop-off point before climbing to the summit. Set amidst natural jungle and approximately 15 mins' walk from the Park HQ, it is isolated but safe, clean,

friendly and with a relaxing atmosphere. Facilities include cooking and washing facilities, camping area, multi-purpose hall and meeting rooms, making it a suitable venue for youth camps or family holidays. Reasonably priced food in the canteen, dorm beds also available.

$$ Kinabalu Rose Cabin
Km18, Ranau–Kinasaraban road, Kundasang, T088-889233, www. kinabalurosecabin.8m.com.
Some 2 km from the park, towards the golf course (30% discount to golfers). There's a range of rooms – in need of a bit of love – and suites, all with mountain views, attached bathroom, hot water and TV.

$$-$ D'Villa Lodge (Rina Ria Lodge)
Batu 36, Jln Tinompok, Ranau, T088-889282, www.dvillalodge.com.
About 1 km from the Kinabalu National Park, rooms have attached kitchen and basic bathroom, armchairs and beautiful views. There's also a shop. Prices increase at weekends. 12-person dorms also available (RM30). Breakfast included.

$$-$ Mile 36 Lodge
Kg Kalanggan, Mile 36, Kalanggan, T088-880161, www.mile36lodge.com
Located 1.3 km from Park HQ. Glorious views and variety of lodgings from an English-style cottage to a kampong-style bungalow. Café and pleasant gardens.

Gunung Kinabalu

Laban Rata Resthouse
Panar Laban.
54 rooms a reasonable though pricey canteen (but sometimes rather limited food – it all has to be walked up the mountain) and hot water showers, plus electricity and heated rooms; bedding provided. Most expensive rooms are the heated deluxe Buttercup rooms at RM765 per night, beds in the dorms go for a pricey RM475 each. Rates include all meals and a packed lunch.

Pendant Resthouse
The Pendant Resthouse is favoured by climbers using the Via Ferrata, and is slightly more basic. However, there is a comfortable lounge area where you can chill out with a book from their Alpine library or pull out a board game. There is a simple café that serves up food until late and starts very early, though for all other meals you'll need to head over to the **Laban Rata** restaurant. Rooms available include a 4-bed dorm and a 38-bed dorm, both of which are non-heated.

Mesilau Nature Resort

$$$ Mesilau Nature Resort
Managed by Sutera Sanctuary Lodges, T088-871733, www.suterasanctuarylodges.com.
A range of tasteful wooden chalets that blend neatly into their surroundings, housing up to 4 people (RM2275 per unit) with all meals, personal butler, cable TV, heater and hot water bathroom. More budget accommodation provided in dorms in the hostel (RM120 per bed). Laundry, gift shop and regular educational talks. The nature reserve is situated close to the **Mount Kinabalu Golf Club**, a few mins' drive away.

Poring
Booking recommended. Camping RM6. The following are all in the $ price bracket. **Serindit Hostel**, dorms with space for 20 people, RM120 per person; **Serindit twin share**, 2 people, RM350 per chalet, shared bathroom; **Jungle Lodge**, 2 people, huge rooms, jungle shower, living room with cable TV, RM420 per unit; **River Lodge**, 4 people, RM740 per unit, comfortable, **Palm Villa** RM3500, 6 people, personal butler. All meals available.

Ranau and Kundasang

$$$-$$ Mount Kinabalu Heritage Resort and Spa
Visible on the hill above Kundasang (a further 1 km down the road from Kinabalu Pine Resort, below), T088-889511, www. mountkinabaluheritageresort.com.my.

Accommodation is in stilted chalets with excellent views. Other rooms in the main block are less impressive. Very professional spa centre on the 6th floor offering rejuvenating therapies to tired walkers.

$$$-$$ Zen Garden Resorts
Km 2, Jln Mohimboyan Kibas, T088-889242.
The biggest resort in the area. Accommodation is in 3- to 4-room lodges with equipped kitchen, living room with TV, and bedroom. Considerably cheaper is room only (TV and some with fridge). A very pleasant environment with wonderful views of the mountains.

$$ Kinabalu Pine Resort
Kampung Kundasang, T088-889388, www.kinabalupineresort.com.
Reasonably priced cabins built with *selangan batu* hardwood come with huge mountain-facing balconies and Wi-Fi. This place has wholesome mountain vibes in abundance and spectacular views.

$$ Little Hut
Off the main road, Kundasang, T016-860 1416, www.littlehutmesilou.blogspot.sg.
Gorgeous little venture with a selection of quirkily named huts (Bizza Hut, Unbreak My Hut) with tasteful furnishings and a good range of facilities including DVD player and rice cooker. The garden is an excellent spot for star gazing.

$$-$ Sabah Tea House
KM 17 Ranau–Sandakan road, Kampung Nalapak, T088-889330, www.sabahtea.com.
Good selection of accommodation including clean chalets, a funky Rungus longhouse with shared bathroom, and a campsite with space for 100.

Restaurants

Breakfast is included in the price of all accommodation. There are cooking facilities at the hostels plus good quality meals are provided for guests at **Rajah Lodge**, **Summit Lodge**, **Garden Lodge** and **Kinabalu Lodge**. The best places to stay are at Park HQ but the restaurants are rather spread out, requiring a walk between buffet and bed.

$$ Liwagu
Open 1100-2130.
Beer chips, curries and other international treats.

$ Balsam Cafeteria
Open 0630-2130.
The cheaper option for filling Malay staples.

Mesilau Nature Resort

$ Renanthera Café
Open 0700-2200.
Has a stunning veranda offering great views of the mountain.

$ Renanthera Terrace
Open 0700-2200.
Provides the 3 main meals.

Poring
There are a number of quite good Chinese and Malay food at the springs and stalls outside the park.

$$ Rainforest
Open 0700-2200.
Comfortable place to kick back and get stuck into Malay, Chinese and international fare.

Ranau and Kundasang
There are several restaurants along the roads serving simple food in Kundasang. Open 0600-2100.

$$ Tinompok
*At Mount Kinabalu Heritage Resort and Spa
(see Where to stay), Kundasang.*
Local and Western dishes, good service,
excellent food.

$ Five Star Seafood
Opposite the market, Ranau.
Chinese food.

$ Sin Mui Mui
*Top side of the square near the market.
Closed Fri afternoons.*
Simple but hearty Chinese coffee shop fare.

Festivals

Oct **Kinabalu Climathon**, www.climbathon.
com.my. One of the world's toughest
mountain races.

Shopping

Ranau and Kundasang
Cheap sweaters and waterproofs for the
climb can be bought from **Kedai Kien Hin**
in Ranau. A *tamu* (market) is held near Ranau
on the 1st of each month and every Sat.
Kundasang *tamu* is held on the 20th of
every month and also every Fri.

What to do

Ranau and Kundasang
Mount Kinabalu Golf Club, *3 km behind
Kundasang, T088-889445.* Club and shoe hire
available. Fees RM100 weekdays/RM200
weekends +5% tax. Truly spectacular golfing
at 1500 m above sea level. Check out the
14th hole which features a deep ravine and
fast flowing river.

Transport

Bus
All buses heading to **Sandakan** and **Ranau**
will drop you off at the turn-off to the park
(RM12-15). Try and get on a bus departing
before 0800 and sit on the left-hand side
of the bus to ensure beautiful morning
mountain views.

Minibus
Regular connections from **KK** to **Ranau**,
ask to be dropped at the park, 2 hrs (RM20).
Departs from KK's Inanam Northern Bus
Terminal and leaves when full. Return
minibuses (roughly every hour) must be
waved down from the main road.

Taxi
RM150-200 negotiable, taxi from outside
the Padang Merdeka in KK or try and hop in
a shared cab for RM15-18 but be prepared
to wait until the cab is full (usually 6 or
7 passengers).

Poring
Minibuses can be shared from **Ranau**
for RM5. Buses running between **KK** and
Sandakan stop in town on Jln Kibarambang.
Taxis are also available.

Ranau and Kundasang
Minibuses leave from the market place to
Park HQ, **KK** and **Sandakan** (4 hrs).

East
coast

From Ranau it is a smooth drive to Sandakan by road. Several key sights are within reach of Sandakan: the Turtle Islands National Park, 40 km north in the Sulu Sea; Sepilok Orang-Utan Rehabilitation Centre; and the Kinabatangan Basin, to the southeast. From Sandakan, the route continues south to the wilds of Lahad Datu and Danum Valley and on to Semporna, the jumping-off point for Pulau Sipadan, an island that has achieved legendary status among snorkellers and scuba-divers. Tawau Hills State Park has some unusual natural features that draw visitors at weekends.

Sandakan is at the neck of a bay on the northeast coast of Sabah and looks out to the Sulu Sea. It is a postwar town, much of it rebuilt on reclaimed land, and is Malaysia's biggest fishing port; it even exports some of its catch to Singapore. Sandakan is often dubbed 'mini Hong Kong' because of its Cantonese influence; its occupants are well-heeled and the town sustains many prosperous businesses, despite being rather scruffy as a whole. It is now also home to a large Filipino community, mostly traders from Mindanao and the Sulu Islands. Manila still officially claims Sabah in its entirety – Sandakan is only 28 km from Philippines' territorial waters. Large numbers of illegal Indonesian workers have made Sandakan their home in recent years, further adding to the town's cosmopolitan atmosphere.

New developments of bright, cheery locks are slowly encircling the generally charmless heart of the town. The waterfront area around Sandakan Harbour Square has a few fancy shops, hotels and a smart promenade, pointing the way to a more attractive future for the city.

Sights

Sandakan is strung out along the coast but in the centre of town is the riotous **daily fish market**, which is the biggest and best in Sabah. The best time to visit is at 0600 when the boats unload their catch. The **Central Market** along the waterfront, near the local bus station, sells fruit, vegetables, sarongs, seashells, spices and sticky rice cakes.

The **Australian war memorial** ⓘ *near the government building at Mile Seven on Labuk Rd, between Sandakan and Sepilok, take Labuk bus service Nos 8, 12 and 14 and stop at the Esso petrol station (RM.1.50) or take a taxi (RM30 return including waiting time – bargain hard)*, stands on the site of a Japanese prison camp and commemorates Allied soldiers who lost their lives during the Japanese occupation. Each year on ANZAC day (24 April) crowds of former servicemen and their families come to the memorial park to commemorate the lives of those that died in the bloody conflict in Sabah. The Japanese invaded North Borneo in 1942 and many Japanese also died in the area. In 1989, a new **Japanese war memorial** ⓘ *walk 20 mins up Red Hill (Bukit Berenda)*, was built in the Japanese cemetery, financed by the families of the deceased soldiers.

St Michael's Anglican church is one of the very few stone churches in Sabah and

Essential Sandakan

Finding your feet

The airport is 10 km north of town. There are daily connections with KL, KK, Kudat and Tawau. Taxis cost RM25 and local buses run into town until 1700 (RM 2). Minibuses travel from the airport to the bus station at the southern end of Jalan Pelabuhan. From the long-distance bus terminal, 5 km to the west of town, there are connections with KK, Tawau, Ranau, Lahad Datu, Semporna and several other destinations. Ferries from Zamboanga in the Philippines call into Sandakan once a week. See also Transport, page 263.

Getting around

Sandakan is not a large town and it is easy enough to explore the central area on foot, although it does stretch some way along the coast. Minibuses provide links with out-of-town places of interest.

BACKGROUND

Sandakan

The Sandakan area was an important source of beeswax for the Sulu traders and came under the sway of the Sultans of Sulu. William Clarke Cowie, a Scotsman with a carefully waxed handlebar moustache who ran guns for the Sultan of Sulu across the Spanish blockade of Sulu (later becoming the managing director of the North Borneo Chartered Company), first set up camp in Sandakan Bay in the early 1870s. He called his camp, which was on Pulau Timbang, 'Sandakan', the Sulu name for the area for 200 years, but it became known as Kampong German as there were several German traders living there and early gunrunners tended to be German. The power of the Sulu sultanate was already waning when Cowie set up. In its early trading days, Europeans, Africans, Arabs, Chinese, Indians, Javanese, Dusun and Japanese all lived here. It was an important gateway to the interior and used to be a trading centre for forest produce like rhinoceros horn, beeswax and hornbill ivory, along with marine products like pearls and sea cucumbers (*tripang*, valued for their medicinal properties). In 1812, English visitor John Hunt estimated that the Sandakan/Kinabatangan area produced an astonishing 37,000 kg of wild beeswax and 23,000 kg of birds' nests each year.

The modern town of Sandakan was founded by an Englishman, William Pryer, in 1879. Baron von Overbeck, the Austrian consul from Hong Kong who founded the Chartered Company with businessman Alfred Dent, had signed a leasing agreement for the territory with the Sultan of Brunei, only to discover that large tracts on the east side of modern day Sabah actually belonged to the Sultan of Sulu. Overbeck sailed to Sulu in January 1878 and on obtaining the cession rights from the Sultan, dropped William Pryer off at Kampong German to make the British presence felt.

is an attractive building, designed by a New Zealander in 1893. Most of Sandakan's stone churches were levelled in the war and, indeed, St Michael's is one of the few colonial-era buildings still standing. It is just off Jalan Singapura, on the hill at the south end of town. In 1988 a large **mosque** was built for the burgeoning Muslim population at the mouth of Sandakan Bay. The main Filipino settlements are in this area of town. The mosque is outside Sandakan, on Jalan Buli Sim Sim where the town began in 1879, just after the jetty for Turtle Islands National Park, and is an imposing landmark. There is also a large water village here.

There are a couple of other notable Chinese temples in Sandakan. The oldest one, the **Goddess of Mercy Temple** is just off Jalan Singapura, on the hillside. Originally built in the early 1880s, it has been expanded over the years. Nearby is **Sam Sing Kung Temple**, which becomes a particular focus of devotion during exam periods since one of its deities is reputed to assist those attempting examinations. The **Three Saints Temple**, further down the hill at the end of the padang, was completed in 1887. The three saints are Kwan Woon Cheung, a Kwan clan ancestor, the goddess Tien Hou (or Tin Hau, worshipped by seafarers) and the Min Cheong Emperor.

The **Forest Headquarters** (Ibu Pejabat Jabatan Perhutanan) ⓘ *Mile 6 Labuk Rd, T089-660811*, next to the Sandakan Golf Course, contain an exhibition centre and a well-laid out and interesting mini-museum showing past and present forestry practice.

Pryer's wife Ada later described the scene: "He had with him a West Indian black named Anderson, a half-caste Hindoo named Abdul, a couple of China boys. For food they had a barrel of flour and 17 fowls and the artillery was half a dozen sinder rifles." Pryer set about organizing the three existing villages in the area, cultivating friendly relations with the local tribespeople and fending off pirates. He raised the Union Jack on 11 February 1878.

Cowie tried to do a deal with the Sultan of Sulu to wrest control of Sandakan back from Pryer, but Dent and Overbeck finally bought him off. A few months later Cowie's Kampong German burned to the ground, so Pryer went in search of a new site, which he found at Buli Sim Sim. He called his new settlement Elopura, meaning 'beautiful city', but the name did not catch on. By the mid-1880s it was renamed Sandakan and, in 1884, became the capital of North Borneo when the title was transferred from Kudat. In 1891 the town had 20 Chinese-run brothels and 71 Japanese prostitutes; according to the 1891 census there were three men for every one woman. The town quickly established itself as the source of birds' nests harvested from the caves at Gomantong and shipped directly to Hong Kong, as they are today.

Timber was first exported from this area in 1885 and was used to construct Beijing's Temple of Heaven. Sandakan was, until the 1980s, the main east coast port for timber and it became a wealthy town. In its heyday, the town is said to have boasted one of the greatest concentrations of millionaires in the world. The timber-boom days are over: the primary jungle has gone, and so has the big money. In the mid-1990s the state government adopted a strict policy restricting the export of raw, unprocessed timber. The hinterland is now dominated by vast plantations of cocoa and palm oil.

Following the Japanese invasion in 1942, Sandakan was devastated by Allied bombing. In 1946 North Borneo became a British colony and the new colonial government moved the capital to Jesselton (later to become Kota Kinabalu).

The **Sandakan Heritage Trail** is a loop which supposedly takes in the historical highlights of this scruffy town. The walk takes a leisurely 90 minutes; the tourist office has trail maps. It starts off at the town mosque and nips up the 'stairs with 100 steps', a nice shady climb with a lookout point at the top where young local couples gather to whisper sweet nothings to each other and smoke clandestine cigarettes. It's rather dark here at night, so lone travellers are advised to climb in the day.

From here the trail passes through **Agnes Keith's House** ① *Jln Istana, T089-221140, daily 0900-1700, RM15 (discounts for children),* the restored British colonial government quarters built on the site of her home (see box, page 258). Inside the grounds, there's an **English Tea House** (www.englishteahouse.org) serving cream teas and pastries on manicured lawns. From here, the trail takes in the Goddess of Mercy Temple, St Michael's Anglican Church and ends up at the **Sandakan Heritage Museum** ① *next to the tourist office, daily 0900-1700, free,* a rather slipshod affair with some early photos of the town and an unexplained mannequin dressed in a kilt. There is, however, a good wall photo of Sandakan razed to the ground taken in 1945.

Tanah Merah

Pertubuhan Ugama Buddhist (Puu Jih Shih Buddhist Temple) overlooks Tanah Merah town, west of Sandakan. The US$2 million temple was completed in 1987 and stands at

BACKGROUND

Agnes Keith's house

American authoress Agnes Keith lived with her English husband in Sandakan from 1934 to 1952. He was the conservator of forests in North Borneo and she wrote three books about her time in the colony.

The Land Below the Wind tells stories of dinner parties and tiffins in pre-war days. Three Came Home is about her three years in a Japanese internment camp during the war on Pulau Berhala, off Sandakan, and in Kuching, and was made into a film. White Man Returns tells the story of their time in British North Borneo. The Keiths' rambling wooden house on the hill above the town was destroyed during the war, but was rebuilt by the government to exactly the same design when Harry Keith returned to his job when the war ended.

the top of the hill, accessible by a twisting road that hairpins its way up the hillside. The temple is very gaudy, contains three large Buddha images and is nothing special, although the 34 teakwood supporting pillars, made in Macau, are quite a feature. There is a good view of Sandakan from the top, with Tanah Merah and the log ponds directly below, in Sandakan Bay. The names of local donors are inscribed on the walls of the walkway.

Pulau Lankayan

This dive resort is on a near uninhabited island, 90 minutes by boat from Sandakan in the Sulu Sea. **Lankayan Island Dive Resort** (see page 260) offers more than 40 dive sites including a couple of wrecks. Sightings of whale sharks are common from April to May.

Pulau Berhala

To get to the beach charter a boat from the fish market.

Famed for its 200-m rust-coloured sandstone cliffs on the south end, with a beach at the foot, this island is within easy reach by boat, but there isn't a great deal to do here. There are plans to develop the island for tourism in the near future. The island was used as a leper colony before the Second World War and as a prisoner of war camp by the Japanese. Agnes Keith was interned here during the war (see box, above).

Listings Sandakan *map page 260.*

Tourist information

Sabah Parks office
Room 906, 9th floor, Wisma Khoo, Lebuh Tiga, T089-273453.
Bookings for Turtle Islands National Park.

Tourist office
Next to the municipal council building opposite Lebuh Empat, T089-229751. Mon-Fri 0800-1600.

The privately run information office is a useful starting point for visitors to Sandakan.

Where to stay

Sandakan

$$$ Four Points Sandakan
Sandakan Harbour Square, T089-244888, www.fourpointssandakan.com.
Luxurious 4-star hotel towering over the town and boasting a rooftop pool and bar

offering unrivalled views over Sandakan Bay. Rooms are modern, well-equipped and staff are professional.

$$ 2 Inn 1 Boutique Hotel & Spa
Lot 1-7, Block B, Bandar Fajar, Jln Leila, T089-202121, www.2inn1.com.my.
With its orange and white swirly exterior and pseudo-oriental interior, this hotel is difficult to miss. Though it is not located in the heart of town (5 mins by bus, RM1), the rooms are good value, newly decorated and have all mod cons.

$$ Borneo Cove Hotel
Lot 2, Mile 1.5, Jln Buli Sim-sim, T089-248777, www.borneocove.com.
Located on the edge of town, the free shuttle bus service makes this a viable mid-range option. It gets plus points for its fast internet but minus points for not having individually controlled a/c. Rooms are spacious and modern and the pool is a good place to lounge after a sweaty day out.

$$ Ibis Styles Waterfront
HS12 Sandakan Harbour Square, T089-240888, www.accorhotels.com.
Budget business hotel in the heart of town and a stone's throw from some of Sandakan's markets, this place offers clean, bright rooms with views over the old town or the Sulu Sea. A good-value and practical option though not brimming with local character.

$$ Nak
Jln Pelabuhan Lama, T089-272988, www.nakhotel.com.
Abundant Chinese decor, this hotel has basic but spacious rooms with clean bathrooms, cable TV and Wi-Fi. There's a decent rooftop bar with excellent views over the bay.

$$ Sabah
Km 1, Jln Utara, T089-213299, www.sabahhotel.com.my.
Surrounded by lush forest, with tremendous views over the treetops, this great value 4-star hotel is perched on a hill on the outskirts of town and has comfortable

rooms with and marble bathrooms. Facilities include gym, pool, tennis court, spa and its own nature trail.

$$ Sanbay
Mile 1.25, Jln Leila, T089-275000, www.sanbay.com.my.
This is a reasonable 3-star retro option hotel with bright and spacious en suite rooms, homely furnishings, piped music and cable TV. It's a bit of a stroll into town from here.

$$ Sandakan
4th Av, T089-221122, www.hotelsandakan. com.my.
Despite the old-fashioned carpets and heavy decor, rooms here are reasonable value, though could do with a bit of modernizing as some rooms are musty and window seals are falling out. Deluxe rooms are spacious and have views over the rooftops of Sandakan and down to the Sulu Sea. Good Cantonese restaurant and bar. Wi-Fi access and cable TV in all rooms.

$ Borneo Sandakan Backpackers
Block HS5, Lot 54&55, Sandakan Harbour Square, T089-215754, www.borneosandakan.com.
This well-regarded option is one of the better budgets option in town with spacious bright rooms with Wi-Fi access and a/c, and friendly staff. Highly recommended.

$ City View
Lot 1, Block 23, 3rd Av, T089-271122, www.citystar.com.my.
Hotel with functional, comfortable rooms with a/c, cable TV, Wi-Fi and attached bathroom in the heart of town. Popular restaurant downstairs. Fair value, given the dearth of decent backpacker accommodation in town.

$ Hsiang Garden
Mile 1.5, Leila Rd, T089-273122, www.hsianggarden.com.
Recently refurbished, this place is some way from the centre of town and is really only suitable in the unlikely event that

everywhere else is booked out. Fair rooms, bar and friendly staff.

$ London
Lot D1, Block 10, Jln Empat, T089-216372.
Excellent mid-range place offering a/c spotless rooms with cable TV with HBO movies, Wi-Fi and attached bathroom. There's a pleasant rooftop garden

$ Sandakan Backpackers,
Lot 108, Sandakan Harbour Square, T089-215754, www.sandakanbackpackers.com.
A decent budget option with simple rooms. Facilities include a friendly common area with a pool table and rooftop garden

with excellent sea views. Can arrange tours to local attractions. Popular with the backpacking fraternity.

Pulau Lankayan

$$$$ Lankayan Island Dive Resort
Run by Pulau Sipadan Resort & Tours, 1st floor, 484 Bandar Sabindo, Tawau, T089-765200, www.lankayan-island.com.
This stunning resort, on a deserted tropical island, offers 23 spacious and quiet wooden chalets by the beach, with attached bathroom. There are more than 40 dive sites nearby including a couple of wrecks. Sightings of whale sharks are common here Mar-May.

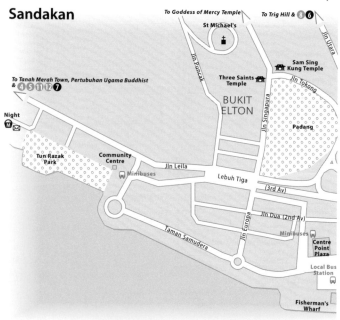

Sandakan

100 metres
100 yards

Where to stay
2 Inn 1 Boutique & Spa **4**
Borneo Cove **9**
Borneo Sandakan
  Backpackers **14**
Boutique Hotel & Spa **12**
City View hotel &
  Hawaii restaurant **1**

Four Points Sandakan **10**
Hsiang Garden **5**
Ibis Styles Waterfront **13**
London **3**
Nak hotel & Balin Rooftop
  Garden restaurant **2**
Sabah hotel &
  Ming restaurant **8**

Sanbay **11**
Sandakan hotel &
  Palm Garden restaurant **6**
Sandakan Backpackers **7**

Restaurants
English Tea House **1**

There is an open-air café for meals and a TV room where dive fanatics gather to watch footage of the day's diving trip.

Restaurants

Sandakan is justifiably renowned for its inexpensive and delicious seafood.

$$ English Tea House & Restaurant
Agnes Keith House, T089-222544, www.englishteahouse.org.
Step back in time at this wonderful place with shady outdoor garden seating overlooking the bay, an immaculate croquet lawn and jugs of Pimms. An afternoon here could easily be mistaken for a freakishly hot day in Devon circa 1930. Scones, clotted cream and pots of tea are proffered alongside excellent fusion cuisine that makes this one of Malaysia's most charming eateries.

$$ Ming Restaurant
Sabah Hotel, Km 1, Jln Utara, T089-213299.
Cantonese and Sichuan cuisine, renowned for dim sum (breakfast).

$$ New Seoul Garden
Hsiang Garden Estate, Mile 1.5, Leila Rd.
Korean food with all the usual suspects.

$$ Palm Garden
Hotel Sandakan. Lunch and dinner.
Well known for its steamboats and dim sum buffets, this place is a good spot to sample Sandakan's Cantonese cuisine. There's an international buffet every Friday in the **Palm Café** downstairs.

$$ Restoran Seafood Sim Sim 88
Pier 8, Water Village.
A short drive out of town, this restaurant stands in watery harmony with its environs and serves up wickedly good seafood. Punters rave about the prawns here and crabs are sold at bargain prices.

$ Balin Rooftop Garden
Nak Hotel, Jln Pelabuhan Lama. Open 1630-2400.
The lovely rooftop bar serving simple Western fare and cold beer, makes this an ideal spot for a sundowner with great views. They occasionally run out of cocktail ingredients, so approach the booze menu with a flexible outlook.

$ Hawaii
City View Hotel, Lot 1, Block 23, 3rd Av.
Pseudo Western and local food, busy at 1200 as workers come for the cheap set lunch.

$ Kedai Makanan King Cheong
Jln Dua. Breakfast and lunch.
The quality of this great place is testified to by the lunchtime crowds that ram in daily.

To Airport, Australian & Japanese War Memorials,
Crocodile Farm, Labuk Road, Sepilok & Forest HQ

Agnes Keith House **1**

100 steps

To Wisma Khoo Siak,
Mosque, Chiew Long Distance
Bus Station & Turtle Islands Jetty

Wisma Sandakan **6**

Lebuh Empat

Sandakan Heritage Museum

Jln Buli Sim Sim

Lebuh Tiga

To Sabah
Parks Jetty

To Central Market, Fish Market & **8**

MAS   Air Asia

Jln Pelabuhan

Jln Lima (5th St)

Lebuh Dua **4**

Jln Empat (4th St)

Jln Tiga (3rd St)

Jln Pryer

2   **7**   **14**

5   **13**

Sandakan Harbour Square **10**

To Turtle Islands

Kedai Makanan
King Cheong **4**
Lemongrass Pancake
House **3**
My Harbour **5**
New Seoul Garden **7**
Restoran Hikmah **6**

Restoran Seafood
Sim Sim 88 **8**
Santai **2**

Trolleys of dim sum weave between tables of punters getting stuck into simple Cantonese fare and some interesting oddities: Marmite fans will want try the *nasi ayam marmite*.

$ Lemongrass Pancake House,
126 Jln Dua, Lot 125. Open 1000-1700.
A haven for vegetarians, this trendy place serves up a variety of yummy vegetarian dishes. The most popular dish is the pumpkin curry though the spinach pancakes and milkshakes also seem to fly out of the kitchen at a rapid pace.

$ My Harbour Restaurant
Ground floor, Sandakan Harbour Square, T089-244888.
Sea views and bargain prices make this one of the best places to grab excellent seafood delights and a variety of Malaysian noodles with an ice cold beer. Those with a sweet tooth should leap at the chance to indulge in an ABC Special of shaved ice with avocado and mango. It sounds weird, but it works.

$ Restoran Hikmah
Jln Batu Empat, Mile 4.
Reputed to be the best spot in town for Malay food, with good seafood dishes and some *asam pedas*.

$ Santai
Sandakan Harbour Square.
Serving cheap seafood dishes, including superb noodles and fried rice, this popular spot is right on the waterfront and offers a relaxing view of the fishing boats on the horizon. Busy in the evenings.

Foodstalls
There are foodstalls next to minibus station, just before the community centre on the road to Ramai Ramai, and at the summit of Trig Hill.

Entertainment

There is a karaoke parlour on just about every street, though some are a tad seedy. The **Best Brew** is a quality bar offering a variety of drinks and live music at the Four Points Sandakan hotel (see Where to stay). You can hone your pool and darts skills here and mix with an international crowd.

Shopping

Almost everything in Sandakan is imported. There are some inexpensive batik shops and some good tailors. **Harbour Mall** is a bog standard shopping mall selling all the usual global brands and makes a pleasant a/c break, but it's not an exciting shopping spot. **Handicrafts Sabakraf** (opposite Hotel Sandakan, see Where to stay), sells basketry, pearls and souvenirs.

What to do

Bowling
Champion Bowl, *Mile 1¼, Jln Leila (the main road that heads out of Sandakan), Bandar Ramai Ramai, T089-211396.*

Golf
Sandakan Golf Club, *Jln Kolam, Bukit Padang, T088-660557, 10 km out of town (RM25 taxi ride).* Open to non-members.

Tour operators
Borneo Ecotours, *1st floor, Blok J, Jln Utara Batu 4, Bandar Pasaraya, T089-220210, www.borneoecotours.com.* Award-winning operator with a large selection of eco-friendly packages including Danum Valley, Kinabalu, Sipidan, Maliau basin and Kinabatangan River. Highly recommended.
Capac Travel Service, *ground floor, Rural District Building, Jln Tiga, T089-217288.* Ticketing, tour and hotel services.
Crystal Quest, *Sabah Park Jetty, Jln Buli Sim Sim, T089-212711, cquest@tm.net.my.* The only company running accommodation on Pulau Selingan, Turtle Islands National Park.
SI Tours, *Lot no 59, Block HS-5, Sandakan Harbour Square Phase 2, T089-213502, www.sitoursborneo.com.* Well-established company running tours to Gomantong

Caves, Kinabatangan and Turtle Islands National Park. Recommended.

Tropical Gateway, *117, Block 12, Sandakan Harbour Square, T089-202333, www.tropicalg. com.* Offers Sabah-wide packages including trips to Kinabatangan, Gomantong Caves and Selingan turtle islands, Danum Valley and Maliau Basin.

Wildlife Expeditions, *Room 903, 9th floor, Wisma Khoo Siak Chiew, Lebuh Tiga, Jln Buli Sim-Sim, T089-219616, www.wildlife-expeditions. com.* Well-regarded agency offering day tours and longer trips around Sabah.

Transport

Air
The airport is 10 km north of the town centre (RM25-30 by taxi into town). Early morning flights from **KK** to Sandakan allow breathtaking close-up views of Mt Kinabalu as the sun rises. **AirAsia** (Lot 2, 1st floor, Airport, T603-2171 9222) and **MAS** (Block 31, Sabah Building, Jln Pelabuhan, T089-273962) have daily connections with **KL** and **KK**. **MASwings** flies daily to **Tawau, Kudat** and **KK**.

Boat
The *MV Kristle Jane 3* sails to **Zamboanga** in the southern Philippines. The journey takes 22 hrs and departs weekly from Sandakan (RM283 economy, RM 323 for a cabin). Contact **Aleson Shipping Lines**, Ramai Ramai Block G (T089-216 9963) for tickets and the latest timetable.

Boats to the **Turtle Islands National Park** run from the Sabah Park Jetty, Jln Buli Buli Sim.

Bus and minibus
Local minibuses from the bus stop between the Esso and Shell stations on Jln Pryer.

Sandakan's a/c long-distance buses leave from the bus station at Mile 2.5. Some buses and all minibuses don't leave until they are full, so be prepared for a long wait. There are regular connections with most towns in Sabah including **KK** (RM43, 6 hrs), **Ranau** (RM29, 4 hrs), **Lahad Datu** (RM22, 3-4 hrs). Buses start at 0715, and depart regularly until 1100. After this you will have to take a Tawau bus, get off at Simpang Assam and take a minibus into Lahad Datu (RM1). **Tawau** buses every 30 mins 0630-1100, 1 bus at 1400 (RM42, 6 hrs). **Semporna**, departs 0800 (RM42, 6 hrs).

Turtle Islands National Park
protected islands where turtles come to lay their eggs

Located 40 km north of Sandakan, Turtle Islands are at the south entrance to Labuk Bay. The park is separated from the Philippine island of Bakkungan Kecil by a narrow stretch of water. These eight tiny islands in the Sulu Sea are among the most important turtle-breeding spots in Southeast Asia. The turtle sanctuary is made up of three tiny islands (Pulau Selingan, Pulau Bakkungan Kecil and Pulau Gulisan) and also encompasses the surrounding coral reefs and sea, covering 1700 ha. On Pulau Bakkungan Kecil there is a small mud volcano.

The islands
The islands are famous for their green turtles (*Chelonia mydas*), which make up 80% of the turtles in the park, and hawksbill turtles (*Eretmochelys imbricata*), known locally as *sisik*. There have also been rare reported sightings of Olive Ridley turtle (*Lepidochelys Olivacea*) but not for many years. Most green turtles lay their eggs on Pulau Selingan. The green turtles copulate 50-200 m off Pulau Selingan and can be seen during the day, their heads popping up like submarine periscopes. Hawksbills prefer to nest on Pulau Gulisan.

Both species come ashore, year-round, to lay their eggs, although the peak season is between July and October. Even during the off-season between four and 10 turtles come up the beach each night to lay their eggs. Pulau Bakkungan Kecil and Pulau Gulisan can only be visited during the day but visitors can stay overnight on Pulau Selingan to watch the green turtles.

Only the females come ashore; the male waits in the sea nearby for his mate. The females cautiously crawl up to nest after 2000 or with the high tide. The nesting site is above the high-tide mark and is cleared by the female's front and hind flippers to make a 'body pit', just under a metre deep. She then digs an egg chamber with her powerful rear flippers after which she proceeds to lay her eggs. The clutch size can be anything between 40 and 200; batches of 50-80 are most common.

When all the eggs have been laid, she covers them with sand and laboriously fills the body pit to conceal the site of the nest, after which the exhausted turtle struggles back

Essential Turtle Islands National Park

Finding your feet

Boats to the island leave from the Sabah Parks jetty at Jalan Buli Buli Sim in Sandakan; the ride to Selingan takes an hour.

Park information

Permission to visit the park must be obtained from **Sabah Parks** (see page 258), where you pay a conservation fee RM60, plus a camera fee of RM10 (no flash photography permitted). All accommodation must be booked through **Crystal Quest** (see page 262). This is booked up weeks, sometimes months, in advance.

Turtle watching

The number of visitors is restricted to 50 per night in an effort to protect the female turtles, which are easily alarmed by noise and light. Visitors are asked not to build campfires, shine bright torches or make noise at night on the beach. The turtles should be watched from a distance to avoid upsetting the nesting process.

When to go

The driest months and the calmest seas are between March and July. The egg-laying season is July to October. Seas are rough October to February.

Sandakan Bay

Sulu Sea

PHILIPPINES

Pulau Selingan
Pulau Gulisan
Turtle Islands National Park ◆
Pulau Libaran
Pulau Bakkungan Kecil

Tanjung Pisau

Tanjung Lari Lari

MALAYSIA

Samawang

Pulau Berhala

Sandakan
Sepilok Orang-utan
Rehabilitation Centre
Sandakan Harbour

Tanjung Aru

Segaliud

Sandakan Bay

Sekong River

Suan Lamba

Sukau

Lamag
Batangan
Gomantong Caves
Malapi
Bilit
Kinabatangan River

N

Batu Tulug

To Lahad Datu

10 km
10 miles

BACKGROUND
The tough life of a turtle

Historically, green and hawksbill turtles have been hunted for their meat, shells and their edible eggs (a Chinese delicacy). They were a favourite food of British and Spanish mariners for centuries. Japanese soldiers slaughtered thousands of turtles for food during the Second World War. Dynamite fishermen are also thought to have killed off many turtles in Indonesian, Malaysian and Philippines waters in recent years.

Malaysia, Hong Kong, Japan and the Philippines, where green turtle meat and eggs are in demand, are all signatories of the Convention in International Trade in Endangered Species (CITES) and trading in sea turtles has been banned under the Convention since 1981.

In his book *Forest Life and Adventures in the Malay Archipelago*, the Swedish adventurer and wildlife enthusiast Eric Mjoberg documents turtle egghunting and shell collecting in Borneo in the 1920s. He tells of how the Bajau would lie in wait for hawksbills, grab them and put them on the fire so their horny shields could be removed.

"The poor beasts are put straight on the fire so that their shield may be more readily removed, and suffer the tortures of the damned. They are then allowed to go alive, or perhaps half-dead into the sea, only to come back again after a few years and undergo the same cruel process."

The Bajau, he says, used an "ingenious contrivance" to hunt their prey. They would press pieces of common glass against their eyes "in a watertight fashion" and would lie face-down on a piece of floating wood, dipping their faces into the water, watching for hawksbills feeding on seaweed. They would then dive in, armed with a small harpoon, and catch them, knocking them out with a blow to the head.

to the sea, leaving her Range Rover-like tracks in the sand. The egg-laying process can take an hour or two to complete. Some say the temperature of the sand affects the sex of the young: if it is warm the batch will be mostly female and if cold, mostly male. After laying her eggs, a tag reading "If found, return to Turtle Island Park, Sabah, East Malaysia" is attached to each turtle by the rangers, who are stationed on each island. Over 27,000 have been tagged since 1970; the measurements of each turtle are recorded and the clutches of eggs removed and transplanted to the hatchery where they are protected from natural predators, like monitor lizards, birds and snakes.

The golf ball-sized eggs are placed by hand into 80-cm-deep pits, covered in sand and surrounded by wire. They take up to 60 days to hatch. The hatchlings mostly emerge at night when the temperature is cooler, breaking their shells with their one sharp tooth. There are hatcheries on all three islands and nearly every night a batch is released into the sea. Millions of hatchlings have been released since 1977. They are released at different points on the island to protect them from predators: they are a favoured snack for white-bellied gulls and sadly only about 1% survive to become teenage turtles.

Tourist information

Crystal Quest
Sabah Park Jetty, Jln Buli Sim-Sim, Sandakan, T089-212711, cquest@tm.net.my.
To book accommodation.

Sabah Parks Office
Room 906, 9th floor, Wisma Khoo, Lebuh Tiga, Sandakan, T089-273453; or Lot 45 and 46, 1st-5th floor, Block H, Signature Office, Times Square, KK, T088-523500; www. sabahparks.org.my.
To obtain permission for visiting the park.

Where to stay

The number of visitors to the islands is restricted, even in peak season. Accommodation comprises 3 chalets (one with 2 doubles, 2 with 6 doubles) on Pulau Selingan (RM260-370 per person, minimum 2 people). Book well in advance through Crystal Quest (see above). Tour agencies can also organize trips to the island.

The average cost of a 1-night tour including accommodation and boat transfer is RM600-800. An expedition to the islands needs to be well planned; the vagaries, such as bad weather, which can prevent you from leaving the islands as planned, can mess up itineraries. Most visitors book trips well in advance.

★ Sepilok Orang-Utan Sanctuary and Rehabilitation Centre
join an orang-utan for breakfast and learn about Borneo's sun bears

Sepilok, a reserve of 43 sq km of lowland primary rainforest and mangrove, was set up in 1964 to protect the orang-utan (*Pongo pygmaeus*) from extinction. It is the first and largest of only three orang-utan sanctuaries in the world and now has 40,000 visitors a year. Logging has seriously threatened Sabah's population of wild orang-utan, as has their capture for zoos and as pets. The orang-utan lives on the islands of Borneo and Sumatra and there are estimated to be as few as 10,000 still in the wild. In Sabah there are populations of orang-utan in the Kinabatangan basin region (see page 270), Danum Valley Conservation Area (see page 276) and a few other isolated tracts of jungle.

The sanctuary
Sepilok is an old forest reserve that was gazetted as a forestry experimentation centre as long ago as 1931, and by 1957 logging had been phased out. Orphaned or captured orang-utans that have become too dependent on humans through captivity are rehabilitated and protected under the Fauna Conservation Ordinance and eventually returned to their natural home. Many, for example, may have been captured by the oil-palm planters because they eat the young oil palm trees. Initially, the animals at the centre and in the surrounding area are fed every day but, as they acclimatize, they are sent further and further away or are re-released into the Tabin Wildlife Reserve near Lahad Datu. In 1996, researchers placed microchip collars on the orang-utans enabling them to be tracked over a distance of up to 150 km so that a better understanding of their migratory habits and other behaviour could be acquired.

After an initial period of quarantine at Sepilok, newly arrived orang-utans are moved to Platform A and taught survival skills by rangers. At the age of seven they are moved

Essential Sepilok Orang-Utan Sanctuary and Rehabilitation Centre

Finding your feet

The park is 25 km west of Sandakan and there are several buses a day. **Labuk Road Bus Company** buses depart from outside Sandakan Town Council starting at 0600 (RM2.10, 45 minutes). These buses stop at a junction on the main road, from where it's 1.9 km to the centre. Public bus No 14 takes visitors straight to the centre (RM5) but departs infrequently. Alternatively, a one-way taxi from Sandakan should cost around RM40. See http://www.sabahtourism.com/destination/sepilok-orangutan-rehabilitation-centre

Park information

The park is open Saturday-Thursday 0900-1200 and 1400-1600, Friday 0900-1100 and

Tip...
The morning feed is packed with tour groups; the afternoon feed is generally quieter.

1400-1600. Entry costs RM30 (children RM15), camera RM10. It is worth getting to the park early before the crowds arrive.

The **Information Centre** is next to the Park HQ. It runs a nature education exhibition with replicas of jungle mammals and shows films (0830, 1100, 1200, 1410 and 1530). If you want to do the walks, arrive at the centre in the morning so you can get a permit. Feeding takes place at Platform A at 1000 and 1500.

deeper into the forest to Platform B, about 30 minutes' walk from Platform A and not open to the public. At Platform B, they are encouraged to forage for themselves. Other animals brought here include Malayan sun bears, wild cats and baby elephants.

Sepilok also has a rare Sumatran rhinoceros (*Didermoceros sumatrensis*), the Asian two-horned rhinoceros, see box, page 278. This enclosure is sometimes closed to the public.

The **Mangrove Forest Trail** takes two to three hours one way and passes transitional forest, some pristine lowland rainforest, a boardwalk into a mangrove forest, water holes and a wildlife track.

Bornean Sun Bear Conservation Centre
Next to the Orangutan Rehabilitation Centre, sharing gates and ticketing facilities, T089-534491, www.bsbcc.org.my, daily 0900-1530, RM30.

This well-organized centre offers the chance to get close to the Malayan Sun Bear, the world's smallest bear species. There is a boardwalk and visitor centre, but no stipulated feeding times. Plan to visit in the morning when the bears are most active.

Rainforest Discovery Centre
Jln Sepilok, T089-533780, www.forest.sabah.gov.my/rdc, daily 0800-1700 (trails and canopy are closed at 2000), RM15, children RM7. A free booklet is available; for more details contact the Forest Research Centre, PO Box 14-07, T089-531522. Guided night walks are available on Mon, Wed, Fri 1800-2000 for RM30 per person, minimum 4 people.

This centre, located within the Kabili-Sepilok Forest Reserve, is 2 km from the Orang-utan Rehabilitation Centre and provides detailed displays about the vegetation in the area. It is run by the **Forest Research Centre**, also found on this road. Emphasis is on participation, with questionnaires, games and so on; it offers a wide range of information about all aspects of tropical rainforests and the need for conservation. It is situated in the Forest

Research Centre's arboretum and there is an 800-m rainforest walk around the lake. There also a 378-m **canopy walkway** offering the opportunity to walk above the forest canopy and spot wildlife. Keep your eyes peeled for hornbills, slow lorises, tarsiers, civet cats, kingfishers and the Bornean bristlehead.

Listings Sepilok Orang-Utan Sanctuary and Rehabilitation Centre

Tourist information

Sabah Wildlife Department
Batu 14, Jln Labuk, Sandakan, T089-531180, www.wildlife.sabah.gov.my.
For information on visiting the park.

Where to stay

$$$-$ Sepilok Forest Edge Resort
Jln Rambutan off Jln Sepilok, Mile 14, T089-533245, www.sepilokforestedgeresort.com
A 10-min walk from the bus stop on Jln Sepilok. This resort is decorated with Kadazan flourishes and has large wooden rooms with spacious verandas overlooking the forest. There is also a good-value dorm (RM40 a bed) and a communal area and jungle trail. The attached café serves a good range of international and locally inspired fusion fare. One of the owners, Robert Chong, is a birdwatching guide and can arrange tailored trips for birders.

$$-$ Sepilok B&B
Jln Fabia, off Jln Sepilok, Mile 14, T089-534050, www.sepilokbednbreakfast.com.my.
Around 1 km from the sanctuary and a short walk to the Rainforest Discovery Centre and the Bornean Sun Bear Conservation Centre. 20 comfortable, bright rooms with polished wooden floors, varying from dorms to a deluxe double with TV and private balcony. All have attached bathroom with hot water, Wi-Fi, and free breakfast.

$$-$ Sepilok Jungle Resort (and Wildlife Lodge)
Jln Rambutan, Sepilok Mile 14 (5 mins' walk from Sepilok Orang-Utan Sanctuary), T089-533031, www.sepilokjungleresort.com.

This resort is the realization of a dream for John and Judy Lim, who have gradually purchased all the land on the edge of the forest and landscaped the area surrounding 3 man-made lakes. They've planted many flowering and fruiting trees, attracting butterflies and birds. The resort offers clean and comfortable dorms with shared hot-water bathrooms; double rooms with fan, a/c and hot water bathrooms; comfortable a/c double and family rooms; and more luxurious rooms, with cable TV, a/c, large balcony and tasteful tropical flourishes, surrounded by forest. There's a pleasant restaurant in a great setting, and a campsite. Boats for fishing available. The resort also has a large pool, children's pool, gym and jacuzzi as well as a café serving up Malaysian and Western fare. Wi-Fi is available in the pricier rooms and around the reception area.

The same team have opened **Bilit Adventure Lodge**, offering mid-range rooms along the Kinabatangan River (see page 270). Rooms, with either a/c or fan, are usually offered in combination with tour packages.

$ Uncle Tan Bed and Breakfast
Jln Sepilok, Lot 1, Mile 14, T089-531639, www.uncletan.com.
This renowned bed and breakfast offers bargain basement dorms and rooms and a convivial jungle holiday camp ambience. All meals are provided. Staff have a wealth of knowledge and can help organize all-inclusive package trips to their famed **Wildlife Camp** in Kinabatangan (see page 272). Recommended.

Restaurants

$$ Lindung Gallery Restaurant
Jln Sepilok, Mile 14, T089-533979.
Open 0900-2100.
Decent Western and Malaysian fare, good bakery options and a variety of drinks (including cider!) in an arty contemporary setting. Service can be a bit slow so take in some art whilst you wait

Transport

Bus
There are 5 direct daily public buses from **Sandakan**, from the central minibus terminal in front of Nak Hotel from 0900-1400 (RM4, 40 mins). Ask for the Sepilok Batu 14 line. From the airport, the most convenient way to reach Sepilok is by taxi. Sepilok is 1.9 km from the main road. A taxi should cost around RM40 into Sandakan. There are 6 buses to Sandakan from 0700-1600 (40 mins RM4).

Gomantong Caves

bat-filled caves and a wild population of orang-utan and mouse deer

The Gomantong Caves are 32 km south of Sandakan Bay, between the road to Sukau and the Kinabatangan River, or 110 km overland on the Sandakan–Sukau road. The name Gomantong means 'tie it up tightly' in the local language and the caves are the largest system in Sabah. They are located in the 3924-ha Gomantong Forest Reserve.

The caves and reserve
There are sometimes orang-utan, mouse deer, wild boar and wild buffalo in the reserve, which was logged in the 1950s. There are several cave chambers. The main limestone cave is **Simud Hitam (Black Cave)**. This cave, with its ceiling soaring up to 90 m overhead, is just a five-minute walk from the Park HQ and picnic area. The smaller and more complex **Simud Putih (White Cave)** is above. It is quite dangerous climbing up as there is no ladder

Essential Gomantong Caves

Finding your feet

It is easiest to visit the caves on a tour (see Sandakan What to do, page 262). The caves are 95 km from Sandakan (1½ hours) and are accessible by an old logging road, which can be reached by bus from the main Sandakan–Sukau road. The timing of the bus is inconvenient for those wishing to visit the caves, so it's a good idea to stop off on the way to Sukau, where you can stay overnight. Alternatively take a taxi (around RM200 from Sandakan).

Park information

The park is open daily 0800-1800, RM30. At the Park HQ there is an information centre, a small cafeteria where drinks and simple dishes are served. Accommodation is available at the **Gomantong Rainforest Chalet**. For information see www.forest.sabah.gov.my.

Good walking shoes are essential, as is a torch. If you're squeamish about cockroaches give this cave a miss. If you arrive independently then one of the nest workers, a person from the information centre or a ranger will show you around. The bats can be seen exiting from the caves between 1800 and 1830.

to reach the caves and the rocks are slippery. Between 200,000 and 300,000 bats of two different species are thought to live in the caves; at sunset they swarm out to feed. Some 64 species of bat have been recorded in Sabah; most in these caves are fruit- and wrinkled-lipped bats whose guano is a breeding ground for cockroaches. The squirming larvae make the floor of the cave seethe. The guano can cause an itchy skin irritation. The bats are preyed upon by birds like the bat hawk, peregrine falcon and buffy fish owl.

There are also an estimated one million swiftlets that swarm into the cave to roost at sunset, the birds of bird's nest soup fame (see box, page 99). The swiftlets of Gomantong have been a focus of commercial enterprise for 400 or 500 years. However, it was not until 1870 that harvesting birds' nests became a serious industry here. The caves are divided into five pitches and each is allocated to a team of 10-15 people. Harvesting periods last 10 days and there are two each year (February-April and July-September). Collecting nests from hundreds of feet above the ground is a dangerous business and deaths are not uncommon. Before each harvesting period a chicken or goat is sacrificed to the cave spirit; it is thought that deaths are not caused by human error, but by an angry spirit. Birdlife around the caves is rich, with crested serpent eagles, kingfishers, Asian fairy bluebirds and leafbirds often sighted. Large groups of richly coloured butterflies are also often seen drinking from pools along the track leading from the forest into the caves.

★ Sungai Kinabatangan

take a river cruise to explore this fauna-rich flood plain

At 560 km, this river is Sabah's longest and Malaysia's second longest, snaking its way from the mountains of central Sabah out into the Sulu Sea. Much of the lower basin is gazetted under the Kinabatangan Wildlife Sanctuary and meanders through a flood plain, creating numerous oxbow lakes and an ideal environment for some of Borneo's most notable fauna making this one of Southeast Asia's best spots for viewing wildlife. Increasing logging activity in areas neighbouring Kinabatangan means that wildlife is hemmed in alongside the river. This makes it easier to spot animals as they have nowhere else to roam.

Kinabatangan Riverine Forest area

One of the principal reasons why the Kinabatangan has remained relatively unscathed by Sabah's rapacious logging is because much of the land is permanently waterlogged and the forest contains only a small number of commercially valuable trees. In addition, there has been little disturbance from human settlements as Kinabatangan basin has always been sparsely inhabited due to the inhabitable land and the threat from piracy. Due to the diversity of its wildlife, the Kinabatangan Riverine Forest area has managed to retain its wildlife reserve status, despite increased pressure from palm oil companies requesting ever more land for their plantations.

Just some of the animals include: tree snake, crocodile, civet cat, otter, monitor lizard, long-tailed and pig-tailed macaque, silver-, red- and grey-leaf monkey and proboscis monkey. It is the most accessible area in Sabah to see proboscis monkeys, which are best viewed from a boat in the late afternoon, when they converge on treetops by the river banks to settle for the night. Herds of wild elephant pass through the park. The birdlife is particularly good and includes oriental darter, egret, storm's stork, osprey, coucal owl, frogmouth, bulbul, spiderhunter, oriole, flowerpecker and several species of hornbill.

The night trip is well worth doing as you can get close to the sleeping birds and they look very colourful.

The inhabitants of the Kinabatangan region are mostly Orang Sungai or people of mixed ancestry including Tambanua, Idahan, Dusun, Suluk, Bugis, Brunei and Chinese. A good destination for a jungle river safari is not on the Kinabatangan itself, but on the narrow, winding Sungai Menanggol tributary, about 6 km from Sukau. The Kinabatangan estuary, largely mangrove, is also rich in wildlife and is a haven for migratory birds. Boats can be chartered from Sandakan to Abai (at the river mouth).

Batu Tulug, also known as Batu Putih (white stone), on the Kinabatangan River 100 km upstream from Sukau, is a cave containing wooden coffins dating back several hundred years. Some of the better examples have been removed to the Sabah State Museum in KK. The caves are about 1 km north of the Kinabatangan Bridge, on the east side of the Sandakan–Lahad Datu road.

Essential Sungai Kinabatangan

Finding your feet

Most people visit as part of a package, which includes transport to their lodge or camp; some offer tours of Gomantong and/or Sepilok en route. **Uncle Tan's** picks up from its base in Sepilok. Others have transport from Sandakan, Tawau, Danum Valley and Semporna. Trips can be booked at tour operators in Sandakan (see page 262) or KK (see page 204).

Most visitor accommodation is at Sukau, two hours by road from Sandakan, or in jungle lodges along the river. Tours include boat trips in the late afternoon through freshwater swamp forest to see proboscis monkeys and other wildlife. There are also walks through the jungle.

Those who wish to visit for a day can charter a cab from Sandakan for around RM400 and upwards.

Listings Sungai Kinabatangan

Where to stay

Most companies running tours to the Kinabatangan put their guests up in Sukau or in camps along the river. See also **Sepilok Jungle Resort**, page 268. Many of the prices here are all-inclusive packages and a stay usually includes wildlife boat tours and meals. Check with resort in advance.

$$$$ Sukau Rainforest Lodge
Borneo Eco-Tours, Lot 1, Pusat Perindustrian, Kolombong Jaya, Km5.5, T088-438300, www.sukau.com.
Award-winning operator with a large selection of packages. This resort is accessible by boat from Sukau, and is run with eco-friendly ideals. There's accommodation for 40 in traditional

Malaysian-style chalets on stilts. All 20 rooms have solar-powered fans, twin beds, mosquito netting, and attached tiled bathroom with hot water. There's an excellent restaurant, 2 boardwalks (including the 1500-ft Hornbill boardwalk), gift shop, pleasant garden and sundeck overlooking the rainforest. Friendly, efficient service. A shining example of ecotourism at its best. Shoe-string package available for budget travellers. Highly recommended.

$$$ Bilit Rainforest Lodge
Kg Bilit Seberang Jln Sukau, T088-448489, www.bilitrainforestlodge.com.
Accommodation here is in wooden chalets and is functional and clean, though not luxurious. A/c chalets with attached bathroom and hot water and large thatched

communal dining area good for taking in the areas rich birdlife.

$$$ Borneo Nature Lodge
No 41, Blk 3, 1st floor, Prima Square, Mile 4, North Rd, Sandakan, T089-210718, www.borneonaturelodge.com.my.
12 comfortable rooms in a lodge designed to blend into the surrounding forest with the design purporting to create a jungle canopy ambience. Built along eco ideals, the lodge composts its food waste and uses glass to filter natural light into the rooms. Rainwater is also used in the toilets. A good place to get a feel for the jungle with a variety of river tours on offer.

$$$ Bukit Melapi Proboscis Lodge
Run by Sipadan Dive Centre, 10th floor, Wisma Merdeka, KK, T088-240584, www.sdclodges.com.
A more upmarket Kinabatangan experience, near Sukau, not in the heart of the jungle like the jungle camps. Chalets with hot-water showers, a/c and 24-hr electricity. Lovely large airy main building for meals and socializing and sun deck for observing riverine happenings. Visitors are limited to a maximum of 47 at a time, so it never feels too hectic. Various packages available.

$$ Nature Lodge Kinabatangan
Nasalis Larvatus Tours, Lot 226, 2nd floor, Wisma Sabah, Jln Tun Adbul Razak, KK, T088-230534, www.naturelodgekinabatangan.com.
Excellent wildlife viewing lodge on a quiet section of the river about 1 hr by boat from Sukau. Accommodation is in simple Orang Sungei huts with electricity. The more expensive Agamind chalets have attached bathrooms with hot water. Good night walks and knowledgeable and professional guides. All meals included. Variety of packages offered, including transfers from Sandakan and entrance to the Sepilok Orang-utan Sanctuary. The lodge is located in the village of Kampong Bilit, home to around 150 Orang Sungei people and there are opportunities to spend some interacting with the local community.

$$-$ Uncle Tan Wildlife Adventures
Jln Sepilok, Lot 1, Mile 14, T089-531639, www.uncletan.com.
A long-established budget option for exploring the lower Kinabatangan Valley. Accommodation is in simple huts with no doors or window and lino flooring. Guests are provided a clean sheet, a thin mattress and a mosquito net and all rooms are shared. There is a bath house with water pumped from the river for bathing and visitors are reminded not to leap in the river as there are several resident large crocodiles. All meals are provided and vegetarians catered for. This is a great way to get back to nature. A 3-day/2-night package including van transport to the river from the B&B on Jln Sepilok, several river cruises including an amazing night cruise, jungle treks and all meals (simple but hearty) costs RM455 (extra nights for RM106 each). It's also possible to do a 2-day/1-night trip for RM349 though a longer stay is recommended. Prepare to get very muddy; wellies are available. Bring a raincoat and torch. The camp is very remote and in the middle of the jungle. It is run by enthusiastic young locals who speak pretty good English, love to mix with guests and, while not expert naturalists, are knowledgeable about the wildlife. Some have been working here for years. The camp was started by Uncle Tan, who began taking tourists out to the jungle in 1988. A colourful character, he fought stridently for conservation issues in the region. He died in 2002 and the running of the resort has been taken over by his brother, based in Singapore. This place is deservedly popular, so book ahead. Recommended.

Lahad Datu is Malaysia's 'wild East' at its wildest and its recent history testifies to its reputation as the capital of cowboy country. The population is an intriguing mixture of Filipinos, Sulu islanders, Kalimantan migrants, Bugis, Timorese and a few Malays. Nowadays there are so many migrants few can find employment in this grubby and uninteresting town. There are reckoned to be more illegal Filipino immigrants in Lahad Datu than the rest of the population put together.

During the Second World War, the Japanese made Lahad Datu their naval headquarters for east Borneo. After the war, the timber companies moved in and the **British Kennedy Bay Timber Company** built Lahad Datu's first plywood mill in the early 1950s. The palm oil industry grew in the hinterland after the timber boom finished in the 1970s, attracting migrants from far and wide to work on the plantations.

In recent years, piracy in the Sulu Sea and the offshore islands in Kennedy Bay has been rife; local fishermen live in terror. In October 2003, a band of Abu Sayyaf rebels kidnapped six Filipino and Indonesian workers from **Borneo Paradise Resort** near Kunak. Eight months later, four hostages were freed. It is thought a Malaysian businessman paid a ransom. In 2013 Lahad Datu, normally a fairly sleepy place, made international headlines after a band of Filipino militants landed and holed up in a village outside the town. They were under orders from a claimant of the Sultanate of Sulu who wished to assert his rights for sovereignty of eastern Sabah (see box, page 274).

Sights
Kampong Panji is a water village with a small market at the end of Jalan Teratai, where many of the poorer immigrant families live.

The only good beaches are on the road to Tungku; **Pantai Perkapi** and **Pantai Tungku**. They can be reached by minibus from Lahad Datu or by boat from the old wharf. It is possible to get to the nearby islands from the old wharf behind the **Mido Hotel**, but because of lawlessness in the area, particularly at sea, a trip is not advisable.

Madai Caves are about 2 km off the Tawau–Lahad Datu road, near Kunak. The caves are an important archaeological site; there is evidence they were inhabited over 15,500 years ago. Birds' nests are harvested from the caves three times a year by local Idahan people whose lean-to kampong goes right up to the cave mouth. Independent transport is required for this trip as it's not catered for by tour operators.

Another 15 km west of Madai is **Baturong**, another limestone massif and cave system in the middle of what was originally Tingkayu Lake. The route is not obvious so it is advisable to take a local guide. Stone tools, wooden coffins and rock paintings have been found there. Evidence of humans dating from 16,000 years ago, after the lake drained away, can be found at the huge rock overhang (take a torch; it is possible to camp here). To get to Baturong, take a minibus from Lahad Datu.

At **Gunung Silam**, 8 km from Lahad Datu on the Tawau road, a track leads up the mountain to a Telekom station at 620 m and from there, a jungle trail to the summit. There are good views over the bay, when it isn't misty, and out to the islands beyond. It is advisable to take a guide.

The 2013 Lahad Datu Standoff

The sleepy town of Lahad Datu was unexpectedly thrust into the global limelight in early 2013 after 235 militants, many of whom were armed, arrived by boat from Tawi-Tawi in the Sulu archipelago of the southern Philippines. The group was sent by Jamalul Kiram III, one of the claimants to the throne of the Sultanate of Sulu with the aim of asserting his unresolved claim to eastern Sabah as part of his sultanate.

The militants were encircled by the Malaysian military in the remote village of Tanduo outside Lahad Datu and diplomats hurried to resolve the situation peacefully. President Acquino of the Philippines appealed to Kiram, stating "It must be clear to you that this small group of people will not succeed in addressing your grievances, and that there is no way that force can achieve your aims". There was no response from Kiram, but tensions slowly increased to boiling point and on the 1 March 2013 a skirmish led to the deaths of 12 militants and two members of the Malaysian military in Tanduo. A further attack in a village off the coast of Semporna led to significant bloodshed on both sides including claims of black magic and torture being used on captured Malaysian police officers proved that hopes of a peaceful resolution were unlikely.

The Malaysian military launched Ops Daulat (Operation Sovereignty) on 5 March 2013 with fighter plane bombardments and mortars being used to clear out the militants' base around Tanduo. By 11 March the village was declared clear and 22 bodies of militants were recovered.

The village of Tanduo is now a camp and the Malaysian military has significantly stepped up its presence in eastern Sabah. As a result of the standoff, many Filipinos residing in Sabah have reported harassment and discrimination from Sabahan indigenous groups in reprisal for the deaths of Malaysian police officers who came from regional ethnic groups. It is claimed that by early 2014 over 25,000 Filipinos illegally residing in Sabah had been forcibly repatriated. Jamalul Kiram III died in 2013 of a heart attack, though his family continue to press their territorial claims for Sabah.

Tabin Wildlife Reserve

Book at Tabin Wildlife Holidays, Lot 11-1, Blk A, Damai Point, Jln Damai, KK, T088-267266, www.tabinwildlife.com.my.

Gazetted in 1984 as a protected forest area, Tabin is one of Sabah's largest and most important reserves, classified as Grade 7, meaning that it cannot be logged and exists fundamentally as a protected zone for conserving wildlife. Since 2015, the Sumatran rhino has been declared extinct in the wild in Sabah, and Tabin's **Borneo Rhino Sanctuary** offers refuge in its safe protected zone for any that may be translocated from areas where they are found and not effectively breeding. Tabin is home to Sabah's largest mammals including the pygmy elephant and the banteng.

The **Tabin Jungle Resort**, around 50 km or one hour's drive from Lahad Datu, is also one of the easiest and most comfortable jungle resorts to visit. In addition, it's in one of the most exciting settings, close to a large mud-volcano – favoured as a mineral lick by mammals. The reserve offers a wide variety of trails and various wildlife habitats. There are several huge bubbling mud volcanoes an easy trek from the resort.

The reserve is particularly good for observing Bornean mammals, due its considerable size, covering 120,500 ha, and the fact it consists of large areas of previously logged and now recovering forest. Pygmy elephants (see box, page 277), wild pigs, civets and macaques are often seen on evening safaris close to palm oil plantations; otters make their homes in the river below the jungle resort; and by staking out the mud volcano for a night a close encounter is even possible with a sun bear (see box, page 292).

There are various packages available to visit the reserve, including day trips that start at RM570 per person (minimum two people) and include transfers from Lahad Datu. All-inclusive two-day packages start at RM1780 and make sense for those who really want to get an insight into the reserve and its wildlife.

Listings Lahad Datu and around

Where to stay

Lahad Datu is not a popular tourist spot and accommodation is generally not good value for money though there is the occasional diamond to be found.

$$$$ Tabin Jungle Resort
Tabin Wildlife Reserve, book at Lot 11-1, Blk A, Damai Point, Jln Damai, KK, T088-267266, www.tabinwildlife.com.my.
Great for serious wildlife enthusiasts or anyone on a romantic weekend or escaping to nature for a few days. Beautifully designed wooden cabins with balconies overlooking the Lipad River in the Tabin Wildlife Reserve. All cabins have ceiling fan and hot showers. Variety of packages available. Recommended.

$$ Bike and Tours Bed & Breakfast
Lot 62, Taman Happ Heng, Jln Segama, T017-293 6376, www.bikeandtours.com.
There are homely vibes in abundance at this B&B with 5 comfortable rooms, pool and an excellent breakfast to set you up for a day of exploring. The owner, Simon, is highly knowledgeable about bikes and can organize a variety of bike trips around Lahad Datu and beyond.

$$ Kingston Hotel
MDLD Level 4, 5, Lahad Datu Centre Point, Jln Kastam Lama, T089-881000.
If you get stuck, this is a reasonable business hotel with clean a/c rooms in the centre of town and surrounded by a good selection of halal eateries

$$ My Inn Hotel
Lot 264 Bandar Sri Perdana, T089-863388, www.myinnhotel.com.
Located on the edge of town and convenient for those on their way into or out of the Danum Valley, this good-value hotel has simple but comfortable rooms, a decent breakfast and good views over the town from the upper floors.

Restaurants

Seafood is a safe bet in Lahad Datu.

$$ Melawar
2nd floor, Block 47, off Jln Teratai (around the corner from the Mido Hotel).
Seafood restaurant, popular with locals.

$$ Ping Foong
1.5 km out of Lahad Datu, on Sandakan Rd.
Open-air seafood restaurant. Highly recommended by locals.

$ Bismi Bistro Restaurant
Darvel Bay Plaza.
Halal fare with super-sweet tea, milo dinosaur (an iced chocolate drink) and delectable crispy Indonesian *ayam penyet* (crushed chicken).

$ Golden Key
On stilts over the sea opposite the end of Jln Teratai.

A humble wooden coffee shop, but well known for its seafood.

$ Restoran Dovist
Fajar Centre.
Good spot for a Chinese-style fish curry, chicken rice or fishball soup. Popular with local families.

$ Secret Recipe
Lot 9-10, Level 1, Harbour Square.
Generic Malaysian chain restaurant/café serving up sweet treats, drinks and a few decent Malaysian main courses. The *laksa* is worth a punt.

Foodstalls
The market (see Shopping, below) has foodstalls upstairs with attractive views out to sea. **Pasar Malam** (behind the Mido Hotel on Jln Kastam Lama), has recommended spicy barbecued fish (*ikan panggang*) and skewered chicken wings.

Shopping

The central market is on Jln Bungaraya and there is a spice market off Jln Teratai where Indonesian smugglers tout Gudang Garam cigarettes and itinerant dentists and *bomohs* (witch doctors) draw large crowds.

What to do

Tour operators
Bike and Tours, *Lot 62, Taman Hap Heng, Batu 1 1/4, Jln Segama, T089-868198, www. bikeandtours.com.* A variety of bike tours around Sabah, led by knowledgeable and friendly hosts.
Borneo Nature Tours, *Block 3, Fajar Centre, T089-880207, www.borneonaturetours.com.*

Transport

Air
Lahad Datu Airport is 1 km north of town, T089-880237. Connections to **KK** with **MAS**.

Boat
Fishing boats take paying passengers from the old wharf (end of Jln Kastam Lama) to **Tawau** and **Semporna**, although time-wise (and, more to the point, safety-wise) it makes much more sense to go by road or air.

Minibus
Minibuses and what are locally known as 'wagons' (7-seater, 4WD Mitsubishis) leave from the bus station on Jln Bunga Raya (behind Bangunan Hap Seng at the mosque end of Jln Teratai) and from opposite the Shell station. Regular connections with **Tawau** (RM20, 2½ hrs), **Semporna**, **Sandakan** (RM22) and **Madai**.

★ Danum Valley Conservation Area
virgin rainforest with prehistoric grave sites

Danum Valley's 438 sq km of virgin jungle is the largest expanse of undisturbed lowland dipterocarp forest in Sabah. The Segama River runs through the area and past the field centre. The Danum River is a tributary of the Segama joining it 9 km downstream of the field centre. Gunung Danum (1093 m) is the highest peak, 13 km southwest of the field centre. Within the area is a tightly controlled Yayasan Sabah timber concession.

Features include a canopy walkway, a heart-stoppingly springy platform 107 m long and 27 m above the ground, an ancient Dusun burial site, waterfalls and a self-guided trail. There are also guided nature walks on an extensive trail system.

WILDLIFE
The gentler beast of Borneo

It was dung that eventually solved the mystery surrounding Borneo's rare elephants. For a long time scientists couldn't decide whether the animals were native to the island or introduced by human settlers. One argument suggested that the British East India Company gave the beasts as gifts to the Sultan of Sulu in the 17th century.

Using evidence gleaned from DNA analysis of the mucus which sticks to elephant droppings, scientists from Columbia University in the US discovered the pachyderm is indeed indigenous. From genetic data they concluded the Borneo variety is a distinct sub-species of Asian elephant, having been isolated from its cousins 300,000 years ago. In recognition of its new status, the animal was rechristened the Borneo pygmy elephant in 2003.

The animals are smaller than the Asian elephant, growing to be on average 2.5 m tall compared to their larger Asian elephant cousins who average 3 m. Borneo pygmy elephants also have larger ears, longer tails and straighter tusks and are said to be gentler in temperament. Scientists believe elephants trooped across swampy land joining Borneo with Sumatra when sea levels were lower during the ice ages.

Like much of the flora and fauna in Borneo, their situation is dire. The number of remaining Borneo elephant is thought to have decreased by at least 50% over the past two generations and an elephant census carried out between 2007 and 2008 estimated that between 1200 and 3700 are left in the wild with the remaining population threatened by ivory poachers and loss of habitat. For the best chance of seeing the elephant in relatively sensitive surroundings head to the Tabin or Kinabatangan areas.

Flora and fauna

Due to its size and remoteness, Danum Valley is home to some of Sabah's rarest animals and plants. The dipterocarp forest is some of the oldest, tallest and most diverse in the world, with 200 species of tree per hectare; there are over 300 labelled trees. The conservation area is teeming with wildlife, including the Sumatran rhinoceros, elephant, clouded leopard, orang-utan, proboscis monkey, crimson langur, pig-tailed macaque, sambar deer, bearded pig, Western tarsier, sun bear (see box, page 292) and 275 species of bird including hornbill, rufous picolet, flowerpecker and kingfisher. A species of monkey, which looks like an albino version of the red-leaf monkey, was first seen on the road to Danum in 1988 and appears to be unique to this area.

The valley

This area has never been inhabited, although there is evidence of a burial site that is thought to have been for the Dusun people who lived here about 300 years ago. There is also growing evidence of prehistoric

Essential Danum Valley

Finding your feet

From Lahad Datu, turn left along the logging road at Km 15 on the Lahad Datu–Tawau road to Taliwas, and then left again to field centre. Unless you are a scientist (see Field Centre, below), visits must be organized through **Borneo Rainforest Lodge** (see Where to stay, page 279). The lodge provides a transfer service (two hours). Guides charge RM5 per hour.

WILDLIFE

The Sumatran rhinoceros

Although not as rare as its Javan brother, the Sumatran, or Asian two-horned rhinoceros (*Didermoceros sumatrensis*) is critically endangered. The species has suffered from the destruction of its natural habitat and the price placed on its head by the value that the Chinese attach to its grated horn as a cure-all. A kilogram of rhino horn is thought to sell for around US$30,000. Should the Sumatran rhino disappear so, too, it is thought, will a number of plants whose seeds will only germinate after passing through the animal's intestines.

It was once widespread through mainland and island Southeast Asia but there are now thought only to be around 80-100 remaining in the wild, mostly in the most remote mountainous forests of Sumatra but with a possible tiny population in West Kutai, East Kalimantan and unconfirmed reports that there may be a small population in Sarawak.

A captive breeding programme to ensure against extinction, proved spectacularly unsuccessful with around a third of the animals dying during capture or shortly thereafter. According to naturalists Tony and Jane Whitten, the only recorded birth in captivity was in Calcutta in 1872.

In 2015 researchers made the sad announcement that the Sumatran rhino is now extinct in Malaysia, with only nine remaining in captivity. Researchers also announced that the animal is functionally extinct in Borneo. The last three rhinos captured in the wild were a male in 2008 and females in 2011 and 2014. The females were infertile as a result of a lack of breeding which damaged their reproductive systems. It is now a protected species. Only on Sumatra does it seem to have a slight chance of surviving.

In a startlingly similar Darwinesque manner to Borneo's bears and elephants, Asian two-horned rhinos have evolved dwarf characteristics, a feature that has helped them to survive in dense undergrowth. The Sumatran rhino is the smallest of all the family, only growing to 600-900 kg. It is a shy, retiring creature, inhabiting thick forest. Tracks have been discovered as high as 3300 m in Mount Leuser National Park, Sumatra. It lacks the armoured skin of other species and has a soft, hairy hide. It also has an acute sense of smell and hearing, but poor eyesight.

Help is needed if species survival is to become a reality. Hopes are now pinned on better conservation in Indonesia and capturing any remaining rhinos in the jungles of Borneo so that advanced reproductive technology can be used for breeding. At present, the prognosis is bleak. Find out more at www.borneorhinoalliance.org.

cave dwellers in the Segama River area. Not far downstream from the field centre, in a riverside cave, two wooden coffins have been found, together with a copper bracelet and a *tapai* jar, all of uncertain date. There is evidence of some settlement during the Japanese occupation; townspeople came upstream to escape from the Japanese troops. The area was first recommended as a national park by the WWF's Malaysia Expedition in 1975 and designated a conservation area in 1981. The field centre was officially opened in 1986.

The main aims of this large area are to research the impact of logging on flora and fauna and to try and improve forest management, to understand processes that maintain tropical rainforest and to provide wildlife management and training opportunities for Sabahans. Many are collaborative projects between Malaysian and foreign scientists.

Danum Valley Field Centre

The field centre, 85 km west of Lahad Datu and 40 km from the nearest habitation, was set up by the Sabah Foundation (Yayasan) in 1985 for forest research, nature education and recreation; the centre is only open to visiting scientists and researchers. If you are a biologist or an educator you may be able to get permission to visit the centre; contact the **Sabah Foundation** ⓘ *Likas Bay, T088-326327, www.ysnet.org.my*, for permission.

Listings Danum Valley Conservation Area

Where to stay

$$$$ Borneo Rainforest Lodge
97 km from Lahad Datu. Bookings via Borneo Nature Tours, Block D, Lot 10, 3rd floor, Sadong Jaya Complex, KK, T088-243245, www.borneonaturetours.com.
One of the finest tourism developments in Sabah. Designed by naturalists, the centre aims to combine a wildlife experience in a remote primary rainforest with comfort and privacy and provide high-quality natural history information. 18 bungalows in a magnificent setting beside the river, built on stilts from *belian* (ironwood) and based on traditional Kadazan design with connecting wooden walkways. The 28 rooms have private bathroom and balcony overlooking the river. Facilities include a good restaurant, jacuzzi (solar-heated water), conference hall, excellent guides, library, after-dinner slide shows and a gift shop. Rafting is available and night drives can be organized, as well as a visit to a centre for forest management. Mountain bikes, fishing rods and river tubes can be hired. Electricity is available all day. Expensive but well worth it. Price includes meals and guided jungle trips.

$ Danum Valley Field Centre
Jln Danum Valley Conservation Area, T088-326300, www.danumvalley.info.
Ostensibly a research centre and hostel for scientists and researchers visiting the valley, the Field Centre offers clean, simple rooms with cold water showers and limited electricity. Those wishing a more tropical experience, you can camp out on the walkways. There is a canteen for meals. No guide service is provided from here, though rangers will be on hand to point visitors in the right direction.

Semporna

good seafood and a jumping-off point for divers to Sipadan

Semporna is a small Bajau fishing town at the end of the peninsula and is the main departure point for Sipadan Island. It has a lively and very photogenic market, spilling out onto piers over the water, and is known for its seafood. There are scores of small fishing boats, many with outriggers and square sails, and a regatta of these traditional boats is held every March. The town is built on an old coral reef, said to be 35,000 years old, which was exposed by the uplift of the seabed.

Many illegal Filipino immigrants pass through Semporna as it is only two hours from the nearest Philippine island, which gives the place quite a different feel from that of other Malaysian towns. The town is grubby and charmless with street corners populated by gangs of lingering youths, but it's a friendly enough place.

Semporna Proboscis River Cruise

Sungai Buaya, Kampung Tunggulangan, T089-785088, daily, RM125.

A popular attraction, this daily sunset cruise takes visitors down the river in the hope of glimpsing a proboscis monkey or two, though these seem rather shy. There are plenty of macaques, fruit bats, hornbills and kingfishers to be seen along with fireflies after the sun has gone down. The trip includes a decent buffet meal at the end and is a good way to spend a tropical Semporna evening.

Fishing villages

Locals live in traditional boats called *lipa-lipa* or in pilehouses at the water's edge and survive by fishing. In the shallow channels off Semporna there are three fishing villages built on stilts: **Kampong Potok Satu**, **Kampong Potok Dua** and **Kampong Larus**.

Semporna Marine Park

Some reefs and islands, including Sibuan, Sebangkat, Maigu and Selakan, can be reached by local fishing boats from the main jetty by the market.

The islands off Semporna stand along the edge of the continental shelf, which drops away to a depth of 200 m to the south and east of **Pulau Ligitan**, the outermost island in the group. Darvel Bay and the adjacent waters are dotted with small, mainly volcanic, islands, which are all part of the 9300-ha marine park. The bigger ones are **Pulau Mabul**, **Pulau Kapalai**, **Pulau Si Amil**, **Pulau Danawan** and **Pulau Sipadan**. There are many more islands than are marked on the map; most are hilly, uninhabited and have beautiful white sandy beaches.

The reefs surrounding these islands have around 70 genera of coral, placing them, in terms of their diversity, on a par with Australia's Great Barrier Reef. More than 200 species of fish have also been recorded in these waters. Reefs in Semporna Marine Park include **Sibuan Ulaiga**, **Tetugan**, **Mantabuan Bodgaya**, **Sibuan**, **Maigu**, **Selakan**, **Sebangkat** and **Bohey Dulang**. The latter is a volcanic island with a Japanese-run pearl culture station. Visitors can only visit if there is a boat from the pearl culture station going out. The **Kaya Pearl Company** leases part of the lagoon and Japanese pearl oysters are artificially implanted with a core material to induce pearl growth. The oysters are attached to rafts moored in the lagoon. The pearls are harvested and exported direct to Japan.

Listings Semporna

Where to stay

$$ Scuba Tiger
Kampung Tampi-tampi, T019-896 6996, www.scubatiger.com.my.
A 10-min drive from town around the coast, this resort has a selection of chalets catering to divers and consequently offers a good selection of diving and accommodation packages. A good option for those wanting to stay outside Semporna.

$$ Seafest
Jln Kastam, T089-782333, www.seafesthotel.com.
This is the biggest hotel in town, and its modern façade stands somewhat out of character with the rest of the buildings. Rooms are comfortable but characterless, though front-facing ones have a great view of the bay. There's a restaurant and pool. A lack of business has forced them into offering very good walk-in promotional rates.

$$ Sipadan Inn
Block D, Lot No19-24, seafront, T089-782766, www.sipadan-inn.com.

Conveniently close to the main jetty, this modern hotel is popular with divers. It has spacious well-furnished deluxe rooms with massive TV, attached bathroom and lounge area. The smaller a/c standards are a bit of a squeeze, but comfortable and clean. Wi-Fi is fast here. Its sister hotel, **Sipadan Inn 2**, is down the road at Block B, Lot 14-11, and has slightly cheaper rooms.

$ Borneo Global Backpackers
Bangunan Seafest, Jln Causeway, T089-785088, www.bgbackpackers.com.

A bright and cheery place on the waterfront with large a/c dorms with attached bathroom or spacious family rooms. Rooms at the front have excellent views over the bay. Very clean and well managed. Arranges dive trips and packages to Sipadan and Mabul.

$ City Inn
Lot 2, Block K, Bangunan, Hing Loong, close to the Dyana Express bus office, T089-784733, www.cityinn-semporna.com.

This is probably the best budget option in town for those seeking a bed for the night. Rooms are reasonably clean with cable TV and a/c but a bit on the old side. Staff are friendly. The main drawback is its location – it's a good 5-min walk to the jetty, but handy for the bus station. Wi-Fi access in the lobby.

$ Dragon Inn
Jln Kastam (next to the jetty), T089-781088, www.dragoninnfloating com.my.

A unique budget place to stay as all the rooms are in wooden longhouses over the sea. Unfortunately much of the sea here is filled with the detritus of urban coastal life, which detracts from the charm. Some very large, well-furnished doubles and smaller twins with a/c, TV and attached bathroom. Cavernous dorms are excellent value with over 20 beds that are often empty. Great experience to have a shower and see the green ocean through the wooden slatted floor.

$ Scuba Junkie Backpacker
Block B Lot 36, seafront, T089-785372, www.scuba-junkie.com.

Opposite **Scuba Junkie's** dive shop and with a bar/restaurant attached. Good location with a variety of rooms from dorms to en suites. Excellent value with breakfast and internet included and discounts for those on SJ's dive packages. Some private rooms are a little cave-like with no windows and not always perfectly clean. Book ahead as this place is often rammed.

Restaurants

This grubby little town is no diner's fantasy, but there is some good seafood on offer and plenty of little eateries offering Malay curries. Don't leave it too late for dinner in the evening as Semporna goes to bed early.

$$ Pearl City Restaurant
Attached to the Dragon Inn hotel (see Where to stay, above).

Chinese-style seafood in a wooden restaurant over the sea. Check prices before ordering. Great setting. Recommended.

$ Fat Mother
Lot B4, seafront.

Right on the water's edge and with gorgeous views, Fat Mother gets busy in the evening and has friendly owners, quality seafood dishes and usually throws in free tea and desserts with meals.

$ Lee's Café
Next to Lee's Hotel.

This place is the best eatery in town with excellent Chinese dishes at very good prices. The prawns here are plump, the beer cold and the staff friendly. Simple Western breakfasts are available from 0700 onwards. Recommended.

$ Mabul Café
A few shops down from Scuba Junkie (see Where to stay).

Friendly service and a menu leaping between Western and Chinese fare, this place offers large portions and is justifiably famous for its mango juice.

$ Ocean Treasure Seafood
Lot C1, ground floor, seafront.
This place is owned by a dive instructor and has an outdoors terrace with sea views and a seafood menu. It is possible to buy your own fish and pay to have it cooked for you.

$ Sinar Harapan
Next to Mabul Café.
Simple Malay place with curries, noodles and *tom yam*. A friendly spot to neck a plate of *pisang goreng* on a listless tropical afternoon.

Shopping

Cultured pearls are sold by traders in town. Filipino handicrafts are also sold.

What to do

Tour operators
Today Travel Services, *No 90, Lot 2, Tingkat Bawah, T089-781112.* Sells **AirAsia** and **MAS** flights to KK and KL from Tawau, the nearest airport.

Transport

Air
The nearest airport is Tawau (see page 287). A minibus runs to the airport (RM10, though tourists are frequently asked to pay more).

Bus and minibus
The minibus station is in front of USNO HQ. There are regular connections with **Tawau** (RM14, 1½ hrs) and **Lahad Datu**. Most departures are in the morning. 1 daily bus to **Sandakan** (RM42, 6 hrs). 2 daily buses to **KK** (0730 and 1930, RM75, 11 hrs), though the mid-morning **AirAsia** flight from Tawau to KK is a better option.

★ Sipadan Island Marine Reserve

some of the world's greatest diving adventures

The venerable French marine biologist Jacques Cousteau 'discovered' Sipadan in 1989 and, after spending three months diving around the island from his research vessel, *Calypso* said: "I have seen other places like Sipadan 45 years ago, but now no more. Now we have found an untouched piece of art." Since then Sipadan has become a sub-aqua shangri-la for serious divers. It is regularly voted one of the top dive destinations in the world by leading scuba magazines. The reef is without parallel in Malaysia and the island itself is magnificent with pristine beaches and crystal-clear water.

The island's tourist facilities are run by a handful of tour companies (see What to do, page 286). In 2004, after much legal wrangling, the operators agreed to close all resort facilities on Sipadan to protect the environment. Boats can still take dive groups to the island, but numbers are limited.

Background
While Sipadan may win lots of points from dive enthusiasts, it has also been in the news for less savoury reasons. In April 2000 Abu Sayyaf, a separatist group in the Philippines, kidnapped 21 people including 10 foreign tourists from the island. Abu Sayyaf, linked to Osama bin Laden's al-Qaeda, spirited the hostages to the Philippine island of Jolo. Here they remained under guard and threat of execution while the armed forces of the Philippines tried, sometimes incompetently, to rescue them. The hostages were freed in dribs and

drabs with the final batch being released in September 2000, but it wasn't the sort of publicity that Sipadan was looking for. There is a heavy Malaysian navy presence on the island and around Semporna.

The island is disputed territory by the Indonesian and Malaysian governments. Indonesia has asked Malaysia to stop developing marine tourism facilities on Sipadan. Malaysia's claim to the island rests on historical documents signed by the British and Dutch colonial administrations. Periodically the two sides get around the negotiating table, but neither is prepared to make a big issue of Sipadan. Occasionally guests on the island see Indonesian or Malaysian warships just offshore. A third party also contests ownership of Sipadan: a Malaysian who claims his grandfather, Abdul Hamid Haji, was given the island by the Sultan of Sulu. He has the customary rights to collect turtle's eggs on the island, although the Malaysian government disputes this.

Pulau Sipadan

Pulau Sipadan is the only oceanic island in Malaysia; it is not attached to the continental shelf and stands on a limestone and coral stalk, rising 600 m from the bed of the Celebes Sea. The limestone pinnacle mushrooms out near the surface, but a few metres offshore drops off in a sheer underwater cliff to the seabed. The reef comes right into the island's small pier, allowing snorkellers to swim along the edge of the coral cliff, while remaining close to the coral-sand beach. The edge is much further out around the rest of the island. The tiny island has a cool, forested interior and it is common to see flying foxes and monitor lizards. It is also a stopover point for migratory birds, and was originally declared a bird sanctuary in 1933. It has been a marine reserve since 1981 and a large wildlife department and anti-poaching group is now permanently stationed on the island. In addition, the island is a breeding ground for the green turtle; August and September are the main egg laying months. With the exception of the beach close to the jetty, beaches now also have restricted access in order to protect turtle nesting sites.

Sipadan is known for its underwater overhangs and caverns, funnels and ledges, all of which are covered in coral. A cavern, known as the **Turtle Cave**, is located on the drop-off in front of the island's accommodation area. The cave originally acquired its fame due to turtles being encountered within the cave's depths – some of these turtles had become disorientated and died in the caves and, with the deaths of a few panicked divers, venturing far into the caverns is now reserved for experienced divers only. The island's

Essential Sipadan Island Marine Reserve

Finding your feet

Tourist permits are restricted to 120 per day (RM 40) and visitors can only be on the island 0800-1500. Tourists can stay on Mabul, Kapalai or Mataking, and these islands are likely to be developed further. As of 2013 only Advanced Open Water Divers (certified) or certified divers with 20 logged dives are allowed to dive at Sipadan due to the strong underwater currents.

When to go

The best diving season is from mid-February to mid-December when visibility is greater (20-60 m). July and August are the busiest times and visitors may find it hard to secure a permit at this time.

Tip...

Due to the limited number of permits issued, visitors are advised to book a trip at least two to three weeks in advance. Those showing up without a booking are unlikely to find a slot at short notice.

geography and location focus nutrient-rich upwellings towards the island, and in areas such as **South Point** and **Barracuda Point**, large pelagic (open sea) species such as grey reef sharks and sometimes even hammerheads are spotted.

Pulau Mabul

Located between Semporna and Sipadan, this 21-ha island is considerably larger than Sipadan and is partly home to Bajau fishermen who live in traditional palm-thatched houses. In contrast to Sipadan's untouched forest, the island is predominantly planted with coconut trees. Diving has been the most recent discovery; an Australian diver claims it is "one of the richest single destinations for exotic small marine life anywhere in the world". It has already become known as the world's best **muck diving**, so called because of the silt-filled waters and poor visibility (usually around 12 m, which is quite reasonable compared with many other places in the area). The island is surrounded by gentle sloping reefs with depths of 3-35 m and a wall housing numerous species of hard corals. Since the closure of Sipadan's resorts, several companies have moved their accommodation to Mabul, only 20 minutes away by fast boat. Places to stay at affordable backpacker budget places are available with island homestays or through Semporna tour operators (see page 282). Depending on your bargaining skills, RM100 should get you a return boat trip to the island. Bajau culture remains fairly traditional on the island and while visitors will be stared at, especially women in Western dress, people are friendly, albeit in an intense manner.

Mataking, Kapalai and Bohedulang

As a resort, **Mataking** has grown increasingly popular since the closure of Sipadan. There are about 30 good dive sites around the island including various reefs (plenty of good shallow ones, making it an ideal spot for beginner divers), a sea fan garden, a 100-m crevice called Alice Channel that runs to Pulau Sipadan and Sweet Lips Rock, a good night-diving spot. Accommodation is at the upmarket **Mataking Island Reef Dive Resort** (see Where to stay, below).

Kapalai is a sandbar, heavily eroded and set on top of Ligitan Reefs between Sipadan and Mabul. Semporna tour operators take people diving in Sipadan and in the shallow waters around Kapalai. Accommodation is available in the stilted **Sipadan-Kapalai Dive Resort** (see page 286), which straddles the sandbar.

Bohedulang is a volcanic, mountainous island east of Semporna, reminiscent of many Thai islands in the Andaman Sea. You pass its thickly forested slopes if heading for dive sites or resorts at Mataking, Bohayan or Mantabuan. The area is exceptionally beautiful above and below the waves.

Listings Sipadan Island Marine Resort

Where to stay

Mabul

Visitors intending to dive at Sipadan need to ensure they book diving packages early enough for the resort to obtain a Sipadan diving license.

As all Sipadan resorts are closed, Mabul Island is a convenient place to stay. There are several resorts here, plus some cheaper options. Food is often included in the price.

$$$$ Mabul Water Bungalows
Book via Explore Asia Tours, Lot A-1-G, Block A, Signature Office, KK Times Square, off the Coastal Highway, T088-486389, www.mabulwaterbungalows.com.
A pricey and luxurious resort built on stilts above the Mabul reef. Dive packages and

facilities including nitrox and cave diving are available. A good choice for people who want all their home comforts, with cable TV, minibar, a/c and business centre with internet access.

$$$ Borneo Divers Mabul Resort
Head Office, 9th floor, Menara Jubili, 53 Jln Gaya, KK, T088-222226, www.borneodivers. info. There's also a small office just outside the entrance to Dragon Inn next to Uncle Chang's (see below).
This is a mid-range offering which includes meals. It's not particularly stylish, but it's decent value and faces the beach and Seaventures platform, with a pool and all diving facilities.

$$$ Seaventures Dive Resort
Run by Sea Ventures Dives, 4th floor 422-423, Wisma Sabah, KK, T088-251669, www.seaventuresdive.com.
Just offshore is the strange site of a refurbished oil rig, which has been converted into accommodation including a family room, twin/double rooms and a dorm. It offers boat dives to Sipadan and other nearby islands and is locally famous for its excellent muck diving directly beneath the platform. Good value and an exciting location for divers who enjoy macrolife and underwater photography.

$$$ Sipadan Mabul Resort
Same contact details as Mabul Water Bungalows (see above).
At the southern tip of the island overlooking Sipadan and a pleasant beach. 25 beach chalets with a/c, hot-water showers, balcony, pool and jacuzzi, restaurant serving Chinese and Western buffet food, all-inclusive price, PADI diving courses, snorkelling, windsurfing, deep-sea fishing, volleyball, diving boats.

$$$ Sipadan Water Village
Reservations: PO Box 62156, T089-751777, www.sipadan-village.com.my.
Constructed on several wharves in Bajau, the water village-style resort sits on ironwood

stilts over the sea. Facilities include 45 chalets with private balconies, hot-water showers, restaurant, well-organized dive shop and deep-sea fishing tours. 3 daily boat dives are usually included in packages and there's quite a bit of marine life on the house reef directly below the resort. A relaxing, tranquil place with unforgettable views.

$$ Scuba Junkie Mabul
www.scuba-junkie.com.
A newly opened resort with 24 en suite rooms next to the water. Rooms are simple, comfortable, spacious and each has a private balcony. There's a good restaurant and bar area for sharing tales and beers into the wee hours. Accommodation discounts for divers.

$ pp Uncle Chang's
T017-897 0002, www.ucsipadan.com.
Another good backpacker option, located in the Bajau village on the far side of Mabul Island with rooms standing on stilts over the sea. Rates include food and Uncle Chang has all the diving kit, plus years of experience above and below the waves in the region. A brilliant place to experience the sunset over the Celebes Sea.

Mataking and Kapalai

$$$$ Mataking Island Reef Dive Resort
Reservations at Jln Bunga, Tawau, T089-770022, www.mataking.com. Also has a counter in Semporna at the jetty on Jln Kastam.
The resort has 3 speedboats daily from the Semporna jetty and the journey takes 45 mins. The resort has a/c chalets and deluxe rooms, some with sea view and balcony. Facilities at the resort include a *jammu* (native medicinal) spa, satellite TV, internet, bar and restaurant. In 2006 the resort sank an old cargo boat and renamed it the *Mataking 1*, with the hopes that this will encourage a new reef to grow. The wreck is home to an underwater post office – postcards are placed in a special plastic bag and receive a waterproof rubber stamp.

\$\$\$\$ Sipadan-Kapalai Dive Resort
Run by Pulau Sipadan Resort & Tours,
1st floor, 484 Bandar Sabindo, Tawau,
T089-765200, www.sipadan-kapalai.com.
This resort straddles Kapalai's sandbank
on stilts and is modelled as a water village.
The 40 twin-sharing wooden chalets,
with attached bathrooms and balconies,
have amazing sea views from every angle.
Chalets are linked by a network of wooden
platforms. Dive centre, internet access.

What to do

Tour operators

Most dive centres offer PADI courses.
Each operator arranges permits, rents out
equipment (RM80-100 per day) and provides
all food and accommodation. Pre-arranged
packages operated by the companies
sometimes include air transfer to and from
Kota Kinabalu. Walk-in rates are cheaper.
Book trips to Sipadan well in advance as only
120 permits are issued daily.
Borneo Divers, *Rooms 401-412, 4th floor,*
Wisma Sabah, KK, T088-222226, www.borneo
divers.info. A major Sipadan player; it
organizes trips from KK to Sipadan with
accommodation on Mabul. A 3-day
package with accommodation, 9 guided
dives and unlimited dives on their house
reef costs RM1800.
Pulau Sipadan Resort, *484, Block P,*
Bandar Sabindo, Tawau, T089-765200,
www.sipadan-resort.com. Organizes dive
tours and instruction, food and lodging,
snorkelling equipment is also available,
maximum of 30 divers at any one time. It
also runs accommodation on Pulau Kapalai.

Scuba Junkie, *Blk B, Lot 36, Semporna*
seafront, T089-785372, www.scuba-junkie.com.
Well-run outfit that offers a variety of courses
and trips to Mataking, Sipadan, Kapalai and
Mabul. Accommodation on Mabul available.
4-day/3-night dive package to Sipadan
costs RM2280. A 3-dive trip to Sipadan costs
RM350. Snorkelling to outer islands and night
dives also arranged.
Sipadan Dive Centre, *Lot A1026, 10th floor*
Wisma Jln Tun Razak, KK, T088-240584, www.
sdclodges.com. All-inclusive 3-day/2-night
packages cost approximately RM1045 in a
chalet and RM885 in a dorm. Recommended.
Uncle Chang's, *entrance to Dragon Inn,*
Semporna, T089-781002, www.ucsipadan.com.
Uncle Chang, entrepreneur extraordinaire,
offers the budget traveller everything. He can
get discount bus tickets, offers shuttle service
to the airport, gets discounts for the **Dragon
Inn**, has an efficient laundry service and runs
some great dive trips out to Sipadan including
courses. 3 boat dives including all equipment
hire and lunch for RM750 Snorkelling day
trips to Siamil (RM180) and Mabul (RM110),
plus night diving at Mabul. Excellent-value
accommodation on Mabul. Recommended.

Transport

Mataking and Kapalai
Air and boat

The nearest airport is **Tawau**. Take a minibus,
taxi or resort van to **Semporna** (1½ hrs), from
where speed boats depart for the islands
(30-60 mins). Boats are run either by dive
companies or as a transfer to a resort. Lots
of boats leave daily but generally only in
the morning at around 0730, for day trips
(around RM150).

Tawau is a timber port in Sabah's southeastern corner. It is a busy commercial centre and the main entry point of Indonesian workers into Sabah. A great contrast to the newly built hotel and business area, the waterfront has plenty of colourful markets and foodstalls and some picturesque views across the bay towards Kalimantan. In the last few years Tawau has begun to develop rapidly as a regional hub of transport and commerce. Tawau centre has been tidied up and has a few decent hotels and restaurants. The town has wide, clean streets and an air of prosperity not seen in many other Sabahan towns.

The town was developed in the early 19th century by the British who planted hemp. The British also developed the logging industry in Sabah using elephants from Burma. The **Bombay Burma Timber Company** became the **North Borneo Timber Company** in 1950, a joint British and Sabahan government venture.

Tawau is surrounded by plantations and smallholdings of rubber, copra, cocoa and palm oil. The local soils are volcanic and very fertile and palm oil has taken over from cocoa as the predominant crop. Malaysian cocoa prices dropped when its quality proved to be 20% poorer than cocoa produced in Nigeria and the Ivory Coast and this, coupled with disease outbreaks in the crop, caused many of the cocoa growers to emigrate to the Ivory Coast. Now that the Sandakan area has been almost completely logged, Tawau has taken over as the main logging centre on the east coast. The forest is disappearing fast but there are some reforestation programmes. At **Kalabakan**, west of Tawau, there is a well-established, large-scale reforestation project with experiments on fast-growing trees such as *Albizzia falcataria*, said to grow 30 m in five years. There are now large plantation areas. The tree is processed into, among other things, paper for making money.

To Kalimantan

With a couple of days' notice you can obtain a 60-day Indonesian visa and cross into eastern Kalimantan. As with many sections of Indonesian Borneo, transport is poor and very few Westerners make this journey; of those that do, a large proportion head for pre-booked and exclusive diving operations off the coast. Although mud logging tracks exist on the Indonesian side of Sebuku Bay, most people usually find boat transport to the Indonesian towns of Nunukan and Tarakan further south much more comfortable and efficient.

Tawau Hills State Park

24 km northwest of Tawau. Contact the Ranger Office, Tawau Hills Park, T089-810676, 0700-1800, RM10. A taxi from Tawau costs

Essential Tawau

Finding your feet

The airport is 33 km east of Tawau and has regular connections with KK, Sandakan, KL and Tarakan (Kalimantan). Shuttle buses run into town every two hours (RM10) or there are fixed-price taxis (RM45). Many travellers heading for Semporna and the islands now fly directly to Tawau.

Tawau has regular ferry connections with Kalimantan in Indonesia. It's also possible to drive from Sapulut (south of Keningau) across the interior to Tawau on logging roads (4WD vehicle is required, seven hours). A new road between Keningau and Tawau is under construction. There is currently no public transport along this route.

RM30 one-way. There is no public transport to the park, so it's best to arrange for a return trip with the taxi driver.

This park protects Tawau's water catchment area. The Tawau River flows through the middle of the 27,972-ha park and forms a natural deep-water pool, at **Table Waterfall**, which is good for swimming. There is a trail from there to hot springs and another to the top of **Bombalai Hill**, an extinct volcano. Most of the forest in the park below 500 m has been logged; only the forest on the central hills and ridges is untouched. The park is popular with locals at weekends. Camping is possible but bring your own equipment. Access to the park is via a maze of rough roads through the **Borneo Abaca Limited** agricultural estates.

Listings Tawau

Where to stay

Rock-bottom places in Tawau are generally grim and visitors are advised to spend a few more ringgit to get somewhere safe and clean. There are a number of mid-range places aimed at local business travellers which have good-value walk-in rates. Hotels are concentrated around the intersection of Jln Bunga and Jln Haji Karim.

$$ Belmont Marco Polo
Jln Abaca/Jln Clinic, T089-777988.
Upmarket though somewhat dated hotel primarily aimed at business travellers, but offering great walk-in promotional rates. Rooms are clean and feature cable TV, Wi-Fi access, and rather stiff, formal furnishings. Bathrooms have bathtubs. There's also a health centre, café and good Chinese restaurant.

$$ Heritage
Jln Bunga, Fajar Complex, T089-766222, www.heritagehotel.com.my.
Well-managed hotel with basic rooms with sofas and complimentary daily newspapers. More expensive rooms have bathtubs, free Wi-Fi access and jacuzzi.

$$ King Park
30 Jln Haji Karim, T089-766699, www.tawau.kingparkhotel.com.my.
Fair mid-range option with 100 clean rooms in a mint-green tower block overlooking the city. Rooms at the front have views of the sea in the distance. All rooms have cable TV, a/c, attached bathroom and Wi-Fi access. Good promotional rates.

$$ LA Hotel
MPT 299, Jln St Patrick, off Jln Belunu, T089-762299, www.lahotel.com.my.
Excellent-value hotel in the heart of town with contemporary rooms with all mod cons and a rooftop café serving a variety of Asian and Western fare. Rooms on the higher floors have sea views.

$$ MB
Jln Masjid, T089-701333.
Limited in character but with all the facilities needed for a moderately comfortable stay. Good promotional rates. Some rooms smell better than others, so ask to see a selection. Recommended.

$$ Monaco
214 Jln Haji Karim (on the corner of Jln Bunga), T089-769912.
Carpeted a/c rooms (some windowless) with Wi-Fi access, cable TV and attached bathroom. Staff are friendly and rooms on the corner have good views over the rooftops to the hills surrounding Tawau. This hotel is run by the same groups that runs the **Monaco Dynasty Hotel ($$)** and **Istana Monaco Hotel ($$)**, opposite on Jln Bunga. All 3 hotels have similar facilities, but the **Istana** has the newest rooms. Rooms at the **Dynasty** are looking a little tatty and are mostly windowless.

$$ My Inn Hotel
TB254, A/B Block, 25 Jln Dunlop, T089-736699, www.myinnhotel.com.
Another sterile but safe offering from this business hotel chain. Rooms are clean and tidy but not bursting with atmosphere. Nevertheless, this hotel represents excellent value for money.

$ VS Guesthouse
TB1194, Jln Stephen Tan, T014-671 1610.
Popular with Indonesian visitors, this is the best of the bunch in Tawau's budget accommodation choices with clean functional rooms with fast Wi-Fi and cheerful staff.

Restaurants

There are foodstalls along the seafront.

$$ Dreamland Coffee House
4497 Ba Zhong Commercial Centre (in a complex of Jln Persisaran).
Popular and informal grill serving up a good blend of Western and Asian staples. Try the lobster thermidor and the *sago gula Melaka* for a true fusion meal. Head here on Sun for their famed Sunday Curry Set Lunch.

$$ Kam Ling Seafood
25 Sabindo Square.
Delicious fresh seafood including crab and huge prawns. The fresh lime juice here is excellent. Very popular.

$$ Maxim's Seafood Restaurant
Jln Barui, T089-771800.
Excellent Chinese fare at very reasonable prices and well regarded in Tawau for its seafood offerings. Diners rave about the prawns in butter sauce and the local vegetables cooked with *sambal belacan* (spicy shrimp paste). Don't be put off by the formal Chinese vibes and the uniformed waiters – just get stuck in, like the locals.

$ Dragon Court
1st floor, Lot 15, Block 37 Jln Haji Karim.
Chinese, popular with locals, lots of seafood and noodles with spicy condiments.

$ Olive Bistro
Lot 4, Jln Masjid. Open 1100-1430 and 1800-2230.
Family-oriented eatery serving glasses of red wine, cold beer and a menu of pizza, tapas and pasta dishes. Don't expect the real deal with these prices, but not a bad spot nevertheless.

$ Tawau Citi Café
TB101 Jln Abaca, T089-757888.
The food is not bad (they do a good chicken soup) but the real reason to come here is that it's one of few places in Tawau you can sit outside and enjoy an ice-cold beer.

$ Yasmin
Jln Chester.
Excellent selection of *nasi campur* dishes served with an interesting cinnamon-infused chicken soup.

$ Yassin Curry House
Sabindo Square (near the minibus terminal).
Biryani, tandoori chicken, kebabs and outrageously sweet lassis, 10 mins' walk from the town centre. A/c seating.

$ Yun Lo
Jln Abaca (below the Hotel Loong).
Good Malay and Chinese. A popular spot with locals, good atmosphere. Recommended.

Entertainment

Cinema (Jln Stephen Tan, next to central market). There are **karaoke** bars on every street corner. Several hotels have nightclubs and bars.

Shopping

There's a general market and fish market at the west end of Jln Dunlop, near the customs wharf.

What to do

Diving

Pulau Sipadan Resort & Tours, *1st floor, Bandar Sabindo, Tawau, T089-765200.*
Reef Dive Resort and Tours, *Jln Bunga, T089-770022, www.mataking.com.* Arranges packages to the upmarket **Reef Dive Resort** on Mataking.

Golf

Shan Shui Golf & Country Resort, *9th Mile, Apas Rd, T089-916888, www.shanshuigolf.com.* An award-winning course designed by Nelson and Haworth, noted for its 15th hole. Course fees from RM150 for 18 holes.

Transport

Air

To get to the airport take a taxi (RM45) or shuttle bus (RM10). There are regular connections with **MAS** (Airport Terminal Building, T089-950 191) and **AirAsia** (office at the airport) to **KK** and **KL** and **MASwings** to **KK**, **Sandakan** and **Tarakan** in Kalimantan (Indonesia).

Boat

Packed boats leave Tawau's customs wharf (behind Pasar Ikan) for Pulau Nunukan Timur and Tarakan, in **Kalimantan** (Indonesia). All visitors need to get an Indonesian visa in advance as these are not visa-free entry points (you can get one fairly painlessly at the consulate in Tawau). Tickets are available from offices near the Pasar Ikan (fish market). Agents include **Saumdera Indah**, T089-753320.

To **Pulau Nunukan Timur**, boats leave twice daily at 1000 and 1500 (RM75, 1 hr). There is limited onward transport available from Nunukan, and travellers will need to travel to Tarakan for more options (there are daily **Kal Star** and **Susi Air** flights from Nunukan to Tarakan www.kalstaronline.com, www.fly.susiair.com). Nunukan is connected to Pare Pare, **Pantoloan**, by **PELNI** ferry.

More convenient is the boat to **Tarakan** (Mon, Wed, Fri at 1130 and Tue, Thu, Sat at 1030, RM140, 4 hrs). Tarakan is connected to **Balikpapan** and **Surabaya** by air with **Toli Toli Surabaya**, and **Jakarta** with **PELNI** ferry.

PELNI ferries in Indonesia generally call in every 2 weeks. Travellers wishing to catch a ferry should time their arrival in Nunukan or Tarakan to meet the ferry. Schedules are available at www.pelni.co.id.

Bus and minibus

The bus station is on Jln Wing Lock, at the west end of town. The minibus station is on Jln Dunlop (centre of town). There is a direct overnight service from Tawau to **KK**, leaving at 2000 to arrive 0500 (RM71.50). A better option is to take the mid-morning flight to KK on **AirAsia**, from RM70. Minibuses to **Semporna** leave when full from the Sabindo Complex (RM13, 1½ hrs).

Maliau Basin Conservation Area
a lost world of untouched jungle and incredible biodiversity

In the rugged forest-clad hills in Sabah's heart lies an area known as Sabah's Lost World. Covering an area of 390 sq km, the Maliau Basin is one of the state's last areas of primary rainforest largely unaffected by agriculture or large-scale logging. It has remained undisturbed partly due to the difficulty of access and the geography of the basin. From the air, it looks like a vast meteor crater, measuring up to 25 km in diameter and surrounded by steep cliffs up to 1700 m in height on all but the southern and southeastern sides. Scientists believe that the crater was made through sedimentary forces over 15 million years ago, combined with major geological shifts, creating more than 30 spectacular waterfalls in the valley.

Essential Maliau Basin

Finding your feet

There isn't much public transport to Maliau; however, due to road improvements this may change in the near future. If you don't have your own transport you can arrange to hire a 4WD and driver through the Maliau Basin Conservation Area organization (www.maliaubasin.org). Vehicles can carry up to five people and their gear. The return four- to five-hour trip to the basin from either Tawau or Keningau (on the west coast) will cost upwards of RM900 per vehicle.

Getting around

Most visitors book an all-inclusive package through an agency such as **Borneo Nature Tours**, www.borneonaturetours.com. A five-day/four-night all-inclusive trekking package costs in the region of RM3610 based on a group of two people with prices

dropping per person as the group size increases. Each trip is individually tailored to match trekkers' needs.

If you prefer to organize your visit semi-independently, **Yayasan Sabah Group** (see below) which runs the park, can arrange an itinerary including accommodation, guides and permits. Expect to spend around RM2500 for a three-night stay (including two nights sleeping at satellite camps and one in the resthouse at Agathis Camp), including transport. Porters are also available.

Park information

Access to the basin is strictly controlled and entry permits must be arranged in advance from Conservation and Environmental Management Division of **Yayasan Sabah Group**, PO Box 11622, T088-326300, http://maliaubasin.org. The website has details of essentials to bring.

Granted government protection in the late 1990s and subject to growing scientific interest, Maliau finally opened its doors to the public in 2011 when the **Maliau Basin Studies Centre** opened. This is an excellent first port of call. There is a resthouse complex with 14 rooms, a hostel with 62 beds and a café and exhibition centre. There is rudimentary accommodation at various research camps in the park which varies from tents to hostel-style accommodation with hammocks.

Flora and fauna

Maliau Basin is an area of incredible biodiversity featuring areas of lowland rainforest, heath forests and oak conifer, with cloud forests on the higher elevations. With over 1800 species of plant being recorded here, including 80 species of orchid, it is also only one of two sites in Sabah to have the rare rafflesia.

For wildlife watchers the park contains the full range of Bornean mammals, with animals such as the sun bear (see box, page 292), clouded leopard, Bornean gibbon, proboscis monkey and orang-utan being recorded in the park. These and other wildlife like the rare banteng (Asian wild cattle), elephant and pangolin are sometimes spotted on night safaris. However, it's unlikely you'll ever be lucky enough to spot the rarest resident, the secretive Sumatran rhino, which is on the verge of extinction (see box, page 277). There are also nearly 300 species of bird. After the rains this area becomes packed with leeches, so specialized leech socks are a good investment.

Trekking

A network of trails linking a series of comfortable but basic scientific camps provides some of the best, and toughest, trekking in northern Borneo. The treks pass numerous

WILDLIFE
It's a bear's life

The least studied and understood of all the bears, the Malayan sun bear or honey bear has differing names in the scientific community. The largest potentially carnivorous mammal in Borneo, sun bears are nevertheless the smallest of the world's eight bear species. A male sun bear weighs up to 65 kg, the female up to 50 kg, and bears are covered in short black fur, except for a yellow chest patch, unique to each bear in shape. It roams the dense forests of Southeast Asia, from Assam in India to southern China and the lush islands of Sumatra and Borneo.

Using outsized claws tailored for an arboreal lifestyle, sun bears are excellent climbers, sometimes reaching up to 50 m in the forest canopy in search of food as diverse as palm hearts, termites, birds, small mammals, eggs and wild honey, which they love, lapping it up with their 20-cm-long tongues. Bears often use their long claws like safety hooks to sleep high in the branches. Rare to see on the forest floor, sun bears are quite aggressive if cornered or startled, and with poor eyesight, they have been known to charge. If you're lucky enough to find a bear in the forest, it would be advisable to back away quietly while facing the bear, keeping as calm as possible. Remember, this is the bear's territory, not yours.

Massive forest destruction in southern Asia means that the habitat of sun bears is under threat. Bears are widely hunted for their body parts, for use in traditional medicines; claws, gall bladders and other bones are found in markets throughout China and Southeast Asia. Sun bears are also illegally exported and farmed for their bile which is used in traditional medicines across Asia. The sun bear is classified as vulnerable and is facing a grim future due to continued deforestation of its habitat and continued poaching. It is estimated that the population of the sun bear has declined by over 30% over the past three bear generations.Bears also face competition from other predators – pythons and crocodiles in Borneo sometimes hunt bears and in mainland Asia they share a shrinking habitat with tigers and leopards, plus Asian black bears and sloth bears in Eastern India.

To protect bears, follow these rules:

- Never buy bear products in markets. In many countries (including Malaysia, Brunei and Indonesia) this is illegal. If you see these products, report them to the local authorities.
- Support projects to protect the rainforest and its habitat. WWF's Heart of Borneo programme aims to protect and conserve national parks and Borneo's most valuable forest areas. See www.panda.org for more information.
- Support environmentally sustainable ecotourism projects by visiting and perhaps volunteering to protect or replant forest areas.
- Encourage local people to become involved in ecotourism or forest-friendly industries. Hiring local and especially indigenous guides such as those from Kelabit, Penan and Iban tribal groups helps both the people and the forest.
- If you have to buy wooden products, choose sustainably produced forest products such as those certified by the FSC (Forest Stewardship Council).
- The US-based Rainforest Action Network, www.ran.org, is another good source of information.

spectacular waterfalls, including the famous multi-tiered **Maliau Falls** and **Takob Akob Falls**, over 38 m high. If you're lucky with the weather you should get some panoramic views of the conservation area from the ridge tops.

To make the most of the conservation area's facilities, a trek of a minimum five days and four nights is recommended. For truly serious trekkers and those with lots of time (and money) it may be possible to arrange a two-week expedition to **Strike Ridge Camp** in the north of the basin. As well as trek-based activities there's also a canopy walkway at **Belian Camp** and an observation platform, 30 m up a huge primary forest tree close to **Camel Trophy Camp**. This is a suggested basic five-day circuit, covering 30 km:

Day 1 Arrive at **Agathis Camp**, on the southern edge of the conservation area, about 20 km north of the security gate. Keep your eyes open for wildlife along the road and get some rest for a tough trek the next day.

Day 2 There's a tough climb uphill for a few hours through magnificent primary forest to the ridge top bordering Maliau's southern edge. Gibbons are often heard calling in forest here, a beautiful, emotional sound that encapsulates the spirit of the jungle. The 7-km-long trail leads to the basic **Camel Trophy Camp**. Behind is the 33-m-high observation tower in an Agathis tree. Additional trails lead to the spectacular **Takob Akob Falls**, two hours' walk away, and the nearer **Giluk Falls**. Don't underestimate the hikes after the initial six hours. This is a wildlife-rich area worthy of time and exploration. **Note** Watch out for poisonous red centipedes.

Day 3 A big day. You hike over highlands, mist-clad montane forest and stunted heathlands. These areas are crammed with orchids and pitcher plants, a botanist's dream. A five-hour walk takes you to **Lobah Camp**. From here, you can get to **Maliau Falls**, another few hours' return hike to the spectacular multi-level cascade.

Day 4 Take a break to enjoy the forest and the falls. A couple of hours' walk to **Ginseng Camp**.

Day 5 Another six- to eight-hour hike brings you back to your starting point, **Agathis Camp**, a good spot for a night hike or a drive to spot some wildlife. Civets, pangolins, small cats and deer are often spotted. You can even get a certificate to state that you've completed the circuit.

Listings Maliau Basin

Where to stay

$$-$ Maliau Basin Studies Centre
Book through Borneo Nature Tours (usually as part of a package), Block D, Ground Floor, Lot 10, Sadong Jaya Complex, KK, T088-267637, www.borneonaturetours.com.

Simple twin and double rooms with a/c and fan, hot water showers in the resthouse and dorm beds with cold water showers in the hostel.

$ pp Maliau Basin camps
Basic dorms, beds must be booked in advance due to limited availability. Camps generally have 20-40 beds.

Background

The name Sabah is probably from the Arabic *Zir-e Bad* (the land below the wind). This is appropriate, as the state lies just south of the typhoon belt. Officially, the territory has only been called Sabah since 1963, when it joined the Malay federation, but the name appears to have been in use long before that. When Baron Gustav Von Overbeck was awarded the cession rights to North Borneo by the Sultan of Brunei in 1877, one of the titles conferred on him was Maharajah of Sabah. In the *Handbook of British North Borneo*, published in 1890, it says: "In Darvel Bay there are the remnants of a tribe which seems to have been much more plentiful in bygone days – the Sabahans". From the founding of the Chartered Company until 1963, Sabah was British North Borneo.

Sabah has a population of just over 3.5 million. Sabah's inhabitants can be divided into four main groups: the Kadazan Dusun, the Bajau, the Chinese and the Murut, as well as a small Malay population. These groups are subdivided into several different tribes (see page 299). Around 25% of the population of Sabah are non-Malaysian citizens, predominately from Indonesia and the Philippines.

History

Prehistoric stone tools have been found in eastern Sabah, suggesting that people were living in limestone caves in the Madai area 17,000-20,000 years ago. The caves were periodically settled from then on; pottery dating from the late Neolithic period has been found, and by the early years of the first millennium AD, Madai's inhabitants were making iron spears and decorated pottery. The Madai and Baturong caves were lived in continuously until about the 16th century and several carved stone coffins and burial jars have been discovered in the jungle caves, one of which is exhibited in the Sabah State Museum. The caves were also known for their birds' nests; Chinese traders were buying the nests from Borneo as far back as AD 700. In addition, they exported camphor wood, pepper and other forest products to Imperial China.

There are very few archaeological records indicating Sabah's early history, although there is documentary evidence of links between a long-lost kingdom, based in the area of the Kinabatangan River, and the Sultanate of Brunei, whose suzerainty was once most of North Borneo. By the early 18th century, Brunei's power had begun to wane in the face of European expansionism. To counter the economic decline, it is thought the sultan increased taxation, which led to civil unrest. In 1704 the Sultan of Brunei had to ask the Sultan of Sulu's help in putting down a rebellion in Sabah and, in return, the Sultan of Sulu received most of what is now Sabah.

The would-be White Rajahs of Sabah

It was not until 1846 that the British entered into a treaty with the Sultan of Brunei and took possession of the island of Labuan, in part to counter the growing influence of the Rajah of Sarawak, James Brooke. The British were also wary of the Americans; the US Navy signed a trade treaty with the Sultan of Brunei in 1845 and in 1860 Claude Lee Moses was appointed American consul-general in Brunei Town. However, he was only interested in making a personal fortune and quickly persuaded the sultan to cede him land in Sabah. He sold these rights to two Hong Kong-based American businessmen who formed the

American Trading Company of Borneo. They styled themselves as rajahs and set up a base at Kimanis, just south of Papar. It was a disaster. One of them died of malaria, the Chinese labourers they imported from Hong Kong began to starve and the settlement was abandoned in 1866.

The idea of a trading colony on the North Borneo coast interested the Austrian consul in Hong Kong, Baron Gustav von Overbeck, who, in turn, sold the concept to Alfred Dent, a wealthy English businessman also based in Hong Kong. With Dent's money, Overbeck bought the Americans' cession from the Sultan of Brunei and extended the territory to cover most of modern-day Sabah. The deal was clinched on 29 December 1877, and Overbeck agreed to pay the sultan 15,000 Straits dollars a year. A few days later Overbeck discovered that the entire area had already been ceded to the Sultan of Sulu 173 years earlier, so he immediately sailed to Sulu and offered the sultan an annual payment of 5000 Straits dollars for the territory. On his return, he dropped three Englishmen off along the coast to set up trading posts; one of them was William Pryer, who founded Sandakan (see page 255). Three years later, Queen Victoria granted Dent a royal charter and, to the chagrin of the Dutch, the Spanish and the Americans, the British North Borneo Company was formed. London insisted that it was to be a British-only enterprise however, and Overbeck was forced to sell out. The first managing director of the company was the Scottish adventurer and former gunrunner William C Cowie. He was in charge of the day-to-day operations of the territory, while the British government supplied a governor.

The new chartered company, with its headquarters in the City of London, was given sovereignty over Sabah and a free hand to develop it. The British administrators soon began to collect taxes from local people and quickly clashed with members of the Brunei nobility. John Whitehead, a British administrator, wrote: "I must say, it seemed rather hard on these people that they should be allowed to surrender up their goods and chattels to swell even indirectly the revenue of the company". The administration levied poll tax, boat tax, land tax, fishing tax, rice tax, *tapai* (rice wine) tax and a 10% tax on proceeds from the sale of birds' nests. Resentment against these taxes sparked the six-year Mat Salleh rebellion (see box, page 193) and the Rundum Rebellion, which peaked in 1915, during which hundreds of Muruts were killed by the British.

Relations were not helped by colonial attitudes towards the local Malays and tribal people. One particularly arrogant district officer, Charles Bruce, wrote: "The mind of the average native is equivalent to that of a child of four. So long as one remembers that the native is essentially a child and treats him accordingly he is really tractable." Most recruits to the chartered company administration were fresh-faced graduates from British universities, mainly Oxford and Cambridge. For much of the time there were only 40-50 officials running the country. Besides the government officials, there were planters and businessmen: tobacco, rubber and timber became the most important exports. There were also Anglican and Roman Catholic missionaries. British North Borneo was never much of a money-spinner – the economy suffered whenever commodity prices slumped – but it mostly managed to pay for itself until the Second World War.

The Japanese interregnum

Sabah became part of Dai Nippon, or Greater Japan, on New Year's Day 1942, when the Japanese took Labuan. On the mainland, the Japanese Imperial Army and Kempetai (military police) were faced with the might of the North Borneo Armed Constabulary, about 650 men. Jesselton (Kota Kinabalu) was occupied on 9 January and Sandakan

BACKGROUND
The Borneo Death March

The four years of Japanese occupation ended when the Australian ninth division liberated British North Borneo. Sandakan was chosen by the Japanese as a regional centre for holding Allied prisoners. In 1942 the Japanese shipped 2750 prisoners of war (2000 of whom were Australian and 750 British) to Sandakan from Changi Prison, Singapore. A further 800 British and 500 Australian POWs arrived in 1944. They were ordered to build an airfield (on the site of the present airport) and were forced to work from dawn to dusk. Many died, but in September 1944 2400 POWs were force-marched to Ranau, a 240-km trek through the jungle which only six Australians survived. This 'Death March', although not widely reported in Second World War literature, claimed more Australian lives than any other single event during the war in Asia, including the building of the notorious Burma-Siam railway.

For more information on the march, including details of sensitive tours and walks take a look at www.sandakan-deathmarch.com.

10 days later. All Europeans were interned and when Singapore fell in 1942, 2740 prisoners of war were moved to Sandakan, most of whom were Australian, where they were forced to build an airstrip. On its completion, the POWs were ordered to march to Ranau, 240 km through the jungle. This became known as the Borneo Death March and only six men survived (see box, above).

The Japanese were hated in Sabah and the Chinese mounted a resistance movement which was led by the Kuching-born Albert Kwok Hing Nam. He also recruited Bajaus and Sulus to join his guerrilla force which launched the Double Tenth Rebellion (the attacks took place on 10 October 1943). The guerrillas took Tuaran, Jesselton and Kota Belud, killing many Japanese and sending others fleeing into the jungle. But the following day the Japanese bombed the towns and troops quickly retook them and captured the rebels. A mass execution followed in which 175 rebels were decapitated. On 10 June 1945 Australian forces landed at Labuan, under the command of American General MacArthur. Allied planes bombed the main towns and virtually obliterated Jesselton and Sandakan. Sabah was liberated on 9 September and thousands of the remaining 21,000 Japanese troops were killed in retaliation, many by Muruts.

A British military administration governed Sabah in the aftermath of the war and the cash-strapped chartered company sold the territory to the British crown for £1.4 million in 1946. The new crown colony was modelled on the chartered company's administration and rebuilt the main towns and war-shattered infrastructure. In May 1961, following Malaysian independence, Prime Minister Tunku Abdul Rahman proposed the formation of a federation incorporating Malaya (ie Peninsular Malaysia), Singapore, Brunei, Sabah and Sarawak. Later that same year, Tun Fuad Stephens, a timber magnate and newspaper publisher formed Sabah's first-ever political party, the United National Kadazan Organization (UNKO). Two other parties were founded soon afterwards: the Sabah Chinese Association and the United Sabah National Organization (USNO). The British were keen to leave the colony and the Sabahan parties debated the pros and cons of joining the proposed federation. Elections were held in late 1962 in which a UNKO-USNO alliance (the Sabah Alliance) swept to power and the following August Sabah became an independent country ... for 16 days. Like Singapore and Sarawak, Sabah opted to join the federation to the indignation of the Philippines and Indonesia who both had claims on the territory. Jakarta's objections resulted in the Konfrontasi, an undeclared war with Malaysia (see page 130) that was not settled until 1966.

Modern Sabah

Politics

Sabah's political scene has always been lively and never more so than in 1994 when the then Malaysian prime minister, Doctor Mahathir Mohamad, pulled off what commentators described as a democratic coup d'état. With great political dexterity, he out-manoeuvred his rebellious rivals and managed to dislodge the opposition state government, despite the fact that it had just won a state election.

Following Sabah's first state election in 1967, the Sabah Alliance ruled until 1975 when the newly formed multi-racial party, Berjaya, swept the polls. Berjaya had been set up with the financial backing of the United Malays National Organization (UMNO), the mainstay of the ruling Barisan Nasional (National Front) coalition on the peninsula. Over the following decade that corrupt administration crumbled and in 1985 the opposition Sabah United Party (PBS), led by the Christian Kadazan Datuk Joseph Pairin Kitingan, won a landslide victory and became the only state government in Malaysia that did not belong to the UMNO-led coalition. It became an obvious embarrassment to then Prime Minister Doctor Mahathir Mohamad to have a rebel Christian state in his predominantly Muslim federation. Nonetheless, the PBS eventually joined Barisan Nasional, believing its partnership in the coalition would help iron things out. It did not.

When the PBS came to power, the federal government and Sabahan opposition parties openly courted Filipino and Indonesian immigrants in the state, almost all of whom are Muslim, and secured identity cards for many of them, enabling them to vote. Doctor Mahathir has made no secret of his preference for a Muslim government in Sabah. Nothing, however, was able to dislodge the PBS, which was resoundingly returned to power in 1990. The federal government had long been suspicious of Sabahan politicians, particularly following the PBS's defection from Doctor Mahathir's coalition in the run-up to the 1990 general election, a move which bolstered the opposition alliance. Doctor Mahathir described this as "a stab in the back", and referred to Sabah as "a thorn in the flesh of the Malaysian federation". But in the event, the prime minister won the national election convincingly without PBS help, prompting fears of political retaliation. Those fears proved justified in the wake of the election.

Sabah paid heavily for its 'disloyalty'; prominent Sabahans were arrested as secessionist conspirators under Malaysia's Internal Security Act, which provides for indefinite detention without trial. Among them was Jeffrey Kitingan, brother of the chief minister and head of the Yayasan Sabah, or Sabah Foundation (see page 194). At the same time, Joseph Pairin Kitingan was charged with corruption. The feeling in Sabah was that the men were bearing the brunt of Doctor Mahathir's personal political vendetta.

As the political feud worsened, the federal government added to the fray by failing to promote Sabah to foreign investors. As investment money dried up, so did federal development funds; big road and housing projects were left unfinished for years. Many in Sabah felt their state was being short-changed by the federal government. The political instability had a detrimental effect on the state economy and the business community felt that continued feuding would be economic lunacy. Politicians in the Christian-led

PBS, however, continued to claim that Sabah wasn't getting its fair share of Malaysia's economic boom. They said that the agreement which enshrined a measure of autonomy for Sabah when it joined the Malaysian federation had been eroded.

The main bone of contention was the state's oil revenues, worth around US$852 million a year, of which 95% disappeared into federal coffers. There were many other causes of dissatisfaction, too, and as the list of grievances grew longer, the state government exploited them to the full. By 1994, anti-federal feelings were running high. The PBS continued to promote the idea of 'Sabah for Sabahans', a defiant slogan in a country where the federal government was working to centralize power. Because Doctor Mahathir likes to be in control, the idea of granting greater autonomy to a distant, opposition-held state was not on his agenda. A showdown was inevitable.

It began in January 1994. As Datuk Pairin's corruption trial drew to a close, he dissolved the state assembly, paving the way for fresh elections. He did this to cover the eventuality of his being disqualified from office through a 'guilty' verdict: he wanted to have his own team in place to take over from him. He was convicted of corruption but the fine imposed on him was just under the disqualifying threshold and, to the prime minister's fury, he led the PBS into the election. Doctor Mahathir put his newly appointed deputy, Anwar Ibrahim, in charge of the National Front alliance campaign.

Datuk Pairin won the election, but by a much narrower margin than before. He alleged vote buying and ballot rigging. He accused Doctor Mahathir's allies of whipping up the issue of religion. He spoke of financial inducements being offered to Sabah's Muslim voters, some of whom are Malay, but most of whom are Bajau tribespeople and Filipino immigrants. His swearing-in ceremony was delayed for 36 hours; the governor said he was sick; Datuk Parin said his political enemies were trying to woo defectors from the ranks of the PBS to overturn his small majority. He was proved right.

Three weeks later, he was forced to resign; his fractious party had virtually collapsed in disarray and a stream of defections robbed him of his majority. Datuk Parin's protestations that his assemblymen had been bribed to switch sides were ignored. The local leader of Doctor Mahathir's ruling party, Tan Sri Sakaran Dandai, was swiftly sworn in as the new chief minister.

In the 1995 general election the PBS did remarkably well, holding onto eight seats and defeating a number of Front candidates who had defected from the PBS the previous year. Sabah was one area, along with the east coast state of Kelantan, which resisted the Mahathir/BN electoral steamroller.

The March 1999 state elections pitted UMNO against Pairin's PBS. Again the issues were local autonomy, vote rigging, the role of national politics and political parties in state elections, and money. A new element was the role that Anwar Ibrahim's trial might play in the campaign but otherwise it was old wine in old bottles.

The outcome was a convincing win for Mahathir and the ruling National Front who gathered 31 of the 48 state assembly seats – three more than the prime minister forecast. Mahathir once again used the lure of development funds from KL to convince local Sabahans where their best interests might lie. "We are not being unfair" Mahathir said. "We are more than fair, but we cannot be generous to the opposition. We can be generous to a National Front government in Sabah. That I can promise."

But, worryingly for the National Front, the opposition Parti Bersatu Sabah (PBS) still managed to garner the great bulk of the Kadazan vote and in so doing won 17 seats. As in Sarawak, the election, in the end, was more about local politics than about the economic crisis and the Anwar trial.

However, in the 2004 state and federal elections, the PBS rejoined the National Front and, faced only with the disunity of opposition parties, the BN-PBS coalition won resounding victories in both polls. A legitimate alternative to KL's ruling steamroller has all but died. The BN gave itself half the seats, one third to non-Malays, and distributed the rest between Chinese representatives. The message is that Sabahans accept dominance by the Malay minority from KL in return for money and development. The Sabah state elections were held simultaneously with the federal elections in 2008, and were again won comfortably by the BN-PBS coalition with only one of the 60 contested seats going to another party, the Democratic Action Party. The 2013 Sabah state elections saw a marked decrease in popularity for the BN. Though the party won a comfortable majority of 48 seats, the newly formed Pakatan Rakyat gained 10 seats, thus providing more opposition to the ruling party.

A key bone for contention in Sabah is the state's ethnic mix, especially in light of the Lahad Datu standoff in 2013 (see page 274) and an increase in violence related to Filipino sovereignty claims. The population of Sabah is growing faster than anywhere else in Malaysia, primarily as a result of apparently state-sponsored naturalization of illegal immigrants from Indonesia and Muslim areas of the southern Philippines. These newly naturalized citizens were put in the same ethnic stock as Malays (bumiputeras) and as a result, many of the non-Muslim Sabahans are increasingly becoming a minority in the state and this has become the cause of a great deal of tension between the Sabahans and the Malaysian government. In June 2012, the prime minister announced a Royal Commission to investigate illegal immigration into Sabah. Since the Lahad Datu standoff, thousands of illegal Filipino immigrants have been repatriated.

Culture

People

According to Malaysia's Population and Housing Census, the main ethnic group in Sabah is Kadazan Dusun (17.2%), followed by Bajau (14%) and Chinese (9%). The Kadazan mostly live on the west coast, the Murut inhabit the southern interior and the Bajau are mainly settled around Gunung Kinabalu. There are more than 30 tribes, more than 50 different languages and about 100 dialects. Sabah also has many illegal Filipino immigrants.

Bajau The Bajau, the famous cowboys of the Wild East, came from the south Philippines during the 18th and 19th centuries and settled in the coastal area around Kota Belud, Papar and Kudat, where they made a handsome living from piracy. The Bajau who came to Sabah joined forces with the notorious Illanun and Balinini pirates. They are natural seafarers and were dubbed sea gypsies or sea nomads; today, they form the second largest indigenous group in Sabah and are divided into subgroups, notably the Binadan, Suluk and Obian. They call themselves 'Samah'; it was the Brunei Malays who first called them Bajau. They are strict Muslims and the famous Sabahan folk hero, Mat Salleh, who led a rebellion in the 1890s against British Chartered Company rule, was a Bajau (see box, page 193). Despite their seafaring credentials, they are also renowned horsemen and (very occasionally) still put in an appearance at Kota Belud's *tamu* (see page 235). Bajau women are known for their brightly coloured basketry – *tudong saji*. The Bajau build their *atap* houses on stilts over the water and these are interconnected by a network of narrow wooden planks. The price of a Bajau bride was traditionally assessed in stilts, shaped from the trunks of bakau mangrove trees. A father erected one under his house on the day a daughter was born and replaced it whenever it wore out. The longer the daughter remained at home, the more stilts he got through and the more water buffalo he demanded from a prospective husband.

Chinese The Chinese accounted for nearly a third of Sabah's population in 1960; today they make up just under 10%. Unlike Sarawak, however, where the Chinese were a well-established community in the early 1800s, Sabah's Chinese came as a result of the British North Borneo Chartered Company's immigration policy, designed to ease a labour shortage. About 70% of Sabah's Chinese are Christian Hakka, who first began arriving at the end of the 19th century, under the supervision of the company. They were given free passage from China and most settled in the Jesselton and Kudat areas; today most Hakka are farmers. There are also large Teochew and Hokkien communities in Tawau, Kota Kinabalu and Labuan while Sandakan is mainly Cantonese, originating from Hong Kong.

Filipinos Immigration from the Philippines started in the 1950s and refugees began flooding into Sabah when the separatist war erupted in Mindanao in the 1970s. Today there are believed to be upwards of 700,000 illegal Filipino immigrants in Sabah (although their migration has been undocumented for so long that no one is certain) and the state government fears they could soon outnumber locals. There are many in Kota Kinabalu, the state capital, and a large community – mainly women and children – in Labuan, but the bulk of the Filipino population is in Semporna, Lahad Datu, Tawau and Kunak (on the east coast) where they heavily outnumber locals by a majority of three to one. One Sabah government minister, referring to the long-running territorial dispute between Malaysia and the Philippines, was quoted as saying "We do not require a strong military presence at the border any more: the aliens have already landed".

Although the federal government has talked of its intention to deport illegal aliens, it is mindful of the political reality: the majority of the Filipinos are Muslim, and making them legal Malaysian citizens could ruin Sabah's predominantly Christian, Kadazan-led state government, though many have been naturalized and awarded citizenship. The Filipino community is also a thorn in Sabah's flesh because of the crime wave associated with their arrival: the Sabah police claim 65% of crime is committed by Filipinos. The police do not ask questions when dealing with Filipino criminal suspects; about 40 to 50 are shot every year. Another local politician was quoted as saying: "The immigrants take away our jobs, cause political instability and pose a health hazard because of the appalling conditions in which some of them live".

There are six different Filipino groups in Sabah: the Visayas and Ilocano are Christian as are the Ilongo (Ilo Ilo), from Zamboanga. The Suluks are Muslim; they come from south Mindanao and have the advantage of speaking a dialect of Bahasa Malaysia. Many Filipinos were born in Sabah and all second-generation immigrants are fluent in Bahasa. Migration first accelerated in the 1950s during the logging boom and continued when the oil palm plantation economy took off. Many migrants have settled along the roadsides on the way to the Danum Valley; it is easy to claim land since all they have to do is simply clear a plot and plant a few fruit trees.

Kadazan The Kadazan are the largest ethnic group in Sabah and are a peaceful agrarian people with a strong cultural identity. Until Sabah joined the Malaysian Federation in

BACKGROUND

The Kadazan in Borneo

Formerly known as Dusuns (peasants or orchard people), a name given to them by outsiders and picked up by the British, the Kadazan live in Sabah and East Kalimantan.

The Kadazans traditionally traded their agricultural produce at large markets, held at meeting points, called *tamus* (see box, page 230).

They used to be animists and were said to live in great fear of evil spirits; most of their ceremonies were rituals aimed at driving out these spirits. The job of communicating with the spirits of the dead, the *tombiivo*, was done by priestesses, called *bobohizan*. They are the only ones who can speak the ancient Kadazan language, using a completely different vocabulary from modern Kadazan. Most converted to Christianity, mainly Roman Catholicism, during the 1930s, although there are also some Muslim Kadazan.

The big cultural event in the Kadazan year is the harvest festival that takes place in May. The ceremony, known as the Magavau ritual, is officiated by a high priestess. These elderly women, who wear black costumes and colourful headgear with feathers and beads, are now rarely seen. The ceremony ends with offerings to the *Bambaazon* (rice spirit). After the ceremonies Catholic, Muslim and animist Kadazan all come together to play traditional sports such as wrestling and buffalo racing. This is about the only occasion when visitors are likely to see Kadazan in their traditional costumes. Belts of silver coins (*himpogot*) and brass rings are worn round the waist; a colourful sash is also worn. Men dress in a black, long-sleeved jacket over black trousers; they also wear a *siga*, colourful woven headgear. These costumes have become more decorative in recent years, with colourful embroidery.

1963, they were known as Dusuns. It became, in effect, a residual category including all those people who were not Muslim or Chinese. Kadazan identity is therefore not particularly straightforward. In Malaysia's 2000 census, they were called Kadazan Dusun. The 1991 census, however, lists both Kadazan (110,866) and Dusun (229,194). The 1970 census listed all as Kadazan, while the 1960 census listed all as Dusun. In 1995 the Malaysian government agreed to add the common language of these people to the national repertoire to be taught in schools. This they named Kadazandusun. The others are Malay, Chinese, Tamil and Iban.

Most Kadazans call themselves after their tribal names. They can be divided into several tribes including the Lotud of Tuaran, the Rungus of the Kudat and Bengkoka Peninsulas, the Tempasuk, the Tambanuo, the Kimarangan and the Sanayo. Minokok and Tengara Kadazans live in the upper Kinabatangan River basin, while those living near other big rivers are just known as Orang Sungai (river people).

The majority of Kadazans used to live in longhouses; these are virtually all gone now. The greatest chance of coming across a longhouse in Sabah is in the Rungus area of the Kudat Peninsula; even there, former longhouse residents are moving into detached, kampong-style houses while one or two stay for the use of tourists.

All the Kadazan groups used to have similar customs and modes of dress (see below). Up to the Second World War, many Kadazan men wore the *chawat* loin cloth. The Kadazans used to hunt with blowpipes and in the 19th century were still headhunting.

BACKGROUND
The Murut in Borneo

The Murut live in the southwest of Sabah, in the Trusan Valley, North Sarawak and in Northeast Kalimantan. Some of those in more remote jungle areas retain their traditional longhouse way of life, but many Murut have opted for detached kampong-style houses.

Murut means hill people and is not the term used by the people themselves. They refer to themselves by individual tribal names.

The Nabai, Bokan and Timogun Murut live in the lowlands and are wet-rice farmers, while the Peluan, Bokan and Tagul Murut live in the hills and are mainly shifting cultivators. They are thought to be related to Sarawak's Kelabit and Kalimantan's Lun Dayeh people, although some of the tribes in the south Philippines have similar characteristics. The Murut staples are rice and tapioca; they are known for their weaving and basketry and have a penchant for drinking *tapai* (rice wine; see box opposite). They are also enthusiastic dancers and devised the *lansaran*, a sprung dance floor like a trampoline. The Murut are a mixture of animists, Christians and Muslims and were the last tribe in Sabah to give up headhunting, a practice stopped by the British North Borneo Chartered Company.

Today, however, they are known for their gentleness and honesty; their produce can often be seen sitting unattended at roadside stalls and passing motorists are expected to pay what they think fair. The Kadazan are farmers, and the main rice producers of Sabah.

For the May harvest festival, villages send the finalists of local beauty contests to the grand final of the Unduk Ngadau harvest festival queen competition in Penampang, near Kota Kinabalu. It is the Kadazans who dominate the Pasti Bersatu Sabah (PBS), a critical piece in Sabah's political jigsaw.

Murut The Murut live around Tenom and Pensiangan in the lowland and hilly parts of the interior. They were the last tribe in Sabah to give up headhunting, a practice stopped by the British North Borneo Chartered Company. See also box, above.

Arts and crafts

Compared with neighbouring Sarawak and Kalimantan, Sabah's handicraft industry is rather impoverished. Sabah's tribal groups were less protected from Western influences than Sarawak's and traditional skills quickly began to die out as the state modernized and the economy grew. In Kota Kinabalu today, the markets are full of Filipino handicrafts and shell products; local arts and crafts are largely confined to basketry, mats, hats, beadwork, musical instruments and pottery.

The elongated Kadazan backpack baskets found around Mount Kinabalu National Park are called *wakids* and are made from bamboo, rattan and bark. Woven food covers, or *tudong saji*, are often mistaken for hats, and are made by the Bajau of Kota Belud. Hats, made from nipah palm or rattan, and whose shape varies markedly from place to place, are decorated with traditional motifs. One of the most common motifs is the *nantuapan* (meeting), which represents four people all drinking out of the same *tapai* (rice wine) jar. The Rungus people from the Kudat Peninsula also make linago basketware from a strong wild grass; it is tightly woven and not decorated. At *tamus*, Sabah's big open-air markets

BACKGROUND

Tapai: Sabah's rice wine

Tapai, the fiery Sabahan rice wine, is much loved by the Kadazan and the Murut people of Borneo. It was even more popular before the two tribal groups converted to Christianity in the 1930s. Writer Hedda Morrison noted in 1957 that "The squalor and wretchedness arising from [their] continual drunkenness made the Murut a particularly useful object of missionary endeavour."

In the Sabah State Museum there is a recipe for *tapai*, which reads: "Boil 12 lbs of the best glutinous rice until well done. In a wide-mouthed jar, lay the rice in layers of no more than two fingers deep, and between layers, place about 20½-oz yeast cakes. Add two cups of water, tinctured with the juice of six beetroots. Cover jar with muslin and leave to ferment. Each day, uncover it and remove dew which forms on the muslin. On the fifth day, stir the mixture vigorously and leave for four weeks. Store for one year, after which it shall be full of virtue and potence and smooth upon the palate."

Oscar Cook, a former district officer in the North Borneo civil service, noted in his 1923 book *Borneo: the Stealer of Hearts*: "As an alternative occupation to headhunting, the Murut possess a fondness for getting drunk, indulged in on every possible occasion... Births, marriages, deaths, sowing, harvesting and any occasion that comes to mind is made the excuse for a debauch. It is customary for Murut to show respect to the white man by producing their very best *tapai*, and pitting the oldest and ugliest women of the village against him in a drinking competition." Cook admits that all this proved too much for him and when he was transferred to Keningau, he had to employ an 'official drinker'. "The applicants to the post were many," he noted.

(see box, page 230), there are usually some handicrafts for sale. The Kota Belud *tamu* is the best place to find the Bajau horseman's embroidered turban, the *destar*. Traditionally, the Rungus people, who live on the Kudat Peninsula, were renowned as fine weavers and detailed patterns were woven into their ceremonial skirts (*tinugupan*). These patterns all had different names but, like the ingredients of the traditional dyes, many have now been forgotten.

Practicalities

Getting there 305
Getting around 310
Essentials A-Z 313

Getting there

Air

The majority of visitors will be touching down at one of three international airports: Kuala Lumpur (page 308), Singapore (page 306) or Bandar Seri Begawan (page 146). Around 60-70 international carriers serve Kuala Lumpur and Singapore making the cities extremely well connected to the rest of the world. From Singapore or KL there are a number of budget airlines flying to the key cities of Malaysian Borneo and Bandar Seri Begawan.

Flights from Europe

Royal Brunei Airlines ⓘ *49 Cromwell Rd, London, SW7 2ED, T020-7584 6660, www.brunei air.com*, is the only airline that flies direct to Borneo from the UK; regular flights between London Heathrow and Bandar Seri Begawan take 16 hours, including a brief stop in Dubai for refuelling, and cost in the region of £680.

Direct flights from Europe to Kuala Lumpur (KL) and Singapore leave from London Heathrow (12½ hours), Manchester, Amsterdam, Istanbul, Frankfurt, Milan, Moscow, Paris, Rome and Zurich. From other cities a change of plane is often necessary en route. Many of the best deals can be found on Middle Eastern carriers and involve a brief stopover in the Gulf.

Flights from Australasia

Royal Brunei Airlines ⓘ *45 William St, Level 6, Melbourne, T03-8651 1000, T02-8267 5300, www.bruneiair.com*, has direct daily flights from Melbourne.

You can fly direct to KL and Singapore from Adelaide, Sydney, Melbourne, Brisbane, Darwin, Perth, Christchurch and Auckland; flight times vary from five to nine hours. Budget airlines **AirAsia** ⓘ *www.airasia.com*, **Jet Star Asia** ⓘ *www.jetstarasia.com*, and **Scoot** ⓘ *www.flyscoot.com*, connect Singapore and KL with Australasia. From other cities a change of plane is often necessary.

Flights from North America

There are no direct flights to Borneo from the USA and Canada. To Singapore, there are direct flights from Los Angeles, Houston and New York. Many other North American carriers stopover in Asia on the way.

Flights from Southeast Asia

There are flights to KL and Singapore from all the regional centres in Southeast Asia. Connecting flights from KL and Singapore go to: Bandar Seri Begawan (Brunei); Kuching, Bintulu, Miri and Sibu (Sarawak); Kota Kinabalu, Pulau Labuan, Sandakan and Tawau (Sabah). The main airlines serving these destinations are budget ones. **AirAsia** ⓘ *www. airasia.com*, operates flights to various cities in Borneo out of both KL and Singapore. **Malindo** ⓘ *www.malindo.com*, offers daily connections to Kuching and Kota Kinabalu from KL. Full service carriers include **Malaysian Airlines (MAS)** ⓘ *www.malaysiaairlines.com*, **Royal Brunei Airlines** ⓘ *www.bruneiair.com*, and **Singapore Airlines** ⓘ *www. singaporeair.com*. There are also flights to Borneo from other Southeast Asian hubs, including Manila, Jakarta, Johor Bahru, Guangzhou and Bali on **AirAsia**; Hong Kong, Tokyo, and Shanghai on **MAS**.

48 hours in Singapore

Singapore is a gentle introduction to Asia. Unfairly labelled as sterile and dull, it's a city filled with dynamism and pragmatic forward thinking. Recent years have seen the completion of a number of tourist draws, including Marina Bay Sands, National Art Gallery, Gardens by the Bay and Universal Studios. Don't let this unrelenting drive towards modernism deter you from the fact that, at its heart, the country is still a deeply traditional place of temples, churches and mosques with beautiful heritage quarters. Singapore also has some of the most diverse food on the planet and its hawker centres and food courts are an excellent place to get to grips with Asian cuisine.

Finding your feet

Singapore's Changi Airport, www.changiairport.com, has three main terminals and another due to open in 2017. To get into the city, take a westbound train from Tanah Merah (accessible from Terminals 2 and 3), which runs until 2318 (S$2, 30 minutes). Public bus 36/36A runs to the city (0600-2355, S$2.50, one hour) from the basement of Terminals 1, 2 and 3. There are taxi stands at each terminal; a journey into town costs S$20-40 (30 minutes). There is also a Budget Terminal, www.btsingapore.com, for low-cost carriers with a shuttle bus connecting it to the main terminals.

Getting around

Most of Singapore is connected by the Mass Rapid Transit (MRT) subway service which is cheap, safe and efficient. Fares range from S70¢ to S$2. Taxis are affordable. Bus routes are comprehensive but can be complex; single journeys cost S80¢ to S$1.80. Stored-value EZ-Link fare cards can be used on the subway or on buses. Alternatively, a **Singapore Tourist Pass** allows unlimited travel on trains and buses for one to three days, S$8 per day. Tickets and passes can and bought at TransitLink offices in MRT stations. You can pick up free MRT maps at any station; the *TransitLink Guide* (S$2) is a helpful publication.

Day 1

Start your day at the **Singapore Botanical Gardens** (1 Cluny Road, Botanic Gardens MRT, www.sbg.org.sg). This 183-acre garden was founded in 1859 and is beautifully laid out, with free guided tours on weekend mornings and a number of cafés. A walk along the rainforest trails and a visit to the Palm Valley and Symphony Lake are highly recommended. Next, hop on a bus along the shopping belt of **Orchard Road**. If you want the full shopping mall experience get off at ION Orchard (www.ionorchard.com) where there's a free city viewing gallery on the 56th floor. Otherwise alight at the iconic **Raffles Hotel** (1 Beach Road, www.raffles.com/singapore). If it's too early for a Singapore Sling, pop into Ah Teng's Bakery for a scone and tea before heading for the newly opened **National Art Gallery** (1 Saint Andrew's Road, www.nationalgallery.sg), in the former City Hall Supreme Court building, home to a fantastic selection of Asian art, or to the **Asian Civilisations Museum** (1 Empress Place, www.acm.org.sg), which gives an excellent overview of Asian cultures. To satisfy any rumbling stomachs head to Chinatown's Maxwell Food Centre (1 Kadayanullur Street) and try out some of the city's legendary hawker food. **Chinatown** has a wealth of attractions including

Buddha Tooth Relic Temple and touristy Pagoda Street. Pop into Singapore's oldest shopping centre, **People's Park Centre**, for an authentic Chinese foot massage and a plate of cold noodles or head to the basement for some authentic *hokkien mee* before settling down for a few beers along gorgeous Club Street.

Day 2

Head to **Little India** for a breakfast of *dosai* and *teh Tarik* at Ananda Bhavan (Syed Alwi Road). Just opposite you'll find the **Mustafa Centre** (Syed Alwi Road), an Indian department store selling everything you can imagine at bargain prices. The new **Indian Heritage Centre** (5 Campbell Lane, www.indianheritage.org.sg/en) has interesting exhibits on Indian culture in Singapore and a free trail map. It's a 20-minute walk to **Arab Street**, home to Malay and Indonesian restaurants such as renowned **Maimunah's** (Jalan Pisang) and Warung Pariaman (742 North Bridge Road), textile shops and Singapore's very own hipster alley, Haji Lane, which has quirky cafés and independent boutiques. The beautiful Sultan Mosque can be visited outside prayer time and the nearby **Malay Heritage Centre** (85 Sultan Gate, www.malayheitage.org.sg) gives a fantastic insight into Malay and archipelago influence on Singapore. Enjoy an afternoon walk towards **Marina Bay Sands** and check out the mall and casinos before heading up to the Ce-La-Vi rooftop bar for sunset drinks, or towards the **Esplanade** for a great viewing spot of the nightly light show and fireworks. **Gardens by the Bay** (www.gardensbythebay.com.sg/en) is a short walk from here and is well worth a visit to see the glowing Supertrees after dark. There's a decent hawker centre here though those with a penchant for nightlife will want to head to **Clarke Quay** for a few ales and maybe a dance in one of the many clubs or catch a show in the Esplanade or Marina Bay Sands before heading home.

Where to stay

Little India and Chinatown have the highest concentration of places to stay, though recent years have seen new ventures around Arab Street. Decent budget accommodation is notoriously scarce.

$$$$ Amoy
76 Telok Ayer St, T065-6580 2888, www.stayfareast.com.
Drawing inspiration from its location in Telok Ayer St, the Amoy is designed with traditional shophouses in mind, though there are plenty of concessions to modernity with contemporary design features offering a twist on traditional southern Chinese design.

$$$ The Arton Hotel
176 Tyrwhitt Rd, T065-6571 9100, www.artonhotel.com.

Slick hotel with smart if somewhat small rooms a short walk from Farrer Park MRT. Late check-out and early check-in available. The eco-wall makes for a pleasant burst of greenery in the mornings.

$$$ The Perak Hotel
12 Perak Rd, T065-6299 7733, www.theperakhotel.com.
Cosy guesthouse in the heart of Little India, with a good selection of comfortable rooms with cable TV and Wi-Fi, and a pleasant breakfast area.

$$-$ Prince of Wales
51 Boat Quay or 101 Dunlop St, T065-6299 0130, www.pow.com.sg.
2 Australian-owned hostels, both in a great location, with cheap beds (with anti-bed bug mattresses), a bar and café and plenty of late-night socializing.

ON THE ROAD

48 hours in Kuala Lumpur

Malaysia's capital, Kuala Lumpur, is a slow moving and charming capital city with big plans. Whilst parts of the city remain scruffy, the government has made significant efforts to bring the city into the 21st century and there are a number of gleaming glassy towers in the city centre. The skyline is dominated by the iconic Petronas Towers, with its Skybridge offering great views. The city has a number of good museums, including the Islamic Arts Museum, neighbouring colonial architecture and Chinese shophouses. Visitors can explore bustling markets, cutting edge malls and enjoy urban greenery in one of the city's parks or head out on a day trip to visit the Hindu pilgrimage site at the Batu Caves.

Finding your feet

Kuala Lumpur International Airport (KLIA), www.klia.com.my, is at Sepang, 55 km south of the city. The new terminal, klia2, is connected by a rail link (three minutes). The KLIA Ekspres Train, www.kliaekspres.com, runs to KL Sentral station (every 30 minutes 0500-0100, RM35, 28 minutes), a transport hub from where buses, trains and the LRT run to the rest of the city. An Airport Coach Service runs from KLIA to KL Sentral 0630-2400 and costs RM10 but takes 1½ hours. Expect to pay RM80-100 in a taxi.

Getting around

With the exception of Central Market, Chinatown and Dayabumi, distances between sights are large and difficult to cover on foot. Roads can also get congested, especially during rush hours. The best way to get about is on the city's three train lines: the Light Rail Transit (LRT), the Monorail and the KMT Komuter, which provide an elevated view of the city. The KL City Bus is a free service which runs to the most popular districts, train stations, shops and landmarks. See www.myrapid.com.my for details of KL transport.

Day 1

Get up early and head to the **Petronas Twin Towers** (www.petronastwintowers. com.my) to get a free ticket for the Skybridge for excellent views over the city. Tickets are issued at 0830 (closed Monday) and are snapped up quickly. Next jump on the LRT to **Central Market** and enjoy a brunch of *nasi lemak* washed down with a sweet cup of the *teh halia* (ginger tea) from a coffee shop before enjoying a leisurely stroll of the boutiques in the market. Pop into **Chinatown** for a cool juice and a bit of hustle and bustle on Jalan Petaling, before heading to the KL City Gallery (27 Jalan Raja, free, www.klcitygallery.com), with a number of fantastic exhibits on the city. The gallery sits close to **Merdeka Square**, where Malayan independence was declared in 1957, backed by the beautiful Moorish Sultan Abdul Samad building with its iconic copper domes roof and high clock tower. To avoid the heat, hop on a train to KLCC where the **Petrosains Discovery Centre** (KLCC, Tues-Fri 0930-1730, adult RM30, child RM18, www.petrosains.com.my) has interactive exhibits on the science and technology of Malaysia's oil and gas industry. As the sun goes down, wander around **KL City Centre Park**, a fantastic spot for photos of the towers, before heading over to

Bukit Bintang for a satay feast at **Fat Brother Satay** (Jln Alor, Bukit Bintang). Night owls should pop up to **Fuego** (Troika Sky Dining, 19 Persiaran KLCC) for cocktails and fantastic city views or for more of an earthy experience head to the **Taps Beer Bar** (One Residency, 1 Jalan Nagasari), with 14 beers on tap.

Day 2

Wake up early and hop on a bus (take bus 11/11d from Puduraya) out to the **Batu Caves**, the world's most visited Hindu shrine outside India, renowned for its 272 steps leading to the labyrinth of caves. Head back into town and pop into **Tanglin Food Court** (Jalan Cendarasari), and outdoors foodcourt renowned for its diverse local dishes (try the stingray or the *hokkien mee*) before heading to the nearby **National Mosque**, which can be visited between prayer times. In the afternoon head to the **Perdana Botanical Garden** (0900-1900, free, formerly known as Lake Gardens) established by the British in 1888 and covering 91 ha. You can join informative guided tours here or enjoy an afternoon stroll by the lake before taking a short walk to the **Bird Park** (0900, 1800, adult RM50/child RM41, www.klbirdpark.com/index.cfm) famed for having the world's largest walk-in aviary. For dinner, walk over to the streets of **Little India** and enjoy some fantastic subcontinental vegetarian food among flowers and spices and shops playing the latest tunes imported from Chennai. A good bet here is **Radhey's Pure Veg** on Lorong Padang Belia.

Where to stay

Kuala Lumpur has an excellent selection of accommodation in all price brackets though the best bargains can definitely be found in the mid-range section.

$$$$ Trader's Hotel
City Centre, T03-2332 9888, www.shangri-la.com/kualalumpur/traders.
Slick hotel in the heart of town with extraordinary night views and fantastic rooftop infinity pool. Rooms are plush as expected for the price, with facilities to match. Good discounts at weekends.

$$$ PNB Perdana On The Park
10 Persiaran KLCC, T03-7490 3333, www.pnbperdanaonthepark.com.
With good deals for online bookings, the huge rooms here have kitchenette, bathtubs, great city views and plenty of space for kids to roam. A short walk from the MRT, and 7 mins from the KLCC City Centre Park.

$$ Hotel Maison Boutique
36 & 38 Jln Baba Off Changkat Thambi Dollah, T03-2145 2929, www.hotelmaison.com.my.
Boutique hotel with themed rooms including Elvis, the Eiffel Tower and Cinderella. Though rooms aren't huge, this is more than made up for with the excellent price and excellent and friendly service.

$ Rainforest Bed and Breakfast
27 Jln Mesui off Jln Nagasari, T03-2145 3525, www.rainforestbnbhotel.com.
A verdant guesthouse designed to look like a hill, decorated with oriental flourishes. Well located for bars, shops and restaurants in Bukit Bintang, the rooms here are heavily accented with bamboo and are well furnished, with Wi-Fi and attached bathrooms. The 4-bed family suite is great value.

Getting around

With frequent and inexpensive flights between the main towns, flying is by far the easiest way to cover large distances around Sabah, Sarawak and Brunei though road conditions continue to improve. Speedboat ferries also skirt the north coast of Borneo, with immigration points either en route or at the departure and arrival points. The cheapest (and slowest) means of travelling around Borneo is by bus. Remember that Sarawak has its own immigration rules (independent to those of Malaysia), with most visitors receiving a free 90-day permit on arrival, which needs to be renewed in Kuching for longer stays (see Visas and immigration, page 325).

Air

Malaysian Airlines (MAS) ① *www.malaysiaairlines.com.my*, its subsidiary MASwings and the budget airline AirAsia ① *www.airasia.com*, have extensive flight networks in Borneo. Flights are relatively inexpensive but get booked up quickly, especially on public holidays (see page 315). MASwings offers services to many rural parts of Sabah and Sarawak on its ATRs and Twin Otters. It serves Ba'kelalan, Bario, Bintulu, Kota Kinabalu, Kuching, Lahad Datu, Pulau Labuan, Lawas, Limbang, Long Akah, Long Banga, Long Seridan, Long Lellang, Marudi, Miri, Mukah, Mulu, Sandakan, Sibu, Tanjung Manis and Tawau. Internationally, the airline connects Sabah with Tarakan in Kalimanatan. MAS offices can be found at most airports.

AirAsia serves Bintulu, Manila, Johor Bahru, Kota Kinabalu, Kuching, Pulau Labuan, Miri, Penang, Sandakan, Sibu and Tawau. There is a thrice-weekly flight between Pontianak and Kuching operated by Malaysian Airlines departing on Mondays, Thursdays and Saturdays.

In addition, Royal Brunei Airlines ① *www.bruneiair.com*, flies from Bandar Seri to Kuching and Kota Kinabalu. Note that it is usually cheaper to fly from Malaysian Borneo into Brunei rather than vice versa. For the best prices, book online as early as possible.

Rail

Trains are not a feasible way of getting around Borneo as the infrastructure is virtually non-existent and the rolling stock very old. In the state of Sabah, however, there is one railway line, the North Borneo Railway which passes through the spectacular Padas River Gorge (see page 207).

River and sea

There are speedy ferry services to Brunei every day from Limbang and Lawas (Sarawak) and from Pulau Labuan, which in turn has an onward service to Kota Kinabalu in Sabah. Tawau, in Sabah, is the main crossing point between Malaysian and Indonesian Borneo, with ferries leaving for Nunakan and Tarakan.

There are excellent coastal and upriver express boat services in Sarawak and Sabah, where local water transport comes into its own, as lack of roads makes it the only viable means of travel.

TRAVEL TIP

Packing for Borneo

When packing, remember that most items are available in Borneo's main towns and cities – often at a lower price than in Western countries – and that laundry services are cheap and rapid, so there is no need to bring lots of supplies. You may wish to pack your favourite brand of sun cream or insect repellent, for instance, but even these will be fairly easy to track down in the major department stores, particularly in Brunei, where large shops are as sophisticated as their counterparts in the West. Of course, if you're heading to more remote areas, you will need to stock up in advance, as items may be unavailable or in short supply in local towns and villages.

The following lists provide an idea of what to take with you on a trip to Borneo: bumbag, first-aid kit, insect repellent, international driving licence, passport (valid for at least six months), photocopies of essential documents, spare passport photographs, sun protection, sunglasses, Swiss Army knife, torch, umbrella and phrase book. Those intending to stay in budget accommodation might also include: cotton sheet sleeping bag, money belt, padlock (for room and pack), soap, student card, towel and travel wash. For women travellers: a supply of tampons (although these are available in most towns) and a wedding ring for single female travellers who might want to ward off the attention of amorous admirers. There is a good smattering of camping grounds in Sabah and Sarawak. If you're intending to camp, then all the usual equipment is necessary: a tent, stove, cooking utensils, sleeping bag, etc. Iodine drops – good for purifying water, sterilizing jungle cuts and scratches, and loosening leeches – are difficult to come by in Malaysia but easily obtained in UK camping and outdoor shops. They are distributed by Lifesystems, www.lifesystems.co.uk.

Road

The road network in Borneo is improving and there are good connections between major urban centres in Sabah, Brunei and Sarawak. However, away from towns and cities the network is limited and some routes are not in a good state of repair. In some places road surfacing has outpaced public transport, which has yet to establish itself in many areas. Air or water travel may be a more comfortable way to travel, and the only choice in some areas.

It is possible to cross overland from Sarawak and Sabah to Kalimantan and Brunei. The main crossing point into Kalimantan is in the west, between Kuching (Sarawak) and Pontianak (Kalimantan), with frequent buses between these two towns. From Miri (Sarawak) there are regular buses to Kuala Belait and Bandar Seri Begawan (Brunei), with an immigration post on either side of the border where passengers disembark briefly for customs formalities. Less regular bus services run between Sipitang (Sabah) to Bangar (Brunei), from where there is a ferry service to the capital.

Bus

Air-conditioned buses connect major towns across the region; seats can be reserved and prices are reasonable, varying according to whether the bus is express or regular. Be warned that the air conditioning can be very cold so keep a jumper handy. In larger towns there may be a number of bus stops and some private companies may operate directly from their own offices. Beyond the main towns, buses are less reliable and road conditions are poorer.

Car hire

Visitors can hire a car provided they have an international driving licence, are aged 23 to 65 years and have at least one year's driving experience. In Sabah and Sarawak, car hire costs approximately RM100-250 per day depending on the model. Shop around online for the best deals. 4WDs are expensive but they are readily available and are de rigueur in Sabah. Cheaper weekly and monthly rates and special deals are often available.

Driving is on the left; give way to drivers on the right. The wearing of seat belts is compulsory for front seat passengers and the driver. Most road signs are international but note that *awas* means caution.

Hitchhiking

It is easy for foreigners to hitch in Borneo, as long as they look reasonably presentable. However, hitching is not advisable for women travelling alone.

Taxi

There are two types of taxi in Borneo – local and 'out-station' (long-distance). Local taxis are fairly cheap in Sabah and Sarawak, but it is rare to find a taxi with a meter, so you will need bargaining skills. Taxis in Brunei are metered.

Out-station taxis connect towns and cities. They operate on a shared-cost basis: as soon as four passengers turn up the taxi sets off. Alternatively, it is possible to charter the whole taxi for the price of four single fares. Taxi stands are usually next to major bus stations. If shared, taxis usually cost about twice as much as buses but are much faster. For groups, taking a taxi makes good sense.

Maps

Maps are widely available in Malaysia and Singapore. The Malaysian tourist board produces good maps of Kuala Lumpur and a series of not-so-good state maps. The Sabah and Sarawak tourist boards also publish reasonable maps. Soviet-era air charts are often the most detailed maps available, but these must be ordered from a specialist such as Stanfords (see below) with plenty of time to spare. Availability isn't always guaranteed. Recommended maps include **Bartholomew Singapore and Malaysia** (1:150,000); **Nelles Malaysia and Brunei** (1:1,500,000); **Nelles Indonesia** (1:4,000,000).

In the UK, the best selection is available from **Stanfords** ⓘ *12-14 Long Acre, London, WC2E 9LP, T020-7836 1321, www.stanfords.co.uk.* Also recommended is The **Map Shop** ⓘ *www.themapshop.co.uk.*

Essentials A-Z

Accident and emergency

Sabah and **Sarawak**: ambulance and police T999; fire T994. **Brunei**: ambulance T991; police T993; fire T995.

Children

Travelling with children in this part of the world is a lot easier and safer than in many other so-called 'developing' countries. Food hygiene is good, bottled water is sold almost everywhere, public transport is cheap (including taxis) and ubiquitous and most attractions provide good discounts for children. Powdered milk and baby food and other baby/child items, including disposable nappies, are widely sold and high chairs are available in most restaurants. Naturally, taking a child to a developing country is not something to be taken on lightly; there are additional health risks and travelling is slower. But it can also be a most rewarding experience. Children are excellent passports into a local culture.

Children in Borneo are rarely left to cry and are carried for most of the first 8 months of their lives since crawling is seen as animal-like. A non-Asian child is still a novelty and parents may find their child frequently taken off their hands; either a great relief (at mealtimes, for instance) or most alarming.

The advice given in the health section (see page 318) on food and drink should be applied even more stringently where young children are concerned. Be aware that some expensive hotels may have squalid cooking conditions; the cheapest street stall can be more hygienic. Where possible, try to watch the food being prepared. Stir-fried vegetables and rice or noodles are the best bet; meat and fish may have been pre-cooked and then left out before being reheated. Fruit is cheap; papaya, banana and avocado are all excellent sources of nutrition and can be peeled ensuring cleanliness. If your child is at the 'put it in mouth' stage, disinfectant wipes are useful. Frequent wiping of hands and tabletops can help to minimize the chance of infection. Always carry a pack or 2 of wet wipes with you for peace of mind and to clean dirty high chairs and grubby fingers.

At the hottest time of year, a/c may be essential for a baby or young child's comfort when sleeping. This rules out some cheaper hotels, but a/c accommodation is available in all but the most remote spots. Guesthouses probably won't have cots but more expensive hotels should (email or phone to check). Be aware that the water could carry parasites, so avoid letting children drink it when bathing. Public transport may be a problem; long bus journeys can be restrictive and uncomfortable so try and break up your journeys into manageable chunks of a few hours and also look into the possibility of boat travel, which is infinitely more fun and roomy eg Labuan to KK or Kuching to Sibu. Hiring a car is the most convenient way to travel with a small child. You can rent cars with child seats in the main towns.

Checklist Pack your own standard baby/child equipment and include baby wipes, a brimmed hat; child paracetamol; disinfectant; first-aid kit; immersion element for boiling water; oral rehydration salts (such as Dioralyte); sarong or backpack for carrying child; Sudocreme (or similar); high-factor sunblock (this is freely available in supermarkets and drugstores in main towns but not out in the sticks); sunhat; thermometer and powdered or instant food. Always pack an umbrella and pull it out to provide shade to you and your child on sunny days. Even when it's cloudy in the tropics the UV can be strong so make sure your child is wearing a hat at all times and apply suncream regularly.

Customs and duty free

Duty-free allowance in **Sabah** and **Sarawak** (Malaysia) is 200 cigarettes, 50 cigars or 250g of tobacco and 1 litre of liquor or wine. Cameras, watches, pens, lighters, cosmetics and perfumes are also duty free in Malaysia. Visitors bringing in dutiable goods, such as film equipment, may have to pay a refundable deposit for temporary importation. It is advisable to carry receipt of purchases to avoid this problem. Export permits are required for gold, platinum, precious stones, jewellery (except reasonable personal effects) and antiques.

The duty-free allowance in **Brunei** for those over 17 is 60 ml of perfume and 250 ml eau de toilette and non-Muslims are allowed 2 bottles of liquor and 12 cans of beer for personal consumption. All alcohol must be declared on arrival. There is a yellow declaration form that needs to be presented at a counter along with a valid passport before clearing customs. Duty is payable on all tobacco products. Trafficking illegal drugs carries the death penalty in Brunei.

Disabled travellers

For travel to this area, it would be best to contact a specialist travel agent or organization dealing with travellers with special needs. In the UK, contact **Disability Rights UK**, CAN Mezzanine, 49-51 East Rd, London, N1 6AH, T020-7250 8181, www. disabilityrightsuk.org. In North America, contact **Society for Accessible Travel & Hospitality (SATH)**, Suite 610, 347 5th Av, New York, NY 10016, T1-212-447 7284, www.sath.org.

Disabled travellers are not well catered for in **Sabah** and **Sarawak**. Pavements are treacherous for those in wheelchairs, crossing roads is a hazard, and public transport is not well adapted for those with disabilities. However, it is not impossible for disabled people to travel in this region. For those who can afford the more expensive hotels, the assistance of hotel staff makes life a great deal easier, and there are also lifts and other amenities. Even those staying in budget accommodation will find that local people are very helpful.

Facilities for disabled travellers in **Brunei** are better than those in Sabah and Sarawak, though still limited by Western standards. Contact **Brunei Tourism**. The top hotels have pretty good facilities for disabled travellers.

Electricity

Borneo's supply is 220-240 volts, 50 cycle AC. Some hotels supply adaptors.

Embassies and consulates

For all embassies and consulates of Malaysia and Brunei abroad and for all foreign embassies and consulates in Borneo, see http://embassy.goabroad.com.

Etiquette

Conduct

As elsewhere in Southeast Asia, in Borneo 'losing face' brings shame. Even when bargaining, using a loud voice or wild gesticulations will be taken to signify anger and, hence, 'loss of face'. By the same token, the person you shout at will also feel loss of face, particularly if it happens in public. In Muslim company it is impolite to touch others with the left hand or with other objects – even loose change. You should also not use your left hand to pick up or pass food. Muslim men shake hands in Malaysia but it is not usual for a man to shake a woman's hand. Ethnic Chinese men and women shake hands. However, in general, excessive personal contact should be avoided. Using the index finger to point at people, even at objects, is regarded as insulting. The thumb or whole hand should be used to indicate something, or to wave down a taxi. Before entering a private home, remember to remove your shoes; it is also usual to take a small gift for the host, which is not opened until after the visitor has left.

Dress

Clothes are light, cool and casual most of the time, but also fairly smart. Some establishments, mainly exclusive restaurants, require a long-sleeved shirt with tie or local batik shirt and do not allow shorts in the evening. For jungle treks, a waterproof is advisable, as are canvas jungle boots, which dry faster than leather. Those heading to the highlands or making an ascent of Gunung Kinabalu should bring some warm, lightweight clothing that dries fast. Dress codes are important to observe from the point of view cultural and religious sensitivities. Women should be particularly careful not to offend. Dress modestly and avoid shorts, short skirts and sleeveless dresses or shirts (except at recognized beach resorts). Public nudity and topless bathing are not acceptable. Remove shoes before entering mosques and temples; in mosques, women should cover their heads, shoulders and legs and men should wear long trousers.

Festivals

Islam is the dominant religion in Borneo. The timing of Islamic festivals is an art rather than a science and is calculated on the basis of local sightings of various phases of the moon. Muslim festivals move forward by around 9 or 10 days each year. For exact dates of local festivals, see **www. tourism.gov.my** or **www.holidays.net**. Chinese, Indian (Hindu) and some Christian holidays are also movable. To make things even more exciting, each state has its own public holidays when shops close and banks pull down their shutters. This makes calculating public holidays in advance a bit of a quagmire of lunar events, assorted kings' birthdays and tribal festivals.

Islamic festivals

Maal Hijrah (Awal Muharram) (public holiday in Sabah, Sarawak and, Brunei) marks the first day of the Muslim calendar and celebrates the Prophet Muhammad's journey from Mecca to Medina on the lunar equivalent of 16 Jul AD 622. Religious discussions and lectures mark the event. **Maulidur Rasul** (public holiday in Sabah and Sarawak), **Maulud Nabi** (public holiday in Brunei), commemorates Prophet Muhammad's birthday in AD 571. Koran recitals and processions in most towns; public gatherings and coloured lights in BSB. **Israk Mekraj** (public holiday in Brunei), **Al Miraj**) celebrates the Prophet's journey to Jerusalem, led by the archangel Gabriel, and his ascension through the 7 heavens. He speaks with God and returns to earth the same night, with instructions, which include the 5 daily prayers.

Awal Ramadan (public holiday in Brunei) is the 1st day of Ramadan, a month of fasting for all Muslims. Muslims abstain from all food and drink (as well as smoking) from sunrise to sundown. The elderly and pregnant or menstruating women are exempt from fasting.

Nuzul Al-Quran (public holiday in Brunei) is the Anniversary of the Revelation of the Koran. Includes various religious observances, climaxing in a Koran-reading competition. **Hari Raya Puasa/Hari Raya Aidil Fitri/ Lebaran/Eid** (public holiday in Sabah, Sarawak and, Brunei) celebrates the end of Ramadan, the Islamic fasting month, with prayers and celebrations. In order for Hari Raya to be declared, the new moon of Syawal has to be sighted; if it is not, fasting continues for another day. It is the most important time of the year for Muslim families to get together. This is not a good time to travel; planes and buses are booked up weeks in advance and hotels are also often full. Muslims living in towns and cities return home to their village, where it is open house for relatives and friends, and special local delicacies are served. In Brunei, families keep themselves to themselves on the 1st day but on the second they throw their doors open. Everyone dresses up in their best clothes; men wear a length of *tenunan* around their waist, a cloth woven with gold thread.

Hari Raya Qurban (public holiday in Sabah and Sarawak), **Hari Raya Haji** (public holiday in Brunei), Held on the 10th day of Zulhijjah, the 12th month of the Islamic calendar, this is the 'festival of the sacrifice' and marks the willingness of Abraham to sacrifice his son. The festival also marks the return of pilgrims from the Haj to Mecca. The Haj is one of the 5 keystones of Islam. In the morning, prayers are offered and later, families hold open house. Those who can afford it sacrifice goats or cows to be distributed to the poor. Every year 4000 Bruneians go on the Haj. If any pilgrim has difficulty making ends meet, the Ministry of Religious Affairs will provide a generous subsidy. Muslim men who have been on the Haj wear a white skullhat.

Sarawak and Sabah

Schools in Sabah and Sarawak have 5 breaks in the year, generally falling in Jan (1 week), Mar (2 weeks), May (3 weeks), Aug (1 week), and October (4 weeks). State holidays, which can last several days, may disrupt travel itineraries, so confirm your travel plans in advance. In addition, note that some government offices are closed on the 1st and 3rd Sat of each month.

In addition to festivals celebrated throughout the country – including Chinese New Year, Christmas and Hari Raya – Sabah and Sarawak have their own festivals. Exact dates are available from the tourist offices in the capitals.

1 Jan **New Year's Day** (public holiday).

Jan/Feb **Thaipusam** (movable) is celebrated by Hindus throughout Malaysia in honour of their deity Lord Subramanian (also known as Lord Muruga), who represents virtue, bravery, youth and power. Held during full moon in the month of Thai, it is a day of penance and thanksgiving.

Jan/Feb **Chinese New Year** (movable; public holiday) a 15-day lunar festival. Chinatown streets are crowded for weeks with shoppers buying traditional oranges, which signify luck. Lion, unicorn or dragon dances welcome in the New Year and thousands of firecrackers are ignited to ward off evil spirits. Chap Goh Mei is the 15th day of the Chinese New Year and brings celebrations to a close. The Chinese believe that in order to find good husbands, girls should throw oranges into the river/sea on this day. In Sarawak the festival is known as **Guan Hsiao Cheih** (Lantern Festival).

1 Feb **Federal Territory Day** (state holiday in Pulau Labuan).

Mar/Apr **Easter** (movable). Good Fri is a public holiday in Sabah and Sarawak.

1 May **Labour Day** (public holiday). Kurah Aran is celebrated by the Bidayuh tribe in Sarawak (see page 132) after the paddy harvest is over.

May **Kadazan Harvest Festival** or **Tadau Keamatan** (movable; state holiday in Sabah and Labuan). Marks the end of the rice harvest in Sabah; the magavau ritual is performed to nurse the spirit back to health in readiness for the next planting season. Celebrated with feasting, *tapai* (rice wine) drinking, dancing and general merrymaking. There are also agricultural shows, buffalo races, cultural performances and traditional games. The traditional *sumazal* dance is a highlight.

May (movable) **Borneo International Jazz Festival** is held in Miri and is a well-received international jazz extravaganza, which attracts performers from as far away as New Orleans, Cuba, Morocco and Europe. See www.jazzborneo.com for the latest on the upcoming treats and more.

May **Wesak Day** (movable; public holiday except Labuan). The most important day in the Buddhist calendar, celebrates the Buddha's birth, death and enlightenment. Temples are packed with devotees offering incense, joss sticks and prayers. Lectures on Buddhism and special exhibitions are held.

May/Jun Gawai Dayak (movable; state holiday in Sarawak) is the major festival of the year for the Iban of Sarawak; longhouses party continuously for a week. The Gawai celebrates the end of the rice harvest and welcomes the new planting season. The main ritual is called magavau and nurses the spirit of the grain back to health in advance of the planting season. Like the Kadazan harvest festival in Sabah (see above), visitors are welcome to join in, but in Sarawak, the harvest festival is much more traditional. Urban residents return to their rural roots for a major binge. On the 1st day of celebrations everyone dresses up in traditional costumes and sings, dances and drinks *tuak* rice wine until they drop.

Jun Dragon Boat Festival (movable) honours the suicide of an ancient Chinese poet hero, Qu Yuan. To press for political reform and protest against corruption, he drowned himself in Mi Luo River. To try and save him fishermen played drums and threw rice dumplings to try and distract vultures. His death is marked with dragon boat races and the enthusiastic consumption of rice dumplings.

Jun Gawai Batu (Sarawak) is a whetstone feast held by Iban farmers.

3 Jun Official birthday of HM the Yang di-Pertuan Agong (public holiday Malaysia).

Jun/Jul/Aug Rainforest World Music Festival (movable). This popular festival takes place just outside Kuching at the superb and aptly green venue of the Sarawak Cultural Village (see page 61). Indigenous performers, from Borneo and further afield, combine with well-known world music acts to share music, performance skills and their diverse cultures and experiences. Workshops, jamming sessions and talks are a major feature of the multi-day event. For details of the 2017 festival and beyond, see www.rwmf.net or contact the Sarawak Tourism Board in Kuching (see page 47).

Mooncake or **Lantern Festival** (movable). This Chinese festival marks the overthrow of the Mongol Dynasty in China; celebrated, as the name suggests, with the exchange and eating of mooncakes. According to Chinese legend secret messages of revolt were carried inside these cakes and led to the uprising. Children light festive lanterns while women pray to the Goddess of the Moon.

31 Aug Hari Kebangsaan/National Day (public holiday) commemorates Malaysian Independence (*merdeka*) in 1957. In Sarawak it's celebrated in a different place each year.

Aug/Sep Festival of the Hungry Ghosts (movable), on the 7th moon in the Chinese lunar calendar, when souls in purgatory are believed to return to earth to feast. Food is offered to these wandering spirits. Altars are set up in the streets and candles with faces are burned on them.

14 Sep Governor of Sarawak's birthday (state holiday in Sarawak).

16 Sep Governor of Sabah's birthday (state holiday in Sabah).

Oct Festival of the Nine Emperor Gods or Kiew Ong Yeah (movable) marks the return of the spirits of the 9 emperor gods to earth. Devotees visit temples dedicated to the 9 gods. A strip of yellow cotton is often bought from the temple and worn on the right wrist as a sign of devotion. Ceremonies usually culminate with a fire-walking ritual.

Oct/Nov Deepavali (movable; public holiday except Sarawak and Labuan), the Hindu festival of lights commemorates the victory of light over darkness and good over evil: the triumphant return of Rama after his defeat of the evil Ravanna in the Hindu epic, the Ramayana. Every Hindu home is brightly lit and decorated for the occasion.

Nov/Dec Gawai Antu/Gawai Nyunkup/Rugan (Sarawak) is an Iban tribute to departed spirits. In simple terms, it is a party to mark the end of mourning for anyone whose relative has died in the previous 6 months.

25 Dec Christmas Day (public holiday). Christmas in Malaysia is a commercial spectacle with decorations and tropical Santa Clauses, although it doesn't compare with celebrations in Singapore. Midnight mass is the main Christmas service held in churches.

Other tribal festivals (*gawai*) in Sarawak include **Gawai Burung**, honouring the Iban war god, Singallang Burong; **Gawai Mpijong Jaran Rantau**, celebrated by the Bidayuh before grass cutting in new paddy fields; **Gawai Bineh**, celebrated by the Iban after harvest to welcome back the spirits of the paddy from the fields; and **Gawai Sawa**, celebrated by the Bidayuh to offer thanksgiving for last year and to make next year a plentiful one.

Brunei

1 Jan **New Year's Day** (public holiday).
Jan/Feb **Chinese New Year** (public holiday), a 15-day lunar festival.
23 Feb **Hari Kebangsaan Negara Brunei Darussalam/National Day** (public holiday), processions and fireworks in BSB.
31 May **Armed Forces Day** (public holiday), celebrated by the Royal Brunei Armed Forces who parade their equipment around town.
15 Jul **Sultan's Birthday** (public holiday) is celebrated until the end of the 2nd week in Aug. There's a procession, with lanterns and fireworks and a traditional boat race in BSB.
25 Dec **Christmas Day**.

Health

See your GP or travel clinic at least 6 weeks before departure for general advice on travel risks and vaccinations. Try phoning a specialist travel clinic if your own doctor is unfamiliar with health conditions in Malaysia and Brunei. Make sure you have sufficient medical travel insurance, get a dental check, know your own blood group and, if you suffer a long-term condition such as diabetes or epilepsy, obtain a **Medic Alert** bracelet/necklace (www.medicalert.co.uk). If you wear glasses, take a copy of your prescription.

Vaccinations

Vaccinations for hepatitis A and tetanus are recommended and vaccinations for diphtheria, cholera, hepatitis B, rabies and Japanese B encephalitis and typhoid may be recommended for Borneo. The final decision, however, should be based on a consultation with your GP or travel clinic. You should confirm your primary courses and boosters are up to date (diphtheria, tetanus, poliomyelitis, hepatitis A, typhoid). A yellow fever certificate is required by visitors over 1 year old, who are coming from or have recently passed through an infected area.

Health risks

The most common cause of travellers' **diarrhoea** is from eating contaminated food. In Malaysia and Brunei, drinking water is rarely the culprit, although it's best to be cautious (see below). Swimming in sea or river water that has been contaminated by sewage can also be a cause; ask locally if it is safe. Diarrhoea may be also caused by viruses, bacteria (such as E-coli), protozoal (such as giardia), salmonella and cholera. It may be accompanied by vomiting or by severe abdominal pain. Any kind of diarrhoea responds well to the replacement of water and salts. Sachets of rehydration salts can be bought in most chemists and can be dissolved in boiled water. If the symptoms persist, consult a doctor. Tap water in the major cities is in theory safe to drink but it may be worth drinking only bottled or boiled water to be sure. Avoid having ice in drinks unless you trust that it is from a reliable source.

Travelling in high altitudes can bring on **altitude sickness**. On reaching heights above 3000 m, the heart may start pounding and the traveller may experience shortness of breath. Smokers and those with underlying heart or lung disease are often hardest hit. Take it easy for the first few days, rest and drink plenty of water, you will feel better soon. It is essential to get acclimatized before undertaking long treks or arduous activities.

TRAVEL TIP
Dive safety

If you plan to dive make sure that you are in good health. Check that any dive company you use is reputable and has appropriate certification from the **British Sub Aqua Club (BSAC)** or **Professional Association of Diving Instructors (PADI)**, Unit 7, St Philips Central, Albert Rd, St Philips, Bristol BS2 0TD, T0117-300 7234, www.padi.com. Should you fall victim to decompression sickness, immediately contact the 24-hr **Malaysian Diving Emergency Hotline**, T05-930 4114, for advice. Recompression facilities are available at the **Labuan Recompression Chamber**, Labuan Pejabat Selam, Markas Wilayah Laut Dua, 87007, Labuan, T087-412122, operated by the Malaysian Navy, and at the **Naval Medicine and Hyperbaric Centre**, 36 Admiralty Rd, West Singapore 759960, T6750 5632 (appointments), T6758 1733 (24-hr emergencies). Note that air evacuation services, if available, are extremely expensive and hyperbaric chambers can charge up to US$800 per hr.

Good dive insurance is imperative. It is inexpensive and well worth it in case of a problem. Many general travel insurance policies do not cover diving. Contact DAN (the Divers Alert Network), www.diversalertnetwork.org, DAN Europe, www.daneurope.org, or DAN South East Asia Pacific, www.danseap.org, for more information. If you have no insurance you can purchase online.

Mosquitoes are more of a nuisance than a serious hazard but some, of course, are carriers of serious diseases such as **malaria**, so it is sensible to avoid being bitten as much as possible. Malaria is present in the Malaysian states of Sabah and Sarawak and is making a comeback worldwide. Sleep off the ground and use a mosquito net and some kind of insecticide. Mosquito coils release insecticide as they burn and are available in many shops, as are tablets of insecticide, which are placed on a heated mat plugged into a wall socket. Those travelling away from coastal areas of Sabah and Sarawak are advised to speak to a doctor about suitable anti-malarial medication. Malarone is widely available in Europe and can be purchased in Singapore with a doctor's prescription. Doxycycline can be bought from pharmacists in Kuala Lumpur. Dengue, a disease also carried by mosquitoes, is common in the region. Fortunately, travellers rarely develop a severe form of dengue, although fatal cases do occur annually.

Medical services

Contact your embassy or consulate for a list of doctors and dentists who speak your language, or at least some English. Good-quality healthcare is available in the larger centres of Sarawak, Sabah and Brunei, but it can be expensive, especially hospitalization. Make sure you have adequate insurance.

Bandar Seri Begawan (Brunei)
Jerudong Park Medical Centre, Jerudong, T261 1433, www.jpmc.com.bn.
RIPAS Hospital, Jln Putera Al-Muhtadee Billah, T222 2366.

Kota Kinabalu (Sabah)
Damai Specialist Hospital, DSC Building, Lorong Tepus 1, Taman Damai, T088-250060, http://www.kpjdamai.com/. Well-established hospital.
Gleneagles, Riverson@Sembulan, Block A-1, Lorong Riverson@Sembulan, T088-518888, www.gleneagleskk.com.my/. Reliable private hospital.

Kuching (Sarawak)

Apex Pharmacy, 1st floor, 125 Sarawak Plaza, open 1000-2100. **Doctor's Clinic**, Main Bazaar, opposite Chinese History Museum, said to be excellent and is used to treating travellers' more minor ailments (around RM30 for a consultation). **Normah Medical Specialist Centre,** 937 Jln Tun Datuk Patinggi Haji Abdul Rahman Yaakub, Petra Jaya, T082-440055, www.normah.com.my, private hospital with a good reputation. **Sarawak General Hospital**, Jln Hospital, T082-276666, consultations from RM60. **Timberland Medical Centre**, Rock Rd, T082-234466, www.timberlandmedical.com, recommended. **UMH Pharmacy**, Ban Hock Rd, Mon-Fri 0900-2030, Sat 0900-1800. **YK Farmasi**, 22 Main Bazaar, 0830-1700.

Miri (Sarawak)

Hospital, on the edge of town on Jln Cahaya, T085-420033.

Useful websites

www.btha.org British Travel Health Association.

www.cdc.gov US government site that gives excellent advice on travel health and details of disease outbreaks.

www.fco.gov.uk British Foreign and Commonwealth Office travel site that has useful information on each country, people, climate and a list of UK embassies/consulates.

www.fitfortravel.scot.nhs.uk A-Z of vaccine/health advice for each country.

www.numberonehealth.co.uk Travel screening services, vaccine and travel health advice, email/SMS text vaccine reminders and screens returned travellers for tropical diseases.

Internet

Sabah, Sarawak and Brunei are fairly well connected to the internet and it is possible to buy a top-up SIM card with pre-loaded data allowance (see Telephone, page 323). You'll need a passport to get hold of a SIM and the best bet for data coverage and cell coverage is **Celcom** followed by **Maxis** and **DiGi**. In Brunei, get connected with **DST**, though if you are there only for a few days it makes sense to rely on the many free Wi-Fi options. Wi-Fi is commonly available in many hotels, hostels, cafés and restaurants thought he speed can be patchy and you might find yourself browsing in hotel lobbies from time to time. If you go out into the wilds of Borneo, you can forget internet access altogether, but enjoy the liberation that this brings! If you want to keep it strictly old school and leave the smartphone at home, internet cafés are widely available with rates of RM2-5 per hr. There are plenty of internet cafés in **Brunei**, too, and all the top-end and most of the mid-range hotels offer internet access. Free Wi-Fi is less widely available in Brunei than in Malaysia, but many mid-range cafés and the more expensive hotels offer it.

Language

Bahasa Melayu (the Malay language, normally shortened to Bahasa) is the national language in **Sarawak**, **Sabah** and **Brunei**. It is very similar to Bahasa Indonesia, which evolved from Malay. All communities, Malay, Chinese and Indian, as well as tribal groups in Sabah and Sarawak, speak Malay, as most are schooled in the Malay medium. Nearly everyone in Malaysia speaks some English, except in remote rural areas. In Brunei, English is widely spoken and is taught in schools. Chinese is also spoken, mainly Hokkien, but also Cantonese, Teochew, Hakka and Mandarin.

The best way to take a crash course in Malay is to buy a teach-yourself book; there are several on the market, but one of the best ones is *Everyday Malay* by Thomas G Oey (Periplus Language Books, 1995), which is widely available. You could also try Oey's 2012 Everyday Malay: phrase book and dictionary (2012). A Malay/ English dictionary or phrasebook is a useful companion too; these are also readily available in bookshops.

The basic grammar is very simple, with no tenses, genders or articles, and sentence structure is straightforward. Pronunciation is not difficult either as there is a close relation between the letter as it is written and the sound. Stress is usually placed on the 2nd syllable of a word. The **a** is pronounced as *ah* in an open syllable, or as in *but* for a closed syllable; **e** is pronounced as in *open* or *bed*; **i** is pronounced as in *feel*; **o** is pronounced as in *all*; **u** is pronounced as in *foot*. The letter **c** is pronounced *ch* as in *change* or *chat*. The **r** is rolled.

For further information, see Useful words and phrases, page 329.

LGBT travellers

Malaysia – officially at least – is not particularly accepting of what might be regarded as alternative lifestyles, and homosexuality remains a crime. (Bear in mind that even Malaysia's former deputy prime minister and leading opposition voice, Anwar Ibrahim, was charged with sodomy in 1999 and in 2015 commenced a 5-year spell in prison after a charge of sodomy was upheld.) However, there is a small gay and lesbian scene in Kota Kinabalu and Kuching. There are 2 good websites for gay and lesbian travellers to the region: **www.fridae. com** and **www.utopia-asia.com**. But the site's homepage states: "Gay life in Malaysia is blossoming. However, Muslims, both Malay and visitors, are subject to antiquated religious laws which punish gay or lesbian sexual activity with flogging and male transvestism with imprisonment. Police may arrest and harass any gay person (Muslim or non-Muslim) in a public place (ie cruise spots), so discretion is advised."

As in Malaysia, **Brunei** is not a good place to be gay: homosexual sex is illegal and the recent implementation of sharia law ensures very harsh punishments for homosexuals.

Money

Currency

The unit of currency in **Malaysia** is the Malaysian dollar or ringgit (RM), which is divided into 100 cents or sen. Bank notes come in denominations of RM1,2, 5, 10, 50, and 100. Coins are issued in 5, 10, 20 and 50 sen. The exchange rate in Jul 2016 was RM4.1 = US$1/RM4.9 = €1.

The official currency in **Brunei** is the Brunei dollar (B$), which is interchangeable with the Singapore dollar. Notes are available in denominations of B$1, B$5, B$10, B$25, B$50, B$100, B$500, B$1000 and B$10,000 (about US$6000!). There are 1, 5, 10, 20 and 50 cent coins. The exchange rate in Jul 2016 was B$1.35 = US$1/B$1.5 = €1. Singapore dollars can be used as legal tender in Brunei with a rate of 1:1.

Exchange

Most of the bigger hotels, restaurants and shops in **Sarawak** and **Sabah** accept international credit cards, including American Express, MasterCard and Visa. The latter 2 are the most widely accepted. Cash advances can be issued against credit cards in most banks, although some banks limit the amount that can be drawn. A passport is usually required for over-the-counter transactions. There are ATMs all over major centres in Sabah, Sarawak and Brunei which accept credit or debit cards. In Malaysia, **Maybank** and **OCBC** will accept both Visa and MasterCard at its ATMs; cards with the Cirrus or Maestro mark will also be accepted at most banks' ATMs. Traveller's cheques can be exchanged at banks and money changers. Money changers often offer the best rates, but it is worth shopping around.

Brunei banks charge a commission of B$10-15 for exchanging cash or traveller's cheques. Money changers often don't charge a set commission at all, but their rates won't be quite so good. ATMs are widespread in Brunei and many accept debit cards and credit cards. Most hotels and many shops and establishments accept credit cards, too.

Cost of travelling

Sabah and **Sarawak** are relatively cheap for overseas visitors. However, with the currencies dipping and rising, stock markets plunging and oil prices at a low it's difficult to know where the ringgit in particular is heading (the Brunei dollar is a steady currency). Nevertheless, Malaysian Borneo remains an excellent-value destination. It's possible to travel on a shoestring budget of RM70-100 (US$16-24) per day – including accommodation (dorms), meals and transport – if you stay in the bottom-end guesthouses, eat at stalls or in hawker centres and use public transport. Cheaper guesthouses charge around RM50 a night for 2 (US$12). Dorm beds are available in most budget guesthouses and can be superb value at less than RM25 (US$6). It's possible to find a simple a/c room for RM50-100 (US$12-24). A room in a top-quality, international-class hotel will cost RM300-500 (US$70-120) and in a tourist-class hotel (with a/c, room service, restaurant and probably a pool), RM100-150 (US$24-35). Eating out is also comparatively cheap: a good filling curry can cost as little as RM5 (US$1.20). Finally, overland travel is a bargain and the bus network is not only extremely good, but fares are excellent value. Booking plane tickets well in advance gives superb deals. However, if you're planning to do any diving, stay in a jungle lodge or hire a guide for a week's trek, your budget will need to increase significantly.

Per capita, **Brunei** is one of the wealthiest countries in the developing world, with a GDP not far off that of Singapore. This means that everything, from hotel rates to groceries and transport, is significantly more expensive than in Sarawak and Sabah and unless you hire a car, you may have to rely on taxis (the bus network is skimpy at best) and these are not cheap. By Western standards, however, Brunei is not particularly expensive. And, when it comes to local food at market stalls or in *kedai kopi* (traditional coffee shops), prices are only slightly higher than just across the border.

Newspapers

The main English-language newspapers in **Sarawak** and **Sabah** are the *Daily Express* (www.dailyexpress.com.my) and the New Sarawak Tribune (www.newsarawaktribune.com). The initial *Sarawak Tribune* was forced out of business in 2006 in a controversy over the Jyllands-Posten Mohammed cartoons, about which the paper claimed the cartoons had made no impact in Sarawak, and reprinted the cartoon, generating enormous criticism from the pro-Islamic Malaysian government. The paper was subsequently relaunched in 2010. *Aliran Monthly* (www.aliran.com) is a high-brow but fascinating publication offering current affairs analysis from a non-government perspective. *The Rocket* (www.therocket.com.my) is the Democratic Action Party's opposition newspaper, and also presents an alternative perspective. International editions of leading foreign newspapers and news magazines can be obtained at main newsstands and bookstalls, although some of these are not cleared through customs until mid-afternoon. One of the most popular online news portals is Malaysia Kini (www.malaysiakini.com), with independent coverage of news and politics.

There are 2 daily newspapers in **Brunei**: the English-language *Borneo Bulletin* (www.borneobulletin.com.bn) and the *Media Permata* (Malay), which cover both local and international news.

Opening hours

In **Sabah** and **Sarawak** business hours are Mon-Thu 0800-1245, 1400-1615, Fri 0800-1200, 1430-1615, Sat 0800-1245. Note that offices and banks are shut on the 1st and 3rd Sat of every month.

In **Brunei**, business hours are Mon-Fri 0900-1500, Sat 0900-1100 (banks), but most shopping malls are open daily 1000-2130. For post office opening hours, see below.

Post

Malaysia's post is cheap and quite reliable, although incoming and outgoing parcels should be registered. To send postcards and aerograms overseas costs RM0.50, letters cost or RM1.20 (up to 20g). Post office opening hours are Mon-Sat 0830-1700 (closed 1st Sat of every month). Fax services are still available in most state capitals. Poste restante, at general post offices in major cities, is reliable; make sure your surname is capitalized and underlined. Most post offices have a packing service for a reasonable fee (around RM5). You can also buy **AirAsia** tickets at post offices.

Post offices in **Brunei** are open Mon-Thu and Sat 0745-1630, Fri 0800-1100 and 1400-1600. Most hotels provide postal services at reception. The cost of a stamp for a postcard to Europe is around 50 cents (45c for an aerogramme) and it costs 90c for letters up to 10 g.

Prohibitions

The trafficking of illegal drugs into Malaysia and Brunei carries the death penalty.

Brunei is a 'dry' country: sale of alcohol is banned, while consumption is prohibited for Muslims. Non-Muslims may consume alcohol that has been declared at customs (2 bottles of liquor or 12 cans of beer; see page 314), but not in public. Certain restaurants will allow non-Muslims to bring their own alcohol, but always check in advance. See also LGBT travellers, above.

Safety

Normal precautions should be taken with passports and valuables; many hotels have safes. Pickpocketing and bag snatching are problems in Kuching. Generally women travelling alone need have few worries – although take the usual precautions like not walking alone in deserted places at night. Drink driving is a problem in Sabah and Sarawak especially in more rural areas.

Student travellers

Anyone in full-time education is entitled to an International Student Identity Card (ISIC). These are issued by student travel offices and travel agencies across the world and offer special rates on transport and other concessions. See www.isic.org. Students can get discounts on some entry fees and transport, but there is no institutionalized system of discounts for students.

Tax

There is a 6% GST (Goods and Sales Tax) in **Malaysia**. There is no GST or VAT tax in **Brunei**.

Telephone

There are public telephone booths in most towns in **Sarawak** and **Sabah**; telephones take RM0.10 and RM0.20 coins. Card phones are widespread and make good sense if phoning abroad. **iTalk** offers the best IDD (international direct dialling) rate. Cards come in denominations from RM10 to RM100 and are available from airports, petrol stations, most **7-Eleven** and magazine stalls. International direct calls can be made from any telephone with an IDD facility, including most **Kedai Telekom** booths in major towns.

You should be able to use your mobile phone in Malaysia with no problems. To get a pre-paid SIM card when you arrive you'll need to show your passport. SIM cards are available from most mobile phone shops, with **Maxis**, **Celcom** and **DiGi** offering the widest service. International calls from these are very good value.

There are no area codes in **Brunei**. With a **Hallo Kad** phonecard (widely available) you can make international calls from any phone.

You can also make international calls from some hotel rooms. Coin phones take 10 and 20 cent pieces. Getting a mobile prepaid SIM card is expensive in Brunei and only really worth it if staying longer than a few days.

Telephone information

Numbers are shown as they should be dialled long distance **within** the country. If phoning from abroad, dial your country's international access code, the country code for Malaysia or Brunei followed by the area code (minus the initial zero) and then the number.

IDD access codes Malaysia: 00; 020 for calls to Malaysia (no country code needed) or 00 for other countries; Brunei: 00.

International country codes Malaysia: +60; +65; Brunei: +673.

Operator Malaysia: T101; Brunei: T113.

Directory enquiries Malaysia: T102/103; Brunei: T0213.

International assistance Malaysia: T108; Brunei: T113.

Time

Official time in Malaysia and Brunei is 8 hrs ahead of GMT.

Tipping

Tipping is unusual in Malaysia, as a service charge of 10% is automatically added to restaurant and hotel bills, plus a 6% goods and services tax (indicated by the + and ++ signs). Nor is tipping expected in smaller restaurants where a service charge is not automatically added to the bill. For porters a modest tip may be appropriate.

Tour operators

In the UK
Audley Travel, New Mill, New Mill Lane, Whitney, Oxfordshire, OX29 9SX, T01993-838000, www.audleytravel.com. Tailor-made eco-tour itineraries.

Exodus, Grange Mills, Weir Rd, London, SW12 0NE, T020-8675 5550, www.exodus.co.uk. Wide range of trips including river journeys and caves at the Niah National Park.

Explore Worldwide, Nelson House, 55 Victoria Rd, Farnborough, Hampshire, GU14 7PH, T0870-333 4001, www.explore.co.uk. Small-group tours, including cultural trips, adventure holidays and natural history tours.

Kuoni Travel, Kuoni House, Dorking, Surrey, T01306-747002, www.kuoni.co.uk. Consistently high-quality tour operator.

Paradise Vacations, 1 Olympic Way, Wembley, Middlesex, HA9 0NP, T020-8166 5050, www.paradisevacations.co.uk. Tailor-made holidays to Borneo and beyond.

Realworld-travel, Lower Farm, Happisburgh, Norwich, NR12 0QQ, T0709-23322, www.4real. co.uk. Self-drive tours and rainforest treks.

Regaldive, 58 Lancaster Way, Ely, Cambs, CB6 3NW, T0870-220 1777, www.regal-diving. co.uk. Diving tours around Sipadan and Mabul islands on Sabah's southeast coast.

Trans Indus, Northumberland House, 11 The Pavement, Popes Lane, London, W5 4NG, T020-8566 2729, www.transindus.com. Tailor-made and group tours and holidays.

Travel Mood, 214 Edgware Rd, London, W2 1DH; 1 Brunswick Ct, Bridge St, Leeds, LS2 7QU; 16 Reform St, Dundee DD1 1RG, T0207-087 8400, www.travelmood.com. More than 30 years of experience in tailor-made travel to the Far East and specialists in adventure and activity travel.

Trekforce Expeditions, Way to Wooler Farm, Wooler, Northumberland, NE71 6AQ, T0845-241 3085, www.trekforce.org.uk. A UK-based charity offering programmes consisting of sustainable projects, language, teaching and cultural experiences.

In North America
Asian Pacific Adventures, T+1-800-825 1680, www.asianpacificadventures.com. Small-group, tailor-made and family adventure tours.

In Australia

Intrepid Travel, 11 Spring St, Fitzroy, Victoria, T+61-1300-360887, www.intrepidtravel.com.au. Australian company with agents all over the world. Dozens of different tours of Malaysia.

Tourist information

Sarawak and Sabah

Visit the Tourism Malaysia site for a list of overseas offices at www.tourism.gov.my.

Brunei

For tourist information, contact the relevant embassy in your country (see page 314) or send queries to the Brunei Tourism office in BSB, see www.bruneitourism.travel.

Useful websites

www.brunei.gov.bn The government of Brunei's official website.

www.journeymalaysia.com A great web resource that covers most of Malaysia's tourist sites in an entertaining and factual way.

www.sabahtourism.com A well-designed but hard-to-navigate site about Sabah by the state's tourism board.

www.sabahtravelguide.com A great travel site with interactive maps, tour agents, up-to-date information and good travel advice.

www.sarawaktourism.com Heaps of information on the state.

www.skyscanner.com Find cheap flights in the region and beyond.

www.tourismbrunei.com Brunei's official tourism site.

www.tourismmalaysia.gov.my Tourism Malaysia's website.

www.tripadvisor.com Information on hotels, restaurants, things to see and avoid.

Visas and immigration

No visa is required for a stay of up to 3 months in **Malaysia** (provided you are not going to work) for citizens of the UK, the US, Australia, New Zealand, Canada, Ireland and most other European countries. If you intend to stay in the country for longer, 2-month extensions are usually easy to get from immigration offices. Note that Israeli passport holders are not allowed to enter Malaysia.

Visitor passes issued for entry into Peninsular Malaysia are not automatically valid for entry into the states of **Sabah** and **Sarawak**. (The reason for this anomaly is that Sabah and Sarawak maintain control over immigration and even Malaysian visitors from the peninsula are required to obtain a travel permit to come here.) On entry into these states from Peninsular Malaysia, visitors will have to go through immigration and receive a new stamp in their passport, usually valid for a month. If you want to stay for longer, then you must ask the official. Apply to the immigration offices in Kota Kinabalu and Kuching for a 1-month extension; 2 extensions are usually granted with little fuss. There are certain areas of East

Malaysia where entry permits are necessary; for example the Rejang River. These can be obtained from the residents' offices (see appropriate sections).

All visitors to **Brunei** must have valid passports, onward tickets and sufficient funds to support themselves while in the country (though the latter is rarely checked). Visitors from the UK and other EU states, USA, Malaysia and Singapore do not need a visa for visits of up to 90 days. New Zealanders are offered 30 days visa-free access to Brunei, and Australian passport holders are issued visas on arrival at Brunei International Airport for stays of up to 30 days. Many other nationalities such as Canada, Japan and South Korea are given visa-free access for 14 days. Check with your nearest Brunei diplomatic mission. For all visitors, getting permission to extend your stay is usually a formality; apply at the immigration department in Bandar Seri Begawan, see below.

Immigration offices in Borneo
Bandar Seri Begawan Jln Menteri.
Kota Kinabalu 4th floor, Government Building, Jln Haji Yaakub.
Kuching 1st floor, Bangunan Sultan Iskandar (Federal Complex) Jln Simpang Tiga, T082-230 280.
Sandakan Federal Bldg, Jln Leila.
Tawau Jln Stephen.

Weights and measures

Metric, although road distances are marked in both kilometres and miles.

Women travellers

Unaccompanied women often attract unwarranted attention. Most male attention is bravado and there have been few serious incidents involving foreign female tourists (or male, for that matter). However, remember that both Malaysia and Brunei are mainly Muslim so dress appropriately, avoiding short skirts and vest tops. In beach resorts, clothing conventions are more relaxed but topless bathing remains unacceptable to most Muslims. If swimming outside beach resort areas bear in mind that local women usually bathe fully clothed, so think twice before wearing a bikini. Keep to public transport and travel during the day. Hitching is not advisable for women travelling on their own.

Working in Borneo

If you're interested in working in Sabah, Sarawak and Brunei, **Escape Artist**, www.escapeartist.com/as/pac.htm, has useful tips and links. The **Centre for British Teachers**, www.cfbt.com, has teaching opportunities for qualified teachers to work in Brunei and Malaysia and offers fairly reasonable recompense. The Malaysian government has an incentive programme for foreigners to move or retire to the country called 'Malaysia: My Second Home'. This scheme offers a renewable 5-year multiple-entry visa called a Social Visit Pass. The catch is you need at least RM500,000 banked for under-50s and at least RM350,000 for over 50s (depending on age and pension income) in Malaysia and a minimum RM10,000 monthly income. If you are retired, you only need one of these. Apply at Malaysian embassies or **Tourism Malaysia** offices. Check **www.mm2h. com** for more information. The **Ministry of Human Resources (MOHR)**, www.mohr. gov.my, provides details of labour law and practice in Malaysia.

Footnotes

Useful words & phrases 329
Glossary........................331
Books 334
Index..........................336
Credits 340

Useful words & phrases

Bahasa Malaysia known globally as Malay and locally as Melayu is the most commonly used language in the region and is also mutually intelligible to Indonesian speakers, of which there are many in Sabah and Sarawak. See also page 320.

Basic phrases

Yes/No	*Ya/tidak*
Thank you	*Terimah kasih*
Good morning	*Selamat pagi*
Good afternoon (early)	*Selamat tengahari*
Good afternoon (late)	*Selamatpetang*
Good evening/night	*Selamat malam*
Welcome	*Selamat datang*
Goodbye (said by the person leaving)	*Selamat tinggal*
Goodbye (said by the person staying)	*Selamat jalan*
Excuse me/sorry	*Ma'af saya (Ma'af)*
Where's the ...?	*Dimana…*
How much is this ...?	*Ini berapa?*
I [don't] understand	*Saya [tidak] mengerti*

Sleeping

How much is a room?	*Bilik berapa?*
Does the room have air conditioning?	*Ada bilik yang ada air-con-kah?*
I want to see the room first please	*Saya mahu lihat bilik dulu*
Does the room have hot water?	*Ada bilik yang ada air panas?*
Does the room have a bathroom?	*Ada bilik yang ada mandi-kah?*

Travel

Where is the railway station?	*Stesen keretapi dimana?*
Where is the bus station?	*Stesen bas dimana?*
How much to go to ...?	*Berapa harga ke ...?*
I want to buy a ticket to…	*Saya mahu beli tiket ke ...*
Is it far?	*Ada jauh?*
Turn left/turn right	*Belok kiri/belok kanan*
Go straight on!	*Turus turus!*

Days

Monday	*Hari Isnin*	*Hari Senin*
Tuesday	*Hari Selasa*	
Wednesday	*Hari Rabu*	
Thursday	*Hari Khamis*	
Friday	*Hari Jumaat*	
Saturday	*Hari Sabtu*	
Sunday	*Hari Minggu*	
Today	*Hari ini*	
Tomorrow	*Esok*	*Hari Besok*

Numbers

1 *satu*	9 *sembilan*	101 *se-ratus satu* ...etc
2 *dua*	10 *sepuluh*	150 *se-ratus limah puluh*
3 *tiga*	11 *se-belas*	200 *dua ratus*
4 *empat*	12 *dua-belas* ...etc	1000 *se-ribu*
5 *lima*	20 *dua puluh*	2000 *dua ribu*
6 *enam*	21 *dua puluh satu* ...etc	100,000 *se-ratus ribu*
7 *tujuh*	30 *tiga puluh*	1,000,000 *se-juta*
8 *lapan*	100 *se-ratus*	

Basic vocabulary

In Malay, with the Indonesian version in parenthesis if the difference is significant.

a little *sedikit*
a lot *banyak*
all right/good *baik*
bank *bank*
beach *pantai*
beautiful *cantic*
bed sheet *cadar*
boat *perahu*
big *besar*
bus *bas*
buy *beli*
can *boleh*
cheap *murah*
chemist *rumah ubat*
clean *bersih*
closed *tutup*
day *hari*
delicious *sedap*

dentist *doktor gigi*
dirty *kotor*
doctor *doktor*
eat *makan*
excellent *bagus*
expensive *mahal*
food *makan*
hospital *rumah sakit*
hot (temperature) *panas*
I/me *saya*
hot (spicy) *pedas*
island *pulau*
market *pasar*
medicine *ubat ubatan*
open *masuk*
please *sila*
police *polis*
police station *pejabat polis*

post office *pejabat pos*
restaurant *kedaimakanan*
room *bilik*
sea *laut*
ship *kapal*
shop *kedai*
sick *sakit*
small *kecil*
stop *berhenti*
taxi *teksi*
that *itu*
they *mereka*
toilet – female/male
tandas–perempuan/lelaki
town *bandar*
very *sangat*
water *air*
what *apa*

Glossary

A

Adat custom or tradition
Amitabha the Buddha of the Past (see Avalokitsvara)
Atap thatch
Avalokitsvara also known as Amitabha and Lokeshvara, the name literally means 'World Lord'; he is the compassionate male Bodhisattva, the saviour of Mahayana Buddhism and represents the central force of creation in the universe; usually portrayed with a lotus and water flask

B

Bahasa language, as in Bahasa Malaysia and Bahasa Indonesia
Bajaj three-wheeled motorized taxi
Barisan Nasional National Front, Malaysia's ruling coalition
Batik a form of resist dyeing
Becak three-wheeled bicycle rickshaw
Bodhi the tree under which the Buddha achieved enlightenment (*Ficus religiosa*)
Bodhisattva a future Buddha. In Mahayana Buddhism, someone who has attained enlightenment, but who postpones nirvana to help others become enlightened
Brahma the Creator, one of the gods of the Hindu trinity, usually represented with four faces, and often mounted on a *hamsa*
Brahmin a Hindu priest
Budaya cultural (as in Muzium Budaya)
Bumboat small wooden lighters, now used for ferrying tourists in Singapore

C

Cap batik stamp
Chedi from the Sanskrit *cetiya*, meaning memorial. Usually a religious monument (often bell-shaped)with relics of the Buddha or other holy remains. Used interchangeably with stupa
Cutch see Gambier

D

Dalang wayang puppet master
Dayak/Dyak tribal peoples of Borneo
Dharma the Buddhist law
Dipterocarp family of trees characteristic of Southeast Asia's forests
Durga the female goddess who slays the demon Mahisa, from an Indian epic story

G

Gambier also known as *cutch*, a dye derived from the bark of the bakau mangrove and used in leather tanning
Gamelan Malay orchestra of percussion instruments
Ganesh elephant-headed son of Siva
Garuda mythical divine bird, with predatory beak and claws, and human body; the king of birds, enemy of naga
Gautama the historic Buddha
Geomancy feng shui
Godown Asian warehouse
Goporum tower in a Hindu temple
Gunung mountain

H

Hamsa sacred goose, Brahma'smount; in Buddhism it represents the flight of the doctrine
Hinayana 'Lesser Vehicle', major Buddhist sect in Southeast Asia, usually termed Theravada Buddhism

I

Ikat tie-dyeingmethod of patterning cloth
Indra the Vedic god of the heavens, weather and war; usually mounted on a three headed elephant

J

Jataka(s) birth stories of the Buddha, of which there are 547

K

Kajang thatch
Kala (makara) literally, 'death' or 'black'; a demon ordered to consume itself; often sculpted over entranceways to act as a door guardian, also known as *kirtamukha*
Kampong or kampung, village
Kerangas from an Iban word meaning 'land on which rice will not grow'
Kinaree half-human, half-bird, usually depicted as a heavenly musician
Klotok motorized gondolas of Banjarmasin
Kongsi Chinese clan house
Kris traditional Malay sword
Krishna an incarnation of Vishnu
Kuti living quarters of Buddhist monks

L

Laterite bright red tropical soil/stone
Linga phallic symbol and one of the forms of Siva
Lokeshvara see Avalokitsvara
Lunggyi Indian sarong
Losmen guesthouse

M

Mahabharata a Hindu epic text written about 2000 years ago
Mahayana 'Greater Vehicle', major Buddhist sect
Mandi Indonesian/Malay bathroom with water tub and dipper
Maitreya the future Buddha
Makara a mythological aquatic reptile, a little like a crocodile and sometimes with an elephant's trunk; often found, along with the kala, framing doorways
Mandala a focus for meditation; a representation of the cosmos
MCA Malaysian Chinese Association
Meru the mountain residence of the gods; centre of the universe, the cosmic mountain
MIC Malaysian Indian Congress
Mudra symbolic gesture of the hands of the Buddha
Musium museum

N

Naga benevolent mythical water serpent, enemy of Garuda
Naga makara fusion of *naga* and *makara*
Nalagiri the elephant let loose to attack the Buddha, who calmed him
Nandi/Nandin bull, mount of Siva
Negara kingdom and capital, from Sanskrit
Negeri also negri, state
Nirvana enlightenment, the Buddhist ideal

O

Ojek motorcycle taxi

P

Paddy/padi unhulled rice
Pantai beach
Pasar market, from the Arabic 'bazaar'
Pasarmalam nightmarket
Pelni Indonesian state shipping line
Perahu/prau boat
Peranakan mixed race, usually applied to part-Chinese and part-Malay people
Pradaksina pilgrims' clockwise circumambulation of a holy structure
Prang form of stupa built in the Khmer style
Prasat residence of a king or of the gods (sanctuary tower), from the Indian *prasada*
Pribumi indigenous (as opposed to Chinese) businessmen
Pulau island
Pusaka heirloom

R

Raja/rajah ruler
Raksasa temple guardian statues
Ramayana the Indian epic tale
Ruai common gallery of an Iban longhouse, Sarawak
Rumah adat customary or traditional house

S

Sago multi-purpose palm
Sakyamuni the historic Buddha
Sal the Indian *sal tree* (*Shorea robusta*), under which the historic Buddha was born

Silat or *bersilat*, traditional Malay martial art

Singha mythical guardian lion

Siva one of the Hindu triumvirate, the god of destruction and rebirth

Songket Malay textile interwoven with supplementary gold and silver yarn

Sravasti the miracle at Sravasti when the Buddha subdues the heretics in front of a mango tree

Sri Laksmi the goddess of good fortune and Vishnu's wife

Stele inscribed stone panel or slab

Stucco plaster, often heavily moulded

Stupa see Chedi

Sungai river

T

Tamu weekly open-air market

Tanju open gallery of an Iban longhouse, Sarawak

Tara also known as Cunda; the four-armed consort of the Bodhisattva Avalokitsvara

Tavatimsa heaven of the 33 gods at the summit of Mount Meru

Theravada 'Way of the Elders'; major Buddhism sect also known as Hinayana Buddhism ('Lesser Vehicle')

Tiffin afternoon meal – a word that was absorbed from the British Raj

Timang Iban sacred chants, Sarawak

Tong or *towkay*, a Chinese merchant

Totok 'full blooded'; usually applied to Chinese of pure blood

Towkay Chinese merchant

Triads Chinese mafia associations

Tunku also *tuanku* and *tengku*, prince

U

Ulama Muslim priest

Ulu jungle

UMNO United Malays National Organization

Urna the dot or curl on the Buddha's forehead, one of the distinctive physical marks of the Enlightened One

Usnisa the Buddha's top knot or 'wisdom bump', one of the physical marks of the Enlightened One

V

Vishnu the Protector, one of the gods of the Hindu trinity, generally with four arms holding the disc, the conch shell, the ball and the club

W

Waringin banyan tree

Warung a foodstall – a simple place to eat on the street. The alternative Malay name is *Kedai Makan*. The word originally comes from Indonesia.

Wayang traditional Malay shadow plays

Books

Fiction

Godshalk, CC *Kalimantan* (1998) Little Brown. A fictional account of an ambitious Englishman's quest to build his own kingdom on the north Borneo coast in the mid-19th century. It's a superb book, detailing the violence, duplicity, waves of pitiless disease and dark colonial attitudes that epitomized the lives of the first white settlers in Borneo.

Keith, Agnes *Land below the Wind* (1969) Ulverscroft: Leicester. Perhaps the best-known English-language book on Sabah.

Maugham, William *Somerset Maugham's Malaysian Stories* (1969) Heinemann: London and Singapore. Another British novelist who wrote extensively on Malaysia. These stories are best for the insight they provide of colonial life, not of the Malay or Malay life. The *Outstation* (1953) is a novel set in Borneo.

History and culture

Amman, Heribert *Textiles from Borneo: The Iban, Kantu, Ketungau and Mualang Peoples* (2013) 5Contintents. 150-page book crammed with gorgeous photos from some of the world's finest private selections of north Borneo textiles shed light on the area's rich cultures and traditions.

Barley, Nigel *White Rajah* (2003) Abacus. Extremely readable account of the life and extraordinary achievements of James Brooke, filled with ingenuity and dark, bloody violence.

Case, Gerard *Operation Borneo: The last untold story story of the War in the Pacific, 1945* (2004). Absorbing account of the American and Australian offensives to defeat the Japanese at the end of the Second World War.

Harrisson, Tom *World Within* (1959) Hutchinson: London. During the Second World War, explorer, naturalist and ethnologist Tom Harrisson was parachuted into Borneo to help organize Dayak resistance against the occupying Japanese forces. This is his extraordinary account.

Payne, Robert *The White Rajahs of Sarawak* (1960). Readable account of the extraordinary history of this East Malaysian state.

Turnbull, Mary C *A History of Malaysia, Singapore and Brunei* (1989) Allen and Unwin. A very orthodox history of Malaysia, Singapore and Brunei, clearly written for a largely academic/student audience.

Natural history

Briggs, John *Mountains of Malaysia: a Practical Guide and Manual* (1988) Longman: London. He has also written *Parks of Malaysia* (Longman: Kuala Lumpur); useful for those intending to visit Malaysia's protected areas.

Cubitt, Gerald and Payne, Junaidi *Wild Malaysia* (1990) London: New Holland. Large-format, coffee-table book with lots of wonderful colour photos, reasonable text and a short piece on each national park.

Garbutt, N and Prudente, J *Wild Borneo: The Wildlife and Scenery of Sabah, Sarawak, Brunei and Kalimantan* (2006) The MIT Press. Beautiful photos and engaging narrative providing deep insight into what natural treasures to expect in Borneo.

Hanbury-Tenison, Robin *Mulu, the Rain Forest* (1980) Arrow/Weidenfeld. The product of a Royal Geographical Society trip to Mulu in the late 1970s; semi-scholarly and useful.

Myers, S *Birds of Borneo: Brunei, Sabah, Sarawak and Kalimantan* (2009). Princeton Field Guides. The most authorative field guide to the birds of Borneo with over 1600 illustrations and more than 600 maps, this is a tropical twitcher's delight.

Wallace, Alfred Russel *The Malay Archipelago* (1869). A classic of Victorian travel writing by one of the finest naturalists of the period. Wallace travelled through all of island Southeast Asia over a period of some years. Only 3 out of 20 chapters are on Borneo.

Travel

Bock, Carl *The Headhunters of Borneo* (1988, first published 1881) Graham Brash: Singapore. Bock was a Norwegian naturalist and explorer and was commissioned by the Dutch to make a scientific survey of southeastern Borneo. His account, though, makes much of the dangers and adventures that he faced, and some of his 'scientific' observations are, in retrospect, highly faulty. Nonetheless, this is an entertaining read.

Hansen, Eric *Stranger in the Forest: On Foot Across Borneo* (2000) Penguin. A fascinating account of Hansen's trek through Sarawak and Kalimantan.

Hose, Charles *The Field Book of a Jungle Wallah* (1985, first published 1929) OUP: Singapore. Hose was an official in Sarawak and became an acknowledged expert on the material and non-material culture of the tribes of Sarawak. He was one of that band of highly informed, perceptive and generally benevolent colonial administrators.

McNamee, Brian *With Pythons and Head Hunters in Borneo: the Quest for Mount Thiban* (2009) Xlibris. Exhilirating adventure account of two separate journeys deep into the heart of Borneo in 2003 and 2006 as the author seeks to scale a mystical and revered mountain on the Malaysian-Indonesian border.

O'Hanlon, Redmond *Into the Heart of Borneo* (1985) Salamander Press: Edinburgh. One of the best more recent travel books on Borneo. This highly amusing and perceptive romp through Borneo in the company of poet and foreign correspondent James Fenton includes an ascent of the Rejang River and does much to counter the more romanticized images of Bornean life.

Walker, H. Wilfrid *Wanderings Among South Sea Savages and in Borneo and the Philippines* (2014). Short book crammed full of literature's classic and timeless accounts of past travels in the region.

Index

Entries in bold refer to maps

A

accident and emergency 313
accommodation 23
    price codes 23
activities 19
air travel 305, 310
Australian war memorial 255

B

background
    Brunei 174
    Sabah 294
    Sarawak 126
Bajau, Sabah 299
Bako National Park 65, **67**
Bandar Seri Begawan 145, **148**
    Arts and Handicraft Centre
        152
    Bubongan Dua Belas 152
    Gadong 153
    Kampong Ayer 147
    listings 154
    Omar Ali Saifuddien Mosque
        150
    Royal Regalia Museum 152
    tourist information 154
Bandar Sri Aman 69
Bangar 165
Baram River 100
Bario 121
Batang Ai National Park 70
Batang Ai River 70
Batang Duri 167, 168
Batu Apoi Forest Reserve 166
Baturong 273
Batu Tulug 271
Bau 58
Beaufort 230
Belaga 85
Belait District 170
Berhala, Pulau 258

Bintulu 90, **91**
bird's nest soup 99, 270
birdwatching 19
    Tempasuk River 236
Brooke, Charles 176
Brooke, Charles Vyner 128
Brooke, James 126, 175, 294
Brunei 142-185
    flora and fauna 183
    history 174
    people 185
    wildlife 184
Brunei Muara District 162
Brunei Museum 150
Brunei Tourism 154
Bukit Pagon 167
Bukit Patoi 168
Bukit Peradayan 168
Bukit Shahbandar Reserve 164
Buntal 60
buses 311

C

car hire 312
caving 19
    Bau 58
    Gomantong 269
    Gunung Mulu National
        Park 113
    Niah National Park 97
children, travelling with 313
Clearwater Cave 118
climate 17
climbing 19
cookery courses 20
Crocker Range National Park
    228
culture
    Brunei 184
    Sabah 299
    Sarawak 132
customs and duty free 314

D

Damai Peninsula 60
Danum Valley Conservation
    Area 276
    flora and fauna 277
Deer Cave 118
disabled travellers 314
diving 20, 21
    Kuching 54
    Labuan 225
    Layang Layang 211
    Miri 103
    practicalities 21
    Pulau Mantanini 240
    safety 319
    Sipadan 282
    Tunku Abdul Rahman
        National Park 216
drink 25

E

electricity 314
elephant, Borneo Pygmy 277
embassies and consulates 314
etiquette 314

F

Fairy Cave 58
festivals 18, 315
food 25

G

Gadong 153, 156
Gawai Padi 60
Gomantong Caves 269
guesthouses 23
Gunung Api (Fire Mountain)
    118
Gunung Gading National
    Park 57

Gunung Kinabalu National
    Park 241, **247**
    flora and fauna 244
    practicalities 243
    treks 242
Gunung Mulu 115
Gunung Mulu National Park
    112, **114**
Gunung Murudi 121
Gunung Penrissen 56
Gunung Santubong 63
Gunung Silam 273
Gunung Trusmadi 228

H

Hassanal Bolkiah 178
Hawaii Beach 101
Headhunter's Trail 110
headhunting 134
health 318
history
    Brunei 174
    Sabah 294
    Sarawak 126
hitchhiking 312
homestays 20
hostels 23
hotels 23
    price codes 23
Hutan Berakas Forest Reserve
    164

I

internet 320
Istana Nurul Iman 162

J

Jalan Labi 172
Japanese interregnum 295
Japanese occupation, Brunei
    177
Japanese war memorial 255
Jerudong Park Playground
    163

K

Kadazan, Sabah 300
Kampong Ayer 147
Kampong Gombizau 238
Kampong Kuala Tutong 169
Kampong Labi 172
Kampong Melilas 173
Kampong Panji 273
Kampong Selungai 229
Kampong Sembiling 168
Kampong Sumangkap 238
Kapalai 284
Kapit 80, **81**
Karambunai Beach 211
Karambunai Peninsula 211
Keith, Agnes 258
Kelabit Highlands 121
Kemabong 230
Keningau 228
Kinabalu, Mount 246
Kinabatangan River 270
Kipungit Falls 249
Klias Wetlands 226
Konfrontasi 178, 297
Kota Belud 235
    market 235
Kota Kinabalu 190,
    192, 195, 209
    history 196
    listings 197
    Masjid Sabah 192
    Sabah Foundation 194
Kuala Balai 172
Kuala Belait 171
Kubah National Park 58
Kuching 36, **40, 57**
    Astana 44
    Chinatown 43
    Civic Centre 44
    Fort Margherita 45
    listings 47
    Petra Jaya 46
    Planetarium 44
    Sarawak Islamic Museum 41
    Sarawak Museum 39
    waterfront 41
Kuching Wetlands 63
Kudat 237
Kundasang 249

L

Labi Hills Forest Reserve 172
Labuan, Pulau 218, **222**
Lahad Datu 273
Lambir Hills National Park 103
Langanan Waterfall 249
Lang's Cave 118
language 320, 329
Lankayan, Pulau 258
Lawas 124
Layang Layang 211
LGBT travellers 321
Likas Bay 194
Limbang 123
Limbang Trail 118
Loagan Bunut National Park
    104
longhouses 20, 71, 83, 91, 134
    Batang Ai River 70
    etiquette 72
    Kemena River (Bintulu) 91
    Keningau 229
    Longhouse Experience 237
    Rejang River (Kapit) 83
    Skrang River 70
    Temburong 168
    visiting 72
Luagan Lalak Recreation Park
    172
Lundu 58

M

Madai Caves 273
Maliau Basin Conservation
    Area 290
Mamutik, Pulau 215
Mantanani Island 239
Manukan, Pulau 215
maps 312
Marine Park 219
markets, Kota Belud 235
Marudi 103
Mataking 284
Mat Salleh 193
Mat Salleh's fort 227
Matunggong 238
Mawah Waterfall 228
Melinau Gorge 116

Mengkabong Water Village 210
menu reader 28
Mesilau Nature Resort 248
   listings 251
Miri 100, **102**
money 321
monkeys, proboscis 163
Monsopiad Cultural Village 208
mountain biking 21
   Kuching 54
Mountain Garden 248
Mount Kinabalu 246
Muara 164
Mulu National Park 112
Murut, Sabah 302
Murut villages 230

N

National Parks and Wildlife
   Booking Office, Kuching 47
newspapers 322
Niah National Park 96, **97**

O

opening hours 322

P

packing 311
Painted Cave 97
Pantai Seri Kenangan 169
Papar 226
Pelagus Rapids 82
Penan 62
Peradayan Forest Reserve 168
Petroleum Museum 101
photography 30
Pinnacles, the 117
Poring Hot Springs 249
Port Victoria 218
post 323
price codes 23
proboscis monkeys 163
prohibitions 323
Pulau Berhala 258
Pulau Gaya 214
Pulau Labuan 218
Pulau Lankayan 258

Pulau Mamutik 215
Pulau Mantanini 239
Pulau Manukan 215
Pulau Ranggu 163
Pulau Satang Besar 59
Pulau Selirong 164
Pulau Sipadan 283
Pulau Tiga National Park 217

R

rafflesia 227
Rafflesia Information Centre
   227
rail travel 310
Rainforest Interpretation
   Centre 267
Rainforest World Music Festival
   64
Ranau 249
Rejang River 83
restaurants 25
   price codes 23
rhinoceros, Sumatran 278
river travel 310
road travel 311
Rumah Panjang Mendaram
   Besar 173
Rumah Panjang Teraja 173

S

Sabah 186-303
   crafts 302
   culture 299
   history 294
   politics 297
Sabah Agricultural Park 230
Sabah State Museum 192
Saberkas Weekend Market 101
safety 323
Salleh, Mat 193
Salleh's fort 227
Sandakan 255, **260, 264**
Santubong 60
Sapulut 228
Sarawak 32-141
   culture 132
   history 126
   politics 130

Sarawak Chamber 119
Sarawak Cultural Village 61
Sarawak Museum 39
sea travel 310
Sematan 58
Semenggoh Nature Reserve
   and Wildlife Centre 56
Semporna 279
Sepilok Orang-Utan
   Rehabilitation Centre 266
Seria 171
Sharif Ali 174
shopping 24
Sibu 74, **76**
Sikuati 237
Similajau National Park 94
Sipadan Island Marine Reserve
   282
Sipitang 231
Skrang longhouses 70
smog 39
student travellers 323
Sultan Abdul Mumin 176
Sultan Awang Alak ber Tabar
   174
Sultan Bolkiah 152
Sultan Hashim Jalilul Alam
   Aqamaddin 176
Sultan Omar Ali Saifuddien
   Mosque 175
Sultan Syarif Ali 152
Sumatran rhinoceros 278
sun bear 267, 292
Sungai Batang Ai 70
Sungai Liang Forest Reserve
   172
Sungai Rejang 83
Sungai Skrang 70

T

Tabin Wildlife Reserve 274
Taman Rekreasi Sungai Basong
   169
Tambunan 226
Tampuruli 210
Tamu Muhibba 100
tamus 230
Tanah Merah 257
Tanjung Aru 208
Tanjung Datu National Park 59

FOOTPRINT

Features

48 hours in Kuala Lumpur 308
48 hours in Singapore 306
A ceramic inheritance 45
Agnes Keith's house 258
A town called Cat 42
Build and be dammed:
  an ecological time bomb 87
Dive safety 319
Diving practicalities 21, 319
Estranged brothers 180
Hazy days in Kuching 39
Headhunter's Trail 115
How to make a swift buck 99
It's a bear's life 292
Mat Salleh: fort builder and folk hero 193
Menu reader 28
Niah's guano collectors: scraping
  the bottom 97
Packing for Borneo 311
Proboscis monkeys 163
Rafflesia: the world's largest flower 227

Sabah's markets and trade fairs 230
Skulls in the longhouse 134
Tapai: Sabah's rice wine 303
The 2013 Lahad Datu Standoff 274
The Borneo Death March 296
The gentler beast of Borneo 277
The Iban in Borneo 133
The Kadazan in Borneo 301
The Kelabit in Borneo 135
The Kenyah and Kayan in Borneo 136
The longhouse: prime location
  apartments 71
The Murut in Borneo 302
The Penan: museum pieces for the
  21st century? 62
The Sumatran rhinoceros 278
The tough life of a turtle 265
Tom Harrisson: life in the fast lane 129
Tribal tattoos 137
Visiting longhouses: house rules 72

Tasek Merimbun 170
Tawau 287
Tawau Hills State Park 287
tax 323
taxis 312
telephone 323
Temburong District 165
Tempasuk River 236
Tenom 229
time 324
tipping 324
Tourism Malaysia, Kuching 47
tour operators 324
transport 305

trekking 22, 66, 95, 98, 116,
  121, 123
  Bario 121
  Gunung Mulu National
    Park 112
  Kelabit Highlands 121
  Niah National Park 98
  Ulu Temburong National
    Park 166
Trusmadi, Gunung 228
Tuaran 210
Tunku Abdul Rahman
  National Park 214
Turtle Islands National Park
  263
turtles 263, 265
Tutong District 169

U

Ulu Belait 173
Ulu Temburong National
  Park 166

V

vaccinations 318

W

Wasai Mendaram 173
weather 17, 37, 146, 191
weights and measures 326
whitewater rafting 22
  Crocker Range 205
  Pelagus Rapids 82
women travellers 326
working in Borneo 326

Credits

Footprint credits
Editor: Nicola Gibbs
Production and layout: Emma Bryers
Maps: Kevin Feeney
Colour section: Patrick Dawson

Publisher: Felicity Laughton
           Patrick Dawson
Marketing: Kirsty Holmes
Sales: Diane McEntee
Advertising and content partnerships:
Debbie Wylde

Photography credits
Front cover: kkaplin/Shutterstock.com.
Back cover top: Yusnizam Yusof/
Shutterstock.com.
Back cover bottom: Faiz Zaki/
Shutterstock.com.
Inside front cover: Ryan M. Bolton/
Shutterstock.com, marcokenya/Shutterstock.
com, Muslianshah Masrie/Shutterstock.com.

Duotones
Page 32: Yusnizam Yusof/Shutterstock.com.
Page 142: AzriSuratmin/Shutterstock.com.
Page 186: Donald Yip/Shutterstock.com.

Publishing information
Footprint Borneo
4th edition
© Footprint Handbooks Ltd
September 2016

ISBN: 978 1 911082 03 3
CIP DATA: A catalogue record for this book
is available from the British Library

® Footprint Handbooks and the
Footprint mark are a registered
trademark of Footprint Handbooks Ltd

Published by Footprint
6 Riverside Court
Lower Bristol Road
Bath BA2 3DZ, UK
T +44 (0)1225 469141
F +44 (0)1225 469461
footprinttravelguides.com

Distributed in the USA by
National Book Network, Inc.

Printed in Spain by GraphyCems

Colour section
Page 1: CORDIER Sylvain/SuperStock.com. **Page 2**: JMcurto/Shutterstock.com. **Page 4**: studio23/Shutterstock.com,
Csaba Vanyi/Shutterstock.com. **Page 5**: Mint Images/SuperStock.com, Rafal Cichawa/Shutterstock.com, Adwo/
Shutterstock.com. **Page 6**: PaulWong/Shutterstock.com. **Page 7**: Nordic Photos/SuperStock.com, Aleksandr
Sadkov/Shutterstock.com, Mint Images/Shutterstock.com, Sainam51/Shutterstock.com. **Page 10**: Faiz Zaki/
Shutterstock.com. **Page 11**: Lyciz Mill/Shutterstock.com. **Page 12**: Jill Goche/SuperStock.com. **Page 13**: Fitri
Mohamad/Shutterstock.com, Lisette van der Kroon/Shutterstock.com, Phil MacD Photography/Shutterstock.
com. **Page 14**: Bunpot/shutterstock.com, CyberEak/Shutterstock.com. **Page 15**: marcokenya/Shutterstock.com,
HitManSnr/Shutterstock.com, Pei Chung Davy/Shutterstock.com. **Page 16**: Hanafi Latif/Shutterstock.com.